T0293644

Cost-Benefit Analysis

Cost-Benefit Analysis: Environmental and Ecological Perspectives

Edited by

Dr. K. Puttaswamaiah

Transaction Publishers
New Brunswick (U.S.A.) and London (U.K.)

Library of Congress Catalog Number: 00-062882
ISBN: 0-7658-0706-8
Printed in the United States of America

Library of Congress Cataloging-in-Publication Data

Cost-benefit analysis : environmental and ecological perspectives / edited by
    K. Puttaswamaiah.
        p. cm.
    A special issue of The Indian journal of applied economics (now The International journal of applied economics and econometrics), with 21 refereed papers by international scholars.
        Includes bibliographical references and index.
        ISBN 0-7658-0706-8 (pbk. : alk. paper)
    1. Economic development—Environmental aspects.   2. Economic development projects—Evaluation.   3. Environmental law—Compliance costs.
4. Ecological assessment (Biology)   5. Environmental protection—Cost effectiveness.   I. Puttaswamaiah, K.

HD75.6 .C693 2000
333.7—dc21   00-062882

CONTENTS

CONTRIBUTORS

David M. Newbery,
Professor, Department of Applied Economics, University of Cambridge, Cambridge, England.

Sardar M.N.Islam,
Director, Victoria University of Technology, Victoria, Melbourne, Australia.

Giuseppe Munda,
Professor, Department of Economics and Economic History, Universitat Autonoma de Barcelona, Barcelona, Spain.

Parameswar Nandakamar,
National Institute of Economic Research, Stockholm, Sweden and Madras School of Economics, Chennai, India.

John C. Whitehead,
Associate Professor, Department of Economics, East Carolina University, Greenville.

Sarah Lumley,
Department of Geography, The University of Western Australia, Nedlands, Western Australia.

Todd Litman,
Director, Victoria Transport Policy Institute, Victoria, Canada.

David K. Lewis,
Associate Professor, Forestry & Adjunct Professor, Agricultural Economics, Department of Forestry, Oklahoma State University, Stillwater, Oklahoma.

Joseph N. Lekakis,
Associate Professor, Department of Economics, The University of Crete, Rethymno, Greece.

Sabine O'Hara,
Assistant Professor of Economics, Department of Economics, School of Humanities and Social Sciences, Rensselaer Polytechnic Institute, New York, USA.

Susan Mesner
Department of Economics, School of Humanities and Social Sciences, Rensselaer Polytechnic Institute, New York, USA.

Peter Clough,
Senior Research Economist, New Zealand Institute of Economic Research, Wellington, New Zealand.

Sardar M.N.Islam, Jim Gigas and Peter Sheehan,
Centre for Strategic Economic Studies, Victoria University of Technology, Melbourne, Victoria, Australia.

David Pimentel,
Professor, Department of Entomology, College of Agricultural and Life Sciences, Cornell University, Ithaca, New York, USA.

Madinah S. Ali,
Department of Agricultural Resource and Managerial Economics, College of Agriculture and Life Sciences, Cornell University, Ithaca, New York, USA.

Karl Steininger,
Department of Economics, University of Graz, Graz, Austria.

Fernando Perna,
Professor, University of Algarve, E.S.G.H.T., Lisbon, Portugal.

Vitor Santos,
Professor, Technical University of Lisboa, I.S.E.G., Portugal.

Peter Seidel Architect,
Urban Planner, Cincinnati, Ohio, USA.

Susan B.Kask,
Associate Professor of Economics, Western Carolina University, Economics, Finance and International Business, College of Business, Cullowhee, USA.

Jason F. Shogren
Distinguished Professor of Natural Resources, Conservation and Management, Economics and Finance Department, University of Wyoming, Laramie, USA.

Todd L. Cherry
Instructor, Economics and Finance Department, University of Wyoming, Laramie, USA.

Jan van der Straaten,
European Centre for Nature Conservation, Warandelaan, Tilburg, The Netherlands.

Jane V. Hall and Victor Brajer
Department of Economics, California State University, Fullerton, USA.

Bernardo Aguilar,
Program Director, Center for Sustainable Development Studies, The School of Field Studies, Alajuela, Costa Rica.

Thomas J. Semanchin,
Center for Sustainable Development Studies, The School for Field Studies, Alajuela, Costa Rica.

PREFACE

In the context of planning for development, particularly when the World is concerned in bridging the developmental gap between the developed and developing countries and with the establishment of a number of funding institutions to the projects including those from the World Bank, the Asian Development Bank and many other agencies, the importance for economically viable projects has come to stay. The Social Cost-Benefit Analysis (SCBA) is an important technique used in project formulation, appraisal and evaluation. Thus, it is an important facet of applied welfare economics which is increasingly being used for identifying and assessing the worthwhileness of public projects, both in the developing and developed countries.

The idea of bringing out this treatise on "Cost-Benefit Analysis" (CBA) arose in my mind, as I had formulated a large number of projects which were accepted by the World Bank and other agencies for funding. The academic urge borne out of this experience spanning a period of three decades added luster to this task. Normally, nay, fundamentally, CBA was being, hitherto applied to major irrigation projects to a large measure and, to some extent, to other projects, the sizes of which have been substantial. As days passed by, more and more projects had to be pressed into the developmental process; other sectors, though not perfectly, started getting the benefits of CBA to evaluate the worthwhileness of them. Now, CBA is being applied to many areas, thanks to the endeavor of the World Bank to take up more varieties of projects and try to formulate techniques appropriate to evaluate them.

In this context, *the environmental and ecological development* on the one hand, *hazards and destruction* on the other are more and more pronounced and this has become a challenge to the planners. The study of environment in different countries of the World remains as before (World Development Report, 1997) and many changes have taken place in other areas of development in this changing World. The fundamental resources, namely forest resources are being decreased, instead of increasing, as could be seen from the indicators given in the above World Development Report, though, much effort has been made to increase it. After five decades of Planning (Indian, for instance), it looks paradoxical. This is really an astonishment and calls for emergent plans covering a period of at least 10 to 15 years. Keeping the importance of environmental protection the World over, seminars and conferences on the subject have been held in plenty and projects are many. These are to be looked into critically by

[[xi]]

an evaluator and the tool necessarily becomes the SCBA. I had myself prepared a project for *"Social Forestry in Karnataka"* (1980) for World Bank Assistance. In fact, it was considered as one of its kind or the first itself to track the social forestry area by the application of SCBA in the World. This project was successfully implemented in Karnataka and a repeat project was also of equal success. At that time, the *"Social Forestry Project"* was altogether a new concept. It is these factors that prompted a Special Issue of the *"Indian Journal of Applied Economics"* (IJAE) on *"Cost-Benefit Analysis with Particular Reference to Environment and Ecology"* which is presented here in book form.

To apply SCBA to any project, one should know the fundamental concepts and methods of evaluating them. My first work; *"Fundamentals of Applied Evaluation,"* which is the quintessence of my experience, was published in 1979 in which, starting from the conceptual framework, methods and issues of investigation, techniques to be used in the current and general contexts which may crop up as we are going on the road to reach the end results of evaluation, and finally presentation of a comprehensive report on the subject of the study are discussed. The evaluation study, when we start, looks fearful as if one is entering the forest. Once one goes through all the hurdles and crosses the thick and evergreen forests which might be full of dreadful beasts and comes to the end, which means the end of the study with full data, he feels totally relieved and he will be impressed that he has at his command full facts and tabulated data necessary for presenting a report. When he sits with all the where-with-all he has collected and is sure of writing a good report, he still faces many problems which were not earlier contemplated. He might have collected multiple data through a questionnaire and that data, to some extent, might have *misfired* and have become useless, because of inappropriate questions in the questionnaire. The presentation of an evaluation report is thus not an easy task even for an experienced evaluator. That sense of exhilaration or despair that the evaluator experiences when he completes the analysis of his data is usually absent when he begins to write the report. The effective scientific writing is rigorously logical and his first task is to visualize and construct a logical pattern or design that he can follow. If the design is not evident, much of the effect is lost. The integration of scientific thinking and writing should begin the moment a problem is conceived. When the final picture emerges, certain creative satisfactions result, some mistakes do occur and it is the duty of the evaluator to introduce correctives. (*"Fundamentals of Applied Evaluation,"* K.Puttaswamaiah, 1979, P.187). Thus, the study results act as a *curtain raiser* suggesting the problems which must be selected for further attention. This book was my early ambition and I reached my goal, to some extent. The whole saga of evaluation is brought out in this work in over 200 pages which is considered to be the first book from

India coming as it did from an individual and the reviewers held that it was also the first such book in the style of a *manual for evaluators in the World.*

The Evaluation Division of the Indian Planning Commission (IPC), after the selection of the subjects for evaluation studies for the next period based on the need of the Government of India for future planning or for introducing correctives in the on-going programmes, would prepare a note on each of the studies, defining the objectives, formulating the hypothesis and developing a methodology. They were also used to prepare questionnaires for studies for different purposes. For example, there may be a questionnaire for collecting the recorded data from the Government of India and the State Governments; then, questionnaires/schedules for canvassing beneficiaries at different levels which have been selected by sampling technique. These sets of papers used to be thoroughly discussed in separate seminars. First, at the Planning Commission Level, they used to be discussed by the Chief, Evaluation Division with the senior officers of the Planning Commission, the Government of India and Heads of the Evaluation Divisions of the State Governments and the Officers belonging to the discipline to which the studies related. At the second stage, these seminars were held at State levels in which the field officers also participated.

In the context of one study, such a seminar was conducted at Bangalore, the capital city of Karnataka, under the aegis of the Planning Department of the State Government in 1978. In this seminar, I raised the subject of the need for a *manual on evaluation* which would serve as a hand book for evaluators and explains all, from the definition of evaluation to field work and writing of the report. The discussion of the note and questionnaires mentioned above used to be normally thorough, a practice which now appears to be not so regular or perhaps lost sight of. I used to be on almost all the Steering Committees of the studies conducted by the Planning Commission. All these prompted me to make a statement about the need for a textbook type manual on evaluation. This seminar was attended by the Chief, the Evaluation Division, Directors of Evaluation of different States and the subject matter specialists relating to the subject under evaluation.

The background for this book was thus in the above context in which I requested bringing out successfully a manual for the use of the evaluators in the country in a short duration of one year, as *"in the long-run, we are all dead."* Dr. P.K. Mukherjee, then Chief, the Evaluation Division of the Indian Planning Commission, who heard me said that such a technical manual/book, which would guide the evaluators in a country like India, which is of continental size, is extremely important and mere discussions about a study without the knowledge of the fundamentals and the methodologies will not give us good report. It was agreed that the IPC would bring out within a year such a manual.

At that time I made a spontaneous joke and said that "if not, we will bring out such a manual/book within that year." We did bring out that most important book, duly published in the very early years of my career, which was well received. It became good material for training, evaluation personnel in the country.

Dr. R.K. Hazari who was then the editor, *"Economic and Political Weekly"* wrote a review article on this book: *"Fundamentals of Applied Evaluation"* under the title: *"Guiding the Evaluators."* He has said, while concluding the review article that *"the task of guiding the evaluators in the country by the Planning Commission of India has been actually done by an individual which is highly creditable."*

By the time this book came out, I had already conducted more than 25 evaluation studies in various sectors of the economy; more important summaries have been published under the title: *"Studies in Evaluation"* (1982). For instance, *"Evaluation of the Roads Programme"* (1970) is a hard nut to crack, unlike other sectors. "The genesis of roads programmes in Karnataka presented by K.Puttaswamaiah wouldn't have been possible but for his background as editor, *Karnataka State Gazetteers,* for nearly a decade. The report on *'Roads Programmes'* contains the criteria and norms at every stage and to every point under discussion–whether it be a road formation stage or a maintenance one. It is a report which is not just useful to Karnataka but is useful anywhere in the world." This has been said by the late Dr. P.K. Bhattacharjee, Chief, the Policy Analysis Division, FAO Rome, prior to which he was Chief, the Evaluation Division, the Indian Planning Commission. Every study has been received very well. That is the only satisfaction that the author has. If one newspaper points out that the report identifies "the zigzags and pitfalls in the roads system," aother newspaper names the author as a *"watch dog of Planning."* Many other sectors of planning have been evaluated similarly with the same success. It is this experience that enabled me to publish the *"Fundamentals of Applied Evaluation"* which defines evaluation objectives, and in many ways, goes on to the Evaluatory Methods– Techniques—and thus the whole saga of the evaluation journey, long indeed, up to the presentation of the report during which the evaluator will have faced many pitfalls to get the final exhilaration. My book on *"Cost- Benefit Analysis–A Theoretical and Applied Critique"* is the result of my experience with the application of CBA to many projects including those sent to the World Bank. When the book came out, even forgetting all the rest, I would be failing in my duty if I did not recollect here the impressions of some well-wishers. Late Prof. Jan Tinbergen, the Nobel Laureate, in a personal letter, considered the book *"as a very useful book for project evaluation; especially since it mentions the methods used by various agencies which have* to evaluate many projects." Prof. Michael Lipton from Sussex also conveyed his appreciation in a letter saying that: "*Your book on Cost-Benefit Analysis should be very useful. I think your closing remarks strike just the right note. We shall have to make do with cost-effective analysis in regard to health projects. While the objections to CBA (and even to cost-effectiveness analysis) have force, the more 'literary' alternatives merely push under the table the problems associated with CBA, rather than solving them. You have presented a very interesting approach. There is, though, a strong argument—maybe even proof— that the UNIDO and Little-Mirrlees methods have given identical results.*"

Prof. Jan Tinbergen, first Nobel Laureate has favored me with his '*Foreword*' in two of my books: (1) "*Nobel Economists–Lives and Contributions*" published in a set of three volumes (1994/5) and (2) "*Econometric Models–Techniques and Applications*" (1994). While he has given a brief '**Foreword**' to the second book in a brilliant language, the '*Foreword*' to the first book relating to "*Nobel Economists–Lives and Contributions*" is a very lengthy one. My academic friends in the Netherlands and elsewhere, wrote to me saying that: "Tinbergen has not given such long 'Forewords' to anybody except for you." It shows his utmost affection for me.

In his letter, Prof. Tinbergen wrote to me saying: "*You know that my mother-tongue is not English. There might be some English errors as the Foreword is long. If you find any error, you are free to correct.*" This shows Tinbergen's openness and simplicity. By then, he had seen chapters 1 to 34 of volumes I-III. He has followed my career by going through my manuscripts for over two decades. In the '*Foreword*' to this book, he has tried to analyze my major works and has chosen three titles for the purpose. These three titles are: (1) "*Economic Development of Karnataka, A Treatise in Continuity and Change*" published in a set of two volumes (1980), (2) "*Nobel Economists–Lives and Contributions*" (1994/5) and (3) *Cost-Benefit Analysis–A theoretical and Applied Critique of Alternative Methodologies*" (1984, 1988), co-authored with S. Venu. His impressions on the last book have already been indicated in the previous paragraph. I once again take this opportunity to express my gratitude to Prof. Jan Tinbergen, the "*Great Man*" of the Twentieth Century, who has supported my works all through my life.

The Cost-Benefit Analysis is normally applied to bigger projects to assess the results–both *ex-ante* and *ex-post*. Normally, small projects were not considered in the early stages, as it was felt that it was waste of time. Even in American conditions, minor projects were not given that importance to apply SCBA vis-à-vis the major ones. The motto was, the minor irrigation works would help "*all as against a few at the cost of all.*" Major projects amount to the lumping of investments and the benefits flow to only a few, while the smaller projects will not only yield quick results and will also give benefits to a larger section of the community. In larger projects, *"covering as large an area as possible"* should be the motto. I was impressed by a paper of the American Administration, probably not published, which is entitled: *"Policies, Standards, Procedures in the Formulation, Evaluation and Review of Plans for use of Water and Related Land Resources,"* a document prepared under the direction of the President's Water Resources Council, U.S. Senate, Document No.97, Washington, 1962, popularly known as *Kennedy's Paper*. Since, I was very much convinced about the views and concepts contained in the paper, I tried to apply them to Indian conditions in a tiny book entitled: *"Irrigation Projects in India towards a New Policy"* (1977) which was very well received. Later, considering the problems which India is facing in the irrigation front like Inter-State Water Disputes, construction of major dams across the rivers which flows in more than one State, scarcity of water and bad management in the water basins, lack of finance and so on, I thought I should prepare a comprehensive study after visiting all the major projects as an extension of the 1977 study published under the title: *"Irrigation Projects in India—Towards a New Policy."*

The new study which is in-depth was brought out under the same title: *"Irrigation Projects in India towards a new policy"* (1994), i.e., under the same title but with a wider scope spelling out in what direction India should go in the Irrigation front for the investment of funds. This latter book is almost like an *"Agenda for Indian Rivers."* The policy implications for major irrigation projects as well as the minor merits and demerits of them are discussed in detail and a number of recommendations have been made. The basis for the latter book was inspired by the Kennedy paper which I mentioned above. This I am quoting just to emphasize that even an affluent country like the United States of America, while prioritizing the projects, gave due importance to minor projects which yielded immediate results. It is not to deny the bigger projects as the resources have to be exploited in full to develop the nation. After the initial irrigation monograph (1977) and after the project for *"Drought Proofing in Karnataka was approved by the World Bank as the only project which was fit for appraisal,"* I took up a couple of minor irrigation works for CBA based on socio-economic studies in the relevant irrigation project areas. This has also been published under the title: *"Cost-Benefit Analysis of Irrigation and Drought Proofing"* (1989). The World Bank team which had come to India for *terminal evaluation* of the drought proofing areas programme had praise for this work and minor irrigation works which were incidentally financed by them.

It is because of the above reasons that I was enthusiastic to bring out a Special Issue of the Journal on the subject taking the environmental aspects of development as the focus. Thus, I have given emphasis to papers on SCBA as *applied to environment and ecology.* I am happy that with the support of the Members of the Advisory Board of IJAE and other colleagues, I have been able to bring out this book.

The genesis of Cost-Benefit Analysis goes back to the publication, "*Water Resources Projects Economics*" by Edward Kuiper (1971) in which SCBA was applied to water resources projects. This may be read with "*Economics of Water Resources Planning*" by L. Douglas James and Robert R. Lee published in 1971. Starting from the water resources planning analysis with the technique of Cost-Benefit Analysis, it took a long time for the Cost-Benefit Analysis to travel to other areas of national problems, but was difficult to evaluate as they were intangibles.

A beginning was made in India by the introduction of a scheme called *Drought Prone Areas Programme* initiated by the World bank in 1973. India was given the opportunity to prepare projects for drought prone areas in 12 districts, two projects of which were given to Karnataka which I had to formulate. These districts are Bijapur in Northern Karnataka and Kolar in Eastern Karnataka. Both are equally drought prone. Starting from the reconnaissance surveys in these districts, the actual formulation of projects, with due consultation with the World Bank and local officials and the people, was a big task, but had to be done in a short time. When all the twelve projects were sent to the World Bank for their appraisal by personal visits, I was happy to read in their appraisal report that "*out of the twelve projects received from India, Bijapur Project was the only one which was fit for appraisal.*" It is difficult to quantify the results of such a project, since major elements contained in it are intangibles. It does not help us to estimate direct benefits too. We made our humble attempt to apply SCBA to some components. Similarly, other projects mainly formulated by me are the Indian National Sericultural Project (1978), Regulated Markets Projects (1973), Karnataka Diary Development Project (1975) and a Project for "Agricultural Extension and Research" popularly called the "Training and Visit (T.V.) System." Karnataka was the first state anywhere in the world to introduce the last project with the assistance of the World Bank, and on an experimental measure. We now find from the latest World Bank evaluation reports that this System initiated in Karnataka is replicated in thousands of countries. The Karnataka Project thus has done its best to give a *multiplier effect.* It has given us sufficient challenges and headaches during the formulation of the project to estimate the benefits, both on *ex-ante* and *ex-post* levels. "*End Evaluation*" has given us much encouragement. These examples are some among many such projects.

Having had experience in the formulation of major projects, only some of which are mentioned above, we did take up some sectoral projects which contained a number of elements that were beyond the scope of evaluation, intangibles. Having experienced this and with the interest on SCBA evinced through practical experience spanning over three decades, it was felt necessary to have a *Special Issue* of the *"Indian Journal of Applied Economics"* on *"Cost-Benefit Analysis."* While doing so, we purposely chose the *'Environment and Ecology'* sector which is the current area of interest, already explained before. Added to this, more and more countries are coming forward with projects relating to areas which were once thought of as beyond the scope of preparation and appraisal. *Environment and Ecology is one such major area.* Denudation of forest areas and pollution are contributing to the destruction. It is the primary duty of everyone, particularly planners, to ensure that environment is properly protected and developed further in every country and region. With this emphasis in mind and with the support and enthusiasm of many contributors who are very well trained in the art and science of SCBA and in the environmental arena it has prompted us strongly to bring out this Special Issue, now in book form.

Before we go to the scope of this book, I wish to point out that there are mainly five methods of social Cost-benefit Analysis (K. Puttaswamaiah, CBA, 1988). Of course, the background for Cost-Benefit Analysis, as mentioned earlier, is the welfare economics. With a detailed theoretical setting relating to welfare economics as introductory to that Book—the five methods are presented—covering both theory and practice. These five methods are: (1) *Consumer's and Producers' Surplus Approach*—Mishan's Contribution, (2) The Little-Mirrlees Method for Project Appraisal, (3) The UNIDO Approach, (4) The World Bank Approach and (5) The 'Value-Added' Approach to Cost-Benefit Analysis. The Methodology followed by the World Bank combines in its ambit the OECD manual, L.M. and the UNIDO guidelines. Not only these three methods are discussed, the merits and demerits are presented in a separate chapter. Much literature and many World Bank methods have come out of late but the basis for it is *"Social Cost-Benefit Analysis: A Guide for Country and Project Economists to the Derivation and Application of Economic and Social Accounting Prices,"* World Bank Staff Working Paper No.239 (Aug. 1976) which has to be read with *"On Shadow Pricing,"* World Bank Staff Working Paper No.792.

My book, which I cited above, namely *"Cost-Benefit Analysis – A Theoretial and Applied Critique of Alternate Methodologies,"* was published in 1984 and reprinted in 1988. With the necessary theoretical background, the five methods are presented from the methodological point of view, as well as applied case studies. This appears to be the only book anywhere that contains all the methods of CBA. The merits and demerits of each of these are also explained and current issues highlighted. Lyn Squire and Herman G. Van der Tak, *"Economic*

Analysis of Projects" a World Bank Research Publication (1975) contains the World Bank Method. A critique of S and T method is now available under the title: *"Cost-Benefit Analysis for Developing Countries"* by Robert J. Brent, published by Edward and Elgar in 1998, as a most comprehensive critical book, we have so far come across on the World Bank method.

Coming to the scope of this Special Issue on *"Cost-Benefit Analysis with particular Reference to Environment and Ecology,"* there has been lots of enthusiasm among authors who have contributed. Almost all professors that have sent their contributions have rich experience in this area. There are in all 21 papers included in this treatise. Of these, the first five papers provide the necessary theoretical setting.

David M. Newbery in his article: *"Spatial General Equilibrium and Cost-Benefit Analysis"* starts with the premise, the transport investments which lower travel costs and land use projects which affect land supply and demand will affect land price and demand. He tries to identify the impacts which arise in making such value judgments in SCBA of such projects. The paper demonstrates this in a series of models and the importance of working with the underlying utility function rather than demand schedules which will move in response to relocations. The author has also computed as an example the size of the result error.

Sardar M. N. Islam in his paper: *"Optimum Growth Theory and Social Time Preference: A Computerised Mathematical Modelling Exercise to Choose a Social Discount Rate"* has tried to analyze how the efforts so far made by the economists for the empirical derivation of the social discount rate for developed and developing countries have ended up with an unsatisfactory outcome. No doubt such a derivation is a difficult task. In this study, the author tries to present illustrative, though realistic exercise of estimating the social discount rate where the rate of growth of per capita GDP and consumption are negative. He has explained limitations of the methodology and suggests further research of resolving the issue by development on a new paradigm.

In the third paper by Giuseppe Munda entitled: *"A Theoretical Inquiry on the Axiomatic Consistency of Distributional Weights used in Cost-Benefit Analysis"* makes a theoretical inquiry to test the consistency and compatability of the axiomatic system, attention is devoted to the relationship between the concept of compensability and meaning of the distributional weights. With a view to tackling this issue, the author has used some results of the multiattribute utility theory and measurement theory literature.

P. Nandakumar in his article: *"The Output Gap: Measurement, Related Concepts and Policy Implications"* compares the various approaches to the measurement of potential output and the NAIRU, and identifies practical policy implications. While doing so, he tries alternative methods like the *Okun's Law approach. The trend-fitting method, the production function approach,* the *simultaneous equations system method* and the *stochastic filter methods* – are discussed in detail. The merits and demerits are pointed out.

John C. Whitehead in his paper: *"A Methodological Comparison of Theoretical Approaches in Dichotomous Choice Contingent Valuation"* tries to explain the choice of a theoretical approach to CBA in a dichotomous choice contingent valuation can have implications for the theoretical validity and bias of willingness to pay estimates. The choice of theoretical approach, according to him should ultimately depend on the type of policy analysis for which the study is designed.

Sarah Lumley in her article: *"Cost-Benefit Analysis, Ethics and the Natural Environment"* explains the ethics part of the natural environment while applying SCBA. This paper examines the issues which arise while making resource allocation to environment and examines some of the reasons for the controversies. This paper is based on the economic analysis applied to a proposed mining project within the boundaries of Kakadu National Park in Northern Australia as a case study. It assesses the ethical implication of using standard economic criteria such as those identified in CBA in making decisions about the long-term use to natural environment.

The next article: *"Transport Cost Analysis: Applications in Developed and Developing Countries"* by Todd Litman concentrates on the transport planning and policy analysis and describes the framework that can be used to evaluate the full cost of the different modes of transport for planning and policy analysis applications. The paper will be useful to policy makers and those who wish to improve transport decision making both in developed and developing regions.

While, David K. Lewis in his paper: *"Cost-Benefit Analysis and the Evaluation of New Technology and Policies in Natural Resources,"* is concerned with the evaluation of new technology and policy in natural resources, Joseph N. Lekakis in his paper: *"Cost-Benefit Analysis and the Environment: A Critical Assessment"* provides a critical evaluation of the selection criteria of environmental projects and describes the criteria which are to rely on a social theory based on ecology, social sciences and humanities. Lekakis illustrates his view point of technology and evaluation and the utility of CBA by examples drawn from genetic improvement, forest fertilization, and the preservation of nesting habitat for the northern spotted owl. The utility of Cost-Benefit Analysis is also illustrated with these examples.

Sabine O'Hara and Susan Mesner in their paper: *"The Limits of Economic Rationality: Social and Environmental Impacts of Recreational Land Use"* the so-called negative externalities of development are discussed. They prefer alternative valuation method which they call discoursive valuation or also called discoursive ethics. Peter Clough in his paper: *"Cost-Benefit Analysis and Wildlife Conservation: A Sustainable Application"* explains the various techniques of non-market valuation that are found wanting and the paper outlines an approach to the valuation of habitats through a set of environmental inventory accounts, encompassing the natural capital-air, water, space, soils, landforms and biological resources-whose contribution to productive sectors and community well-being may be fundamentally transformed by adverse environmental effects. It links these accounts to project appraisal and other environmental economics issues, such as the use of incentives and instruments in implementing policy.

Sardar M.N. Islam, Peter Sheehan and Jim Gigas in their paper: *"Cost-Benefit Analysis of Climate Change: Towards an Operational Decision Making Rule for Climate Change Policy"* discuss the sustainability of CBA as an operational method for policy making to address the issue of climate change. In the next paper entitled: *"The Effect of Social Time Preference on the Future of the Australian Economy and Environment: Findings from the Australian Dynamic Integrated Climate and Economy Model (ADICE),"* Sardar M.N.Islam and Jim Gigas emphasize on the social time preference scenario as applied to inter- generational equity in Australian society. They feel higher efforts for environmental management or higher rates of emission controls are required.

David Pimentel and Madinah S. Ali in their paper entitled: *"An Economic and Environmental Assessment of Herbicide-Resistant and Insect/Pest-Resistant Crops"* describe the use of insecticide and the environmental pollution and attempts to analyze the economic impact of it. Karl Steininger in his paper: *"Spatial Discounting and the Environment: An Empirical Investigation into Human Preferences,"* Fernando Perna and Vitor Santos in their paper: *"The Free-Riding Behaviour in Culatra Island Case Study: Detection and Correction"* and Susan B. Kask, Jason F. Shogren and Todd. Cherry in their paper: *"Valuing Multiple Health Risks from Long-Term Low Dosage Exposure to Hazardous Chemicals"* have given their experiences with reference to their countries in the area of SCBA and natural environment, namely, Australia, Portugal and USA respectively. Fernando Perna and Vitor Santos in their paper: *"The Free-Riding Behaviour in Culatra Island Case Study: Detection and Correction"* relates to an island Culatra placed in the South of Portugal in the heart of Ria Formosa, a natural Park since 1987 and contains a good account of their development and maintenance. Susan B. Kask, Jason F. Shogren and Todd Cherry's paper mainly relates to valuation of multiple health risks, long term low dosage exposure to hazardous chemicals. Jan van der Straaten in his paper:

"Challenges and Pitfalls of Cost-Benefit Analysis in Environmental Issues"
has dealt with the contingent evaluation method, Travel Cost Method, and
Hedonic Pricing or techniques taken for attempting an evaluation and to suggest remedial action to get rid of some of the environmental issues in the
Netherlands. Jane V. Hall and Victor Brajer in their paper: *"Challenges in Valuation: the Health Benefits of Reducing Air Pollutants"* identifies and discusses
some of the challenges for the case of valuing health benefits that result from
better air quality. Bernardo Aguiliar and Thomas J. Semanchin give a very
detailed account of the implications of ecological economic theory of value
and capital, for effecting the estimates of SCBA and suggest several alternative
valuation methods for developing nations with special emphasis on Central
America. Thus, the ecological and economic theory of value and capital can be
used to promote sustainable development in the decision making process. The
author has surveyed the existing trends in ecological economic literature regarding value estimating and their effect on Social Cost-Benefit Analysis. Brief
case studies relating to Central America are presented here and there. The paper
illustrates with a number of figures and is quite an interesting one.

In all, the purpose of this technical volume on SCBA is to bring together the
experiences of different countries in its application of Cost-Benefit analysis
with appropriate new methods and techniques in the areas of environment and
ecology.

Each paper has something new to say about the Cost-Benefit Analysis and
the entire collection put together, it is hoped, will be a good set of new theories
and applications. All authors have done their best in assisting in this exercise
by their wide ranging contributions based on their own country's experience. I
am, in fact, very happy to see these papers in this volume.

I wish to thank all the authors who have co-operated in sending papers as
requested and then in answering queries of mine and the referees. Their unlimited efforts and co-operation are highly appreciated. This exercise had to be
finalized within a year–first for IJAE and for this book. Hence, the mode of
communication, namely, email was an excellent source which we could use for
collecting the feed-back information and as most of the authors have this facility, the task became easy. I once again place on record my heartfelt gratitude to
all the authors who have contributed and co-operated. I specially thank the
referees and those who indirectly or directly supported to modify ideas which
have been carried out. Prof. Rati Ram, Distinguished Professor, Illinois State
University took a very special interest and refereed two very tough articles and
got them revised thrice. I am equally grateful to other referees also who were
kind enough in extending their co-operation in refereeing articles and making
many suggestions.

I am extremely grateful to Prof. Paul A. Samuelson, Institute Professor Emeritus, Massachusetts Institute of Technology and Nobel Laureate, who has been of great support to academics. His blessings have always been there which have inspired my recent research. I am grateful to him. Similarly, Nobel Laureates like Professors Robert M. Solow and Franco Modigliani have supported my work and I wish to express my gratitude to them. Late Prof. Wassily Leontief was also a source of inspiration in my work as he used to readily send his contribution and supported me in my work as a Member of the Editorial Advisory Board. Just at this time when we are bringing out this book, Professors Lawrence R. Klein and M.C. Merton, Nobel Laureates, have joined as Members of the EAB of our journal which has really given me much courage and support for my tasks ahead. I am grateful to them.

I wish to express my gratitude to Prof. M.S. Swaminathan, world's greatest agricultural scientist, who has been giving me all the moral support, guidance and inspiration in India. The other Members of the Editorial Board, particularly Professors G.C. Harcourt (Cambridge U.K.), W.P. Hogan (Sydney Univ.,) and J.W. Nevile (N.S.W. Univ., Australia) have given their support in this work. Prof. John Lodewijks Professor N.S.W Univ., and editor, *History of Economic (Review)* has been a source of inspiration, support and courage to me.

Dr. Irving Louis Horowitz, chairman, Transaction Publishers, Rutgers–The State University of New Jersey, spontaneously agreed to publish this work on my approaching him. I wish to record my appreciation for his support and grateful thanks for his follow up and interest in this work. Ms. Mary E. Curtis, president and publisher, has taken a very keen interest in this publication and followed up the quality of production at every stage. I appreciate her goodness in working with me on this project. Ms. Cristina Kollett, associate editor, in-charge of this publication has worked hard in bringing out this publication so neatly in such a short time. I wish to record my appreciation both to Ms. Mary E. Curtis, and Ms. Cristina Kollett for their unstinted support.

In a work of this nature, it would be difficult to thank everybody. If I have forgotten anyone who has helped me in this task, may I be forgiven.

I am happy that I have been able to bring out this book on *"Cost-Benefit Analysis with Reference to Environment and Ecological Perspectives."*

January 1, 2000   K. Puttaswamaiah

CHAPTER - 1

SPATIAL GENERAL EQUILIBRIUM AND COST-BENEFIT ANALYSIS[†]

David M. Newbery

ABSTRACT

Transport investments which lower travel costs and land use projects which affect land supply or demand will affect land prices and rents. How should these impacts be valued in cost benefit analyses of such projects or polices where agents relocate in response to chaging land and property prices? Surplus measures used in transport evaluation such as the rule-of-one-half continue to work provided agents do not relocate, but are inaccurate when they do. The paper demonstrates this in a series of models and demonstrates the importance of working with the underlying utility functions rather than demand schedules, which will move inresponse to relocations. The size of the resulting error is computed in an example.

1. INTRODUCTION

The discipline of General Equilibrium analysis is particularly important for Cost-Benefit Analysis, where the object is to compare and evaluate the world with and without a project. It is common, for example, to come across news items announcing that a new supermarket is to be located in a particular town, creating n jobs. Leaving aside the obvious problem that the relationship between social net benefit and employment is not direct, there is the deeper problem that the demand for goods bought in shops and supermarkets is primarily determined by total income, rather than the number of stores, so

---

[†]Paper prepared to celebrate Frank Hahn's 70th birthday in Siena in 1995. This work grew out of a research project with Marcial Echenique and Partners, and I am indebted to Marcial Echenique, Simon Milner and Ian Williams for insightful discussions on the problems discussed here.

[1]

opening up a new supermarket must mean that other shops lose custom, and a comparable (possibly larger) number of jobs will be lost from the retail sector elsewhere. Such failures to take account of obvious general equilibrium effects pervade public debate, and are particularly likely to arise in locational decisions, where the repercussions might occur in a different place, and hence are more likely to be overlooked.[1]

General equilibrium effects may be important not only in other locations, but in other markets. Transport projects designed to improve traffic flow (either physically, by increasing the supply of road space, or by improved traffic management, including parking restrictions and road charging) often have complex effects elsewhere on the network, and a proper evaluation would keep track of all these network effects. In addition residents and businesses, in deciding where to locate, must consider the transport costs involved in commuting, shopping, delivering goods, etc., and if a project changes these transport costs, they may decide to move to a better location. Transport projects will therefore have repercussions in the land market, as changes in the demand pattern for different locations lead to changes in land prices and rentals. Similarly, land use projects (new towns, changes in zoning restrictions, etc) will have impacts on transport demand and costs. Any transport or land-use project or intervention will affect prices or costs not only in the immediate market (for transport or land use), but also in the other market. How should these multi-market impacts be evaluated?

Standard transport cost-benefit analysis ignores changes in land prices,[2] on the argument that where such changes are induced by the transport improvements, to include them would involve double counting. If a new transport link (e.g. an extension of the underground) lowers transport costs to a town, and rentals rise in response, these rental increases reflect the improved access, and measure the consumer surplus above any charge for the

---

[1]One fruitful way of handling the general equilibrium effects in cost-benefit analysis or project appraisal is to look for a set of shadow or accounting prices which themselves capture all the repercussions of the project on the economy. The usual problem in deriving these prices is to decide what it is reasonable to hold constant. For example, Dinwiddy and Teal (1987) criticize Blitzer, Dasgupta and Stiglitz (1981) for failing to specify how tax revenue is dealt with, and therefore what meaning attaches to a foreign exchange constraint. See also Mookherjee (1986), Hammond (1986) and Buffie (1987) for examples of general equilibrium derivations of shadow prices.

[2]See, e.g. COBA 9, Department of Transport (1981, updated 1987) which also discusses the complications associated with a variable trip matrix and the possibility of using additional programs such as MATBEN to predict changes in travel patterns in Appendix 1.7.

new link. Provided this consumer surplus is measured directly as part of the transport project evaluation, it is not necessary (and would introduce an error) to include the increased value of land.[3] This argument sounds convincing, but is it correct if the land price changes induce agents to change location? More to the point, is the standard method of measuring consumer surplus as the area under the demand curve valid if the demand curve itself shifts because of changes in the number of commuters?

This paper addresses these questions for a number of test cases that arise in transport and land-use project evaluation, starting with the simpler case of introducing a charge for using previously uncharged but congested roads, and then moving to the broader question of analyzing pure transport policies which involve no change in the supply of land, and finally looking at cases where the supply of land (for specific uses) is changed.

2. COST-BENEFIT ANALYSIS OF ROAD PRICING

If road pricing is introduced into a previously congested road it will reduce the inefficiency caused by the failure of motorists to take account of the social costs of their trips, and it will, by raising the private cost of travelling, induce relocations. In addition to the standard problem of evaluating consumer surplus changes by looking at one market (for transport) when prices change in other markets (land), there may be additional problems caused by a mismatch between private and social costs. Here we consider an extremely simple model to better track the various effects.

There are N households who can choose either to live in the city, or a suburb. Those who live in the suburb must commute to the city to work, while those in the city have no demand for travel. The only travel is commuting,

---

[3]Mishan (1976, p. 79) makes the same point in evaluating a new railroad. Mohring (1976) looks at cost savings in production, and again finds that only transport demand surplus needs to be computed. The more general problem of relating factor and final goods demands is discussed by Carlton (1979) and Jacobsen (1979). Jara-Díaz (1986) summarises the measurement of transport users' benefits and argues that transport consumers' surplus exactly measures the net benefits to all consumers and producers in a competitive economy, but do not necessarily do so if production is imperfectly competitive. This illustrates the more general point that if an intervention (like improved transport) changes the degree of distortion in the economy, there will be an additional benefit equal to the fall in deadweight loss. This paper assumes that the rest of the economy outside the transport sector is competitive and there are no changes in distortions. None of these considers the effect of allowing agents to relocate.

whose volume is q, determined by the number of households living in the suburbs, q. The remainder, $N - q$, live in the city. The total cost of commuting is $p = c(q) + \tau$, where travel costs $c(q)$ increase with traffic, q, as congestion increases trip times, and τ is the road price or toll. The utility function of household is V^{ij} where $i = u, s$ (urban or suburban) is the initial location and the location of the initial property endowment, $\bar{h}^i$, and j is the final location of the household after responding to any changes in road prices, τ, and where residence is rented. The (indirect) utility function is defined over income, y, net of any commuting costs, and housing rents, r: $V = V(y, r)$. Thus

$$V^{ss} = V(s\bar{h}^s - p, s), \qquad (1)$$

where fixed (wage) income is ignored, and only rental income from the initial ownership of housing, $\bar{h}^s$, less the cost of commuting, p, is included. Let subscript 0 denote the initial equilibrium, then social welfare is W given by

$$W = (N - q_0)V^{uu} + (q_0 - q)V^{su} + qV^{ss} + q\tau, \qquad (2)$$

where the first term on the right-hand side is the original set of urban residents, who do not move, the second term is the new immigrants from the suburbs responding to an increase in road charges, the third term is the remaining suburban residents still commuting, and the last term is the revenue from the road charges. To avoid income distributional issues, the marginal social utility of each resident is assumed equal and equal to the value of revenue raised, so

$$V^{uu}_y \equiv \frac{\partial V^{uu}}{\partial y} = V^{su}_y = V^{ss}_y = 1, \qquad (3)$$

where subscripts denote derivatives with respect to that variable.

Commuters can choose to move to the city and rent or remain where they are but pay for commuting, and in equilibrium will enjoy equal utility in each location, implying that $V^{su} = V^{ss}$. Aggregate demand for housing in each location must equal fixed supply, and these two equations, plus the equilibrium condition on location, jointly determine the rents in each location and the size of the suburban population, q. The total derivative of W in (2) with respect to urban rent, r, gives the net supply of urban land, which is zero in equilibrium:

$$\frac{dW}{dr} = (N - q_0)[V_y^{uu} \cdot \overline{h}^u + V_r^{uu}] + (q_0 - q)[V_r^{su}] = \overline{H}^u - H^{ud} = 0. \qquad (4)$$

Here individual housing demand is $- V_r/V_y$ from Roy's identity, $V_y = 1$ in each location as we are ignoring income distribution by assumption, and aggregate urban housing demand and supply are $H^{ua}, \overline{H}^u$ respectively, which must be equal in equilibrium. A similar equation holds when differentiating with respect to suburban rents.

Let the urban rent be r and the suburban rent be s. the impact of an increase in road charge τ can now be evaluated:

$$\frac{dW}{d\tau} = \frac{dW}{dr}\frac{\partial r}{\partial \tau} + \frac{dW}{ds}\frac{\partial s}{\partial \tau} + (V^{ss} - V^{su} + \tau)\frac{dq}{d\tau} - qV_y\frac{dp}{d\tau} + q. \qquad (5)$$

The first two terms on the right-hand side are zero because of demand-supply balance in the two land markets, while the first two elements in the third term cancel because of the mobility equilibrium condition $V^{su} = V^{ss}$. Finally,

$$\frac{dp}{d\tau} = \frac{dc}{dq}\frac{dq}{d\tau} + 1, \qquad (6)$$

and $V_y = 1$, so that

$$\frac{dW}{d\tau} = \left(\tau - q\frac{dc}{dq}\right)\frac{dq}{d\tau}. \qquad (7)$$

The term in brackets is the difference between the actual and efficient road charge, as qdc/dq is the marginal external cost of an extra trip.[4] If road use is efficiently charged, then a small change in the road charge has no effect on social welfare (the normal first-order condition for optimal charging), but otherwise changing the level of road charges will have a first-order effect on social welfare. The equation can be rewritten as

---

[4] The total cost of traffic is $C = qc(q)$, and $dC/dq = c + qdc/dq$. The first term is the private cost borne by the road user, and the remainder is the external cost. See Newbery (1990).

$$\Delta W = \left(\tau - q \frac{dc}{dq} \right) \Delta q, \tag{8}$$

showing that if road taxes increase and reduce trips ($\Delta q < 0$), welfare will increase so long as road charges are below the efficient level.

How would the standard rule-of-a-half (ROH) evaluate the benefit of a change in road taxes? The total gain in welfare would be

$$\Delta W = -\tfrac{1}{2}(q_0 + q)\Delta p + \Delta(q\tau), \quad \Delta = \frac{dc}{dq} \cdot \frac{dq}{d\tau} \Delta\tau + \Delta\tau, \tag{9}$$

which, for small changes Δq, reduces to the previous formula:

$$\Delta W = \left(\tau - q \frac{dc}{dq} \right) \frac{dq}{d\tau} \Delta\tau. \tag{10}$$

Thus the ROH should give the correct answer (subject to the usual reservations about the validity of linear approximations) for this case in which land supply is not externally adjusted, and in which relocations are induced by changes in road pricing.

Another way of seeing why changes in land values can be ignored is to note that the ROH applied to land involves no change in supply, so the income impacts are $\sum h_i \Delta r_i$ which sum to zero as changes in rental income are pure transfers from one side of the market to the other. Summarising:

Changes in road charges can be evaluated by measuring the changes in transport costs alone without taking account of any land price changes.

3. COST-BENEFIT ANALYSIS OF PURE TRANSPORT PROJECTS

The defining character of pure *transport* projects is that they affect the perceived cost of transport services to the user, and, as a consequence, affect the relative attractiveness of different locations, in turn inducing relocations and changes in land and property values. Thus prices change, but overall supplies of each quality of land do not. Land use projects or policies are those that influence locational choice directly by changing the supplies of each quality of land. For example, planning restrictions affect the supply of land with building permission and thereby affect the location of businesses and building. This kind of project will be considered in section 3.

Suppose that locations are indicated as before by sub- or super-scripts i, and that the only prices that change with the project are transport costs facing individuals in each zone, t_i, and property rentals, r_i. Suppose that an individual can only live in one location at a time, but may choose to relocate from i to j in response to price changes. As we are not interested in distributional issues, and to reduce the number of subscripts, suppose that agents need only be distinguished by their initial and final location: ii, ij, jj, or ji. The quantity of property services consumed by an agent in location i will be h_i, of transport services q_i, and the final choices will be distinguished by a dash, e.g. q_i', while the initial position will be undashed. Changes will be denoted by Δ, so that $\Delta q \equiv q_i' - q_i$.

The money value of individual welfare for an agent ij will be $V^{ij}(r, t, y^{ij} + r_i \overline{h_i})$ in the initial location i, where y^{ij} is money income from sources other than land ownership of agent ij. This can be thought of as the indirect utility function measured in money when the individual faces prices r_i, t_i and has total income $y^{ij} + r_i \overline{h_i}$ from all sources, including the ownership of property in amount h_i. For simplicity of notation, assume that individuals continue to own their own property in their initial location, so that they enjoy the implicit rent as income $r_i \overline{h_i}$, and notionally buy housing services and hence face property prices as shown in the utility function.

As before, the function V^{ij} has been normalised to be a money metric, which implies that $\partial V^{ij}/\partial y = 1$. Demand for housing services can be found from Roy's identity as $-\partial V^{ij}/\partial r_y$ and for transport services as $-\partial V^{ij}/\partial t_i$. Consider the subset of individuals who do not relocate from location i after the project. Their change in money welfare is

$$\Delta V^{ii} = V(r_i', t_i', r_i \overline{h_i}) - V(r_i, t_i, r_i \overline{h_i}), \qquad (11)$$

(dropping mention of the unchanging value of other income, y^{ij}), which can be expanded around the initial position in a second-order Taylor's series:

$$\begin{aligned}
\Delta V^{ii} &\approx \Delta r_i (V_r + V_y \overline{h_i}) + \Delta t_i V_t + \tfrac{1}{2}(V_{rr}\Delta r_i^2 + V_{tt}\Delta t_i^2) \\
&= \Delta r_i(-h_i + \overline{h_i}) = q_i \Delta t_i + \tfrac{1}{2}(-\partial h_i/\partial r_i \Delta r_i^2 - \partial q_i/\partial t_i \Delta t_i^2)
\end{aligned} \qquad (12)$$

where subscripts to V refer to partial derivatives, so $V_r = \partial V^{ii}/\partial r_i$, and the cross partial derivatives $V_{rt} = -\partial h_i/\partial t_i$ are assumed to be zero. If in addition h_i and q_i

are approximately linear in prices, then $\partial h_i / \partial r_i \approx \Delta h_i / \Delta r_i$ and (12) can be further approximated as

$$\Delta V^{ii} \approx (\overline{h}_i - h_i)\Delta r_i - q_i \Delta t_i - \tfrac{1}{2}(\Delta h_i \Delta r_i + \Delta q_i \Delta t_i), \tag{12a}$$

Notice that the first-order effect on housing choice cancels out when summed over i as (aggregate) initial demand is equal to (aggregate) initial supply, and only the second order or triangle term $-(1/2)\partial \Delta h_i \Delta r_i$ survives, while the change in transport costs is given by the usual rule-of-a-half that the transport gain is the average level of transport services times the fall in transport costs, $(1/2)(q_i' + q_i) \cdot (-\Delta t_i)$, noting that $q_i + (1/2)\Delta q_i = (1/2)(q_i + q_i')$.

If no individuals relocate, then total benefits will be found by summing over all agents i, and in this case the triangle terms $(1/2)\Delta h_i \Delta r_i$ cancel out as the sum of the changes in housing use in any location are identically zero by definition for a pure transport project. Note also that the result is only strictly accurate for linear demand schedules (for which the second-order expansion is accurate). With these qualifications we have established

Proposition 1. In computing the benefits of a pure transport project in which agents do not relocate, changes in rents do not contribute to overall benefits as they are pure transfers between agents that cancel out.

For individuals who relocate, this approach does not readily translate, as there may be a variety of locationally-specific characteristics that distinguish the quality of life in each location that have to be subsumed into the utility measure, and one cannot assume that $V^{ij}(r_i', t_i', r_i'h_i) = V^{ii}(r_i', t_i', r_i'h_i)$ even if $r_i' = r_i'$ and $t_i' = t_i'$. Instead we need to consider changes arising from prices and movements separately. Introduce the shorthand that $V(i) \equiv V^{ij}(r_i, t_i, r_i h_i)$ and $V(i') \equiv V^{ij}(r_i', t_i', r_i'h_i)$, and consider the total change in welfare of a mover:

$$\begin{aligned} \Delta V^{ij} &= V^{ij}(r_j', t_j', r_i'h_i) - V^{ij}(r_i, t_i, r_i h_i) \equiv V(j') - V(i) \\ &= V(j') - V(i') + V(i') - V(i), \quad \text{or} \\ &= V(j') - V(j) + V(j) - V(i). \end{aligned} \tag{13}$$

In the first case $V(i')$ has been added and subtracted, while in the second case $V(j)$ has been added and subtracted. The individual did not wish to move before prices changed, and did want to move after, so it must have been the case that

$$V(j') - V(i') = \varepsilon_{ij} > 0,$$
$$V(j) - V(i) = -\delta_{ij} < 0, \tag{14}$$

where ε_{ij} is the net benefit of moving after prices have changed, and δ_{ij} would be the net cost of moving before prices changed. Consequently,

$$\Delta V^{ij} = \varepsilon_{ij} + \Delta V^{ii} = \Delta V^{jj} - \delta_{ij}, \tag{15}$$

so that

$$\Delta V^{jj} \geq \Delta V^{ij} \geq \Delta V^{ii},$$

That is, the benefits to a mover are overstated by the benefits someone who has always lived in j would have enjoyed (as there was some cost in moving to j) and are understated by the benefits that would have been enjoyed if the individual had been forced to stay in i, as he chose to move. Since these costs of moving or being prevented from moving are unobservable, these two expressions can be used to place bounds on the benefits of the project.

The total benefits, ΔW, summing over all locations can now be bracketed as follows:

$$\frac{1}{2}\sum_i (q_j' + q_j)(-\Delta t_j) > \Delta W > \frac{1}{2}\sum_i (q_i' + q_i)(-\Delta t_i), \tag{16}$$

where the left-hand sum is taken over all trips that would have been generated at the old and new transport prices *after* all moves have taken place, and the right-hand sum is taken over all trips that would have been generated at the old and new transport prices *before any* moves had taken place. Notice that the triangle terms $(1/2)\Delta h_i \Delta r_i$ only cancel out for the upper and lower bounds on the change in welfare where we are able to appeal to the fact that the sum of the changes in housing use in any location are identically zero by definition for a pure transport project. Even then, they only cancel out to the accuracy of the linearity approximation. As these bounds are based on hypothetical demands and not those observed, they are not immediately useful for the analysis, suggesting that it is preferable to work in terms of the actual impact on individual welfare. Equation (16) is not quite the same as the conventional measure of benefits B:

$$B = \frac{1}{2}\left(\sum_j q'_j(-\Delta t_j) + \sum_i q_i(-\Delta t_i)\right),$$
(17)

where j denotes the final location and trips, and i the original location and trips. Nevertheless, B is likely to be a good compromise estimate, and will normally lie between the bounds given in (16). Thus the errors involved in the standard approach may not be too serious even where transport projects induce relocations and changes in land use, though it would be preferable to check this directly by computing the changes in welfare.

4. LAND USE POLICIES

Policies which affect the *supply* of land designated for particular uses (such as housing or office space) are such that aggregate changes in land use do not cancel out, and must therefore be taken into account: $\Sigma\Delta h_i \neq 0$.[5] Otherwise similar arguments to those advanced above apply, and there is some inaccuracy in applying consumer surplus based approaches such as the rule-of-one-half in computing impacts when agents relocate. To make further progress quantifying these errors it is convenient to use a utility function which produces linear demand schedules for transport and land use and hence for which the rule-of-one-half should be exactly correct. Consider the indirect utility function

$$V = y + r\bar{h} - (\alpha r - \tfrac{1}{2}\beta r^2) - (\gamma t - \tfrac{1}{2}\delta t^2) - w_{ij},$$
(18)

where t is the local area transport cost, and w_{ij} is the price of commuting between area i and j, taken to be zero for $i = j$. Demand for housing and local travel are given by

$$h_i = \alpha_i - \beta_i r_i, \qquad q_i = \gamma_i - \delta_i t_i,$$
(19)

---

[5] Transport policies such as building major new access roads are also likely to be associated with changes in the supply of land for specific purposes such as building.

where subscripts indicate the region of location of the household and hence of demand. Consider a change in land use policies that affects the endowment of land, $\overline{h}$. The change in welfare of a stayer is

$$\Delta V^{ii} = r_i\overline{h}_i' - r_i\overline{h}_i' - \alpha_i(r_i' - r_i) + \tfrac{1}{2}\beta_i(r_i'^2 - r_i^2) - \tfrac{1}{2}\Delta t_i(\gamma_i - \delta_i t_i + \gamma_i - \delta t_i'),$$
$$= \Delta y - \tfrac{1}{2}\Delta r_i(h_i' + h_i) - \tfrac{1}{2}\Delta t_i(q_i' + q_i). \tag{20}$$

where $\Delta y \equiv r_i'h_i' - r_ih_i'$ the change in rental income from land ownership. In the top equation the first two terms are the change in income caused by the change in the endowment of land, while the next two terms are the result of differencing the land price terms in the indirect utility function, and the last term is found in a similar way, but solves for the difference. The second line replaces the demand schedules by the quantities demanded to give the normal rule-of-one-half, which is thus correct *at the household level* for *stayers except for the change in rental income*, Δy.

For movers matters are more complicated. If we ignore the local travel demand (which has the same general form as the housing demand, and can thus be inferred from the final form of the housing term), the change in welfare of a mover is

$$\Delta V^{ij} = r_i\overline{h}_i' - r_i\overline{h}_i' - (\alpha_j r_j' - \alpha_i r_i) + \tfrac{1}{2}(\beta_j r_j'^2 - \beta_i r_i^2)w_{ij}. \tag{21}$$

All households within a zone are assumed identical (though demand coefficients may differ by zone, perhaps reflecting special features of land in each zone), and if there are initially n_i and finally n_i' households in zone i, then aggregate welfare change is

$$\Delta W = \Delta Y - \sum_i (\alpha_i[n_i'r_i' - n_ir_i] - \tfrac{1}{2}\beta_i[n_i'r_i'^2 - n_ir_i^2]) - n_cw, \tag{22}$$

where ΔY is the change in total income caused by the rental income changes, (local transport has again been ignored), and n_c is the number of new commuters each paying commuting cost w. This can be expanded and rearranged to give

$$\Delta W = \Delta Y - \tfrac{1}{2}\sum_i (\Delta r_i[H_i + H_i'] + \Delta n_i[\alpha_i(r_i + r_i') - \beta_i r_i r_i']) - n_cw. \tag{23}$$

The first term in square brackets, $H_i + H_i'$, is the rule-of-one-half term for total land use in zone i, which might be thought (incorrectly) to capture all the impacts. The interesting question is the size and interpretation of the second bracketed term. The term in square brackets can be rewritten as

$$[\alpha_i(r_i + r_i') - \beta_i r_i r_i'] = \alpha_i r_i - \tfrac{1}{2}\beta_i r_i^2 + \alpha_i r_i' - \tfrac{1}{2}\beta_i r_i'^2 + \tfrac{1}{2}\beta_i(\Delta r_i)^2,$$
$$\equiv -u(i) - u(i') + \kappa_i.$$
(24)

Here $u(i) = -(\alpha_i r_i - (1/2)\beta_i r_i^2)$ is the land part of the utility function and $\kappa_i \equiv (1/2)\beta_i(\Delta r_i)^2$. - Consider a mover from i to j who now must commute back to zone i. If he were the sole mover and commuter, he would give rise to $\Delta n = -1$, $\Delta n_i = 1$, $n_c = 1$. Reasoning as in equation (14)

$$u(i) = u(j) - w + \delta_{ij}, \quad u(i') = u(j') - w - \varepsilon_{ij},$$
(25)

so the effect of one person moving from i to j on aggregate welfare, where ΔW^* is the rule-of-one-half measure of the welfare change for housing and non-commuting traffic, including income changes ΔY, and the commuting terms cancel. It will be seen that the error consists of pairs of offsetting terms, and arguably small, though

$$\Delta W = Dy - \tfrac{1}{2}\sum_i \left(\Delta r_i[H_i + H_i']\right) - \tfrac{1}{2}\left(u(i) + u(i') - \kappa_i - u(j) - u(j') + \kappa_j\right) - w,$$
$$\Delta W^* - \tfrac{1}{2}(\delta_{ij} - w - \varepsilon_{ij} - w - \kappa_i \_ \kappa_j) - w,$$
$$\Delta W^* - \tfrac{1}{2}(\delta_{ij} - \varepsilon_{ij} + \kappa_j + \kappa_i),$$
(26)

this needs to be checked. Note that the terms involving κ are second order in Δr_i and do not vanish even when demand schedules are linear so that the rule-of-one-half applies exactly, as here. They arise because the correct measure of welfare keeps track of individual consumer surplus, and some consumers have relocated, whereas the measure in (23) and (26) is the surplus under a changing demand schedule, as illustrated below.

Interpreting equations (23) and (26) in terms of conventional consumer surplus areas is complicated by the fact that the numbers of consumers at each location is changing. There is a special case in which these formulae simplify. Suppose that after the restrictions in land use are imposed, migration continues until the marginal person is indifferent between staying and moving, and suppose that all consumers in each zone are identical (so that all consumers in the final equilibrium are indifferent between staying and moving). Suppose there are just two zones between which consumers locate, and movements give rise to commuting (ie initially everyone works in the zone where they live, and jobs do not relocate with consumers). The counterpart to (22) is

$$\Delta W = \Delta Y + n_1' u(1') - n_1 u(1) + n_2' u(2') - n_2 u(2) - n_c w,$$
$$= \Delta Y + n_1 u(1') - n_c u(1') - n_1 u(1) + n_2 u(2') + n_c u(2') - n_2 u(2) - n_c w,$$
(27)

because $n_i' = n_1 - n_c$ and $n_2' = n_2 + n_c$,, assuming that land restrictions force consumers to move from zone 1 to zone 2. If consumers are indifferent between zones in the final equilibrium,

$$u(1) = u(2) - w + \delta_{ij}, \quad u(1') = u(2') - w, \tag{28}$$

so that (27) can be written as

$$\Delta W = \Delta Y + n_1 u(1') - n_1 u(1) + n_2 u(2') - n_2 u(2),$$
$$= \Delta Y - \frac{1}{2} \sum_i \left(\Delta r_i [H_i + \hat{H}_i] \right), \tag{29}$$

where $H_i' = n_i' h_i'$ is the hypothetical demand for land in zone i assuming no relocation, and would be given by the per capita demand for land times the original number of consumers (an amount incompatible with the actual supply). Note that induced commuting costs have been ignored as we are measuring the impact on welfare by supposing that movers do not actually move, making use of indifference between moving and staying. Note also that this result is not the same as constraining consumers to stay in their original location, because land rents would then have to change more than if consumers are allowed to relocate. Equation (29) has actual changes in land rent but hypothetical demands for land. The result generalises to more than two zones.

A numerical example may clarify the various approaches illustrated above. Let $n_1 = n_2 = 1$, $\alpha_1 = 2$, $\beta_1 = 1$, $\alpha_2 = 1\frac{5}{4}$, $\beta_2 = \frac{5}{4}$. Demand for land in zone i is $\alpha_i - \beta_i r_i$, and if (per capita) land supply is initially $\bar{h}_1 = \bar{h}_2 = 1$, rents initially will be $r_1 = r_2 = 1$. If there is no other income than land rent, initial welfare is $V^i = 1 + u(i)$, with $u(1) = -1.5$, $u(2) = -1.4$, and if $w = 0.25$, $\delta_{12} = 0.15$ from (18). Suppose now that land supply is reduced in zone 1 but not changed in zone 2, so $\bar{h}_1' = \frac{8}{3}$ The new equilibrium will be established at

$n'_1 = \frac{3}{4}, n'_2 = \frac{5}{4}, n_c = \frac{1}{4}, r'_1 = \frac{3}{2}, r'_2 = \frac{5}{4}, \Delta Y_1 = -0.4375, \Delta Y_2 = \frac{1}{4}, \Delta Y = -0.1875,$ $\Delta u(1) = -0.375, \Delta u(2) = -0.225,$ so $\Delta W = -0.7875.$

Following the approach of equation (29), per capita land demand in the new equilibrium is $h'_1 = \frac{1}{2}$, $h'_2 = \frac{5}{4}$, (so that $n'_1 h'_1 = \frac{3}{8} = \bar{h}'_1$, etc) and $\frac{1}{4} \Delta r_i (H_i + \hat{H}'_i) = 0.375$ $(i = 1)$, and -0.225 $(i = 2)$, giving the same result for ΔW as above. Following the approach of equations (23) and (26), $-\frac{1}{2} \Delta r (H_i + H'_i) = -0.34375$ $(i = 1)$, and -0.25 $(i = 2)$, or together -0.59375 and $\Delta W^* = -0.78125$, 99% of the correct answer. The 'error terms' are $\kappa_1 = 0.125$, $\kappa_2 = 0.025$, and $\delta_{12} + \kappa_2 - \kappa_1 = 0.05$, so $-\frac{1}{2} n_c(\delta_{12} + \kappa_2 - \kappa_1) = -0.00625$, and again $\Delta W = -0.7875$. In this numerical example the errors are indeed small, though if the commuting costs had been included, these would have been ten times larger than the 'error', and the final figure would have overstated the disbenefit by 7%, a considerably larger error.

Figs. 1–4 attempt a visual representation of the impact of the land use policy. Figs. 1 and 2 show the per capita land demands for zones 1 and 2. Note that the demand schedule does not change with the policy, as the income elasticity of demand for land is zero (the condition required for surplus analysis to give the same result as the compensating variation). The initial equilibrium in zone 1 is at E, the final one is at C, and the loss in a resident's welfare is BCED, plus any change in rental income, BGHO - DEKO (assuming no compensation for the loss of land). The net loss is the area GCEKH. In Fig. 2, the loss in welfare is MNPQ, plus the increase in rental income, MSLO – QPLO = MSPQ, giving a net benefit NSP. The final equilibrium is established such that the difference in welfare between zones, LNM – ABC, is just equal to the extra commuting cost.

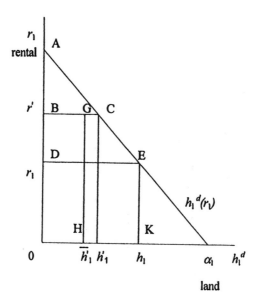

Figure 1. Per capita demands for land in zone 1

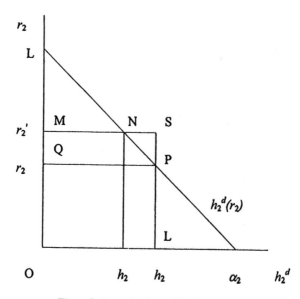

Figure 2. Per capita demand for land in zone 2

16

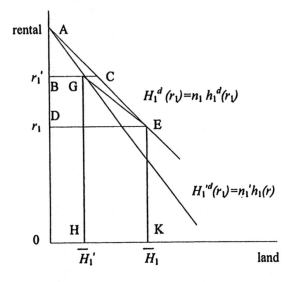

Figure 3. Aggregate demand for land in zone 1

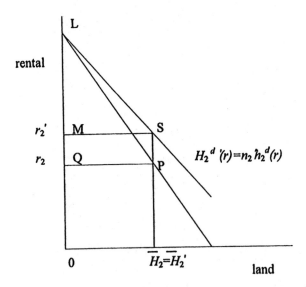

Figure 4. Aggretate demand for land in zone 2

Fig. 3 shows aggregate demand schedules, which do change with relocation. The original demand schedule is AE, which shifts in to AG as consumers relocate to 2. The total demand for land is then equilibrated with total supply, OH, at G. The rule-of-one-half gives the loss in welfare as BGED, to which should be added the change in income as before, to give a loss of GEKH. Note that GE is not a demand schedule, but points on two different demand schedules. Similarly in Fig. 4, the demand shifts from LP to LS, and the apparent loss in welfare is just MSPQ, plus the income change, also MSPQ, netting to zero. The difference between the correct method of Figs 1–2 and this measure is the thin triangle GCE, which understates the loss in Fig. 1, less the benefit NSP in Fig. 2. The difference is thus small.

4. CONCLUSIONS

If agents do not relocate after changes in land use and/or transport policies, then to within the accuracy of a linear approximation, the rule-of-one-half gives a good measure of the welfare changes of the policy and there is no need to look for wider General Equilibrium effects in the land market. But if general agents will move, and then the welfare change is only approximately equal to the rule-of-one-half measure. One way to see why this is so is to realize that consumer surplus measures are reasonable if the underlying utility function stays the same, and in this model, the level of utility attained depends on the location of the household and its work, which will change if they move. Surplus analysis when demand schedules are shifting is treacherous, and prone to error. It is difficult to quantify the error precisely, and in such cases it is preferable to work with the underlying utility functions.

REFERENCES

Blitzer, C., P. Dasgupta and J. E. Stiglitz (1981), 'Project appraisal and foreign exchange constraints', *Econ. Journ.* 91, pp. 58–74.

Buffie, E. (1987), 'Shadow prices and substitution in trade distorted economies', *Journal of Public Economics*, 34, 211–42.

Carlton, D. (1979), 'Valuing market benefits and cost in related output and input markets', *American Economic Review*, 69, 688–96.

Department of Transport (1987), *COBA 9*, Assessments Policy and Methods Division, London: Department of Transport

Dinwiddy, C. and F. Teal (1987), 'Project Appraisal and Foreign Exchange Constraints: A Comment', *Econ. Journ.* June, 479–486

Hammond, P. (1986), 'Project evaluation by potential tax reform', *Journal of Public Economics*, 30, 1–36.

18

Jacobsen, S.E. (1979), 'On the equivalence of input and output market Marshallian surplus measures', *American Economic Review*, 69, 423–28.

Jara–Díaz, S.R. (1986), 'On the relation between users' benefits and the economic effects of transportation activities', *Journal of Regional Science* 26(2), 379–91.

Mishan, E.J. (1976), *Cost-Benefit Analysis*, New York: Praeger

Mohring, H. (1976), *Transportation Economics*, Cambridge, Mass: Ballinger

Mookherjee, D. (1986), 'Shadow pricing with suboptimal policy rules', *Journal of Public Economics*, **31**, 287–305.

Newbery, D.M. (1990), 'Pricing and Congestion: Economic Principles Relevant to Pricing Roads', *Oxford Review of Economic Policy*, 6(2), 22–38.

CHAPTER - 2

OPTIMUM GROWTH THEORY AND SOCIAL TIME PREFERENCE[1]: A COMPUTERISED MATHEMATICAL MODELLING EXERCISE TO CHOOSE A SOCIAL DISCOUNT RATE[2]

*Sardar M.N. Islam**

ABSTRACT

Optimum economic growth models provide the framework for the derivation of the social discount rate. Although modelling of optimum growth is a well developed area in economics, the empirical derivation of the social discount rate remains as one of the most difficult exercises. Considerable efforts have been made by economists for the empirical derivation of the social discount rate for developed and developing countries with unsatisfactory outcomes. Moreover, in many developing countries where the rate of per capita consumption is decreasing and in countries where substantial environmental degradation and resource exhaustion are occurring, any study showing the empirical derivation of the social discount rate has not been undertaken or reported. This study presents an illustrative, though realistic exercise of estimating the social discount rate in an economy where the rates of growth of per capita GDP and consumption are negative. The estimated social discount rate in an illustrative example are reported and the limitations of the methodology in the case of decreasing per capita consumption and environmental degradation are stated. As the theory of optimum economic growth cannot provide a suitable guidance in these situations, concerns have been raised as to what should be the right method for choosing a social discount rate in these cases. The choice is probably a partly political economic one. Further research is necessary to resolve this issue which may require the development of a new paradigm.

*Director, Victoria University of Technology Melbourne, Victoria, Australia.

[1]An earlier version of this paper was prepared in 1993. The author thanks Prof. R. Williams, Prof. H. Hughes, Assoc. Prof. N. Norman and Dr. E. Boehm for their comments on that version of this paper. He also thanks Jim Gigas and Jamie Sanderson for providing research assistance in preparing the present version of the paper. The author is responsible for any remaining errors.

[2]A background research report submitted to the Research and Graduate Studies Committee, Faculty of Business, Victoria University of Technology, and presented at a seminar on 22 July, 1997 at the Centre for Strategic Economic Studies, Victoria University of Technology, Melbourne.

1. INTRODUCTION

Discounting the future has been a controversial issue in economics. Some of the important questions in growth economics (Wan, 1971) and public finance (Stiglitz, 1988) are in this area and are in the following form: Should we discount the future? If the decision is yes, what rate of discount should we adopt in public policy analysis and formulations. Discounting the future, which reflects the positive time preference of the society, is justified on the basis of myopic considerations of mankind, the possibility of extinction etc. In spite of the objections raised against discounting on the grounds of intergenerational equity and welfare, and environmental concerns, discounting the future is a prevalent practice in theoretical and applied economics. The question of what discount rate should be adopted in economic planning, project appraisal and public policy formulation has been one of the oldest, dominating issues in economics, it is still to be resolved. The methods of empirical derivation of the social discount rate (SDR) for developed and developing countries that can be adopted for practical use (see Brent, 1990; Bruce, 1976; Kula, 1984; & 1985; Lal, 1977; Lind, 1982; Ray, 1984) are mainly derived from the theory of optimum economic growth and are based on the assumption that the level of GDP and consumption in the economy will increase in the future and that future generations will be better off compared to the present generation.

However, in many developing countries the rate of per capita GDP or consumption is decreasing (see United Nations, 1990). Any study to empirically derive SDR in an economy where the per capita consumption rate is decreasing has not been undertaken or reported so far. And the choice of the current SDR in the economic situation when substantial environmental degradation is occurring (ibid) which may create catastrophic consequences for future generations making them worse off compared to the present generation (i.e. the growth rate of so called environmental GDP or per capita environmentally adjusted consumption is negative) has not been satisfactory in the existing literature (Islam and Gigas 1995, 1996).

The objectives of this paper are to illustrate the estimation of SDR on the basis of the theory of optimum growth and to point out the limitations of the dominating methodology in the cases with decreasing per capita

GDP or consumption and substantial future environmental degradation which will disadvantage future generations. This paper establishes an agenda for further research on the choice of SDR in the contemporary world characterised by an inadequate rate of growth of the economy, environmental degradation, inappropriate or inadequate technical progress, rapid population growth, etc. (Price, 1993).

In section 2 the theoretical derivation of SDR for a perfectly competitive or ideal economy is presented. This is followed by the discussion of the methodology adopted by this study and the data used in this study. Section 3 presents the estimated results with the suggested SDR, which is followed by a discussion of the limitations of the commonly adopted methodology, and the political economic nature of the choice of SDR (Section 4). The conclusions of this study are summarised in Section 5. In spite of all my efforts for a clear personation of the materials in this paper, the paper may still appear to be confusing, my only excuse for which would be that I would agree with Brent's view (1990, p. 65) that "The literature on the social discount rate is anything but clear."

2. OPTIMUM GROWTH THEORY AND THEORETICAL DERIVATION OF, AND NUMERICAL METHODOLOGY FOR SDR

2.1. The social discount rate

SDR is the rate used by society (policy makers, economic planners or analysts) to convert economic activities (costs and benefits) occurring at different periods of time to common present values by giving particular weights to future events (costs and benefits). SDR, therefore, determines the time value of economic activities occurring at different points of time to make them measurable by the same unit. For example, the present value net benefit (PVNB) stream of a project is given as follows:

$$PVNB = D_0 NB_0 + D_1 NB_1 + \cdots + D_T NB_T \qquad (1)$$

Where D is the relative weight given to the net benefits (NB) at different time periods $(0, 1, ..., T)$ so that these net benefits can be added for comparison. D is set according to the following formula

$$D_t = \frac{1}{(1+\rho)^t} \text{ where, } \rho = SDR \qquad (2)$$

In a perfectly competitive or ideal economy, SDR can be derived from an optimum growth model.

2.2. Optimum Growth Theory and SDR

An extensive literature on the theory of optimum economic growth has developed following the seminal work of Frank Ramsey on optimum saving (Ramsey 1928). The central issue in the determination of optimum economic growth is concerned with the rates at which a society should save and consume out of the national income so that the economy grows at the maximum growth rate (i.e. the optimum rate of accumulation) over an infinite or finite time horizon., a choice which is determined by a discount factor reflecting the time preference of the society. Therefore, the rate of discount used in an optimum growth model is crucial in programming optimum growth of the economy. The solution to a programme for optimum growth also provides the discount rate, the rate that determines the allocation between consumption and savings so that the economy grows at the optimum rate over the planning horizon. This is how the theory of optimum growth determines SDR. A *formal derivation* of SDR from an optimum growth model is given below.

We can define the variables of an aggregate growth model in per capita terms as follows:

$$y = f(k), \ c = C/L \text{ and } k = K/L \tag{3}$$

where: C = consumption, K = capital, L = population, and Y = output. The lower case letters denote variables in per capita form. We also define n as the growth rate of population and δ_k as the depreciation rate of capital. If we specify a social utility function as a non-negative, continuous, concave and twice differentiable function of the level of consumption and assume it to be well-defined (it is necessary for $U(0)$ to be bounded at infinity) and to represent the consumption preference of the society over time, then the problem of finite horizon optimal growth is to find a dynamic solution to the following optimisation problem (Burmeister and Dobell 1971):

$$\text{Max } U = \int_0^T u(c)e^{-\rho t}dt \text{ social welfare function}$$

Subject to $k' = f[k(t)] - c - (n + \delta_k) k(t)$ (accumulation equation) (4)

Initial condition:

$$k(0) = k_0$$

and transversality condition given as:

$$k(T) = k_T.$$

The Hamiltonian method yields the equations of motion (ignoring t arguments) of the maximisation problem characterising the dynamic growth paths of the state and control variables with the transversality condition as follows:

$$c' = U'(c)/U''(c) \, [f'(k) - (n + \delta_k) + \rho] \qquad (5)$$

$$k' = f(k) - c - (n + \delta_k)k \qquad (6)$$

$$k(0) = k_0 \text{ and } k(T) = k_T.$$

To derive the discount rate, the equation of motion for $c(t)$ in (5) can be used. In a steady state equilibrium condition,

$$\rho = f'(k) + (n + \delta_k) \qquad (7)$$

This implies that the discount rate is equal to the marginal product or return of capital, say $q = f'(k) + (n + \delta_k)$. From (4) it appears that in a steady state condition implies that the marginal product of capital is equal to the rate of discount on the welfare function:

$$p = q \qquad (8)$$

This result implies that in a perfectly competitive or ideal economy, SDR is equal to the marginal productivity of capital which is equal to the market interest rate:

$$SDR = \rho = q \qquad (9)$$

In addition to the economic role of SDR in an optimum growth programme as stated above, SDR (ρ) plays a very important technical or philosophical role in the programming of optimum growth (especially in infinite horizon optimisation models) and intertemporal resource allocation and planning as without ρ the above optimum growth model may not possess a convergent solution. This is a fundamental theoretical and mathematical concern in growth economics as was evident in the Ramscy growth model. If we assume the existence of ρ in the optimum growth model, then not only do we need ρ in the model, but we also need it to appear in an exponential form otherwise the growth model will be dynamically inconsistent, which is the so-called Strotz phenomenon in growth economics (Chakravarty, 1969; Heal, 1973). In addition to ρ, the optimum growth model must satisfy other normal mathematical conditions of existence, uniqueness and global optimality in the form the Weierstass theorem which ensures that the production possibility set of the economy is closed and compact (bounded), non-empty and convex and the objective functional is concave.

The above derivation of SDR is based on a single level optimisation approach to growth modelling, however, a multi-level optimisation approach can also be adopted (Islam, 1997). In a second best world, especially in a developing economy, the two rates (q and ρ) diverge due to the isolation paradox, market imperfections and externalities; and the problems of defining, determining and estimating SDR arise.[3] For several reasons such as intergenerational equity, social contact nature of the government, the possibilities for multiple market rate of interest it is argued that SDR should be less than the market interest rate. What we need is to find a *social interest rate*.

2.3. Methodology and Computer Programs for Empirical Derivation of SDR

There are two main methods or schools of thought of estimating or defining SDR. They are the social rate of time preference (SRTP), and the social opportunity cost of capital (SOOC). SRTP is the indication of the society's collective preference between current and future consumption. While the SOOC measures the social rate of return forgone due to the public investment of a certain amount. Since it is generally believed that SRTP and SOOC will diverge in an economy, efforts have also been made to estimate SDR by blending the two rates obtained from the two approaches. The resulting SDR is measured in terms of government income, and indicates the current value of future government income over time. In this approach, explicit considerations are given to the sources of government income and to the benefits derived from the public project. There are several measures of SDR, quantitative or qualitative, in each

---

[3]Economists have not yet agreed on the definition, identification, determination and estimation of the SDR (for the different theories on and views about SDR, see Lind (1982)).

school of thought such as the value of the historical average productivity or the rate of return on investment, the implicit discount rate implied by public sector decisions, the rate of discount socially chosen by growth planning.

Following the synthetic methods for estimating SDR, the formula for SDR developed by Squire and van dar Tak (1975) are commonly used in empirical work in developing countries. The Squire-Tak method falls largely in the SOOC school although it has elements of the SRTP approach. This study adopts the Squire-Tak method for estimating SDR. It is assumed that the economy is characterised by the shortage of capital, which requires a saving premium, and the society has preference for reduced inequality of income which is taken care of by the inequality aversion parameter in the social objective function. This method involves first converting all values to domestic prices by using the Standard Conversion Factor (SCF) (Appendix 1). The consumption rate of interest (CRI) is estimated separately and this value is then used to estimate the social accounting rate of interest (SARI). It should be noted that either CRI and SARI may be used as SDR, depending on the choice of numeraire (consumption or investment).

The methodology adopted in this study is one of the two available operational or numerical methods that exists in literature on SDR. These methods are: (1) Dynamic optimisation growth modelling where the rate of change of the shadow price of capital provides the numerical value of SDR (Newbery, 1972). (2) The enumerative procedure where different formulas are adopted to estimate the numerical value of SDR (see Brent, 1990; Bruce, 1976; Kula, 1984, 1985; Lal, 1977; Lind, 1982; Ray, 1984). The second method has been adopted in this study.

For numerical estimation of different formulas to derive SDR, Lotus 1-2-3 was used in this study. However, other computer programs, especially spreadsheets, can be used (Cartwright, 1993).

2.4. Data

To estimate SDR, data for different subjective and objective variables and parameters are required. These data can be from published sources. The objective data used in the estimation of SDR was obtained from different sources and some data were estimated by the present author. Appendix 2 contains a set of illustrative compiled data. Imports, exports, consumption, price index, GDP, investment, savings, and population are the major data required for our calculation.

Subjective parameters are difficult to reliably quantify or estimate. This is made especially difficult in a developing economy where the statistical bases are not yet developed and the political-economic environment is not yet crystallised enough to provide the needed data to estimate the subjective, quasi-political parameters necessary for project planning. As economists are sharply divided over the issues of methodology, definition or implications of some of these parameters or factors influencing these parameters, and given the illustrative nature of the present study, the commonly adopted practices (Brent, 1990; Bruce, 1976; Ray, 1984) suitable to an economy having the characteristics assumed earlier were adopted in this study.

3. EMPIRICAL DERIVATION OF SDR FOR THE ECONOMY

As noted earlier the estimation of SDR can be accomplished through the derivation of CRI or SARI which will be SDR. The linkage between CRI and the SARI will emerge as the estimation procedure unfolds in the following sections. Section 3.1 discussed the estimation of CRI while section 3.2 discusses the estimation of SARI. Estimation of both involves the calculation of several other parameters which is also discussed in these sections. A comprehensive discussion of the estimation and calculation of CRI, SARI and the associated parameters may be seen in Ray (1984).

The essence of the detailed and technical derivation of different formulas for CRI and SARI which will be reported in the following sections involves the following estimation steps: (1) The estimate of the market rate: To find the market time preference (for CRI) or the marginal products of capital (for SARI). (2) The estimate of the economic SDR: To adjust the market rate for economic considerations by shadow prices or other economic indicators or factors. (3) The estimate of the social SDR: To adjust the economic estimates by social objectives such as equity or poverty eradication by weighting the economic SDR by distribution parameters or basic needs parameters.

3.1. The Consumption Rate of Interest (CRI)

Following the underlying utilitarian approach to social welfare, we assume that the planning problem in the economy is best represented as maximisation of a social welfare function which is of the utilitarian form given by

$$W = [c(t)]^{\eta} e^{\rho t}$$

(where: η = the inequality aversion parameter or elasticity of marginal utility; ρ = the pure rate of time preference), subject to the investment constraint for the economy given by (5). And if consumption is used as the numeraire, the rate of discount is CRI. As CRI is the rate of fall in the value of future consumption streams, CRI is defined as follows:

$$\text{CRI} = -\frac{dW/dt}{W}$$

The formula for CRI is given as follows:

$$\text{CRI} = -\frac{dW/dt}{W} = \eta g + \rho \qquad (11)$$

The above formula can also be derived from the optimum growth model, equation (5), if we assume a social welfare function of the form (10) in model (4). Alternatively, it can also derived by logarithmic or product differentiation of (6) (see Brent (1990, p. 92). In theoretical and applied works ρ and ηg are added to provide an estimate of CRI. The two components of CRI incorporate intra-generational considerations (ηg) and inter-generational consideration (ρ) about the allocation of resources, equity and welfare. Since both these considerations are prevalent in the society, the estimate of CRI will include ρg and η so that the existing social preferences are accommodated in SDR.

In the following sections, definitions and a discussion of the methods for derivation of ηg and ρ are provided.

3.1.1. Elasticity of Marginal Utility (η)

The estimation of the elasticity of marginal utility of consumption (the inequality aversion parameter) with respect to changes in per capita consumption has been a difficult task, particularly in developing countries. The appropriate value of this parameter is important as it determines the relative weights given to income and consumption of different groups, $\eta = 0$: utilitarian position – all groups' income have same weight; $\eta > 0$: egalitarian position – higher weights for groups with lower income. In a developed country context, this parameter can be estimated by several methods using the Stone-Geary utility function, an additive separable function, and a complete demand system, among others. To estimate the elasticity of marginal utility, Squire and van der Tak (1975) have adopted the following function for marginal utility:

$$U_c' = dU / dc = c^{-\eta} \qquad (12)$$

where:

U_c' = marginal utility of consumption.

Elasticity of marginal utility is defined as

$$\frac{\% \text{ change in marginal utility}}{\% \text{ change in consumption}} = \frac{dU_c' / U_c'}{(dc / c)} = -\eta$$

Because of the difficulties in estimating the elasticity of marginal utility of consumption, an approach to determine η a priori on some philosophical or political basis or an approach to determine the weight from the past policy decisions of the Government is adopted very often in the literature. In developing countries a range of assumed values (0 to 2) is generally recommended and adopted (Brent, 1990; Bruce, 1976). The value adopted for the elasticity of marginal utility of consumption in this study was 0.50 as the base case estimate. This figure is also within the range of values of the elasticity of marginal utility of consumption suggested by Squire and van der Tak (1975) for developing countries. For the alternative estimates, η was assumed to be 1.0 and 1.5.

3.1.2. The Rate of Growth of Real per Capita Consumption (g)

The growth rate of real per capita consumption was calculated from the historical data. The exceptional result that we found that it was negative for the sample period. The average growth rate of per capita consumption over the period was found to be – 1.94%, therefore $g = -1.94\%$. It may be stated that the negative growth rate of GDP or per capita income is being experienced in real life in some developing countries. During 1980–87, the per capita GDP growth rates of developing market economies and petroleum exporting countries were –0.5 and –3.5 respectively (United

Nations 1990, p. 36). The environmental GDP growth rate per capita, if estimated properly is certainly negative as well (UN 1990).

3.1.3. The Rate of Pure Time Preference (ρ)

The pure time preference rate is the community valuation of future consumption at current prices. The valuation is very subjective. The values used in this study are 2%, 3% and 4% with the most likely value being 3%.

3.1.4. Estimates of CRI (i)

Table 1 below shows the estimation values of CRI with the growth rate of -1.94%[4].

The range of the estimate and value of CRI is -0.91 to 3.03.

3.2. Social Accounting Rate of Interest (SARI)

If investment or government income is the numeraire, then SDR is measured by SARI. It is a measure of the fall in the value of an additional unit of government income. SARI formulae involve the marginal productivity of capital (q) in the public sector and the social valuation of public income and CRI need also to be used. The formula adopted in this study for the base case estimation of SARI is given below:

$$SARI = s*q + (1 - s)*q/v*B_c \qquad (13a)$$

Table 1
Estimates of CRI

		Pure Time Preference		
		2.0	3.0[a]	4.0
Elasticity	0.5[a]	1.03	2.03	3.03
of Marginal	1.0	0.06	1.06	2.06
Utility	1.5	-0.91	0.09	1.09

[a]Most likely value for a developing economy.

   where:

v = the social value of public income,

s = marginal propensity to save,

---

[4]All of the SDR values in this paper are in % form.

$(1 - s)$ = marginal propensity to consume.
(*s are used some cases to indicate multiplication)

An interpretation of the SARI may be as follows: The return is equal to the rate of return on the saved capital assets (sq) and the imputed return to consumption.5 Other formulas that can be used in estimating the SARI are shown in Appendix 3.

In the following sections, definitions and the methods for derivation of the components of SARI (equation 13) are provided.

3.2.1. The Marginal Product of Capital (q)
The marginal product of capital can be inferred from the internal rate of return of various public sector projects approved by the government in recent years. The internal rate of return of some government projects in a developing economy may vary from 0% to 30%, and even more. But in many cases, no ex-post implementation estimates on the estimate of internal rate of return are available, it is not possible to use the values of the internal rate of return as the value of q.

For illustration the use of $q = 12\%$ (base case) is justified as the SOOC appears to be as high as 12% in some high growth economies, although two other values 10 and 15 were tried. This selection is consistent with other studies, for example Mashayekhi (1980).

3.2.2. The Social Value of Public Income (v)
The social value of public income is the accounting price of public income measured by the welfare value of marginal increases in consumption of a household at the average income, defined as:

$$v = \frac{w(g)}{w(c)} \tag{14}$$

where $w(g)$ = welfare value of public income; $w(c)$ = welfare value of private consumption.

---

[5]If in this case $v = q/(B_c * i)$, this implies that the SARI is equal to ARI = $sq + (1 - s)B_c(\eta g + \rho)$. The term $B_c(\eta g + \rho)$ is the conversion of CRI to the marginal product of capital numeraire while $(1 - s)$ is the consumption expended in this fashion and B_c is the conversion factor. Other formulas for v exist, however, interpretation of their meaning is more complicated.

The estimation of the social value of public income involves subjective and objective parameters. Controversy also surrounds the methodology used in the estimation of these parameters as is evident from the numerous estimation methods some of which are given below in Appendix 4. The following formula was adopted (base case) to estimate the social value of public income:

$$v = q/(B_c * i) \tag{15a}$$

To calculate a numerical v, the value of q was obtained from the procedure discussed above, and the value of CRI estimated using formulas stated in previous sections was adopted.

The other important determinant of v is B_c = consumption goods conversion factor which was estimated by using the standard method as shown in Appendix 1. The SCF for consumption goods for $(B_c) = 0.802$.

3.2.2. The Marginal Propensities to Save (s)

The marginal propensities to consume (global) and save were estimated from the national income accounts in Table 3 in Appendix 2. The value for s was estimated to be 0.618 and thus the value for $(1 - s)$, the propensity to consume is 0.382.

3.2.3. The Estimation of SARI

Table 2 below shows an illustration of the estimation of SARI. The rate of growth (g) in the economy is − 1.94% and assumed to be constant for the estimation of SARI.

3.3. The Estimated Values of SDR

We have stated above either CRI or SARI can be regarded as SDR depending on the choice of numeraire. Tables 1 and 2 show the estimated values of CRI and SARI. The sign of SDR is both positive and negative, and the estimated values are widely spread from −0.91 to 5.5. The three variables in the SARI, s, v, and q are different. In the present case, we have assumed a very high value of v, lower values such as 5 would give a

Table 2

Estimates of SARI

The SCF for the MPC initially was 0.95 and SCF (B_c) for consumption goods is estimated to be .802. The other parameters that are relevant to the calculations are s = 0.3, MPC = 0.12, t = 50, g = −1.94 and a risk aversion parameter value of η = 0.5.

CRI = i	0.010	0.020	0.030
ρ	0.020	0.030	0.040
(1) SARI = sq + (1 − s)q/vB_c	0.041	0.048	0.055
Simple definition of $v = q/B_c^* i$	13.800	7.002	4.691
$B_c^* i$	0.008	0.016	0.024
(2) SARI = sq + (1 − s)q/vB_c	0.010	0.020	0.030
Complex definition of $v(v^*B_c)$	−3.339	−5.741	−20.462
$v = (1 − s)q/((i − sq)^*B_c$	−4.163	−7.158	−25.513
(3) SARI = sq + (1 − s)q/vB_c	0.045	0.048	0.053
$v = a(1−b^{\wedge}(tm))$	9.555	7.115	5.422
$a = (1 − s)q/(i − sq)B_c$	−4.163	−7.158	−25.513
$b= (1 + sq)/(1 + i)$	1.024	1.014	1.004
(4) SARI = i + v'/v	0.044	0.047	0.052
$v'/v = −b^{\wedge}(tm)\ln(b)/(1 − b^{\wedge}(tm))$	0.034	0.027	0.022
$v = (1 − b^{\wedge}(tm))$	−2.295	−0.994	−0.213
$b= (1 + sq)/(1 + i)$	1.024	1.014	1.004

negative estimate of SARI. The CRI is comprised of the variables ρ, η, g. The growth rate is assumed to be constant while ρ (the social time preference) and ρ the marginal utility of consumption are allowed to vary. Thus Table 1 and 2 above shows the effects of risk aversion, social preference for current versus future consumption in an environment that is experiencing negative growth in per capita consumption.

The estimated values of SDR in this study (Tables 1 & 2) may now be compared with the estimates of SDR of different countries (see Brent, 1990; Bruce, 1976; Kula, 1984; and 1985; Lal, 1977; Lind, 1982; and Ray, 1984). In the existing literature, the range of estimated SDR is also wide. For Pakistan, Squire, Little & Durdag estimated SDR = 3. Scott found the range for Great Britain to be 2.13 to 4.57. Many other estimates lie in the range of 8 to 12, while the World Bank generally advocates a rate around 10%. Professional economists traditionally suggested 4 or 5, although present environmental economists are suggesting a zero or even negative rate. Australian estimates are within a range of 2.1 to 7.9. Although the widely used parameter is 6, the Department of Finance recommendation is for a rate of 8 (Department of Finance, 1991).

As the question of estimation or choice of SDR is an important topic in climate change economics since economic theory suggests a higher discount rate will increase the rate of resource extraction and will increase global warming, a large number of different estimates and suggestions have been made, some of which are as follows: Nordhaus (1994) suggests a pure time preference rate of 3, Cline (1992) suggests a pure time preference rate of 0 and a discount rate on goods and services of 1.5, Manne (1995) suggests that a discount rate of less than 5 is unsustainable.

Regarding the negative SARI value in Table 1, the reason for the negative SARI is generally due to the negative growth rate in consumption in the economy. If the growth rate was positive, the value of CRI would be larger representing a preference for current consumption and the calculated SARI would be positive. In real life, developing countries are experiencing a negative per capita income or consumption growth rate and a negative SARI or SDR may be estimated by applying the existing formulas. In this situation, how will SDR be chosen?

4. A POLITICAL ECONOMIC CHOICE OF SDR OR A NEW PARADIGM

This exercise of the determination of SDR provides an insight into the policy problem a nation faces: What SDR can be used for optimum growth planning? All the above measures and estimation of the SARI are based on assumed historical data. The assumption being that once the effects of the past have been determined future policy options can be developed in the light of the expected future developments and past empirical measures. If historical data provide an estimate of the positive discount rate, the choice of SDR is then solved without much difficulty.

Although the theory of optimum economic growth provides a framework for the derivation of SDR, its estimation involves substantial subjective value judgement regarding the values of the parameters, income distribution and intergenerational equity objectives, and the goals of economic management. The situation becomes very complicated if an economy is experiencing a negative income or consumption growth rate and environmental degradation and resource exhaustion. In these situations, the future generations will not be better off as assumed in the theory of optimum economic growth. The author is not familiar with any numerical study dealing with the estimation of negative SDR. Theoretically, the concept of negative time preference or negative SDR is not alien in economics. Wan, (1971, p. 322) has put the issue of negative SDR in the following form: "A negative time preference rate ($\delta < 0$) may appear rather bizarre tothe average economist at first glance. However, our prejudice against such an assumption may be due to the writings of the Austrian school, who tried hard to justify the positive interest rate observed. The adoption of a negative time preference rate may be quite appropriate in the context of the Ramsey model.... The economic consequences of a negative time preference rate is an encouragement to invest".

A negative value of SDR suggests the society will prefer to consume later rather than spend and consume now. The question is then: Can we apply this rule in formulating public policy?

Work in environmental economics to estimate SDR by incorporating the environmental concerns are progressing rapidly. A recent proposal for a suitable methodology in this area may be seen in Islam and Gigas (1996).

The operational guidelines provided by optimum growth theory for the derivation of SDR are not appropriate and the situation requires a partly political economic decision as to what should be the appropriate SDR for the economy in the above conditions. This may involve the development of a new paradigm. A discussion of the logic and principles of political economic choice of SDR can be found in Parkins (1994).

5. CONCLUSIONS

This study has attempted to estimate SDR. Two alternative estimates of SDR are reported. The common method adopted to estimate SDR in a developing country is SARI. The estimated SDR is found to vary substantially. One striking feature of this study is the possibility of negative values of SDR caused by mainly negative g and found when the value of ρ increases. The same situation may arise if there is environmental degradation. Although the issue of the estimation of SDR in countries with the negative income or consumption growth rate and environmental degradation needs further and comprehensive consideration, the choice of SDR remains probably an essentially unsolvable problem in economics. An alternative paradigm, rather than the framework of optimum growth theory, may be necessary. As Howe did, (1979, p. 158) we can ask the question: 'Where does this leave us in selecting an appropriate discount rate for public sector programs?' The answer probably lies in the view of many leading experts in this area that the purpose of studies on SDR should not be to find a numerical value of SDR, rather it should be to provide a better understanding of the issues of intergenerational and intertemporal allocation, planning, equity and welfare (personal discussion with Alan Manne 1996 who is one of the leading authorities in this field). I leave these issues as agenda for further research.

APPENDIX 1. THE STANDARD CONVERSION FACTOR

The Standard Conversion Factor (SCF) was estimated by its standard formula shown below.

$$SCF = \frac{M + X}{M(1 + t_m) + X(1 - t_x)} \tag{16}$$

where:

M = average value of imports
X = average value of exports
t_m = value of rates of taxes on imports
t_x = value of rates of taxes on exports.

The variables are summed over the sample period and used to estimate the SCF. The estimated value of the standard conversion factor is 0.90. This value for the SCF is also consistent with the values for the SCF in other studies.

It is assumed that SCF for consumption goods is: $B_c = 0.95$.

APPENDIX 2.

Table 3

National Income and Economic Statistics ($Million)

	1981	1982	1983	1984	1985	1986	1987	Total	Average
Value of Total Imports (M)	746.9	762.2	863.1	914.9	899.5	1024.3	963.0	6173.9	881.99
Value of Total Exports (X)	565.9	571.4	687.4	822.0	926.2	1000.8	1134.8	5708.5	815.50
Taxes on Local Imports (Tm)	63.7	77.6	88.4	99.5	103.9	122.7	141.0	696.8	99.54
Taxes on Local Exports (Tx)	4.5	4.5	4.9	12.8	13.1	14.3	12.4	66.5	9.50
Subsidies on Exports (-Tx)								0.0	0.00
Net Taxes on Trade	59.2	73.1	83.5	86.7	90.8	108.4	128.6	630.3	90.04
Value of Producer Goods Imports (Mp)	437.1	435.6	514.1	513.9	513.3	565.1	531.1	3510.2	585.03
Value of Producer Goods Exports (Xp)	403.8	433.9	507.8	568.1	689.2	710.5	905.3	4218.6	602.65
Taxes on Producer Goods Imports (Tmp)	37.3	44.4	52.7	55.9	59.3	67.7	63.1	380.3	63.37
Taxes of Producer Goods Exports (Txp)	3.2	3.4	3.6	8.8	9.7	10.2	9.9	48.9	6.98
Subsidies on Producer Goods Exports (-Txp)								0.0	0.00
Net Taxes on Trade	34.1	40.9	49.0	47.0	49.5	57.5	53.2	331.4	47.33
Value of Consumer Goods Imports (Mc)	309.8	326.6	349.0	401.0	386.1	459.3	431.9	2663.7	443.95
Value of Consumer Goods Exports (Xc)	162.1	137.5	179.6	253.9	237.0	290.3	229.5	1489.9	212.84
Taxes on Consumer Goods Imports (Tac)	26.4	33.2	35.7	43.6	44.6	55.0	63.2	301.9	50.31
Taxes on Consumer Goods Imports (Tmc)	1.3	1.1	1.3	4.0	3.4	4.1	2.5	17.6	2.51
Subsidies on Consumer Goods Exports (-Tac)								0.0	0.00
Net Taxes on Trade	25.1	32.2	34.5	39.7	41.3	50.9	60.7	284.3	40.61
Consumption at Current Prices	1558.6	1586.0	1716.3	1849.0	2001.0	2086.0	2165.0	12961.9	1851.70
Consumption at Constant Prices	1558.6	1497.9	1533.1	1551.0	1611.0	1600.0	1584.0	10935.6	1562.22
GDP at Constant Market Prices	1681.2	1649.0	1758.2	1786.4	1818.9	1866.7	1908.2	12468.6	1781.22
Gross Fixed Capital Formation	450.6	544.2	562.2	446.6	383.8	418.1	438.9	3244.8	463.53
Change in Stocks	6.7	-13.2	59.8	26.8	27.3	24.3	19.1	150.7	21.53
Gross Investment	457.3	531.0	622.4	473.4	411.1	442.4	458.0	3395.5	485.07
Gross Domestic Savings (GDS)	110.6	192.7	286.9	318.4	314.7	415.6	500.00	2138.9	305.55
Per Capita Cons. at Constant Prices (C)	498.9	468.7	469.0	463.8	470.9	457.1	431.2	3270.8	467.25
Population (millions)	3.1	3.2	3.3	3.3	3.4	3.5	3.6		

APPENDIX 3. ALTERNATIVE SARI FORMULA

The common formulas which have been used to estimate SARI. A careful consideration of the alternative formulas of SARI is necessary in choosing any particular value of SDR. These alternative formulas are derived from different specifications of public income, distribution parameter and the time period when the need for savings will cease to exist.

The formulas used for estimating the SARI are:

$$1.\ \text{SARI} = sq + (1 - s)q/v \tag{13a}$$

where:

v = the social value of public income,
s = marginal propensity to save,
$(1 - s)$ = marginal propensity to consume.

$$2.\ \text{SARI} = \text{CRI} + v'/v \tag{13b}$$

where:

v' = marginal utility of government income,
v'/v = rate of decline in the marginal utility of government income.

$$3.\ \text{SARI} = \text{CRI} - \frac{b^{(t+1)}\ln(b)}{(1 - b^{(t+1)})} \tag{13c}$$

where:

$$b = \frac{(1-s)q}{(1+i)}$$

APPENDIX 4. FORMULA FOR THE SOCIAL VALUE OF PUBLIC INCOME

The formulas (Bruce 1976; Ray 1984) used for estimation of the alternative social value of public income are:

1. Simple formula

$$v = q/(B_c^* i) \tag{15a}$$

where:
B_c = the standard conversion factor for consumption goods; the factor is equivalent to the factor shown in Appendix 1, except only consumption goods are considered,
i = consumption rate of interest (CRI).

2. Complex formula

$$v = \frac{(1-s)q}{(i - sq)B_c} \tag{12b}$$

where:

 s = marginal propensity to save,
 q = marginal productivity of capital.

3. More complex formula

$$v = \frac{(1-s)q}{(i-sq)B_c}\left[1 - \frac{(1+sq)^{(t+1)}}{(1+i)}\right]$$ (12c)

where: t = the time when the value of public income will be equal to the value of consumption. The determination of t when the country will have no savings deficiency has also been partly subjective. In the previous studies, a range of t from 15 to 100 has been assumed (Brent 1990; Bruce 1976; Ray 1984). In this study, a relatively longer time frame was assumed, t was assumed to equal 30, 50 and 100.

REFERENCES

Arrow, K. (1982), 'The Rate of Discount on Public Investments with Imperfect Capital Markets', in Lind 1982.

Brent, R. J. (1990), *Project Appraisal for Developing Countries*, Harvester Wheatsheaf, New York.

Bruce, C. (1976), *Social Cost-Benefit Analysis*, Staff Working Paper No. 39, World Bank, Washington DC.

Burmeister, E. and Dobell, A. (1970), *Mathematical Theories of Economic Growth*, Macmillan, London.

Cartwright, T. (1993), *Modeling the World in a Spreadsheet*, John Hopkins University Press, Baltimore.

Chakravarty, S. (1969), *Capital and Economic Development Planning*, M.I.T. Press, Cambridge.

Cline, W. (1992), The Economics of Global Warming, Institute of International Economics. Washington.

Department of Finance (1991), Handbook of cost Benefit Analysis, Australian Government Publishing Service, Canberra.

Heal, G. M. (1973), *The Theory of Economic Planning*, North Holland Publishing Company, Amsterdam.

Howe, G. C. (1979), *Natural Resource Economics*, John Wiley and Sons, New York.

Islam, S. M. N. (1997, forthcoming), Mathematical Economics of Multi-level Optimization: Theory and Application (Physica series: *Contributions to Economics*), Springer-Verlag, Heidelberg.

Islam, S. M. N. and Gigas, J. (1996), Economics of Project Appraisal and Sustainable Economic Development, a paper presented at the Pacific Rim Allied Economic Organisations Conference in Hong Kong on January 10 –15, 1996.

Islam, S. M. N. and Gigas, J. (1995), Social Time Preference, Climate Change and the Future of the Australian Economy: Findings from the Australian Dynamic Integrated Climate Economic Model (ADICE), *Proceedings of the Conference of the Australia New Zealand Society of Ecological Economists*, Coffs Harbour, Sydney, November.

Kneese, A. V. and Sweeney, J. L. (eds.) (1993), *Handbook of Natural Resource and Energy Economics: Volume III*, Elsevier Science Publications, Amsterdam.

Kula, E. (1984), 'Derivation of Social Time Preference Rates for the United States and Canada', *Quarterly Journal of Economics*, vol. 99, pp. 873–882.

Kula, E. (1985), 'An Empirical Investigation on the social Time preference Rate for the United Kingdom', *Environment and Planning*, vol. 7, pp. 99–22.

Lal, D. (1977), 'Distributional Weights, Shadow Wages, and the Accounting Rate of Interest: Estimates for India', *Indian Economic Review*, vol. 2, no. 2.

Lind, R. (1982), *Discounting for Time and Risk in Energy Policy*, John Hopkins University Press, Baltimore.

Manne, A (1996), *A Personal Discussion,* Osaka.

Manne A. S. (1995), The rate of time preference: Implications for the greenhouse debate. In: Nakicenovic, N., Nordhaus, W.D., Richels, R., and Toth, F.L., (Editors). Energy Policy. 23, 4/5, pp 391–394.

Mashayekhi, A. (1980), *Shadow Prices for Project Appraisal in Turkey*, World Bank Staff Working Paper 392, Washington DC.

Newbery, D. G. (1972), 'Public Policy in Dual Economy', *Economic Journal*, 37, 47–61.

Nordhaus, W., (1994), *Managing the Global Commons: The Economics of Climate Change*, MIT Press. London.

Parkins, F. (1994), *Practical Cost-Benefit Analysis*, Macmillan Education, Melbourne.

Price, C. (1993), *Time, Discounting and Value,* Blackwell, Oxford.

Ramsey, F. P. (1928), 'The Mathematical Theory of Saving', *The Economic Journal*, Dec, 543–59.

Ray, A. (1984), *Cost-Benefit Analysis*, John Hopkins University Press, Baltimore.

Sen, A. (1967), 'Isolation, Assurance, and the Social Rate of Discount', *Quarterly Journal of Economics*, vol. 81, no. 1.

40

Squire, L. and van dar Tak, H. G. (1975), *Economic Analysis of Projects*, John Hopkins University Press, London.

Squire, L., I. M. D. Little, and Durdag, M. (1979), *An Application of Shadow Pricing to Country Economic Analysis with an Illustration from Pakistan*, World Bank Working Paper No. 330, World Bank, Washington DC.

Stiglitz, J. (1988), *Economics of the Public Sector*, W.W. Norton, New York

United Nations (1990), *Global Outlook 2000*, UN, New York.

Wan, H. Y. Jr. (1971), *Economic Growth: A Critical Review and Summary of the Modern Theories of Economic Growth*, Harcourt Brace Jovanovich, New York.

CHAPTER - 3

A THEORETICAL INQUIRY ON THE AXIOMATIC CONSISTENCY OF DISTRIBUTIONAL WEIGHTS USED IN COST-BENEFIT ANALYSIS

Giuseppe Munda

ABSTRACT

The present paper has as the main objective to analyse the role of distributional weights normally presented in cost-benefit analysis handbooks. In particular, to test the consistency and compatibility of the axiomatic system, attention will be devoted to the relationship between the concept of compensability and meaning of the distributional weights. In order to tackle this issue, some results of the multiattribute utility theory and measurement theory literature are used.

1. INTRODUCTION

The notion of individual preference that is relevant to cost-benefit analysis (CBA) is the preference that is recorded on the market place (or which would be recorded if there were a market), and not the preference recorded by a simple political vote. This kind of "economic voting" is preferred to classical political voting procedures for different reasons [see Mishan, 1971; Pearce and Nash, 1981]. One reason is that "the use of money values permits some expression of the *intensity of preference* in the vote: it enables the individual to say how deeply he wants or does not want the project or good in question" [Pearce and Nash, 1981, p. 7].

[41]

This approach can be related to Borda's [1781] method in the theory of social choice.[1]

The assumption underyling the net present value rule is that of an additive social welfare function, such as $SW = \sum_h U_h$, where the subscript h denotes the individual to whom the utility function applies. Under the assumption that marginal utility of money income (λ) is *identical for all individuals*, the variation of this social welfare function indicating the social worth of a project is:

$$\Delta SW = \sum_h \sum_i \frac{\partial U_{ih}}{\partial Y_{ih}} \cdot \Delta Y_{ih} = \lambda \sum_h \sum_i P_i \Delta Y_{ih} = \lambda \sum_i P_i \Delta Y_i \qquad (1)$$

where h subscript denotes the individual to whom the utility function and quantity of the good Y_i apply. The translation into monetary terms is accomplished by the equation $\lambda(\partial U_i/\partial Y_i = P_i)$ where P_i is the (relative) price of good i.

The use of linear aggregation procedures and the fact that intensity of preference is taken into account have different consequences. These will be investigated in the following section.

2. COMPENSABILITY AND THE MEANING OF WEIGHTS

One has to note that the net present value formula can be considered to be an additive value function, where the different dimensions are condensed by using a simple linear weighting rule or a generalised-linear rule, where suitable non-linear functions transformations are used. Here, the legitimacy of these procedures is investigated. For this purpose, some results of the multiattribute utility theory and measurement theory literature are used. The formal analogy between social welfare functions and multicriteria decision theory was first investigated by Arrow and Raynaud (1986) who noted that it is formally possible to consider a single individual as an attribute.

Multiattribute utility theory is based on the following hypothesis: in any decision problem there exists a *real valued function U* defined on the set A of feasible actions, which the decision maker wishes, consciously or not, to

---

[1]The "Borda rule" can be described as follows. "Each voter reports his preferencec by ranking the p candidates from top to bottom (ties are not allowed). A candidate receives no points for being ranked last, one point for being ranked next to last, and so on, up to $p-1$ points for being ranked first. A candidate with highest **total** score, called a **Borda winner**, wins [Moulin, 1988, p. 229]".

examine [Bell et al., 1977, 1988; Keeney and Raiffa, 1976]. This function aggregates the different attributes taken into consideration, where an attribute i, $i \in \Omega$, consists of a set X_i of at least two elements expressing different levels of some underlying dimensions, and of a total strict order P_i on X_i. As a consequence, the decision problem can be formulated as max $U[v_i(x_i)]$ (where v_i is a value function over X_i). The role of the analyst is to determine this function. The most usual functions are the *linear* or the *multiplicative* form.

The aggregation of several dimensions implies taking a position on the problem of *compensability*. Intuitively, compensability refers to the existence of trade-offs, i.e. possibility of offsetting a disadvantage on some attribute by a sufficiently large advantage on another attribute, whereas smaller advantages would not do the same.

This approach is based on the idea that in order to compare two alternatives $a, b \in A$, we have to consider the differences between the evaluations of **a** and **b** on each attribute and to declare that aPb (**a** is preferred to **b**) if the differences in favour of **a** more than compensate those in favour of **b**. Thus a preference relation is noncompensatory if no trade-off occurs and is compensatory otherwise.

The way each aggregation procedure transforms information in order to arrive at a preference structure can be called its aggregation convention, which is generally well illustrated by the numerical transformation used. Clearly, the convention underlying the additive utility model is complete compensatory. The notion of compensability has been extensively studied by several authors [e.g. Bouyssou, 1986; Fishburn, 1976, 1978; Keeney and Raiffa, 1976; Podinovskii, 1994; Vansnick, 1986].

Given any nonempty disjoint subsets of attributes I and J, I strongly compensates, J if for all x, $y \in X$ such that $x \succ y$, ($\succ$ meaning a preference relation) $P(x, y) = J$, $P(y, x) = I$, (where $P(x, y)$ indicates the subsets of all the relations $x \succ y$ and on the contrary $P(y, x)$ all the relations $y \succ x$) there is a $z \in X$ such that $z \succ x$ or $z = x$ and $z_i = y_i$ for all $i \notin I$. Therefore, a notion of perfect compensability is at hand if we ask for strong compensability to hold both ways between any two disjoint (nonempty) subsets of attributes. The notion of compensability can also be formalised by means of the usual definition of a trade-off ratio whenever $U(x, y)$ can be differentiated.

To use the compensatory approach in practice, we have to determine for each attribute, a mapping $\phi_i : X_i \to R$ which provides an interval scale of measurement and to assess *scaling constants* in order to specify how the compensability should be accomplished, given the scales ϕ_i between the different attributes [Roberts, 1979]. Note that the scaling constants which appear in the compensatory approach depend on the scales ϕ_i; thus they *do not characterise the intrinsic relative importance of the attributes.*

This can be easily shown as follows [see Vincke, 1992]. Let us consider options, it is:

$$z_a = (x_1(a),\ x_2(a),\ ...,\ x_n(a))$$

and

$$z_b = (x_1(b),\ x_2(b),\ ...,\ x_n(b))\qquad \text{then as a first approximation}$$

$$0 = U(z_b) - U(z_a) = \sum_{i=1}^{n}\left(\frac{\partial U}{\partial x_i}\right)_{z_a}(x_i(b) - x_i(a)) = -\left(\frac{\partial U}{\partial x_j}\right)_{z_a} + S_{jr}(a)\left(\frac{\partial U}{\partial x_r}\right)_{z_a}$$

and from the latter

$$S_{jr}(a) = \frac{(\partial U / \partial x_j)(z_a)}{(\partial U / \partial x_r)(z_a)}\qquad (2)$$

When the function U is a weighted sum of all the attributeds, i.e.

$$U(x_1, x_2, ..., x_n) = \sum_{i=1}^{n}\lambda_i x_i \quad \text{it is}$$

$$S_{jr}(a) = \frac{\lambda_j}{\lambda_r} = \text{constant.}\qquad (3)$$

This means that in the weighted summation case, the substition rates are equal to the weights of the attributes upto a multiplicative coefficient. As a consequence, the esimation of weights is equivalent to that of substitution rates: the questions to be asked are in terms of "gain with respect to one attribute allowing to compensate loss with respect to another" and not in terms of "importance" of attributes.

Of course, a too precise specification of weights is utopian and creates false certainties, as a consequence, a sensitivity analysis or the study of the feasible weight space is very important. For example, in the weighted summation model the substitution rates between a reference attribute r and each of the other j $(j \neq r)$ attributes may vary between an upper and lower boundary, that is

$$\underline{S}_{jr} \leq S_{jr} \leq \overline{S}_{jr} \qquad (\forall j \neq r)$$

The function used in cost-benefit analysis can be considered an additive social welfare function, where the assumption of the constancy of the marginal utility of income across individuals needs to be accepted. This is a distributional question, and that assumption embodies particular social values. Given that society is unlikely to be indifferent among relevant distributions of income, some ways of integrating the distributional aspects into the analysis have to be found. The most popular methodology is to introduce distributional weights explicitly; by using different weights for different social groups.

It has to be noted that failures to use any weighting system implies making the value judgements either that the existing distribution of income is optimal and/or the change in income distribution is negligible. If, and only if, one is happy with such value judgment, it is reasonable to use unweighted market valuations to measure costs and benefits. *Therefore, there is no escape from value judgements.*

The methods used to obtain weights are based on a variety of philosophical and methodological principles. A review of the scientific debate on these issues can be found in Dasgupta and Pearce [1972], Dasgupta et al. [1972], Pearce and Nash [1981] and Ray [1984]. Just for giving some examples, a possible approach for getting distributional weights is to observe the weights implicit in past government decisions [Weisbrod, 1968]. Another possibility is an analysis of the progressivity of the income tax schedule [Krutila and Eckstein, 1958]; by means of this approach the marginal rate of tax can be converted into a surrogate for the marginal utility of income, the relevant weights are the inverses of the marginal tax rates. As a consequence the gains (or losses) of lower-income groups are weighted more heavily than the gains of high-income groups. Another approach is to scale down higher incomes and scale up lower incomes to equalise their influence on the cost-benefit outcome; Foster [1960] suggests that gains and losses should be weighted by the ratio of the average national personal income to the individual's income. Lastly, different sets of weights can be obtained by trying to assess the likely shape and elasticity of a marginal utility of income function.

Here we want to stress that given an aggregation procedure, there should be consistency between the aggregation procedure used and the questions asked to the decision-maker in order to elicit a set of weights. Otherwise one runs the risk of combining weighting techniques with aggregation models with which they are not theoretically compatible. All the proposed methods for obtaining weights in CBA are based on the concept of weights as *coefficient of importance:* "if the decision-maker considers individual 2 more "deserving" than individual 1 he will weight 2's losses more heavily than 1's gains i.e. $\lambda_2 > \lambda_1$ [Dasgupta and Pearce, 1972, p. 65]". This concept of importance can be classified as *symmetrical importance,* that is "if we have two non-equal numbers to construct a vector in R^2, then it is preferable to place the greatest number in the position corresponding to the most important criterion" [Podinovskii, 1994, p. 241]. Unfortunately, since CBA is based on a complete compensatory mathematical model, the weights can only have the meaning of a trade-off ratio, as a consequence a theoretical inconsistency exists.

3. CONCLUSIONS

(1) Since in CBA the concept of intensity of preference is used, complete compensability among different dimensions is allowed. Complete compensability implies that weights have to be considered as scaling factors and then their meaning is of a trade-off ratio (depending on the scales of measurement of the various dimensions). As a consequence the weights used in CBA, since are based on the concept of "importance", are not theoretically compatible with the linear aggregation rule.

(2) Since weights can be derived in different ways, there is no guarantee that the ratio between these weights is a constant. Such a ratio may be equal to the trade-off ratio between different income groups only by chance, no theoretical assurance exists.

(3) To identify a monetary trade-off ratio between different income groups implies an interpersonal comparison of utility, that is exactly what CBA tries to avoid.

REFERENCES

Arrow K.J., Raynaud H. (1986). *Social choice and multicriterion decision making*, M.I.T. Press, Boston.

Bell D.E., Keeney R.L. and Raiffa H. (eds) (1977). *Conflicting objectives in decision.* International series on applied systems analysis. J. Wiley and Sons, New York.

Bell D.E. Raiffa H. and Tversky A. (eds.) (1988). *Decision making: descriptive, normative and prescriptive interactions*, Cambridge University Press, Cambridge.

Bouyssou D. (1986). Some remarks on the notion of compensation in MCDM, *European Journal of Operational Research* 26 pp. 150–160.

Borda, J.C. de (1781). Mèmoire sur les elections au scrutin, *Histoire de l'Academie Royale des Sciences.*

Dasgupta A.K. Pearce D.W. (1972). *Cost-benefit analysis*. Macmillan, London.

Dasgupta A.K., Marglin S., Sen A. (1972). *Guidelines for project evaluation*, UNIDO, New York.

Fishburn P.C. (1976). Noncompensatory preferences, *Synthese*, N. 33, pp. 393–403.

Fishburn P.C. (1978). A survey of multiattribute/multicriteria evaluation theories, in Ziontz S. (ed.). *Multicriteria problem solving*, Springer-Verlag, Berlin, pp. 181–224.

Fishburn P.C. (1985). Multiattribute nonlinear utility theory, *Management Science*, N. 30, pp. 1301–1310.

Foster C.D. (1960). Surplus criteria for investment, *Bulletin of Oxford University, Institute of Economics and Statistics*, 22 Nov.

Keeney R., Raiffa H. (1976). *Decision with multiple objectives: preferences and value trade-offs*, Wiley, New York.

Krantz D.H., Luce R.D., Suppes P. and Tversky A. (1971). *Foundations of measurement, vol. 1, Additive and polynomial representations*, Academic Press, New York.

Krutila J.V. Eckstein O. (1958). *Multiple purpose river development*, Resource for the future, Baltimore.

Mishan E.J. (1971). *Cost-Benefit Analysis*, London: Allen and Unwin.

Moulin H. (1988). *Axioms of co-operative decision making*, Econometric Society Monographs, Cambridge University Press.

Pearce D.W., Nash C.A. (1981). *The social appraisal of projects*, Macmillan, London.

Podinovskii, V.V. (1984). Criteria importance theory, *Mathematical Social Sciences*, 27, pp. 237–252.

Ray A. (1984). *Cost-benefit analysis*, The John Hopkins University Press (published for The World Bank), Baltimore.

Robers F.S. (1979). *Measurement theory with applications to decision making, utility and the social sciences*, Addison-Wesley, London.

Vansnick J.C. (1986). On the problem of weights in multiple criteria decision making (the noncompensatory approach), *European Journal of Operational Research.* 24 pp. 288–294.

Vincke Ph. (1992). *Multicriteria decision aid*, Wiley, New York.

Weisbrod B. (1968). Income redistribution effects and benefits-cost analysis, in Chase S.B. (ed.) *Problems in public expenditure analysis*, Brookings Institution, Washington.

CHAPTER - 4

THE OUTPUT GAP: MEASUREMENT, RELATED CONCEPTS AND POLICY IMPLICATIONS

Parameswar Nandakumar

ABSTRACT

This paper compares the various approaches to the measurement of potential output and the NAIRU, and identifies practical policy implications. The respective advantages and disadvantages of each method – the Okun's Law approach, the trend-fitting method, the production function approach, the simultaneous equations system method and the stochastic filter methods – are discussed in detail. It is noted that the production function approach, despite obvious advantages in comparison with the trend and the Okun's Law methods, has the drawback of relying on exogenous or trend values of NAIRU to get equilibrium values of labour inputs. Some of the weakness of this approach is noted to be present even in the 'fully structural' system approach, which does not overcome the limitations of its individual component equations. In search of alternatives, the stochastic univariate and multivariate filter methods are compared to the structural methods. It is reasoned that the extended multivariate filter methods in which additional structural information replaces a priori restrictions of univariate methods may be better-equipped to produce good estimates of potential output. On the NAIRU, a recommendation of the paper is that open-economy influences should not be neglected in its estimation, so that the real exchange rate is given its due role. An implication is that in a situation where a current account surplus that leads to allows a fall in the endogeneous relative price of imports prevails, the NAIRU is lowered, allowing the possibility of beneficial policy action using such a trade-off.

The author would like to thank Bharat Barot, Per Jansson and Mats Kinwal for pointers to relevant literature. He has gained from discussions with them, Hakan Frisen, Alfred Kanis, Lasse Koskinen, Alek Markowski, Thomas Modschean and Lars-Erik Oller. Detailed comments were provided by Lars-Erik Oller, who holds no responsibility for errors that have escaped his argus eyes. The responsibility for remaining errors and omissions rests with the author.

[49]

I. INTRODUCTION

It has been sometimes said that the Non-accelerating Inflation Rate of Unemployment, the NAIRU, is not carved in stone. The same holds for the concept of potential output – even independently of the way the NAIRU is conceived – which has undergone considerable reformation over the years, leading to reappraisals and revisions of the output gap which is the difference between potential and actual output. The way this gap is measured has important consequences for policymaking, especially by central bankers monitoring the relationships between monetary aggregates and inflation.

The concept of an output gap that is linked to inflationary tendencies is present in Keyne's early manuscript, "How to pay for the war", but gained currency really only in inflationary Seventies. Until then, the widely used concept of potential output had a kind of engineering intonation: it is simply the maximum capacity output with all factors of production fully employed and utilized. The peak to peak trend-fitting method embodied this concept: capacity output was assumed to be reached at the peak of each cycle, leaving open the question whether all factors were indeed employed fully, or to the same extent, at all peaks.

Still, the trend-fitting method was thought to provide estimates of potential output at least as good as the somewhat more involved method based on the Okun's Law, a basic macroeconomic relationship popularized by Artur Okum (1962) in his work for the U.S. President's council of economic advisors. This relationship between the changes in unemployment – of labour, just one of the factors of production – and output growth may be considered to be more of a theorem, rather than a rigid law, since the so-called Okun's Coefficient that quantifies this link has been subject to quite a bit of variation over the years. This variation has been mostly attributed to the non-inclusion of the other production factors, which meant for instance that the effects on capital formation of the oil shocks of the seventies were not captured. To correct for this "misspecification", the Okun's Law has sometimes been used embedded in a more general formulation that encompasses the input of other factors of production as well.

The complete production function approach for the measurement of potential output has, of course, been used independently, without any reference to the Okun's Law which has had a foothold basically only in the United States. It has been used – at least by some of the research staff – at the International Monetary Fund (IMF), and is now in vogue at the OECD's Economic Secretariat. The primary advantage of this approach lies in the fact that all the various sources of output growth are represented (though sometimes measurement is arbitrary, as is usually with total factor productivity), and it is often used as complementary input even in stochastic approaches, providing structural information.

However, the concept of potential output to which the production function approach is being applied is no longer that of maximum capacity output. That was discarded hastily after the supply shocks of the seventies brought the necessity of controlling inflation to a level of urgency. Since then, potential output has been increasingly defined as the level of output consistent with non-accelerating inflation; and, accordingly, the NAIRU used as the level of equilibrium unemployment rate that is used in the Okun's Law and production function approaches to the estimation of potential output. It may be added that the popular concept of the NAIRU need not always correspond to that of the NARU, the natural rate of unemployment that Friedman (1969) wrote about, which could have very long-run equilibrium conditions built in.

In fact, in some of the so-called "fully structural" approaches, used for instance by the IMF, the NAIRU and potential output are determined simultaneously. At the other end of the spectrum is the fully stochastic approach that relies on univariate filters. Occupying a promising fertile middle ground are the "structural-stochastic" methods, espoused particularly by the Bank of Canada, which take in considerable structural information for use in their multi-variate filters which are described in a later section.

All these diverse methods for determining potential output and the output gap have their own advantages as well as disadvantages, but a discussion of these is deferred to the end of the paper, which is structured as follows. The next short section disposes of the trend-fitting method, which does not attract much attention now. Section III discusses the Okun's Law approach, and the following section extensions of it. V describes the production function-based method in some detail, followed by an examination of the common ways of estimating the NAIRU. Section

VII takes up the "fully structural" or "system" approach, followed by sections describing the univariate and the extended multivariate filter, or the "stochastic-structural" method of the Bank of Canada, respectively. Before the final section which provides some recommendations, there is a section (X) which discusses the methods adopted by the various national and international organisations, and their respective merits and drawbacks.

II. ESTIMATING POTENTIAL OUTPUT BY THE USE OF LINEAR TRENDS

This method, which is based on a maximum capacity notion of potential output, was commonly used until the 1970s because of its simplicity, and because the other concomitant approaches did depend anyway to varying degrees on trend-fitting. Linear trends are fitted through consecutive peaks, the assumption being that capacity output is reached at all peaks – and that output grows at a constant rate between successive peaks. No consideration is given to the possibility that the employment and utilization of production factors can differ between peaks. Sometimes, as something of a compromise, trends are fitted through centre points in the cycles instead.

In none of its specifications does the method take any account of inflationary pressures, nor is any macroeconomic relation an input into the procedure. During periods of supply shocks, this pure time trend method invariably produces inflated estimates of potential output, the use of time dummies for the supply shock periods being not of much help when a continuous string of supply shocks occur. However, in many of the other estimation methods such as the production function approach, time trend-fitting is resorted to partially, due to its simplicity, providing a weak link in the method.

III. THE OKUN'S LAW AND THE OUTPUT GAP

The Okun's Law is a well-established macroeconomic relationship dating back to the formulation by Okun (1962), who advanced the proposition that a one percent rise in the unemployment rate in the United states will translate into a three percent fall in the growth rate of GNP. Thus, in the following equation, 'a', the so-called Okun's Coefficient, will have a value of around 3:

$$y - y^* = -a \, (u - u^*), \tag{1}$$

where 'y' is the log of output and 'u' the unemployment rate, the superscript * representing potential or natural rate values. These potential values are often purely exogenous in this approach, fixed at some benchmark level, or obtained from underlying variables such as the labour participation rate using time trends.

Kinwall (1996) has used this approach to estimate the GNP gap for Sweden, and compared the results with those derived from an Hodrick-Prescott (H-P) approach. He uses equation (1) in the form

$$y^* = y + a\delta u, \tag{2}$$

with 1986 as the benchmark year when actual and potential output were equal, and the actual unemployment rate equal to the natural rate NAIRU. This assumption follows the usual practice when using this approach, that of making arbitrary assumptions about 'normal years' during which actual and potential output (and unemployment) have coincided. He attributes this to the fact that with the (H–P) method, the restrained growth of actual output in the recession of the early 1990s would have even affected potential output due to the end-point problem associated with this method; however, when he adopted a higher NAIRU – quite realistically – from 1993 onwards, the estimated output gap with the Okun method came closer to that obtained with the H-P filter. Clearly, the exogenous inputs of the potential values are crucial when using the Okun relationship.

There are other difficulties associated with the Okun method; Wage and price dynamics play no role whatsoever, and this is of course the reason why the equilibrium level of unemployment has to be fed in exogenously, unless the Okun's relation is presented as part of a larger system. Also, in any 'abnormal' period, such as that of the supply shocks of the seventies, this approach falters since labour is the only production factor that is explicitly considered; so the increased scrapping rate of the capital stock, for instance, due to higher energy prices, that lowers the growth of potential output, will not be captured. Actually, the Okun's Coefficient has varied considerably in the United States, from around 3 in the sixties to between 2 and 2.5 in the seventies.

All the same, the Okun's Law continues to be regarded as an important macroeconomic relationship between unemployment and growth. And it may well be that given the fact that the determination of the equilibrium levels of output and unemployment lie outside the domain of this approach, the better option would be to forecast changes in unemployment using output growth estimated by other-say, stochastic – methods.

IV. OKUN'S LAW : EXTENSIONS AND RELATED APPROACHES

As noted already, the Okun's Law has been subject to criticism because of its focus on only one of the factors of production. This exclusion of other (factor) influences in fact means that the estimated Okun's Coefficient actually represents a *composite* effect, rather than the sole effect of unemployment changes, as Prachowny (1993) points out. He embeds the Okun's relation in a composite production function relationship:

$$y = \alpha (k + c) + \beta (n + h) + t, \tag{3}$$

where (in logs) y = output, k = capital stock, c = utilisation rate of capital, n = no. of workers, h = no. of hours, t = total factor productivity. A similar expression holds for potential output, with stars representing potential values of the variables in equation (3) :

$$y = \alpha(k^* + c^*) + \beta(n^* + h^*) + t^*, \tag{4}$$

Then, assuming that capital stock is at its potential, from (3) and (4),

$$y - y^* = \alpha(c + c^*) + \beta(n + n^*) \, \beta(h - h^*) + (t - t^*)$$

Or, writing in terms of labour supply 'e' and the unemployment rate 'u',

$$y - y^* = \alpha(c - c^*) + \beta(e - e^*) - \beta(u - u^*) + (t - t^*)$$

From (6), it can be seen that even when unemployment is at its potential level, output can deviate from its potential level. It follows that in the coefficient that is usually interpreted as the Okun's multiplier ('a' in equations 1 and 2) the effects of changes in factor utilisation and the total factor productivity growth are also incorporated; these do not appear formally in the Okun representation because underutilization of production factors or changes in the rate of productivity growth are not concepts encompassed within this framework. In his empirical work, Prachowny (1993) did find that the composite specification (6) provided better estimates than those using (1). The potential values in (6) needed for the estimates were obtained using trend methods.

Perry (1977) follows the Okun's Law tradition in his emphasis on the labour market in the estimation of potential output, but works at a more disaggregated level. He considers altogether ten age groups, differentiating by sex as well, and determines (weighted) total potential manhours based on the estimates of potential participation rates and potential average hours for each group. Estimates of estimates of potential output are then made from total potential manhours and trend labour productivity. A study on the natural rate of unemployment for Canada (Fortin (1989)) has a similar approach, with a stable NAIRU being estimated only for males over 25, with the aggregate NAIRU being more volatile due to labour market composition effects. A detailed description of the methods adopted for the determination of equilibrium unemployment is deferred to section VI.

Even in the extended form discussed above, the Okun's approach is lacking in wage and price dynamics that influence equilibrium unemployment levels. An early attempt at the inclusion of these influences was by Friedman and Wachter (1974), who included expectational variables in an unemployment equation, which in bare elements was an Okun's law formulation. In the system approach to be described in section VII, the Okun's relationship forms part of a system of equations that includes wage and price equations, potential output and the natural rate of unemployment being determined simultaneously. In Vector Autoregression (VAR) approaches also, for instance in Blanchard and Quah (1989), the Okun's relation is part of a whole system, just one of the relations between innovations. The VAR methodology enables a distinction to be made between supply and demand shocks, the former having long-lasting effects, but does not make use of the macroeconomic relationships that form the key inputs into the system approach, used for instance, by the IMF.

V. THE PRODUCTION FUNCTION APPROACH

In this approach, estimates of potential output are obtained from the production relation between factor inputs and output when the former are at their potential level, as are factor productivities – or total factor productivity, when technical progress is of the disembodied form. The definitions of factor inputs used in the estimate are not self-evident; for instance, there is considerable ambiguity about the definition of equilibrium labour inputs, and often it is the actual stock, rather than any estimated potential, of capital that is used. This method is exemplified by the OCED (Giorno, Richardson, Rosevare and Van den Noord (1995)) approach, which is now being used in preference over the H-P filter approach that was opted for earlier:

56

Business sector production is (small letters representing logs),

$$y = a + \alpha n + (1 - \alpha) k + t, \qquad (7)$$

where n is labour input, k capital stock, α is the average labour share (in a Cobb-Douglas formulation), a is a constant and t is total factor productivity. From (7), the factor productivity series is calculated and then smoothed with the H–P filter to get the potential series, which is substituted back into the function, together with actual capital stock and potential labour input to get potential output:

$$y^* = a + \alpha n^* + (1 - \alpha)k + t^*, \qquad (8)$$

stars representing potential values of variables. For obtaining the potential labour input used in (8), the equilibrium level of unemployment is pinned down first. The next section is devoted to a discussion of the concept and estimation of the equilibrium level of unemployment. Here we may just note that while the OECD has chosen to work with the concept of NAWRU, the non-accelerating wage rate of unemployment, the NAIRU is often the preferred concept: primarily because price inflation is a policy target variable, while the control of wages is not a goal in itself.

To get at the NAWRU, it is first assumed that the rate of wage inflation is proportional to the unemployment gap:

$$D^2 \text{Log } W = - b(U - \text{NAWRU}), \qquad (9)$$

where D is the difference operator, W the wage rate, and U the actual unemployment rate. For a period of stable NAWRU, the value of b is obtained from (9), and then substituted back to get a series for the NAWRU, which is then smoothened. It may be noted that the NAWRU series so obtained will tend to move with actual unemployment, in contrast to the constant NAIRU obtained in a long-run equilibrium in the absence of supply shocks with permanent effects.

The NAWRU estimates thus obtained is used in the following way to get the labour input used in (8) in the determination of potential output:

$$N^* = L(1 - \text{NAWRU}) - EG, \qquad (10)$$

where L = smoothed labour force = working population * trend participation rate, and EG is government employment. Potential output for the economy as a whole is obtained by adding *actual* value added in the government sector to the business sector estimates obtained by using (10) in (8). In comparison, potential output estimates fluctuates less from year to year with the H–P filter smoothing method used earlier.

The OECD also uses a more detailed production function approach that can incorporate the effects of energy price changes. Torres and Martin (1990), in their work for the OECD, has the following nested CES specification for the business sector:

$$Q = (a(Le_f)^\rho + b(KE)^\rho)^{1/\rho}, \tag{11}$$

where KE is the actual capital-energy bundle, L is actual employment, ef is the labour efficiency index and a and b are scale parameters. In the production function, the scrapping rate has been endogenized, thus supplying the vintage element; an estimated proportion of the capital stock is adjusted in each period with shifts in real energy prices. Technical progress is labour-embodied, represented by the labour efficiency index, and is assumed to follow the productivity development in the U.S for other OECD countries, a kind of "catch-up" hypothesis.

Potential output is obtained from equation (11) using the actual capital-energy bundle, potential employment and the labour efficiency index. It will be the level of output consistent with non-accelerating wage inflation, since that is the definition (NAWRU) of equilibrium unemployment adopted, leading to the estimation of potential labour input using (10). The labour force variable used there is normalised using a geometric moving average, to eliminate as far as possible the effects of cyclical variations in the participation rate. It may be mentioned that the concept of the NAIRU has also been used by the OECD elsewhere (Coe (1985)), along the lines of the discussion in the next section

The incorporation of energy as a production factor leave – or, rather, along with capital as a composite factor, to be precise – and the endogenization of the scrapping rate seems to be a necessary step to capture the effects of the energy price shocks of the seventies, and the estimates of potential output for the OECD countries studies are lower than those using time trend methods for same period. But it may be mentioned that similar effects on capacity growth for Sweden in the middle of the 1970s has been obtained by Markowski (1988), based solely on real wage costs, using a model similar to Knoester and Sinderen gap (1980).

The merits and drawbacks of the general production function approach are discussed in section X. An innovation of the OECD approach is the user of the "catch-up" hypothesis for the estimation of potential labour productivity, which avoids the common problem associated with the time trend estimation of total factor productivity.

In KOSMOS, the macroeconometric model of the national Institute of Economic Research, Stockholm, the concept of potential output is akin to that of *capacity* output, with *full* employment (actual employment + unemployment) labour input being used in the production function. In the case of industry, actual output is derived using an endogenous capacity utilization index, which is the ratio of actual to potential output, given as (see Ernsater and Markowski (1994))

$$ CU = f\left(\frac{S}{y_p} \frac{RIS}{DIS}, PR \right), $$

Where S is total sales, y_p is potential output, RIS is real inventory stock, DIS is desired inventory stock and PR is profitability. As in Helliwell (1984), actual output will be decided by the level of capacity utilization. But note that in Helliwell's paper the denominator in the capacity utilization index expression is normal output, derived using actual employment: at the actual employment level, utilization varies from the normal due to demand shocks. A case can be made out for measuring potential output using equilibrium labour inputs consistent with an estimated natural rate of unemployment, rather than full employment; then the capacity utilization index will represent deviations from an equilibriumlevel of employment, rather than from a level which is never ever reached.

VI. DETERMINING THE NATURAL RATE OF UNEMPLOYMENT – CONSISTENT WITH NON-ACCELERATING INFLATION

The usual way of obtaining the NAIRU is from an augmented Philips Curve equation (Gordon (1996), Fortin (1989)). Such an estimate need not be synonymous with Friedman's (1969) natural rate of unemployment, which is the level of equilibrium unemployment ground out by a fully-specified general equilibrium equation system, unless additional long-run equilibrium conditions are imposed as will be discussed later in this section. The estimation of NAIRU as commonly done from wage and price equations is as follows in the simplest specification:

$$ w_t = a_0 + a_1 p_{te} - a_2 u_t \tag{12} $$

$$ p_t = b_0 + b_1 (w - q)_t + b_2 z_t \tag{13} $$

Lagged terms have been omitted for simplicity. Also, there will be an additional equation representing price expectations formation based on lagged prices. Equation (12) is a Philips Curve relation for wages – in logged form; w is the wage rate, u actual unemployment, and subscript e represents an expected variable. (13) is a price mark-up equation, where q is the trend productivity growth and z a vector of other relevant variables.

In the "long-run" equilibrium with stable inflation, realized expectations, and full nominal wage adjustment to expectations as well as full mark-up for wage costs, we have

$$p_{te} = p_t = p_{t-1}; a_1 = 1, b_1 = 1. \qquad (14)$$

The NAIRU, the level of unemployment consistent with this non-accelerating inflation equilibrium is solved out to be independent of the price level – representing a vertical long-run Philips Curve – and depends only on the coefficients in the equations. It is, however, influenced by trend labour productivity. Also, when employer's payroll taxes are taken into account, $(w - q)$ in the price mark-up equation will be replaced by $(w + s - q)$, where s is the payroll tax rate, and the NAIRU will be seen to vary with changes in s as well. Now, substituting (13) and (14) into (12), the NAIRU can be solved out as.

$$U^* = ((a_0 + a_1 b_0 - (1 - a_1 b_1)w - a_1 b_1)w - a_1 b_1 q)/a_2.$$

With a_1 and b_1 equal to unity, the natural rate of unemployment is independent of wage inflation.

Of course, there could be other, country-specific, variables which can influence the estimated NAIRUs. These may be incorporated in a simple fashion by writing the wage equation (12) as

$$w_t = a_0 + a_1 p_{te} - a_2 u_t - a_3 u_{t-1} + a_4 x_t. \qquad (15)$$

Here, the presence of lagged unemployment is to capture the possibility of *hysteresis*, the possibility of cyclical changes in actual unemployment affecting the natural rate. A few reasons have been advanced in support of this possibility. Workers laid off for fairly long periods could suffer from "skill deterioration", leading to their permanent alienation from the labour market; or, after their initial discharge in a recession, "insiders" may set wages rates so high that their reentry becomes difficult even when the economy emerges from the downturn.

In (15), x represents a vector of other relevant variables. This could include variables such as the degree of unionization, profits etc., which may be justified by bargaining models of wage determination; there may be also structural variables relating to labour market composition. These structural variables could be directly tested for cointegration relationships with unemployment, as in a Bank of Canada working paper (Cote and Hostland (1996)).

The price mark-up equation (14) could be formulated in error correction terms, as in Torres and Martin (1990):

$$p_t = b_0 + b_1 c_{te} - b_2(p_{t-1} - c_{t-1}) + b_3(R - 1). \qquad (16)$$

where c represents total unit cost, including capital cost (in (13), capital costs would be submerged in the constant term). R is the ratio of actual to potential output. Since the error correction term is in level terms, price will equal cost in long-run equilibrium. Also, then, actual output will equal potential, so that there is consistency between factor and product markets.

The open-economy aspects of NAIRU determination are given prominence in Joyce & Wren–Lewis (1991). Basically, they use a Layard & Nickell (1986) type model, with imperfect competition in goods and labour markets – with a bargaining model of wage determination – complemented by endogenous real exchange rate determination this studence missing determination – complemented by endogenous real exchange rate determination via current account imbalances. But, we can even extend the framework represented by equations (12)–(14) to arrive at the insights that an explicit open economy extension has to offer:

Rewrite (13) as

$$p = b_0 + b_1 (w - q) + b_2 z + b_3 p_m, \qquad (17)$$

where subscript t has been dropped for convenience and "p_m" is the import price that is expected to affect the mark-up of firms. Solving as before by substituting (17) and (14) into (12), the NAIRU is obtained as

$$u^* = \frac{((a_0 + a_1 b_0 - (1 - a_1 b_1)w - a_1 b_1 q + a_1 b_2 p_m))}{a_2}. \qquad (18)$$

with a_1 and b_1 equal to unity, the NAIRU is independent of the wage rate, but varies with the import price. Hence, in a period of supply shocks – which have permanent effects, which is the sense in which they are usually distinguished from demand shocks even in the stochastic filter approaches – the NAIRU will not be constant. For a constant NAIRU, i.e., invariant with respect to import price changes, additional assumptions have to be made: that

$$w = p_m; \; 1 - b_1 = b_2 . \qquad (19)$$

This may be considered to be a long-run condition, domestic and foreign inflation coinciding.

Joyce and Wren-Lewis (1991) derive the following relationship from their wage and price equations:

$$w^* + p^* = a_1 cu - a_2 u + a_3 s + a_4 (m - p), \qquad (20)$$

where starred w and p are target real wage and target profit margin respectively (all in log form), cu is capacity utilization, s is the payroll tax rate (they have other taxes as well), m is import price, and p domestic price. In steady state when inflation is constant, the LHS of (20) will be zero, capacity utilization will be unchanging, and then the level of unemployment consistent with this scenario is the NAIRU, which is seen to depend on the real exchange rate (and the payroll tax rate).

The implications of this dependence can be easily illustrated. Suppose there is a current account surplus as there is in Sweden now; with an endogenous real exchange rate that moves to eliminate trade imbalances (as is in Joyce-Wren-Lewis's larger model), there will be a real exchange appreciation, which from equation (20) above, is seen to *reduce* the NAIRU. In other words, a current account surplus is an indication of a scenario where reductions in actual unemployment and the NAIRU are possible (of course, if the current account is *always* constrained to be balanced, as in Forslund (1995), then this possibility vanishes; but note that the definition of NAIRU does not incorporate current account balance).

Hence the NAIRU can be time-varying. There may be other structural factors which cause this variation, in addition to the supply shocks discussed above, for instance, changes in labour market composition. A study by the Bank of Canada (Cote and Hostland (1996)) found trend unemployment – which does not exactly correspond to the common definition of NAIRU – to be cointegrated with the degree of unionization in the labour market, as well as with payroll tax rates.

Gordon (1996) estimates a time-varying NAIRU in a simple fashion, complementing a Philips Curve equation with the following hystersis – type specification:

$$u_t^* = u_{t-1}^* + \varepsilon_t, \tag{21}$$

where, if the standard deviation of the error term is not zero, a varying NAIRU series is obtained, even if the Philips Curve had implied a constant one. The choice of the standard deviation is here a key step, somewhat similar to the choice of the smoothing parameter in the H–P filter method that will be discussed later.

For estimating the natural rate or structural rate of unemployment, Koskinen & Öller (1996) and Assarson & Jansson (1996) use the method of additive decomposition of the unemployment rate into two unobservable components: a natural rate or a trend component, and a cyclical component. The natural rate here is not synonymous with the NAIRU, since there is no reference to the rate of inflation. Koskinen and Oller use the "median filter" for the decomposition, while Assarson and Jansson use what is commonly known as the unobserved components model: along with the additive decomposition of the unemployment rate into the natural and cyclical components, they have a random walk specification for the cyclical rate, and a formulation where the natural rate depends on its own lagged value and the lagged cyclical rate – so that hysteresis is present. The basic idea behind the unobserved components model is that the unobservable variables – such as the natural rate – are determined from the path of observable variables. Here, for that exercise, further information is needed, and for that the authors use two relationships (in fact, one is sufficient): that between capacity utilization and cyclical unemployment, and that between world demand and domestic cyclical unemployment. The authors choose these relationships as versions of the Okun's Law, with cyclical output-related measures co-varying with cyclical unemployment. The Kalman Filter method is used to estimate the unobserved components of the aggregate Swedish unemployment rate.

Stochastic, univariate, methods of estimating potential output, similar to the approach of Koskinen & Öller (1996), are discussed in section VIII, while semi-structural methods, similar to the work of Assarson & Jansson (1996), but with a richer variety of structural information, including inputs from the wage – price sector, are taken up in section IX.

VII. THE SYSTEM APPROACH

The IMF's (Adams and Coe (1990)) methodology represents the comprehensive "system approach" for determination of potential output and the NAIRU. These are determined *jointly*, based on a system of simultaneous equations. Essentially, what is done is as follows: a number of single-equation estimates are made from wage, price, unemployment and output equations and then these equations are combined and estimated as a system, with appropriate cross-equation restrictions. The estimation is carried out for the U.S. only.

Inputs which are exogenous for the single-equation estimates are endogenized under this approach. For instance, trend output and productivity used in the individual unemployment, wage and price equations can be replaced by expressions for potential output and productivity obtained from the production function. Similarly, the expression for the natural rate of unemployment obtained from the unemployment equation is an input into the wage equation. Such an approach constrains the estimates of equilibrium unemployment and output to be consistent with each other (otherwise, one is often assumed when estimating the other; for instance, when using the Okun's relationship to estimate potential output, equilibrium unemployment is often an exogenous input).

The equation system used is, in its bare elements, as follows :

$$U = \alpha_0 + \alpha_1(y - y^*) + \alpha_2(Z_u) + \varepsilon_u \tag{22}$$

$$dw = dp_e + \beta_1(U - U^*) + \beta_2 dq^* + \beta_3 Z_w + \varepsilon_w . \tag{23}$$

$$y = \delta_0 + \delta_1 h + \delta_2 k + \varepsilon_y \tag{24}$$

$$dp = (dw - dq^*) + \delta_l(y - y^*) + \varepsilon_p . \tag{25}$$

Lowercase letters represent logarithms, and dx stands for a change in variable x. w, q, y, U and p represent the wage rate, productivity, output, the unemployment rate and the price level respectively. The superscript * represents a natural or trend value, while the subscript e represents expectations. Z represents other – often structural-variables. (22) is an Okun's relation, (23) is a Philips Curve equation. The other two relationships represent a production function (h and k are labour and capital inputs respectively) and a price equation where the output gap and unit labour costs determine the growth of prices.

The way the single-equation estimates are combined within a system can be seen by focusing on, say, the unemployment equation. From equation (22), the natural rate of unemployment is estimated. This is done by including a number of structural variables related to the labour market, but without incorporating any information on wage and price developments. Some assumption about trend output will also be required. The equation is estimated in a dynamic form, the long-run version of which is

$$U^* = a_0 + a_1 NWLC + a_2 UIRR + a_3 RMW + a_4 UNN, \qquad (26)$$

UNN being the degree of unionization, *UIRR* the average weekly unemployment insurance replacement ratio, *NWLC* employer's social security contributions as a proportion of total wage costs, and *RMW* the minimum wage – multiplied by the labour force share of the age group 16–24, who are the ones most likely to be affected.

Then, when the system is estimated as a whole, the natural rate term in the Philips Curve equation for wages is replaced by the expression (26) for the natural rate obtained from an individual equation. Similarly, in the unemployment and price equations, trend output term is replaced by the expression for potential output derived from the production function – which is derived from an individual equation with assumptions about the level of equilibrium factor inputs. These substitutions, which amount to cross-equation restrictions, ensure that the estimates of potential output and the equilibrium unemployment rate obtained are consistent with each other.

But though the estimated potential values are consistent, the weaknesses of the individual equations are carried over into the system estimation. Thus, the assumed level of equilibrium factor inputs – note here there is no energy input specified – in the production function do still influence the derived potential values. Though a proxy variable, the input of research and development, is used to capture total factor productivity growth, a time trend is used in addition so that this approach is really not "fully structural".

VIII. STOCHASTIC APPROACHES: UNIVARIATE FILTERS

The system approach described in the previous section attempts to come up with structural determinants of the shifts in potential output and the natural rate of unemployment, avoiding the use of shift dummies and ad hoc trend fitting (as far as feasible, at least). However, the estimates derived by this purely structural approach have been rather wide off the mark. Presumably, there is still insufficient knowledge about the important structural determinants (a common criticism of any macromodelling activity), especially since modelling the political decision making process – even those that lead to supply shocks such as energy price increases – is next to impossible. This has led to the increased adoption of less detailed models that still use structural information, but are well-suited for the stochastic environment. But before coming to the description of such multivariate filters complemented with structural inputs, used for instance extensively by the Bank of Canada, the univariate approach for the determination of potential output will be discussed.

In the use of *univariate* filters for such as the Hodrick-Prescott (HP) filter, the underlying assumption is that the potential output is driven by a stochastic process. The filter helps to decompose an observed shock into a supply (permanent) component and a demand (temporary) component – the identifying difference being that supply shocks have lasting, permanent effects, while demand shocks have only transitory effects. Of course, in practice, when the demand shocks are of a longer duration, it will be difficult to separate the two, especially at the end of a cycle. Nevertheless, such a mode of classification has been used popularly since the work of Blanchard and Quah (1989).

The HP filter is derived by minimizing the sum of the squared deviations of output from its trend, subject to a smoothness constraint that penalizes deviations in the trend. So HP trend values are those that minimize.

$$\phi = \Sigma(y_t - y_{p,t})^2 + \lambda\Sigma((y_{p,t+1} - y_{p,t}) - (y_{p,t} - y_{p,t-1}))^2 \qquad (27)$$

In (27), y is output, with the subscript p representing the trend or potential value. The first term is the so-called global distance, while the second term represents the fluctuating part, the fluctuations assumed to be dominantly transitory, due to demand disturbances. The choice of the smoothing parameter, the multiplicator for the second term that penalizes deviations, plays a key role. With a vary large value chosen for the smoothing parameter, the restriction becomes dominant, and potential output is just modelled as a linear trend – the assumption being that demand disturbances have relatively large variances which are thus minimized, leaving only the supply or the permanent component. A very small value of the smoothing parameter will mean almost no restriction at all, and the potential series will follow the actual very closely.

The Central Bank of Sweden (Apel, Hansen and Lindberg (1996) has used the HP filter method for measuring the output gap, and compared the results with those obtained from an unobserved components method. As mentioned in section II, Kinwall (1996) has made a comparison of the results for the output gaps obtained using the HP filter method and the Okun's Law. The relative merits of these different methods are taken up in section X, which also discusses the approaches of various national and international organizations to this issue.

The *unobserved components* method may be considered to be a combination of univariate filter approach with appropriate – often ad hoc – structural information that helps in locating the path of unobservable potential variable values. The work of Assarson and Jansson (1996) on these lines to differentiate between permanent and cyclical components of unemployment was discussed in section Apel, Jansen and Lindberg (1996) of the Central Bank of Sweden (Riksbanken) have a similar approach, drawing inferences about unobserved potential output from observable changes in actual output and inflation:

$$y_{p,t} = \mu + y_{p,t-1} + \varepsilon_t \tag{28}$$

$$dy_t = \beta_0 + \beta_1 (y_{p,t-1} - y_{t-1}) + u_t. \tag{29}$$

$$d\pi = \gamma_1 (y_{p,t-1} - y_{t-1}) + e_t. \tag{30}$$

In (28)–(30), subscript p represents trend values, while the operator d stands for a one-period change. The last terms in all equations represents random influences. Equation (29) implies that output tends to return to a trend, and resembles the minimization of the deviation of actual from trend values represented by the first term in the HP filter. Equation (30) relates the changes in inflation to the output gap – an effect which may not be all that strong for Sweden, according to Kinwall (1996) and Koskinen and Öller (1996) – who are discussing the unemployment gap instead. The observable variables, actual output and its change, and the change in inflation, are used to determine the level of potential output. The estimation of potential output is carried out using a Kalman filter, which is basically an iterative process: it proceeds by guessing the initial value of potential output in period $t - 1$, and then makes estimates of changes in output and inflation; then, the prediction errors with respect to these variables are used to update the initial estimate of potential output, and the process is repeated until the latest observation is reached, thus generating a time series for potential output.

IX. THE STOCHASTIC-STRUCTURAL APPROACH: MULTIVARIATE FILTERS WITH STRUCTURAL INPUTS

Essentially, if a univariate filter method is complemented by the addition of structural information, it is termed a multivariate filter. But in more elaborate versions the filter is applied to more than just one variable in the process of estimating the potential value for the final target variable.

Laxton and Tetow (1992) present a *multivariate filter* in which the HP filter's univariate approach with its fluctuation restriction is complemented by information from a Philips Curve inflation rate equation and an unemployment rate equation. The general minimization problem has the usual HP filter's penalty function and the global distance term for the output gap, but also gap terms for inflation and unemployment, all the gap term attached with time-varying weights. This allows the incorporation of information from other sources. The intuitive idea is illustrated by the following reasoning: if inflation is rising, and it is not due to other factors, then output must be above its potential level.

The HP filter identifies supply and demand shocks in a rather mechanical fashion, which may falter when the shock occurs towards the end of the sample. Laxton's and Tetlow's extension also does not include much information about the determination of output. However, Butler (1996), in a technical report for the Bank of Canada, uses a decomposition of output combined with considerable structural information to distinguish supply and demand shocks, in an extensive combination of the stochastic and structural approaches. Other work in this area follow the lead set by Blanchard and Quah (1989), and use VAR methods – with their impulse responses – to estimate the supply and demand components of each innovation, only the supply components considered to feed into potential output. The extended multivariate filter of Butler (1996), in contrast to Laxton's filter, which is directly applied to potential output, *decomposes* output into its components and applies the filter at disaggregated levels. The decomposition used has some practical measurement advantages:

Starting out form a Cobb-Douglas production function

$$Y = (TFP)N^a K^{1-a}, \tag{31}$$

Where N is labour input, K capital and a the labour share or labour-output elasticity, and nothing that the marginal product of labour is

$$\frac{\delta Y}{\delta N} = a \frac{Y}{N} \tag{32}$$

Output is, in *log terms*

$$y = n + \mu - \alpha, \tag{33}$$

where the three right hand side variables stand for labour input, marginal product of labour (MPL) and labour-output elasticity respectively.

Equilibrium values of these variables are needed for the estimation of the potential level of output.

The equilibrium level of employment is given as the multiple of the total population, equilibrium participation rate and the equilibrium employment (1-equilibrium unemployment) rate. The *equilibrium* participation rate is obtained by fitting it to the *observed* participation rate and a *trend estimate* of the participation rate. Separate weights are given to these two gaps, and the smoothness parameter – similar to the HP filter smoothness parameter – is also chosen appropriately.

The general method used is to specify an objective function that constrains the weighted average of the squared errors (deviations) from each of the conditioning terms. The value of the unobservable variable that best explains the conditioning terms, or minimizes the squared error terms – subjected to restrictions, here an end-of sample growth restriction and a smoothness constraint similar to that in the HP filter – is the filter's estimate of the unobserved variable. Thus, the filter's estimate of the equilibrium participation rate is that which minimizes the sum of the weighted, squared deviations of the gaps of the equilibrium rate from a trend estimate and an observed participating rate, subject to the restrictions imposed.

The NAIRU estimate – needed for calculating equilibrium labour input, n, – uses a structural estimate of the trend unemployment rate developed in a cointegration analysis by Cote and Hostland of the Bank of Canada (1996), the previous period's NAIRU, and a Philips Curve relation. The objective function that is minimized is given as

$$(u - u_n)^2 W_1 + (u_{n-1} - u_n)^2 W_2 + (c - u_n)^2 W_3 + e^2 W_4,$$

where u is the actual unemployment rate, c is the trend unemployment rate, subscript n denotes the NAIRU, with the additional subscript (-1) representing a lagged value, e is the residual from a Philips Curve equation, and the W_s are the – priori – chosen weights. There is also an end-of-the sample growth restriction, and a smoothness restriction similar to that used in the HP filter.

The use of the growth restriction in the objective function above reduces the importance of the last two observations. The previous period's NAIRU is used to prevent large variations. 'e' is the residual from an asymmetric Philips Curve with the property that a negative gap between actual unemployment and the NAIRU is more inflationary – in absolute terms – than the disinflationary effect of an identically sized positive gap.

The estimation of potention output in (33) also requires an estimate of the equilibrium values of the marginal product of labour and the labour-output elasticity. Under the CD production function assumption and perfect competition, labour's share of income is equal to the labour-output elasticity. To remove cyclical variations in this, the HP filter is applied with the smoothness parameter set to a high value of 10000 (the usual choice is 1600) to the measured income share to get the equilibrium value.

The *equilibrium marginal product of labour* is estimated more elaborately, the following conditioning information being used, with appropriate weights given to the squared gaps: previous period's equilibrium MPL, the real producer wage W, the residual from an inflation-MPL relation, and the residual from a modified Okun's relation relating changes in the output gap to lagged changes in the MPL gap. The Okun's modified relation is included since it can be a pointer, as when the marginal product rises above the equilibrium level, firms hire more, reducing the unemployment gap. The inflation-MPL relation provides another similar pointer. The usual growth and smoothness restrictions are also applied.

In comparison with HP filter estimates of potential output for Canada, the extended multivariate filter estimates fare well, current estimates needing less revision, according to Butler (1996). But it may be possible to improve the quality of the structural information provided (some of the conditioning information in Butler (1996) is of a somewhat indirect nature), taking some inputs from the simultaneous system approach that uses basic macroeconomic relationships with clear causality. Also, open economy aspects may be incorporated more, particularly in NAIRU determination.

X. THE VARIOUS METHODS: THEIR USE IN ORGANIZATIONS, MERITS AND DRAWBACKS

The so-called pure smoothing or trend-fitting methods – which find scarce use now anywhere – are characterised by lack of information concerning the determinants of potential output or the natural rate of unemployment. These totally atheoretic methods derive estimates of potential values by fitting trends to ouput data, usually through the peaks of cycles, embodying the notion of a maximum capacity output as the level of potential output. So the cyclical position of the last observation becomes very important, even when the fit is through a limited number of successive peaks only. The basic advantage of this method is its simplicity, requiring no information at all about economic relationships, the level of factor employment and utilisation etc. But this also constitutes its basic disadvantage in times of economic disturbances, and is bound to give inflated estimates in periods of, say, supply side shocks, regardless of the degree of smoothing and sophistication. In stable periods, the trend estimates thus obtained may be used as rough bench marks to note whether labour and product markets are getting heated.

The Okun's Law, considered a basic macroeconomic relationship between changes in unemployment and the growth rate of output, has been used extensively in the U.S – by the President's Council of Economic Advisors and economists attached to The Brookings Institution, for instance – to derive estimates of potential output. The Okun's Coefficient is quite stable over fairly long periods marked by the absence of supply shocks, which together with the underlying relatively constant output growth and unemployment rates even prompted the belief that simple trend-fitting could do the job as well. The demerits of the Okun's methods are clear: no consideration is given to factor markets other than the labour market; and even for the labour market, the wage and price dynamics which provides the key influences, are ignored. So any period of large relative price changes will push this method's estimates wide off the mark. But authors using this broad approach, for instance, Perry (1977), have often worked at disaggregated levels of the labour market, isolating important structural determinants of unemployment.

The production function approach, in contrast, can claim the merit of decomposing potential output into all its components, and is, in this way, a fully disaggregated approach, especially if aggregated labour input is also disaggregated into its various determinants. In fact, extended versions of the Okun's Law approach use a production function – in which this relation is embedded – to obtain the *isolated* effects of changes in unemployment. Yet, theuse of a production function for estimating potential output values does not amount to a *fully* structural approach, since equilibrium or potential values of the various inputs are exogenous. Often, the natural rate of unemployment that is needed to get the equilibrium labour input is assumed to be the fairly constant rate that has or had prevailed over a period, and potential total factor productivity is determined – at least partially, even when proxies such as the input of research and development are used – by the trend method. Also, the assumption of a particular form of production function itself can be unduly restrictive. The problem of determining the potential input capital is usually got around by the use of the actual stock of capital. The production function approach is now being used by the OECD, in preference to the HP filter method that was in use earlier, and has also been used by the staff at IMF. The Central bank of Sweden (Apel, Jansen and Lindberg (1996)) has also used the production function approach and compared results with those obtained using HP filter and unobserved components methods.

The system approach is more comprehensive than the production function method in that much of the exogenous inputs in the latter are endogenized here – and is thus put forward as being a fully structural, simultaneous approach. As seen in section VIII, the IMF's system method determines the potential level of output and the natural rate of unemployment simultaneously, including inputs from the wage-price sector and considering structural factors in the labour market. Yet, while consistency can be thus maintained between the estimates of potential output and unemployment, some of the weaknesses of the individual equations, which with cross-equation restrictions combine to form the consistent system, remains. For instance, the production function depends at least partially on an estimate of trend productivity from outside the system; in this sense the approach is not fully structural, and an important part of the estimation does not possess the advantage claimed for it.

Thus, not only do methods devoted to comprehensive modelling of the supply side have the irredeemable drawback of being unable to include *all* relevant structural information; they are all dependent to some extent or other on time trend-fitting. But it had been noted earlier that pure time trend methods that tried to handle periods of supply disturbances by using dummy variables didn't work well either. A continuous string of supply shocks permanently lowered potential output in a way that time trends couldn't capture, even with spline and kink modifications. This led to increased adoption of methods that treat the stochastic element of potential output development explicitly, with a basic premise that permanent changes in output are caused by supply shocks.

But *univariate* stochastic methods such as the HP filter method, while they are simple to apply, have the disadvantage that they use only very limited information – even when additional information may be there just for the taking. Only the information from realized output is used to estimate the level of potential output. Given this lack of information, which also implies an inability to distinguish between demand and supply shocks, arbitrary smoothing, based on assumptions about the relative variance of supply disturbances, has to be resorted to for the estimation. There is also the difficulty of separating out persisting demand-side effects from supply disturbances, particularly at the end of the sample.

Multivariate filter methods, in contrast, tend to take in considerable additional information, not restricted to the sole output variable. Often, each of aggregate output's individual components, they themselves disaggregated into structural determinants, are smoothed by filter techniques. Reliance on any pure time trend is avoided, and basic macroeconomic relations as well as ad hoc structural information are used so that they may be termed stochastic-structural methods, which use structural modeling, rather than arbitrary assumptions, about demand and supply shocks. Sometimes informed judgements are also incorporated as inputs, which may be important particularly at end-of-sample points. The Bank of Canada works extensively with these methods for the estimation of potential output and the natural rate of unemployment, which seem to be able to side-step the disadvantages associated with pure structural, time trend, or stochastic methods.

XI. CONCLUSION

A totally structural approach – even of the simultaneous system type – as well as the univariate filter methods seem to have drawbacks that are avoidable. So does the Okun's Law-based method, which may, in fact, be better utilized to predict changes in unemployment using estimates of potential output derived elsewhere – and the Okun's coefficient estimated in a period relatively free of shocks. The output gap may be a better predicator of the unemployment gap than of inflationary surges: the output gap-inflation correlation seems weak for Sweden.

An extended multivariate filter method on the lines of that used by Butler (1996) of the Bank of canada, with additive structural information replacing the a priori restrictions of univariate methods, seems a good candidate for producing better estimates of potential output. It also has the advantage that the filter is applied to each of the component – and often their determinants – of potential output, at a very disaggregated level, and also avoids having to deal with estimations of trend total factor productivity and capital stock (but with some restrictions on the production function). But it should be possible to further improve the quality of structural information fed in, using well-established relationships such as those used in the simultaneous system approach, to replace some of the more indirect or ad hoc relations.

There may be a case for replacing the concept of capacity output in KOSMOS, the macroeconometric model of the National Institute of Economic Research,. Stockholm, with that of potential output based on an estimated natural rate of unemployment. Currently, the level of actual output in industry is derived using an index of deviations in factor utilization from the level of output that corresponds to full employment – that is never ever reached. It may be more intuitive to work with an index of deviations in utilzation from an equilibrium level of employment – that is attainable.

As regards the estimation of the equilibrium level of unemployment, the NAIRU, open-economy influences should be fully incorporated-which is usually not the case even in multivariate filter approaches. Clearly, the NAIRU, as is commonly defined, depends on the real exchange rate. A longer-run equilibrium concept, that imposes strict continuous current account balance may be smacking more of Friedman (1968), and may not be also resonant with the stochastic approaches where supply shocks are deemed to have permanent effects. This does have some identifiable policy implications: in a situation where a current account surplus that leads to or allows a fall in the (endogenous) relative price of imports prevails, the NAIRU is lowered as described in section V. Hence there seems to be an unemployment-current account trade-off which is now in a favorable constellation for beneficial policy action in Sweden.

REFERENCES

Apel, M., J. Hansen and H. Lindberg (1996) "Potential Output and the Output Gap", *Quarterly Review 3, Sveriges Riksbank:* 24–35.

Adams, C. and D. T. Coe (1990) "A System Approach to Estimating the Natural Rate of Unemployment and Potential Output in the United States", *International Monetary Fund Staff Papers*, 37 (2): 232–93.

Artur., J.R. (1977) "Measure of Potential Output in Manufacturing for Eight Industrial Countries, 1955–78", *International Monetary Fund Staff Papers*, Vol. XXIV, 1, March: 1–34.

Assarson, B. and P. Jansson (1996) "Unemployment Persistence: The Case of Sweden", *Revised Version of Working Paper 1995:16, Department of Economics, Uppsala University.*

Blanchard, O. and D. Quah (1989) "The Dynamic Effects of Demand and Supply Disturbances", *American Economic Review*, 79 (4): 65–73.

Butler, L. (1996) "A semi-structural method to estimate potential output: combining economic theory with a time series filter", *Technical report no.77, Bank of Canada*, Ottawa.

Calmfors, L. (1993) "Lessons from the macroeconomic performance of Sweden", *European Journal of Political Economy*, 9 (1): 25–72.

Coe, D. T. (1985) "Nominal wages, the NAIRU and wage flexibility", *OECD Economic Studies*, 5, Autumn, OECD, Paris.

Cote, D. and D. Hostland (1996) "An econometric examination of the trend unemployment rate in Canada", *Working paper 96–7, Bank of Canada*, Ottawa.

Forslund, A. (1995) "Unemployment – is Sweden still different?", *Swedish Economic Policy Review*, Vol. 2, 1, Spring: 15–58.

Fortin, P. (1989) "How 'natural' is Canada's high unemployment rate?", *European Economic Review*, Vol. 33, 1, January: 89–110.

Friedman, B. and M. Wachter (1974) "Unemployment: Okun's Law, labour force and productivity", *The Review of Economics and Statistics*, 56: 167–176.

Friedman, M. (1968) "The role of monetary policy", *American Economic Review*, 58, March: 1–17.

Giorno, C., P. Richardson, D. Rosevare and P. Van den Noord (1995) "Estimating potential output, output gaps and structural budget balances", *Working Paper no. 152. Economics Department*, OECD, Paris.

Gordon, R.J. (1984) "Unemployment and potential output in the 1980s", *Brookings Papers on Economic Activity* (2): 537–568.

Gordon, R.J. (1996) "The time-varying NAIRU and its implications for economic policy", Working paper no. 5735, NBER, August.

Gorter, D. and C. Gorter (1993) "The relation between unemployment benefits, the reservation wage and search duration",*X for d Bulletin of Economics and Statistics*, Vol. 55.2, May: 194–214.

Helliwell, J., P. Sturm, P. Jarrett and G. Salou (1986) "The supply side in the OECD macroeconomic model", *OECD Economic Studies*, 6, OECD, Paris.

Jackman, R., and S.Roper (1987) "Strucutural unemployment", *Oxford Bulletin of Economics and Statistics*, Vol. 49: 9–36.

Joyce, M. and S. Wren-Lewis (1991) "The role of the real exchange rate and capacity utilisation in convergence to the NAIRU", *The Economic Journal*, Vol. 101, 406, May: 497–507.

Kanis, A. and A.Markowski (1990) "The supply side of the econometric model of the NIER", *Working Paper no. 4, Konjunkturinstitutet*, National Institute of Economic Research, Stockhom.

Kinwall, M. (1996) "Output gaps as inflation indicators", Economics Reference Library, 4, *Handelsbanken*, Stockholm, October

Knoester, A. and J. Van Sinderen (1984) "A simple way of determining the supply side in macroeconomic models" *Economics letters*, 1–2

Koskinen, L. and L.E. Oller (1996) "Strukturell arbetsloshet I Sverigeoch NAIRU samt ett forslag om at anvanda medianfilter", *Mineo, Konjunkturinstitutet*, National Institute of Economic Research, Stockholm.

Kuh, E. (1966) "Measurement of Potential Output", *American Economic Review* 56, September, 758–776

Laxton, D., R. Tetlow (1992) "A simple multivariate filter for the measurement of potential output", *Technical Report*, No. 52, Bank of Canada, Ottawa

Layard, P.R.G. and S.J. Nickell (1986) "Unemployment in Britain", *Economica*, Vol. 33, supplement: 121–70.

Lindbeck, A. and D. Snower (1987) "Union activity, unemployment persistence and wage – employment ratchets", *European Economic Review*, Vol. 31: 157–67.

Markowski, A. and L. Ernsater (1994) "The supply side in the econometric model KOSMOS", *Working Paper no. 37, Konjunkturinstitutet*, National Institutee of Economic Research, Stockholm, January.

76

Nickell, S. (1990) "Unemployment, a survey", *The Economic Journal*, Vol. 100, 401, June: 391–439.

Okun, A. (1962) "Potential GNP: its measurement and significance", in Proceedings of the Business and Economics Section, American Statistical Association: 98–104.

Perry, G. (1997) "Potential output and productivity", Brookings papers on Economic Activity 1: 11–61.

Prachowny, M. (1993) "Okun's Law: theoretical foundation and revised estimates", The Review of Economics and Statistics, 331–336.

Setterfield. M. A., D. V. Gordon and L. Osberg (1992) "Searching for a will of the wisp: an empirical study of the NAIRU in Canada", European Economic Review, 36(1): 119–36.

Wyplosz, C. (1994) "Demand and structural views of European high unemployment trap", Swedish Economic Policy Review, Vol. 1, 1–2, autumn: 75–107.

Torres, R., and J. P. Martin (1990) "Measuring output in the seven major OECD countries", OECD Economic Studies 14: 127–49, OECD, Paris.

You, J.K. (1979) "Capital utilization, productivity and output gap", The Review of Economics and Statistics 1, February: 91–100.

CHAPTER - 5

A METHODOLOGICAL COMPARISON OF THEORETICAL APPROACHES IN DICHOTOMOUS CHOICE CONTINGENT VALUATION[1]

John C. Whitehead

ABSTRACT

The choice of theoretical approach in dichotomous choice contingent valuation can have implications for the theoretical validity and bias of willingness to pay estimates. The choice of theoretical approach affects the interpretation of validity tests, and through the implicit selection of the useable sample, sample bias. Data imputation techniques can be used to reduce the bias in willingness to pay at a cost of measurement error and inefficiency. The choice of theoretical approach should ultimately depend on the type of policy analysis for which the study is designed.

1. INTRODUCTION

The use of the contingent valuation (CV) method for measuring benefits in cost-benefit analysis is gaining considerable popularity. Use of the dichotomous choice, or referendum, approach is currently the most accepted questioning format for the CV method (Mitchell and Carson, 1989). For a proposed change in environmental quality, dichotomous choice questions are

---

[1]The data collection for this study was funded by the Department of Economics and Survey Research Laboratory, East Carolina University. The data can be obtained upon request from the author. The author would like to thank Ju-Chin Huang for suggestions which have improved this paper.

[77]

typically in a form such as "Would you be willing to pay $A for a policy with a goal to improve environmental quality ... ?" where $A is a randomly assigned individual policy cost. The dichotomous choice approach is preferred for reasons such as incentive compatibility and the ease of respondents' task. This view is supported by the NOAA Panel on Contingent Valuation (Arrow, et al., 1993) who suggest that referendum surveys should be used in order to achieve reliability of natural resource damage assessments.

Several theoretical approaches have been offered to guide empirical estimation of dichotomous choice CV data. Hanemann (1984) specifies explicit utility functions and derives functional forms for estimation with the logit technique. Seller, Chavas, and Stoll (1986) suggest functional forms that should be used in order to obtain valid estimates of WTP. Cameron and James (1987) and Cameron (1988) specify probit and logit models which can be transformed into valuation functions. In an effort to reconcile the competing approaches, McConnell (1990) develops the theoretical properties of the alternatives and shows that under certain conditions the Hanemann (1984) and Cameron (1988) approaches are equivalent and that the Sellar, et al. (1986) model is inappropriate due to the presence of endogenous variables in the empirical specification.[2]

These results have led most CV researchers to invoke an almost standard assertion that "the choice of empirical approach does not matter." While this may be true for some purposes, when estimating benefits for policy analysis it ignores the potential for sample bias and divergences of theoretical validity tests.[3] The purpose of this paper is to argue the opposite of the standard assertion. The choice of theoretical approach in dichotomous choice CV does matter when conducting policy analysis, especially if differences in approach are not explicitly recognized.

This paper is organized as follows. The purpose of section 2 is to illustrate how the choice of theoretical approach explicitly guides the type of independent variables that are used to explain the dichotomous choice. Section 3 shows how the theoretical approach will implicitly guide decisions about useable sample sizes and describe data imputation procedures that can be used to equalize sample sizes across approaches. Section 4 illustrates a typical comparison of results across theoretical approaches. Finally, section 5 offers

---

[2] Park and Loomis (1992) provide an empirical test of the connections between the Hanemann and Cameron approaches. They find that in terms of the relationships among variables the empirical approaches are not equivalent, but, the welfare estimates predicted by each model are not significantly different.

[3] See Mitchell and Carson (1989) for a discussion of both of these issues in the context of CV.

some conclusions.

2. THE THEORETICAL APPROACHES

Suppose consumers have the utility function u(q,x,θ), where q is the quality of a natural resource, x is the on-site (recreational) use of the resource, and θ is a composite commodity of all other goods. The indirect utility function, $v(q,p,y)$, is found by solving the consumer problem

$$\max u(q, x, \theta) \tag{1}$$
$$\text{s.t. } y = px + \theta$$

where y is income, p is the on-site use price, and θ is the numeraire good, $p_\theta = 1$.[4] The indirect utility function is decreasing in p and increasing in q and y. The expenditure function, $m(q,p,u)$, is found by solving the consumer problem

$$\min [px + \theta] \tag{2}$$
$$\text{s.t. } u = u(q, x, \theta)$$

The expenditure function measures the minimum amount of money a consumer must spend to achieve a fixed utility level and is increasing in p and u and decreasing in q.

The Utility Difference Function

The Hanemann utility difference function approach defines WTP by comparing indirect utility functions

$$v(q=1,p,y\text{-}WTP) = v(q=0,p,y) \tag{3}$$

where q=1 is an improved quality level and q=0 is a degraded quality level. A CV respondent who is presented with a dichotomous choice question faces the following problem

$$v(q = 1, p, y - A \geq v(q = 0, p, y). \tag{4}$$

$<$

---

[4] Related environmental goods and the corresponding cross-prices should also be theoretically specified and empirically tested. The extension is straightforward. In this paper, however, I avoid this step after determining that several choices of cross-prices have little direct or indirect empirical effects.

The respondent will answer yes if utility is higher with improved quality and the deduction in income. The utility difference function is formed by subtracting the right hand side of (4) from both sides

$$\Delta v = v(q = 1, p, y - A) - v(q = 0, p, y) \gtrless 0. \tag{5}$$

The utility difference function is increasing in income

$$\frac{\partial \Delta v}{\partial y} = \frac{\partial v(q = 1, p, y - A)}{\partial y} - \frac{\partial v(q = 0, p, y)}{\partial y} > 0 \tag{6}$$

if $v_{qy} > 0$ and $v_{yy} < 0$, where subscripts denote partial derivatives. The partial effect of price changes on the utility difference function can not be signed without restrictive, and perhaps unrealistic, assumptions[5]

$$\frac{\partial \Delta v}{\partial p} = \frac{\partial v(q = 1, p, y - A)}{\partial p} - \frac{\partial v(q = 0, p, y)}{\partial p} \gtrless 0 \tag{7}$$

The utility difference function is decreasing in the tax payment

$$\frac{\partial \Delta v}{\partial A} = -\frac{\partial v(q = 1, p, y - A)}{\partial A} < 0 \tag{8}$$

if the marginal utility of income is positive.[6] These comparative static results can be used to test for theoretical validity of CV.

The utility difference approach is implemented by specifying functional forms for the indirect utility function. Typically the linear form of $v(\cdot)$ is used

$$v(q = 1, p, y - A) = \alpha_1 - \beta_1 p + \phi_1(y - A) \tag{9}$$
$$v(p, q = 0, y) = \alpha_0 - \beta_0 p + \phi_0 y$$

---

[5] In order for Δvp to be negative several non-intuitive conditions must hold. For example, $v_{qp}=0$. Second, x and q must be gross complements so that as p increases, the consumption of x and q decrease. The marginal utility of q would then increase as a slope effect as p increases. Lastly, $v_{yp}=0$. If all these conditions hold, then $\Delta vp<0$. Several other possibilities are also likely, however.

[6] McConnell (1990) derives similar results for the utility difference function with WTP for price changes.

The utility difference function becomes

$$\Delta v = [\alpha_1 - \alpha_0] - [\beta_1 - \beta_0]p - \phi_1 A + [\phi_1 - \phi_0]y \qquad (10)$$

It is often assumed that $v_{qp} = v_{qy} = 0$ so that $[\beta_1 - \beta_0] = [\phi_1 - \phi_0] = 0$ and the "simple" utility difference function is

$$\Delta v = \alpha - \phi_1 A \qquad (11)$$

where $\alpha = [\alpha_1 - \alpha_0 > 0]$ is the marginal utility of the quality improvement and $\phi_1 > 0$ is the marginal utility of income

$$= \phi_1 \frac{\partial v(q = 1, p, y - A)}{\partial A} < 0 \qquad (8)$$

Setting $\Delta v = 0$ and solving for A* yields the WTP measure which is equal to the marginal utility of the quality change divided by the marginal utility of income

$$WTP = \alpha / \phi_1 \qquad (12)$$

To complicate matters, however, it is possible that $v_{qp}, v_{qy} \neq 0$.[7] In these cases the function must include price and income variables in order to avoid omitted variable bias

$$\Delta v = \alpha - \beta_p - \phi_1 A + \phi y \qquad (13)$$

where

$$\beta = [\beta_1 - \beta_0] \frac{\partial v(q = 1, p, y - A)}{\partial p} \frac{\partial v(q = 0, p, y)}{\partial p} \gtrless 0$$

$$\phi = [\phi_1 - \phi_1] \frac{\partial v(q = 1, p, y - A)}{\partial y} \frac{\partial v(q = 0, p, y)}{\partial y} > 0$$

---

[7] If x and q are gross complements, so that as p increases the consumption of x and q decreases and the marginal utility of q will increase as q decreases, then $v_{qp} < 0$. If other recreation goods purchased by y and q are gross complements or gross substitutes v_{qy} will be either positive or negative, respectively.

Again, setting $\Delta v=0$ and solving for A* yields the WTP measure

$$WTP = [\alpha - \beta p + \phi y]/\phi_1 \tag{14}$$

The benefit of the simple utility difference approach is its theoretical soundness and ease of implementation. The benefit of the extended utility difference approach is the opportunity to conduct theoretical validity tests.

The Valuation Function

The Cameron (1988) logit[8] valuation function approach defines WTP based on the difference in expenditure functions

$$WTP = m(q=0,\iota,u) - m(q=1,\iota,u) \tag{15}$$

where ι is a vector of demand shifters, such as socio-economic and attitudinal variables and WTP is equal to that defined in (3). The valuation function is implemented by specifying WTP to depend on a host of potential independent variables, $WTP = \iota'\beta$, where β is a coefficient vector.

Dichotomous choice CV respondents are assumed to directly compare their WTP values with A. The Cameron WTP function converts the estimate of the marginal utility of income into the scale parameter, κ

$$WTP = \iota'\beta = \kappa[\iota'\delta] \tag{16}$$

where $\kappa = 1/\phi_1$ and ? is a vector of coefficients. The major benefit of this approach is that income, demographic, attitudinal and other variables can be used to explain respondent behavior. This may be important for benefits transfer, distributional analysis, forecasting changes in WTP due to demographic change, or correcting non-response bias through weighting.

One drawback to the valuation function approach, when non-utility theoretic variables are included, is that it is not possible to theoretically link the coefficient estimates with economic theory. McConnell (1990) has shown that the comparative static effects of household characteristics, such as education, on WTP for price changes cannot be signed. Since this result is easily extended to the WTP for quality improvements, any coefficient estimate can only be used to describe changes in WTP in an informal way (i.e., "WTP increases with education as expected") relative to formal theoretical validity testing. A further problem is that measures of tastes and preferences may be correlated with

---

[8] A parallel model for the probit is developed by Cameron and James (1987).

utility-theoretic variables. Education and income are highly correlated and it is likely that the education coefficient will measure both taste and income effects. This correlation will confound the theoretical interpretation of the income effect as noted by McFadden (1994). For this reason, including measures for taste and preference differences should not be simply considered a parameterization of the constant in WTP functions, as is often assumed.

The Variation Function

The McConnell (1990) variation function approach employs a theoretical manipulation of the valuation function. If the reference level of utility is $v(q=1,p,y)$ substitution of the indirect utility function into the expenditure difference function, equation (15) holding ι constant, yields the variation function

$$s = m(q=0,p,v(q=1,p,y)) - y. \tag{17}$$

The effect of income on the variation function for quality improvements is

$$\frac{\partial s}{\partial y} = \frac{\partial m(q=0,p,u)}{\partial v} \frac{\partial v(q=1,p,y)}{\partial y} - 1$$

When evaluating at the same quality arguments, $v_y = 1/m_v$, and

$$\frac{\partial s}{\partial y} = \gamma - 1 \lessgtr 0,$$

where

$$0 < \gamma = \frac{\partial m(q=0,p,u)}{\partial v(q=1,p,y)} \lessgtr 1$$

If q is a normal good the marginal cost of utility will be greater when q=0 and the income effect will be positive.
The effect of the own-price on the variation function is

$$\frac{\partial s}{\partial p} = \frac{\partial m(q=0,p,u)}{\partial p} + \frac{\partial m(q=0,p,u)}{\partial v} \frac{\partial v(1=1,p,y)}{\partial p} \tag{20}$$

which can be rearranged and expressed as

$$\frac{\partial s}{\partial p} = x(q = o, p, y) - \gamma x(q = 1, p, y) < 0 \qquad (21)$$

where $x(q,p,y)$ is the ordinary demand function. Assuming quality is a normal good, the own-price effect will be negative if recreation trips and quality are complements.[9] The major benefit of the variation function approach is that comparative static results can be used to theoretically interpret results of CV empirical models (Whitehead 1995).

3. EMPIRICAL IMPLEMENTATION

Discrete choice econometric models are used to implement all three empirical approaches to dichotomous choice CV data. The utility difference approach specifies the probability of a yes response, π, to the dichotomous choice question to depend on the probability that the utility difference function with random error is positive

$$\begin{aligned} \pi &= \Pr(\Delta v + \varepsilon \geq 0) \\ &= \Pr(\Delta v \geq -\varepsilon) \end{aligned} \qquad (22)$$

where ε is a mean zero error term. Logistic regression employs a functional form to estimate the parameters of the utility difference function

$$\pi = \frac{1}{1 + e^{-\Delta v}} \qquad (23)$$

Substituting the explicit functional form for Δv yields

$$\pi = \frac{1}{1 + e^{-\alpha v \phi_1 A - \beta p \phi y}} \qquad (24)$$

By setting $\pi = 0.5$, so that the respondent is indifferent between paying the policy cost or not, the logistic function can be manipulated to yield

$$0 \; \hat{\alpha} - \hat{\phi}_1 A - \hat{\beta} p + \hat{\phi} y \qquad (25)$$

---

[9] If recreation trips and quality are substitutes the own-price effect is positive or equal to zero, depending on the size of γ.

and solving for A* yields

$$WTP = A* = \frac{\hat{\alpha}- \hat{\beta}p + \hat{\phi}y}{\hat{\phi}_1} \tag{26}$$

The valuation and variation function approaches specify the probability of a yes response to depend on the probability that *WTP* with random error is greater than the policy cost

$$\pi = \Pr(WTP + \mu \geq A) \tag{27}$$
$$= \Pr(WTP - A \geq -\mu)$$

where ? is a mean zero error term. The logistic function is

$$\pi = \frac{1}{1 + e^{(WTP-A)}} \tag{28}$$

which yields

$$\pi = \frac{1}{1 + e^{(\tau\delta-(1/\kappa)A)}} \tag{29}$$

By setting $\pi=0.5$ so that the respondent is indifferent between paying the policy cost or not, the logistic function can be manipulated to yield

$$0 = \tau\delta - \frac{1}{\kappa} A \tag{30}$$

and solving for A* yields

$$\hat{WTP} = A* = \kappa[\hat{\tau'\delta}] \tag{31}$$

The valuation function approach allows the τ vector to contain any variable which might explain the variation in *WTP*. The variation function approach constrains the τ vector to contain only those variables that are theoretically important determinants of *WTP*.

The simple utility difference approach, in which the marginal effects of own-price and income are not estimated, requires data on only two variables: the dichotomous choice response and the policy cost amount. Item non-response on independent variables is therefore not a problem. The probability of item-nonresponse increases with inclusion of additional variables in the model. The useable sample size will fall for the extended utility difference, variation and valuation functions since more independent variables are used relative to the simple utility difference function. Therefore, the choice of theoretical approach is also an implicit sample selection.

Item nonresponse is a typically ignored but potentially serious problem in CV research, especially when conducting policy analysis.[10] The least costly strategy when dealing with item nonresponse, and the one most often observed in CV research, is complete case analysis. One problem with complete case analysis is item nonresponse bias. When incomplete cases are discarded information on other independent variables is lost which creates problems similar to unit nonresponse bias. Throwing out incomplete cases will result in a biased sample unless the discarded cases are a random sub-sample. Further, sample sizes can decrease substantially when cases with missing data are discarded. Another problem is item selection bias. When incomplete cases are discarded information on the dependent variable, the yes and no responses, is lost. If incomplete cases are discarded a form of selection bias may result if respondents systematically select themselves out of the sample.

Data imputation, which requires replacing missing data with estimates of the missing values, allows analysis of the entire sample which reduces item nonresponse bias. If the estimate of the missing values are unbiased, data imputation also reduces the effects of item selection bias. There are several imputation methods available (Little and Rubin, 1987). The least costly is the unconditional mean imputation method in which the univariate mean of the available case data replaces the missing values. This method will increase the sample size, retaining information from incomplete cases, but may not produce an unbiased estimate of the missing variables. Another problem with using unconditional mean imputed data is that the variance of the mean of the variable is reduced which may lead to measurement error.

Another low cost strategy is the conditional mean imputation method which includes regression and hot deck imputation. Regression imputation involves regressing the variable with problematic nonresponse on expected determinants of that variable and replacing the missing value with the fitted value from the regression equation. Hot deck imputation involves replacing missing values with values from similar units in the sample. Conditional mean imputation will obtain an unbiased point estimate of the missing value. The bias in the missing variable is reduced, relative to the unconditional mean method, since the multivariate distribution of known variables is used in determining estimates for missing values.[11] Again, however, the variance of

---

[10] The next few paragraphs closer follow Whitehead (1994).

[11] This is the method employed by Carson, et al. (1994) for missing income values.

the mean will be reduced (although not as much as with the unconditional mean method) since some true variation in the imputed variable is lost which may lead to measurement error. Imputation will decrease sample bias but also decrease theoretical validity due to measurement error.

4. EMPIRICAL RESULTS

The first comparison of the theoretical approaches involves tests to determine if the coefficients on the price and income variables in each approach are significantly different from zero. If so, then the utility difference, valuation, and variation functions are conceptually different in terms of the theoretical interpretation of regression coefficients. If not, price and income are irrelevant variables, theoretical validity tests are of no use (or suggest that CV results are invalid), and the approaches are practically equivalent.[12] The second comparison across approaches is at the implementation stage of analysis which involves comparison of WTP point and confidence interval estimates. If WTP estimates are equal and similarly precise then the reduced sample size of all but the simple utility difference approach does not lead to sample bias.

The data from this study is from a computer assisted telephone interviewer survey conducted by a University survey research laboratory which has an overall response rate of 71%. A contingent market proposed a policy of "tougher laws" to control agricultural and commercial fishing practices that pollute water and destroy wildlife habitat in the Pamlico Sound, North Carolina. The laws are designed to "restore" Pamlico Sound resources by increasing fish catches, reducing disease in crabs, opening shellfish beds, and increasing growth of underwater grasses. Most survey respondents felt that these laws would be at least "somewhat effective" in achieving these goals.

Respondents are told that tougher laws would lead to higher consumer prices and that enforcement of these laws would lead to higher taxes. The willingness to pay question was closed-ended: "If you knew the money would be used to restore water quality and fish and wildlife habitat in the Pamlico Sound, would you and your household be willing to pay $A each year, in

---

[12] There are further tests which must be conducted to ensure the approaches are equivalent even when coefficients on price and income are significantly different from zero. These tests, however, have little practical significance and are not likely to change the outcome of the initial tests. An appendix to this paper, which is available from the author, sketches the remaining theoretical comparison between these approaches and specifies the complete set of statistical tests which could be performed.

higher consumer prices and state taxes?" The individual policy cost (annual prices and taxes = $A) randomly varied ranging from $5 to $300. Follow up questions were used to identify protest and outlier responses which were then deleted.

The overall item nonresponse rate is almost 18% with most of the missing values from the income variable. The conditional means imputed data includes missing income values replaced with regression imputation and other missing demographic values replaced with hot deck imputation. A household wage equation was used to impute missing income values. The wage equation performed reasonably well with wages increasing with education, increasing at a decreasing rate with experience, and with an acceptable adjusted R^2. The number of other missing demographic variables are small and were imputed by matching respondents with like characteristics and replacing missing values from the "donor" respondent with full data.

The complete case data, available case data, unconditional means imputed, and conditional means imputed data are presented in Table 1. Over sixty percent of the sample responded "yes" to the valuation question. The percent "yes" statistic falls from 64.4% with complete case data to 60.83% with available case data. The percentage of yes responses for the portions of the sample with complete case and imputed data are significantly different at the .01 level (χ^2=17.43). In a logit regression, with the probability of yes the dependent variable, a dummy variable for an imputed data point yields a negative and significant coefficient (t=4.17). These results are the initial indication that sample selection by the researcher could lead to item selection bias in the contingent valuation estimates. Only slight differences are found between means of demographic variables in the complete, available, and imputed data sets suggesting that item nonresponse bias on these variables is not a major concern.

The contingent valuation results are estimated using logistic regression and the utility difference, variation, and valuation functions are presented (Table 2).[13] Theoretical validity of the CV data is tested for with the signs and significance level of the dependent variables. CV respondents behaved rationally in the hypothetical market since the proportion of "yes" responses

---

[13] Four different versions of the survey instrument are combined in these models. Three dummy variables for versions were included in the empirical models but results are not reported.

Table 1

Data Summary

Variable	Complete Case Data	Available Case Data	Imputed: Unconditional Means	Imputed: Conditional Means
%YES	64.40	60.83	60.83	60.83
	(47.93)	(48.85)	(48.85)	(48.85)
A (1993 dollars)	116.35	116.75	116.75	116.75
	(104.11)	(103.71)	(103.71)	(103.71)
Own-price (time plus	112.87	112.69	112.68	104.80
travel costs)	(80.65)	(82.10)	(76.75)	(78.09)
Income (1993 dollars)	29,815	30,045	29,762	28,547
	(20,180)	(20,699)	(18,624)	(19,410)
Race (non-white = 1)	0.30	0.30	0.30	0.30
	(0.46)	(0.46)	(0.46)	(0.46)
Age (years)	42.97	44.01	44.38	44.40
	(16.41)	(17.20)	(17.16)	(17.18)
Married (=1)	0.60	0.58	0.57	0.57
	(0.49)	(0.49)	(0.49)	(0.49)
Education (years)	13.27	13.31	13.24	13.23
	(1.92)	(1.94)	(1.93)	(1.93)
Household size	2.71	2.64	2.63	2.63
(number)	(1.27)	(1.29)	(1.27)	(1.28)
Sample size	595	725*	725	725

* Sample sizes are 829 for own-price, 837 for income, 985 for race, 979 for age, 985 for married, 985 for education, 969 for household size.

fell as the price and tax level rose. Regardless of approach, the sign of the own-price coefficient is negative and the sign of the income coefficient is positive. Both results are statistically significant. Employing the variation function interpretations, these results suggest that recreation quality and recreation demand are complements and that quality is a normal good.

The income coefficient in the valuation function approach is measured with bias and less precision as covariates which are correlated with income are entered into the model. The income elasticity of WTP, evaluated at the means of income and WTP, falls from 1.09 to .55 from the variation to the valuation function. This result suggests that demographic variables which are correlated with income are irrelevant variables which confound CV econometric models.

90

Table 2
Complete case data WTP results

Variable	Utility Difference	Utility Difference	Variation Function	Valuation Function
Constant	0.787	0.298	64.8	−159
	(4.54)	(1.24)	(1.11)	(0.80)
A	−0.00454	−0.00459		
	(6.03)	(5.36)		
Own-price		−0.00393	−0.856	−0.815
		(2.07)	(1.89)	(1.79)
Income		0.000036	0.0078	0.0040
		(4.50)	(3.44)	(1.97)
Race				−195
				(3.49)
Age				−4.83
				(2.83)
Married				−36.8
				(0.72)
Education				−38.75
				(2.54)
Household size				38.58
				(1.75)
κ			218	215
			(5.36)	(5.03)
Sample size	725	603	603	595
χ^2	42.08	58.03	58.03	108.25

Unconditional and conditional means data imputation procedures are applied to the data and the resulting variation and valuation functions are presented (Table 3). The variation function results are less valid with imputed data. Own-price coefficients become insignificant due to measurement error on the opportunity cost of time as the imputed data is included. Valuation function estimates are even less valid due to measurement error in addition to including demographic variables which are correlated with income.

Mean WTP and 90% confidence intervals are calculated for each of the estimated logits using the technique of Park, Loomis, and Creel (1991). The benefit estimates for the available case variation and valuation functions are upwardly biased when compared to the available case benefit estimate of the simple utility difference function (Table 4). The extended utility difference

Table 3
Imputed data WTP results

Variable	Unconditional mean		Conditional mean	
	Variation function	Valuation function	Variation function	Valuation function
Constant	53.0	−122	28.3	−116
	(1.01)	(0.73)	(0.58)	(0.68)
Own-price	−0.666	−0.639	-0.336	−0.322
	(1.64)	(1.57)	(0.91)	(0.89)
Income	0.007	0.003	0.006	0.002
	(3.35)	(1.54)	(3.40)	(1.36)
Race		−173		−169
		(3.28)		(3.67)
Age		−5.81		−5.70
		(3.76)		(3.74)
Married		−4.31		−14.8
		(0.10)		(0.35)
Education		40.0		37.7
		(3.08)		(2.89)
Household size		24.9		25.91
		(1.39)		(1.44)
κ	217	205	216	206
	(5.98)	(5.89)	(5.99)	(5.86)
Sample Size	725	725	725	725
χ^2	63.25	135.27	69.34	134.77

function WTP estimate is equal to the variation function WTP estimate. Confidence intervals are larger for the reduced sample benefit estimates as well. Unconditional mean imputation reduces the upward bias but does not eliminate it. The more reliable conditional mean imputation technique does eliminate the upward bias. The benefit estimates of the variation, valuation, and utility difference functions are within $3 of each other when the reduced sample sizes from complete case analysis are increased with conditional mean imputation methods. Confidence intervals for benefit estimates using both imputation techniques are comparable to the simple utility difference function benefit estimate.

Table 4
Mean WTP and 90% confidence intervals

Function	Sample size	Mean	Lower bound	Upper bound
Utility				
Difference				
Complete case	725	$218.59	$186.00	$266.74
Variation				
Complete case	603	258.95	215.51	320.77
Unconditional means	725	236.02	189.25	270.33
Conditional means	725	220.84	190.55	274.45
Valuation				
Complete case	595	264.53	222.07	352.73
Unconditional means	725	234.63	190.91	275.39
Conditional means	725	219.33	189.11	274.35

5. CONCLUSIONS

Several results were identified in this paper. First, the chosen theoretical approach, whether the utility difference, valuation, or variation function, matters when conducting theoretical validity tests and interpreting coefficient estimates. Second, the valuation function can lead to theoretically invalid CV results due to correlation of utility theoretic variables with irrelevant demographic variables. Third, the theoretical approach chosen matters since, implicitly, the useable sample size is simultaneously chosen. The WTP estimates from the resulting sample may be biased. Fourth, data imputation techniques can be used to mitigate the effects of sample bias.

Often CV researchers use only complete case data and ignore the potential for sample bias from item nonresponse. The results of this paper suggest that only the simple utility difference approach will lead to unbiased benefit estimates with complete case data. Theoretical validity testing should be conducted with either the extended utility difference or variation function approaches and complete case data. The valuation function approach with complete case data may generate useful tests of the qualitative effects of socio-demographic variables on WTP. However, the quantitative effects of utility-theoretic or socio-demographic variables on WTP should be viewed with caution due to the potential for irrelevant variable bias.

Data imputation techniques should be used if either the variation or valuation function approaches are designed for policy analysis. The benefit of data imputation is the reduction in the bias in WTP estimates. The cost of data imputation is the loss of statistical efficiency in coefficient estimates. Since imputed data is measured with error, theoretical validity tests conducted with imputed data may be erroneous and conclusions based on them misleading. The valuation function approach with imputed data may be best for purposes such as forecasting changes in WTP over time and benefits function transfer.

REFERENCES

Arrow, K., R. Solow, E. Leamer, P. Portney, R. Radner, and H. Schuman (1993) "Report of the NOAA Panel on Contingent Valuation," Federal Register, 58, 4602-4614, 1993.

Cameron, T. A. (1988) "A New Paradigm for Valuing Non-Market Goods Using Referendum Data: Maximum Likelihood Estimation by Censored Logistic Regression," Journal of Environmental Economics and Management, 15, 355-379.

Cameron, T. A. and M. D. James (1987) "Efficient Estimation Methods for 'Closed-Ended Contingent Valuation Surveys," Review of Economics and Statistics, 69, 269-276.

Carson, R. T., R. C. Mitchell, W. M. Hanemann, R. J. Kopp, S. Presser, and P. A. Ruud (1994) "Contingent Valuation and Lost Passive Use: Damages from the Exxon Valdez," Discussion Paper 94-18, Resources for the Future, Washington, DC.

Hanemann, W. M. (1984) "Welfare Evaluations in Contingent Valuation Experiments with Discrete Responses," American Journal of Agricultural Economics, 66, 332-341.

Little, R. J. A. & Rubin, D. B. (1987) Statistical Analysis with Missing Data, New York: John Wiley.

McFadden, D., (1994) "Contingent Valuation and Social Choice" American Journal of Agricultural Economics, 76, 689-708.

McConnell, K. E. (1990) "Models for Referendum Data: The Structure of Discrete Choice Models for Contingent Valuation," Journal of Environmental Economics and Management, 18, 19-34.

Mitchell, R. C. & Carson, R. T. (1989) Using Surveys to Value Public Goods: The Contingent Valuation Method, Washington: Resources for the Future.

Park, T. and J. Loomis (1992) "Comparing Models for Contingent Valuation Surveys: Statistical Efficiency and the Precision of Benefit Estimates," Northeastern Journal of Agricultural and Resource Economics, 21, 170-176.

94

Park, T., J. Loomis, and M. Creel (1991) "Confidence Intervals for Evaluating Benefits from Dichotomous Choice Contingent Valuation Studies," Land Economics, 67, 64-73.

Sellar, C., J.-P. Chavas, and J. R. Stoll (1986) "Specification of the Logit Model: The Caseof Valuation of Nonmarket Goods," Journal of Environmental Economics and Management, 13, 382-390.

Whitehead, J. C. (1994) "Item Nonresponse in Contingent Valuation: Should CV Researchers Impute Values for Missing Independent Variables?" Journal of Leisure Research, 26, 296-303.

Whitehead, J. C. (1995) "Willingness to Pay for Quality Improvements: Comparative Statics and Theoretical Interpretation of Contingent Valuation Results," Land Economics, 71, 207-215.

CHAPTER 6

COST-BENEFIT ANALYSIS, ETHICS AND THE NATURAL ENVIRONMENT

Sarah Lumley

ABSTRACT

Cost-benefit analysis (CBA) is a technique which is used to assess project options for a wide range of resource allocation issues. The use of CBA in evaluating environmental resource allocation has attracted controversy for a number of reasons. This paper examines some of the reasons for the controversy. It uses the economic analyses applied to a proposed mining project within the boundaries of Kakadu National Park in northern Australia as a case study. Most of the controversy related to the application of CBA in this case arose as a result of difficulties experienced in valuing non-market factors associated with the environment. In addition to these valuation problems, the paper assesses the ethical implications of using standard economic criteria, such as those identified in CBA, when making decisions about the long-term use of the natural environment.

1. INTRODUCTION

Cost-benefit analysis (CBA) is a widely used technique described and discussed in a large body of conceptual and applied economics literature. It was first used as an empirical technique in the United States in the 1930s (Folmer and van Ierland, 1989) and it is now widely used as an evaluative tool in developed and less developed nations (Puttaswamaiah, 1978; Lumley, 1986). Its most common and most uncontroversial use is in its application to choice between discrete infrastructure projects (involving no externalities) where assessment of the relative costs and

[95]

96

benefits of each available option is required for comparison. CBA's popularity stems from its apparently easy to follow methodology, its neat tabulation of costs and benefits, its readily accepted protocols relating to the simple iteration of cash flows, and the ease with which time considerations can be accommodated by its computer-friendly discounted cash flow analyses. However, CBA is not innocent of controversy. While there are many how-to-do-it manuals on the market, those who delve deeper into the literature will find that almost every facet of CBA is subject to some level of disagreement. Some of this disagreement relates to the way in which costs and benefits are identified, some is about the subjects to which the technique is applied (the environment represents a particularly contentious subject), and some is about CBA theory and its treatment of time, particularly the manner in which the present is effectively weighted against the future through the process of discounting (Abelson, 1979; Bennett and Block, 1991; Frost, 1971; Mishan, 1979). A casual reading of CBA texts will reveal that practitioners and critics of the technique often do not agree about what CBA **is** and what it should be used **for** (Harris, 1991).

A cursory appraisal of some of the CBA literature yields a range of definitions and explanations of CBA. Some of these are reproduced below to give an idea of the mix of emphases inherent in applying CBA techniques.

Cost-benefit analysis (CBA) is a quantitative analytical tool to aid decision-makers in the allocation of resources (Department of Finance, 1995, p. 1).

...cost:benefit analysis uses a monetary basis to determine how the values of inputs and outputs are expressed (National Capital Authority, 1996, p. 12).

[CBA is] ...The appraisal of an investment project which includes all social and financial costs and benefits accruing to the project (Bannock et al., 1991, p. 91).

Benefit-cost analysis is a method to assess the relative desirability of competing alternatives in terms of their economic worth to society (Sinden and Thanpapillai, 1995, preface).

*CBA purports to describe and quantify the **social** advantages and disdvantages of a policy in terms of a common monetary unit* (Pearce, 1971, p. 8)

Cost-benefit analysis [is] a technique that aims to identify and measure the losses and gains in welfare that are incurred by society as a whole in relation to a particular project (Resource Assessment Commission, 1991, p. 384).

Social cost benefit analysis is a frequently used method of incorporating more information than that provided by the use only of 'market' prices. It typically employs 'accounting' prices as a means of placing a value on socio-economic factors which are not incorporated into narrower financial analyses (Department of Conservation, Forests and Lands, 1988, p. 1).

The definitions available for reproduction are almost limitless, since there are almost as many definitions of CBA as there are books about it. Some of these definitions are narrowly focussed and some are very broad. However, having digested them, the reader may puzzle over their relative meanings. Are economic, monetary, financial and quantitative values the same? The reader may also wonder if the definitions which call for quantification of costs and benefits without referring to their description refer to the same technique which requires, according to its definition, that they be described **and** quantified. And does the technique which requires the **inclusion** of all social and financial costs and benefits also require that such costs and benefits be quantified? If the cost-benefit analyst wishes to use monetary values why does one definition suggest that such values extend beyond market prices, which seem to be associated with 'narrower financial analyses'? And why do some definitions stress **social** values and society, while other definitions ignore the social dimension?

Clearly, cost-benefit analysis is more complex than it first appears. Whatever the relationship between the different approaches and ideas expressed in the simple definitions above, in all instances CBA appears to have something to do with value. It is, in part, because of differing perceptions of value that CBA becomes controversial.

As mentioned earlier, one use of CBA which is very controversial is its application to the natural environment, and the way it is used as a means of expressing environmental value and comparing it to other more tangible (quantifiable) values (Daly and Townsend, 1993). This paper will focus on the application of CBA to the environment, and it will assess two main issues: the interpretation of value, and the ethical dimension of CBA given different interpretations of its use and application in the context of value.

The three main sources of controversy when cost-benefit analysis is applied to environmental issues (Lumley, 1997, p. 72) relate to:

i) difficulties experienced in placing monetary values on intangible environmental resources,
ii) difficulties in placing monetary values on environmental impacts, and
iii) the process of discounting the streams of identified costs and benefits in such an analysis

None of these problems is satisfactorily addressed in any of the definitions of CBA outlined above. However, in order to examine the problems associated with use of CBA in more detail, the concepts of value and ethics, and how they are addressed in a broader socio-economic context, need to be considered.

2. CONCEPTS OF VALUE AND ETHICS

Concepts of value are embedded in almost every discipline. In English literature, for example, Eagleton (1991, p. 11) states:

> Value is a transitive term: it means whatever is valued by certain people in specific situations according to particular criteria and in the light of given purposes.

We can draw on the body of knowledge and ideas in other disciplines to address difficulties encountered in valuation techniques within the discipline of economics. A common criticism of the neo-classical economics framework is that, because it is based on a utilitarian philosophical approach, it does not operate within a properly defined ethical context (Brennan, 1992). There are many sub-disciplines within philosophy and between them they deal with other more broadly based concepts of ethics, such as responsibility and duty to people other than ourselves (Etzioni, 1988). These approaches differ from the uitiliarian approach, and hence the neo-classical approach, because they are not based on the goal of maximising utility, or individual satisfaction. There is a need to determine which mix of ethical critera should be used for any given purpose. Philosophers are much better equipped to do this than economists.

The definitions of CBA presented above make it clear that, apart from some confusion about how we place values on costs and benefits, the question of to whom the costs and benefits accrue is also unclear. Some definitions of CBA include social considerations and some do not. In addition, the word 'social' is sometimes added so that it is clear we

are talking about social cost-benefit analysis. None of the definitions make it clear whether this is different from private cost-benefit analysis. However, the technique is widely accepted as having its foundations in the social welfare function which is a key concept in neo-classical economics in that "*the maximisation of net benefits should be formally equivalent to the maximisation of social utility, or social welfare*" (Pearce, 1971, p. 18), so 'social' would seem to be implicit in CBA. One of the reasons that ethical criteria are being suggested as an adjunct to CBA is that "CBA is about efficiency not equity" (Common, 1995, p. 169).

CBA is still widely accepted as being a tool that is used to assess government projects in order to best serve the **public** (social) interest because the government is held to act in the interest of society. However, the equation of social utility with social welfare and hence with social **good** precludes consideration of other issues which might motivate individuals in society to make choices, precisely because such choices might not be dependent on them being motivated solely by maximising their own utility. Thus, in neo-classical theory social good does not include ethical or altruistic factors. In reality, individuals might be motivated by considerations which will not lead to maximisation of their own utility. For example, they might be concerned with conserving bio-diversity, with upholding the rights of indigenous people, when they themselves are not indigenous, with ensuring a better quality of life for their grandchildren. Or they might be concerned with improving the distribution of wealth between all members of society.

When Pearce (ibid) was writing back in 1971 the role of CBA was less opaque than it is now because it was identified almost exclusively as a technique used by governments, rather than by corporations. It was also more widely accepted that there may be unquantifiable values (intangible benefits or costs) which could over-ride market or monetary values because they were deemed to have greater (though unquantifiable) social value. Thus a decision might be made contingent upon these other considerations in what Pearce called the 'contingency' approach (ibid,p. 56). Interestingly, when identifying controversies associated with CBA in the '70s, Pearce commented at the end of his critique of the technique that:

> Clearly, the advocates of free markets and private enterprise see cost-benefit as one more weapon which might be used to justify state intervention. As such, it is no accident that the advocates and adversaries of CBA are often split by political persuasions (Pearce, 1971, p. 12).

Contemporary adversaries and advocates of CBA are also split by political persuasions. However, it now tends to be free market-proponents who advocate the use of CBA while those who are of more interventionist persuasion oppose it. This change has come about because in contemporary times CBA is often used as a tool by commercially oriented governments or companies to demonstrate the "economic worth" of a project using financial or market values. Such projects often involve publicly owned natural resources, and might be associated with what many argue are large and unquantifiable environmental costs. The 1991 case of whether to mine Coronation Hill in Australia will be used to illustrate this point.

The disagreement about how CBA should be used and what the technique's results demonstrate is a disagreement about the relative worth of different goods or resources, and to whom such worth accrues. In short it is a disagreement about concepts of value and of equity. As outlined earlier, a criticism of neo-classical economics, and techniques associated with it, is that it has no moral context beyond that of utility maximisation. However, if economics is about the maximisation of social good, then, some argue, inter-generational and intra-generational equity considerations should be included, as well as concepts of care and compassion for others. This would mean though, that social good would have to be defined in a context which is broader than just that of utility. This would run counter to the theoretical foundations of neo-classical economics and CBA. Thus, the exclusion of equity is a problem with the **theory** of CBA and might only be resolved through the development of a new economic theory.

Some of the problems associated with the use of CBA are problems of application. Many of the considerations which affect society, and the ecosystems upon which society depends, have no market price and are excluded from CBA in **application** though not in theory. The values which attach to these are not market values but they may include significant intangible or moral values. If market oriented governments are making decisions on behalf of society, and if such decisions are based on CBA results which exclude a large proportion of (non-market) social values then, it might be argued, that in a broader moral context, such use of CBA is unethical. If society were to take a more pluralist approach to decision making and policy development it would become apparent that it is very difficult to separate concepts of economic value from concepts of ethical value. These issues will be considered in an assessment of the applied economics and the ethical arguments contained in the Coronation Hill case study below.

3. THE CASE OF CORONATION HILL IN THE KAKADU CONSERVATION ZONE

In Australia in the late 1980s and early 1990s a dispute arose about whether the government should permit the establishment of a gold, platinum and palladium mine, to be operated by a joint venture of mining companies, at a place called Coronation Hill in the Kakadu Conservation Zone in the north of Australia's Northern Territory. Coronation Hill was mined for uranium in the 1950s and, as a natural feature, the hill itself was not considered to have a high conservation value, scarred as it was by previous mining activity. However, Coronation Hill lies very close to the source of the South Alligator River which spreads its tributaries across Kakadu National Park, feeding its World Heritage listed wetlands (nominated for environmental and cultural reasons) in one of the world's mega-diverse ecosystems. In fact the boundaries of Kakadu National Park closely approximate the catchment boundary of the South Alligator River, so the main environmental concern was that any mishap at a mine sited on Coronation Hill had the potential to damage much of the extensive (around 25,000 km. sq.) National Park and its wetland ecosystems (ERISS, 1997).

The Kakadu Conservation Zone was Commonwealth Crown land lying within the boundaries of the Kakadu National Park, but not part of it. Under the National Parks and Wildlife Conservation Act 1975 mineral exploration and other activities are permitted in Conservation Zones (CZs) as long as controls which protect and conserve the wildlife and natural features of the areas are established. These controls must remain until it is decided whether to declare the area as parks or reserves (RAC,

1991). In order to settle the dispute in a balanced manner, the government asked the Resource Assessment Commission (RAC) to conduct a comprehensive analysis of all the options available in the Kakadu CZ. The RAC eventually identified seven options for the CZ. Three main values of the CZ were implicit in these options. These were as follows:

i) A unique conservation value for Kakadu National Park, its natural features, (particularly the South Alligator River), and its flora and fauna, and the ecosystem damage which might occur should Coronation Hill be mined.

ii) A spiritual and cultural value for the local Aboriginal people, which was inextricably linked to the environmental value of the place

iii) A financial value for the proposed mine, and its employment possibilities for local communities.

There was a strong view among some Australians that the mine would irrevocably damage the natural environment, especially the unique wetland ecosystems of Kakadu National Park. Amongst most of the local Aborigines the view was that the mine would adversely affect the cultural and spiritual value of the area. Conversely, the mining companies claimed that ... *the economic value of the mine was greater than its environmental worth* (Young, 1996, p. 6).

The case of assessing natural resource use options in the Kakadu Conservation Zone provides a good example of the three main sources of controversy inherent in the application of CBA to the natural environment, and outlined earlier.

The first two problems relate directly to the convention of valuing resources according to their current market price, and the lack of suitable methods of dealing with resources for which there is no market (remembering that according to neo-classical economic theory, non-market values are supposed to be accommodated within CBA). The third point relates to the way discounting might influence intergenerational equity and the fact that the neo-classical theory in which CBA has its foundations does **not** account for equity considerations.

The CBA conducted on the Kakadu Conservation Zone natural resource options was contained within the comprehensive inquiry carried out by the Resource Assessment Commission (RAC) which was established by an Act of the Australian Commonwealth Government in 1989. Under the inquiry's terms of reference the government required the RAC to:

> evaluate and identify the options for the use of those resources [of the Kakadu Conservation Zone, including Coronation Hill and El Sherana], including an assessment of:
>
> - the environmental and cultural values of the Conservation Zone;
> - the impact of potential mining operations in the Conservation Zone on those values and on the values of Kakadu National Park;
> - the national economic significance of potential of potential mining development in the Conservation Zone;
> - the interests of Aboriginals affected by any potential mining development (RAC, 1991, p. 2).

These terms of reference appear to lend themselves well to the technique of CBA, given that they clearly relate to a comparison of competing options and the valuation of those options. Although the various definitions of CBA presented in the introduction to this paper differ in detail they have the valuation and comparison of competing options in common. They are also relevant to main points of contention about the application of CBA to environmental resources, as outlined above.

The variation in understanding and interpretation of the broad goals of CBA, especially as an **economic** technique, led to major disagreements between the main protagonists of the different options in the Conservation Zone. Mining companies, with a commercially oriented view of what constitutes economics and CBA, tended to interpret economic (or social) benefits as those with a commercial value. Aboriginal groups required particular recognition of cultural and spiritual values, while conservationists argued for recognition of aesthetic and bequest values in addition to a range of use values for the environment. Commercial protagonists were far more concerned with present and tangible values, while Aboriginal and conservation protagonists were concerned with future values as much as they were concerned with the present.

3.1. Valuing Coronation Hill and its Environment

Cost-benefit analysis theory requires the inclusion of all costs and benefits, monetary and non-monetary, in order to make an accurate comparison of the avaliable options. Various cost-benefit practitioners have called for the appropriate use of total economic value (TEV) calcuations in order to ensure the incorporation of intangible values in CBA results (Pearce and Turner, 1990; Tisdell, 1991; Barbier et al., 1994). This is because, despite theoretical requirements, factors which have no market price are often excluded from CBA as there is no universally accepted technique for their quantification. This problem was identified earlier in this paper and relates to the first two sources of controversy associated with the application of CBA to the environment. These are: valuing environmental resources and valuing environmental impacts.

The Resource Assessment Commission attempted an exhaustive inquiry into the potential uses and values of Coronation Hill and its environment in order to reflect the TEV of the different options (RAC, 1991a, b). This included an attempt to account, qualitatively and quantitatively, for all possible benefits of environmental resources (including benefits associated with mining) and all possible costs of environmental impacts (including costs associated with mining).

The results of the Kakadu Conservation Zone Inquiry were published by the RAC in a two volume final report in May 1991. The values identified by the RAC associated with the environmental resource and the impacts of its use are shown below in Table 1. These values were accounted for quantitatively or qualitatively, depending on the feasibility of deriving monetary values. There were three sources of value which were deemed to be particularly important. These were the mining value, the environmental value and the spiritual and cultural value to the traditional Aboriginal people.

In order to determine the value of mining activities, the Australian Bureau of Agricultural and Resource Economics constructed a simulation model of the mine, and a cost-benefit analysis was conducted for the years 1992 to 2004, which was assumed to be the close-out year of the mine. Costs and benefits were discounted at a **nominal** rate of 13% per year (8% real) and the net present value (NPV) of the mine was assessed at 82.4 million dollars.

The sometimes controversial contingent valuation method (CVM) was used to determine the monetary value of the existing environmental resource, as perceived by the Australian population. The CVM valued the Coronation Hill environment (including broader aspects which might be affected by mining) at 647 million dollars per year for ten years (RAC, 1991b, p. 268). That is, Australians said they would be willing to pay this amount to avoid damage to the environment from mining Coronation Hill.

The third important value of the area was identified as being the spiritual and cultural value to the traditional Aboriginal population. This was not assessed quantitatively, but was subject to considerable consultation and qualitative assessment involving the local clans, and particularly the Jawoyn people. It was concluded that the Jawoyn people had a long and continuing traditional affiliation with much of the relevant land, and that their cultural and religious values are integrally linked with the land (RAC, 1991a, p. 85–125).

Table 1

Resources and Values Associated with Coronation Hill

Resource	Associated Values
Archaeological Resources	Rock painting and artistic values
	Artefact values
	Engraving values
	Spiritual and cultural values
Physical Resources	Landform values
	Water values
Biological Resources	Vegetation values
	Terrestrial vertebrate values
	Aquatic vertebrate values
	Invertebrate values
	Ecological integrity values
	World heritage values
Mineral Values	Commercial value of gold
	Commercial value of platinum
	Commercial value of palladium
	Employment values
Recreation and Tourism Resources	Wilderness values
	Aesthetic values
	Recreational opportunity values
	Commercial values
	Employment values

Source: RAC (1991a), Chapters 4 and 5, pages 65 to 125.

3.2. The outcome of the Inquiry

The methodology used to assess the costs and benefits of mining Coronation Hill proved to be extremely controversial. The joint venture of mining companies did not want to accept that the CVM reflected the economic value of the environment. Indeed, even among economists what is actually measured by CVM is in dispute (see Blamey et al., 1996). Not surprisingly, the mining companies argued that the mining value of the site was greater than its environmental worth (Young, 1996). One submission presented during the course of the inquiry suggested that the delay to the mining project was "symptomatic of an increasing tendency for governments to interfere in commercial decision making, especially in the mining industry" (RAC, 1991a, p. 238).

The then Australian government requested the RAC inquiry report to help it make a decision about which of the seven options outlined for the conservatiuon zone it should adopt. As a decision making tool, CBA provides information about which option is most economically efficient. As mentioned earlier, it does not use any equity criteria, and this is one reason why some economists have proposed a formal broadening of decision making criteria, especially for environmental issues. With CBA, the option with the highest NPV is indicated for adoption. On the basis of the analyses conducted for the RAC inquiry, if CVM is accepted as providing an estimate of economic value, the economic value of the environment would have been deemed to be higher than the economic value of the mine. This is one reason for the CVM being so controversial. Ultimately, the Government chose the fifth of the seven options:

> Mining and exploration not to be permitted at Coronation Hill or elsewhere in the Conservation Zone, the whole of the zone to become part of Kakadu National Park (RAC, 1991, p. xvii).

What surprised those who were arguing against the economic validity of the CVM was that the government chose this option on the basis of the value of the area to the religion and culture of the Jawoyn people. This might be viewed as an ethical decision, not predicated on the outcome of the quantitatively based cost-benefit analysis.

4. CONTEMPORARY APPROACHES TO VALUATION ISSUES AND MORAL CONSIDERATIONS

Earlier in this paper three aspects of CBA were identified as being a source of controversy. All relate to valuation. The first two have been discussed briefly in the applied study of Coronation Hill. The Coronation Hill case demonstrates:

   i) difficulties experienced in placing monetary values on intangible environmental resources, and,

   ii) difficulties in placing monetary values on environmental impacts.

The CVM technique, which was applied in this case, was originally developed in an attempt to overcome the problem of valuing intangibles. Along with other shadow pricing techniques, such as the travel cost method and the hedonic pricing technique, it is used to enable the inclusion of intangibles within a quantifiable CBA framework. In this way, all costs and benefits might be measured with the same yardstick. These techniques rely on attempting to measure individuals' willingness to pay (WTP) in some manner and are said (in theory) to reflect consumer preference. A lively and interesting debate about environmental valuation methods and techniques designed to measure preference continues (Boxall et al., 1996; Langford and Bateman, 1996; Lockwood, 1996). Some economists argue that CVM may be measuring something other than consumer preference, such as individuals' approval or disapproval of the project in question. In such cases Blamey et al. (1996) argue that CVM surveys might be better used as citizens' referenda than as a measure of consumers' preferences which reflect economic value. As evidenced by the response of the mining sector to the Coronation Hill CVM, such techniques are often not accepted by, or acceptable to, those who have a commercial interest in the outcome of the CBA.

The third source of controversy identified earlier as stemming from the application of CBA to the environment is:

iii) the process of discounting the streams of identified costs and benefits ...

Although not yet discussed, this too is relevant to the Coronation Hill case. Discounting is linked to the valuation issues outlined above because the discount rate is applied to the flows of costs and benefits determined by the valuation procedures (Lumley, 1997).

Problems associated with valuing intangibles and with discounting in CBAs concerning the environment have long been recognised by economists (Pearce, 1971; Frost, 1971; Abelson, 1979). However, despite the development of shadow-pricing techniques, or perhaps because of it, the issue is subject to much debate. Disagreement on how to resolve such problems is exacerbated by disagreement about the validity of discounting (Rabl, 1996; Tisdell, 1991; Sinden and Thampapillai, 1995).

As indicated above, the contemporary debate about valuation issues is alive and largely unresolved. Participants entering the debate from other disiplines tend to disagree with economists, and economists tend to disagree with each other about the best approach to environmental valuation. Barbier et al. (1994, p. 84) summarise the reason for the contention about discounting in environmental CBAs:

> ... it has been argued that if the current population has an ethical responsibility for future generations, then the costs of environmental degradation should not be discounted. Under this scenario, discount rates would effectively be zero. However, in recent years, these arguments for removing or reducing high discount rates have largely been refuted. A low discount rate may be insufficient to avoid imposing environmental costs on future generations.

Sinden and Thampapillae (1995, p. 136) are more ambivalent. They state:

> Both high and low rates can favour conservation of the environment, and both high and low rates can favour development – so there is no consistency in the rate advocated by conservationists.

Consistency in theory and application is very important to the proper conduct of CBA. The issue of discounting and its potential inconsistencies in application can be illustrated in the Coronation Hill case study. Recall that a 13% **nominal** rate of discount was applied to the mining CBA. There is some disagreement about whether or when inflation should be added to the real discount rate, since, as in this case, generally applied (Mishan, 1979). In addition, with respect to the inconsistencies in the Coronation Hill study it appears that while the mining values were discounted (favourably for the NPV), the environmental values from the CVM were not. This could have had the effect of weighting the mining values against the environment values. It also contravenes the theoretical requirements of CBA that:

> There is a presumption that all benefits and costs, regardless of their nature, are to be discounted at the same rate, and that this rate is constant over time (Pearce, 1971, p. 40).

In this context it can be seen that ethics has **at least** two points of relevance to the use of CBA. One is that the choice of discount rate in CBA is viewed by some as being an ethical choice. The second is that if the theory is inconsistently or dishonestly applied to CBA, this might be viewed as unethical. A third point of relevance, and perhaps the most important, is that CBA is based on efficiency not equity considerations. As such, outside of utilitarian ethics, it has no moral context and pays no heed to the possible distributional consequences of project proposals

Contemporary approaches to valuation issues are many and varied. It is the treatment of intangibles in CBA that is currently the most vehemently debated. Brent (1996, p. 183) suggests that:

> People sometimes label intangible items 'unquantifiable'. By definition these cannot be valued. An intangible effect, on the other hand, is merely one that cannot be touched.

Economists who believe that intangibles can be quantified do their best to incorporate them in CBA by using the various shadow pricing techniques. Those who do not believe that they can or should be quantified have sought other alternatives for dealing with them in the decision making process, and some tend to participate actively in the international pluralist debate by arguing to broaden the formal decision making framework. Some suggest that this can be done by including considerations such as ethical criteria. This could mean that economic efficiency might lose some currency as the dominant criterion in policy determination.

The question of whether the discipline of economics should countenance the inclusion of moral criteria as part of the formal decision making framework is one that is attracting much dialogue in contemporary economics literature (Etzioni, 1988; Buarque, 1993; Daly and Townsend,

1993; and Brennan, 1996). This is especially true in the emerging pluralist sub-disciplines of new economics and ecological economics. One of the reasons for this approach is the concern which is being expressed by members of society and by members of other disciplines, about the limitations of CBA. These limitations are viewed as being inherent in the theory and application of CBA, especially when applied to environmental and social justice issues. Some economists argue that the limitations of CBA, and especially its inability to accommodate concerns about inter-generational and intra-generational equity, cannot be overcome. In this they are often joined by practitioners from other disciplines, particularly philosophers, ecologists and other scientists who have increasing access to the debate now that economic questions are often raised in transdisciplinary international forums (Intergovernmental Panel on Climate Change, 1996; International Environmental Justice and Global Ethics Conference, 1997). Greater credence is being given to the idea that moral criteria should be included with economic criteria in decision-making.

6. CONCLUSION

Economic analysis has long been considered by most members of society to be the province of the expert. The language of economics is often held to be arcane, and its jargon opaque. CBA is a prominent economic tool and discussions about its theory and application have been conducted between economists over many years. Generally, members of the public have not attempted to participate in these discussions. However, with the inclusion of economics and CBA in the pluralist dialogue, members of society have increasing access to arguments about economics. Articles about the theory and application of economics are appearing with ever greater frequency in the mainstream press (e.g. Barker, 1997) and members of society are beginning to question the ethical (and other) implications of implementing the dominant economic paradigm.

Some time ago Mishan (1986) considered the question of the public's acceptance of the economist's criterion (economic efficiency) in public policy decision making. He concluded that the influence of such a criterion depends on its acceptability by society in some **non**-political capacity and that

> ... nothing less than an ethical consensus is needed to confer legitimacy on the economist's criterion (p. 95).

A broader global dialogue is enabling members of society to question more openly the legitimacy of the economist's criterion, and to require the inclusion of ethics in decisions which define social good.

This paper has sought to demonstrate some of the continuing problems with the application of CBA to the environment, using Coronation Hill as a case study. In this paper, calls for the inclusion of moral criteria as part of the decision making framework have been supported as a way of helping to overcome the limitations of CBA. In fact, the use of moral criteria is not without precedent. Governments can and occasionally do make ethically based decisions, as the then Australian government did in the case of Coronation Hill. The formal inclusion of ethical criteria in the decision making process might help to stem some of the controversy associated with the theory and application of CBA to social and environmental policy determination. The dialogue relating to this issue will no doubt continue in the international pluralist forum. It is to be hoped that the ethical criteria appropriate to resolving the problems discussed in this paper will be identified as a result of this continuing dialogue.

REFERENCES

Abelson, Peter (1979) *Cost benefit analysis and environmental problems.* Saxon House, Westmead.

Bannock, Graham, Baxter, R.E and Davis, Evan (1991) *The Penguin dictionary of economics.* Penguin, Harmondsworth.

Barbier, E.B., Burgess, J.C. and Folke, C. (1994) *Paradise lost? The ecological economics of biological diversity.* Earthscan Publications, London.

Barker, Geoffrey (1997). The great divide. *The Australian Financial Review Magazine,* June.

Bennett, Jeff and Block, Walter (editors) (1991) *Reconciling economics and the environment.* Australian Institute for Public Policy, West Perth.

Blamey, R.K., Common, M.S. and Quiggan, J. (1996) 'Respondents to contingent valuation surveys: Consumers or citizens?'. *Australian Journal of Agricultural Economics,* 39(3)

Boxall, Peter C, Adamowicz, Wictor L., Swait, Joffre, Williams, Michael and Louviere, Jordan (1996) 'A comparison of stated preference methods for environmental valuation'. *Ecological Economics,* 18(4): 243–253.

Brennan, A. (1992) Moral pluralism and the environment. *Environmental Values,* 1: 15–33.

Brennan, A. (1996) Ethics, ecology and economics. In: *Ecologists and ethical judgements.* Chapman Hall, London.

Brent, Robert, J. (1996) *Applied cost-benefit analysis.* Edward Elgar, Cheltenham.

Buarque, Cristovam (1993) *The end of economics? Ethics and the disorder of progress.* Zed Books, London and New Jersey.

Common, Michael (1995) *Sustainability and policy. Limits to economics.* Cambridge University Press, Cambridge.

Daly, Herman, E. and Townsend, Kenneth, N. (editors) (1993) *Valuing the earth. Economics, ecology and ethics.* The MIT Press, Cambridge, Massachusetts.

Department of Conservation, Forests and Lands (1988) *Project evaluation manual.* DCFL, Government of Victoria.

Department of Finance (1995) *Introduction to cost-benefit analysis for program managers.* Australian Government Publication Service, Canberra.

Eagleton, Terry (1991) *Ideology: An introduction.* Verso, London. Cited in Saunders, Ian (1993) *Open texts, partial maps.* Centre for Studies in Australian Literature, University of Western Australia, Perth.

ERISS (1997) Personal communication. Environmental Research Institute of the Supervising Scientist, Jabiru, Kakadu National Park, May 1997.

Etzioni, A. (1988) *The moral dimension. Towards a new economics.* The Free Press, Collier Macmillan, London.

Folmer, H. and van Ierland, E. (editors) (1989) *Valuation methods and policy making in environmental economics.* Elsevier, Amsterdam.

Frost, Michael J. (1971) *Values for money. The techniques of cost benefit analysis.* Gower Press, London.

Harris, G.T. (1991) 'Cost benefit analysis: Its limitations and use in fully privatised infrastructure projects'. *Australian Journal of Public Administration.* 50(4): 526–537.

Intergovernmental Panel on Climate Change (1996) *Climate change 1995. Economic and social dimensions.* Cambridge University Press, Cambridge.

International Environmental Justice and Global Ethics Conference (1997) To be held at the University of Melbourne, Victoria, Australia. October.

Langford, I.H. and Bateman, I.J. (1996) 'Elicitation and truncation effects in contingent valuation studies'. *Ecological Economics,* 19(3): 265–268.

Lockwood, M. (1996) 'Non-compensatory preference structures in non-market valuation of natural area policy'. *Australian Journal of Agricultural Economics,* 40(2): 85–102.

Lumley, Sarah (1986) Factors influencing the social benefits and social costs of pest plant control. Economics Group, Department of Conservation, Forests and Lands, Victoria, Australia.

Lumley, Sarah (1997) 'The environment and the ethics of discounting: An empirical analysis'. *Ecological Economics* 20: 71–82.

Mishan, E.J. (1979) *Cost-benefit analysis.* George Allen and Unwin, London.

Mishan, Ezra, J. (1986) *Economic myths and the mythology of economics.* Wheatsheaf Books, The Harvester Press, England.

National Capital Authority (1996) *Towards best practice for improved urban management. Social cost: benefit analysis. Technical notes.* Australian Government Publishing Service, Canberra.

Pearce, D.W. (1971) *Cost-benefit analysis.* Macmillan studies in economics. Macmillan, London and Basingstoke.

Pearce, D.W. and Turner, P.K. (1991) *Economics of natural resources and the environment.* Harvester Wheatsheaf, London.

Puttaswamaiah, K. (1978) *Aspects of evaluation and project appraisal.* Popular Prakashan, Bombay.

Rabl, Ari (1996) 'Discounting of long-term costs: What would future generations prefer us to do?' *Ecological Economics,* 17(3): 137–154.

114

RAC (1991a) *Kakadu Conservation Zone Inquiry. Final Report. Volume 1.* Resource Assessment Commission, Australian Government Publishing Service, Canberra.

RAC (1991b) *Kakadu Conservation Zone Inquiry. Final Report. Volume 2.* Resource Assessment Commission, Australian Government Publishing Service, Canberra.

Sinden, J.A. and Thampapillai, D.J. (1995) *Introduction to benefit-cost analysis.* Longman, Melbourne.

Tisdell, C. (1991) *Economics of environmental conservation. Economics for environmental and ecological management. Vol. 1.* Elsevier, Amsterdam.

Young, Liz (1996) 'Rhetoric and strategy: Australian mining and the conflict over Coronation Hill'. *Policy, Organisation and Society.* 11: 1–24.

CHAPTER - 7

TRANSPORT COST ANALYSIS: APPLICATIONS IN DEVELOPED AND DEVELOPING COUNTRIES

Todd Litman

ABSTRACT

Transport planning and policy analysis often focuses on just a few costs, primarily direct costs to users and government agencies. Other costs, particularly indirect, external and non-market costs, tend to be ignored or undervalued by individual consumers and public officials. Recent analysis indicates that such costs are significant. Failing to consider all social costs results in suboptimal transport decisions.

This article describes a framework that can be used to evaluate the full costs of different modes of transport for planning and policy analysis applications. The results indicate that a significant portion of transport costs are either fixed or external, resulting in underpricing and therefore economically inefficient travel behavior, and that many transport costs are indirect and non-market, which tend to be undervalued by transport planners and policy makers. This framework has many potential applications for improving transport decision-making in both developed and developing regions.

INTRODUCTION

If you ask people what it costs to travel, you are likely to receive an incomplete answer. Transit and cab riders will include their fares. Automobile users will typically mention vehicle operation expenses, such as fuel and vehicle wear, and tolls. Some may also include a portion of vehicle ownership costs, such as depreciation, insurance, and residential parking. Some travelers may mention the value of their time. These however are only a portion of the total social costs of transport. In

[115]

addition to these internal costs are various external costs, such as resources used for roads and parking facilities that are not user paid, congestion and accident risk imposed on other road users, and a variety of environmental and social costs. Planners and economists should consider all these costs when evaluating transport policies, plans and investments.

In practice, transportation decision makers sometimes behave like blind men exploring an elephant. As the old story goes, each individual only perceives one aspect of the whole. Consumers are primarily aware of their direct financial and time costs, transport planners focus on congestion problems and roadway construction costs, developers may only consider the costs of providing driveways and parking facilities, traffic safety officials are concerned with accident costs, development economists may focus on macroeconomic impacts of automobile consumption, while environmental planners are concerned with pollution and habitat impacts. Each of these perspectives leads to different conclusions as to what constitutes optimal transport policy. Only by taking into account *all* social costs can economists and policy makers be confident that their analysis results truly reflect society's overall interests.

This article describes a comprehensive transport cost framework which attempts to account for all costs associated with various travel modes. This framework is suitable for use in both developed and developing countries, provided that cost values are adjusted to represent local conditions.

This emphasis on transport costs does not ignore the significant benefits provided by transportation. Analysis of costs is actually the basis for calculating most transport benefits since marginal benefits are usually measured in terms of reduced costs. For example, the benefits of a road improvement comes from reductions in travel time and vehicle operation costs.

Comprehensive analysis of transport costs is increasingly important for a number of reasons. Growing motor vehicle use is causing a number of "problems" (or, as economists would say, "costs") in both developed and developing countries. Public officials need better tools for evaluating alternative transport policies, plans and programs, taking into account a wide range of impacts and social concerns. There is also increasing interest in using marginal cost pricing instruments to optimize travel behavior. Marginal cost implies consideration of all social costs.

Economic efficiency requires marginal cost pricing. This means that prices should equal short run marginal costs (SRMC) based on existing facility capacity and conditions, while long run decisions (such as roadway facility capacity) would consider whether this SRMC pricing provides economic profits (Hau, 1992, 29). The scope of costs typically considered for marginal pricing has expanded over time. Most highway cost allocation literature assumes that road users must simply pay a "fair" share of road construction and maintenance costs (Jones and Nix, 1996; Small, Winston and Evans, 1989). Others emphasize congestion costs (Hau, 1992; Vickrey, 1969). But a truly efficient pricing must include charges that reflect the full variety of costs imposed by motor vehicle use (Komanoff, 1995; Litman, 1997), including road and parking facilities, congestion, accident risk, pollution, and other environmental costs.

Estimates of transportation's full costs are also useful for equity analysis. Although mobility is often considered a "merit" good that deserves government support, beyond a certain point (defined as "basic mobility", which is typically considered to consist of access to education, employment and public services using a low-cost mode), increased personal travel can be considered a luxury. As such, equity demands that society be compensated for costs imposed by such travel as much as is technically efficient. Otherwise, those who bear uncompensated costs are subsidizing other peoples' luxury travel.

FULL-COST RESEARCH

A number of recent studies attempt to estimate the full social costs of land transport (Apogee Research, 1994; Delucchi, 1996–97; IBI, 1995; Kageson, 1994; Litman, 1997; MacKenzie et al., 1992; Maddison et al., 1996; Works Consultancy Services Ltd., 1993). A few focus on the full costs of freight transport (Committee for Study of Public Policy for Surface Freight Transport, 1996; Transport Concepts, 1994). Only one recent study attempts to estimate full transport costs in a developing country (Zegras and Litman, 1997), although many researchers discuss the significant and varied costs of increased motor vehicle use in such regions (Birk and Zegras, 1993; Cullinane and Cullinane, 1995; Dimitriou, 1992; Njoh, 1997; Garb, 1997).

Litman and Rintoul (1996) developed a computer model for evaluating the magnitude and distribution of costs for different types of travel. It

Table 1.
Transportation Cost Categories (Litman, 1997)

Cost	Definition	Internal/External	Fixed/Variable	Market/Non-market
1. Vehicle Ownership	Fixed vehicle expenses.	Internal	Fixed	Market
2. Vehicle Operation	User expenses that are proportional to travel.	Internal	Variable	Market
3. Operating Subsidies	Vehicle expenses not paid by the user.	External	Fixed	Market
4. User Travel Time	Time spent traveling.	Internal	Variable	Non-Mkt
5. Internal Accident	Vehicle accident costs borne by users.	Internal	Variable	Non-Mkt
6. External Accident	Vehicle accident costs not borne by users.	External	Variable	Non-Mkt
7. Internal Parking	Parking costs borne by users.	Internal	Fixed	Market
8. External Parking	Parking costs not borne by users.	External	Variable	Market
9. Congestion	Delay each vehicle imposes on other road users.	External	Variable	Mixed
10. Road Facilities	Road construction and maintenance expenses not paid in proportion to road use.	External	Variable	Market
11. Roadway Land Value	Opportunity cost of land used for roads.	External	Fixed	Market
12. Municipal Services	Public services devoted to vehicle traffic.	External	Variable	Market
13. Equity & Option Value	Reduced travel choices, especially for disadvantaged people.	External	Variable	Non-Mkt
14. Air Pollution	Costs of motor vehicle emissions.	External	Variable	Non-Mkt
15. Noise	Costs of motor vehicle noise.	External	Variable	Non-Mkt
16. Resource Consumption	External costs resulting from the consumption of petroleum and other natural resources.	External	Variable	Mixed
17. Barrier Effect	The disamenity motor traffic imposes on pedestrians and bicyclists. Also called "severance."	External	Variable	Non-Mkt
18. Land Use Impacts	Economic, environmental and social costs resulting from low density, auto oriented land use.	External	Fixed	Mixed
19. Water Pollution	Water pollution and hydrologic impacts from motor vehicles and roads.	External	Variable	Non-Mkt
20. Waste Disposal	External costs from motor vehicle waste disposal.	External	Variable	Non-Mkt

Note: This table summarizes possible transportation costs categories, and their attributes. Not all of these costs apply in every situation.

tracks twenty costs for eleven modes under three travel conditions. Table 1 summarizes the cost categories. The software provides "generic" estimates of these costs representing typical North American conditions.

Full cost studies incorporate costs that transport economists and planners traditionally quantify (vehicle expenses, roadway facilities, travel time, and accident risk), plus additional costs that have frequently been overlooked either because they are indirect (such as parking subsidies and land use impacts), or because they are difficult to value in monetary units (such as environmental and equity impacts). For detailed discussions of the various techniques used to estimate and evaluate total costs see Delucchi (1996–97) and Litman (1997). Some of the issues involved are discussed below.

Quantifying non-market costs
Many of the costs included in these studies are at least partly "non-market", which means that they involve goods which are not normally traded in a competitive market. Travel time and accidents are two non-market impacts that are already widely incorporated into transportation decision making. Comprehensive cost studies include additional non-market social and environmental impacts. There is nothing unusual or mysterious about valuing non-market goods. Individuals and public officials often make decisions which trade non-market goods, such as safety and environmental improvement, against money or market goods. For example:

- Home buyers must decide how much extra they will pay (in dollars or by giving up other amenities) for a residence that is subject to less noise or air pollution.
- Public agencies must decide how much society should spend to achieve goals such as increased health care and environmental protection.
- Individuals choose how much to spend on optional safety equipment, or how much compensation they require for dangerous work.

Various techniques are used to quantify non-market benefits and costs (David James, 1994; Pearce, 1993):

1. *Hedonic Methods* (also called *Revealed Preference*)
   Hedonic pricing infers values for non-market goods from their effect on market prices. A common strategy is to analyze impacts on

property values and wages. For example, if houses on streets with heavy traffic are valued lower than otherwise comparable houses on low traffic streets, the cost of traffic (and, conversely, the value of neighborhood quiet, clean air, safety, and privacy) can be calculated.

2. *Contingent Valuation* (also called *Stated Preference*)

Contingent valuation involves surveying a representative sample of society to determine how much they value a particular non-market good. For example, residents may be asked how much they would be willing to pay for a certain improvement in air quality, or the minimal compensation they would accept for the loss of a recreational site. Such surveys must be carefully structured and interpreted to obtain accurate results.

3. *Control Costs*

A cost can be estimated based on existing control, prevention or mitigation expenses. For example, if industry is required to spend $1,000 per ton to reduce an air pollutant, this implies that society considers the emissions to impose costs of that magnitude.[1] Comparable transportation emissions can therefore be assessed using the same value.

4. *Precedents*

This uses policy and legal judgments as a reference for assessing non-market costs.

5. *Travel Cost*

This method uses visitors' travel costs (monetary expenses and time) to measure consumer surplus provided by a recreation site such as a park or other public lands.

Valuing Human Life

Evaluating some costs (particularly accidents and pollution) require placing a value on human life and health. Although human life is not a commodity, many individual and social decisions trade risk against

---

[1]This, of course, assumes that decision makers who determine control standards are rational from society's perspective.

market goods, which indicate the value society places on risk (Haight, 1994). This analysis does not value any particular person's life, which is essentially infinite, but rather a marginal change in risk of a "statistical" life or injury. There are two general approaches (Miller, 1991). The *Human Capital* method measures only market costs, including property damage, emergency services, medical treatment, and lost productivity. The *Comprehensive* approach adds non-market costs, including pain, grief, and reduced quality of life, as reflected in people's willingness-to-pay (WTP) to avoid a risk, or willingness-to-accept (WTA) compensation for such risk. These can be indicated by revealed preference studies, such as expenditures on vehicle safety equipment or the wage premium demanded for high-risk jobs, and by contingent valuation surveys that ask a representative sample of the population how much they would be willing to pay for a given safety improvement.

Incorporating Uncertainty

If the magnitude of a cost is uncertain, as indicated by a range of estimates, some transportation professionals use a low or zero value, claiming that doing so is "conservative" (Black et al., 1996). However, use of the word *conservative* in this context is confusing because it results in the opposite of what is implied. It is actually more conservative (cautious) to treat uncertain costs as having a relatively high value within the range of available estimates. Using a low or zero value tends to underestimate costs and overestimate net benefits of transportation projects or activities. Uncertainty is best incorporated explicitly into decision making using statistical methods, such as sensitivity analysis based on cost ranges.

Defining Externalities

Another frequent issue of debate is the definition and analysis of external costs, or "externalities". Externalities are impacts imposed by consumption of a good on anybody other than the consumers of the good.[2] Negative externalities violate the economic efficiency requirement that prices (perceived, internal costs) reflect full marginal costs. They are a form of underpricing. They are also inequitable to the degree that

---

[2] It is even conceivable that the same consumer eventually bears an "externality", provided he/she was unaware of that fact at the time of the decision to consume.

external costs are imposed on other people, and therefore represent cross subsidies.

Some costs are external to individual users but borne largely within a group (sector). For example, traffic congestion and some accident costs are external to individual road users but largely internal to road users as a group. It is sometimes assumed that since each vehicle both imposes and bears these cost, the external impacts cancel out, so there is no inefficiency or inequity. This is not true. As Delucchi (1997, #1, 21) explains,

> "It does not matter whether or not motor-vehicle users *as a class* pay for a particular cost generated "within" the class; what matters is whether or not each individual decision maker recognizes and pays the relevant social marginal-cost prices. If the responsible individual decision maker does not account for the cost, it does not matter then who actually pays for it, fellow user or non-user; the resource [usually] is missallocated, regardless of who pays. To account for a cost, a consumer must know its magnitude and be required or feel obliged to bear it".

Group level analysis tends to be arbitrary and easily manipulated, since it depends on how groups are defined. A population may be grouped in countless ways. For example, Green (1995) recognizes only two groups: members of automobile owning households and members of households that do not own an automobile. He assumes that automobile externalities are limited to cross subsidies between these groups. But within these groups there may be tremendous differences in levels of individual automobile *use*. Aggregate analysis hides cross-subsidies within groups. Externalities are therefore better defined in terms of individual vehicle use, not household vehicle ownership.

Which standard should be used to define externalities depends on the type of problem being addressed. If the only concern is group level equity (*"It's not fair that one group imposes uncompensated costs on another group"*), group level analysis may be appropriate. However, if the concern is either individual level equity (*"It's not fair that some people impose uncompensated costs on others".*), or economic efficiency (*"Underpriced goods tend to be used inefficiently".*) then external costs *must* be defined at the individual level.

Consideration of Fixed Costs

Although much of the debate about transportation underpricing focuses on external costs, internal-fixed vehicle costs (costs that the users incur regardless of how much they drive) also contribute to underpricing. Private motor vehicles are expensive to own, but relatively cheap to operate. Vehicle depreciation, ownership taxes and fees, insurance, and residential parking are costs that are internal but usually considered fixed and therefore do not affect consumer's individual trip decisions. Automobile owners have a strong incentive to maximize their driving in order to "get their money's worth". For this reason, the "price" of motor vehicle use is best defined as costs that are perceived by users as internal and variable.

APPLYING TRANSPORTATION COST ANALYSIS IN DEVELOPING REGIONS

The transport cost analysis framework described in this article can be applied in both developed and developing regions, provided that the values are modified to reflect local conditions. Below are some factors to consider when applying cost studies in developing countries.

- Vehicle ownership and operating costs depend on a country's vehicle and petroleum production, tariffs and taxes.
- Travel time, accident risk, and pollution damage costs can be estimated using local studies, or, if such studies are unavailable, by prorating default values based on relative wage rates using purchasing power parity.
- Older fleets and lower emission control standards in many developing countries may result in relatively high emissions per unit of travel.
- Land values (and therefore the opportunity cost of land used for roads and parking) tend to be lower in developing countries, although still relatively high in urban areas.
- A greater portion of accident costs tend to be external in developing countries due to higher per-kilometer accident rates; more pedestrians, animals, bicyclists and motorcyclists; and less comprehensive compensation for crash victims.
- Equity, option value, barrier effect and land use impacts of motor vehicle travel are likely to be greater in developing countries due to the greater portion of the population that do not use automobiles. A policy that

benefits automobile traffic at the expense of other road users is likely to be more inequitable and to impose greater external costs in a country where only 5% of households own an auto-mobile than in countries where 90% of households own an automobile.

- One of the biggest problems with performing transport cost studies in developing countries is the lack of reliable data on everything from the number of vehicles in a city to the amount of land devoted to roads. However, this is a matter of degree; even the most developed countries do not have all the data needed for comprehensive transport cost studies readily available.

Another difference in performing transport cost studies between developed and developing countries is in the time horizon. In developed countries, analysis of automobile costs can focus on existing conditions and problems. In developing countries, high growth rates in automobile use may indicate much higher costs in the future, and significant benefits if such costs can be avoided. Analysis should therefore consider future rather than current costs. For example, a city may have moderate levels of traffic and parking congestion, vehicle accidents and pollution now, but a high growth rate in vehicle ownership would indicate that such costs will increase significantly in the future.

SANTIAGO CASE STUDY

A recent study of transportation costs in Santiago, Chile (Zegras and Litman, 1997) provides an opportunity to demonstrate the application of transportation cost analysis in developing country conditions. Table 2 summarizes cost estimates based on this study, with additional estimates based on Litman (1997).[3]

---

[3]Costs not provided in the Santiago study were estimated by prorating Litman's default values based on Chilean incomes. Critics who consider such estimates to be too arbitrary should note that they represent less than 10% of total estimated costs. Excluding them would not change the main conclusions, but would perpetuate the even more arbitrary practice of treating costs that are difficult to measure as having zero value. This approach probably underestimates the full magnitude of these costs (particularly option & equity value, barrier effect, and land use impacts) due to the portion of non-drivers in the Santiago region, which implies that increased vehicle traffic negatively impacts more people than in North American conditions.

Table 2
Social Transport Costs in Santiago (1994 US $ Per Passenger Kilometer)

Cost	Automobile	Motorcycle	Bus	Bicycle	Walk
1. Vehicle Ownership	0.089	0.014	0.009	0.010	0.000
2. Vehicle Operation	0.080	0.038	0.008	0.008	0.005
3. Operating Subsidies	0.000	0.000	0.000	0.000	0.000
4. User Travel Time	0.050	0.050	0.090	0.170	0.530
5. Internal Accident	0.009	0.027	0.001	0.006	0.009
6. External Accident	0.009	0.036	0.001	0.008	0.016
7. Internal Parking	0.017	0.006	0.001	0.003	0.000
8. External Parking	0.009	0.003	0.000	0.002	0.000
9. Congestion	0.030	0.013	0.002	0.008	0.000
10. Road Facilities	−0.004	−0.001	0.001	0.002	0.004
11. Roadway Land Value	0.016	0.007	0.001	0.000	0.000
12. Municipal Services	0.001	0.002	0.000	0.000	0.000
13. Equity & Option Value	0.001	0.001	0.000	0.000	0.000
14. Air Pollution	0.031	0.114	0.002	0.000	0.000
15. Noise	0.001	0.007	0.002	0.000	0.000
16. Resource Consumption	0.003	0.002	0.001	0.000	0.000
17. Barrier Effect	0.001	0.002	0.000	0.000	0.000
18. Land Use Impacts	0.006	0.009	0.000	0.000	0.000
19. Water Pollution	0.001	0.002	0.000	0.000	0.000
20. Waste Disposal	0.000	0.000	0.000	0.000	0.000
Total	**0.350**	**0.332**	**0.119**	**0.217**	**0.564**

This table indicates estimated transportation costs in Santiago, Chile. Standard font indicates values from Zegras & Litman, 1997. Italicized values based on Litman, 1997.
Notes: Automobile parking costs assume 2 parking spaces per vehicle with annualized value of $270, one of which is fixed (residential), of which 92% of costs are internal, and one of which is variable, of which 40% is internal. Motorcycle parking was assumed to be 1/4th, and bicycle parking 1/7th of automobile parking costs. This cost was separated from vehicle ownership and operating costs. 2. Air pollution costs include road dust. 3. Costs not quantified in the Santiago study were estimated by multiplying default values by the 1:6 average wage ratio between Santiago and North American wages. 4. Due to rounding, costs less than $0.0005 (1/20th of a cent) are not shown on this table, although they may be incorporated into cost totals.

For analysis, these costs are divided into the following three categories according to how they affect transport decisions:

1. *Internal Variable.* These are costs that affect individual trip decisions. They include vehicle operation expenses, travel time, and accident risk.

126

2. *Internal Fixed.* These are vehicle expenses that do not (or at least are not perceived to) accrue in proportion to distance traveled. They include vehicle depreciation, insurance, registration, and residential parking. These costs affect vehicle ownership, but once a vehicle is purchased they do not affect individual trip decisions.
3. *External.* These are costs that are not borne directly by users. They include congestion delay imposed on other road users, accident externalities, free parking, roadway services (police and emergency services), and various environmental impacts of automobile use.

Figure 1 illustrates the estimated magnitude and distribution of these costs. Figure 2 shows the overall distribution of these cost categories for five modes. There are several interesting findings from this analysis:

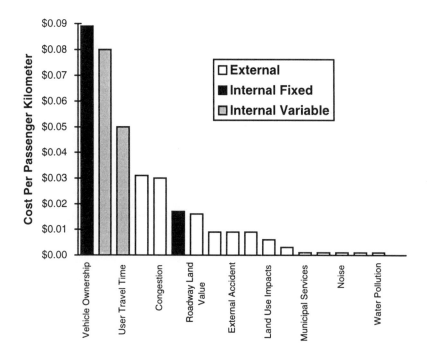

Source: Table 2

Figure 1. Components of Average Automobile Costs in Santiago, 1994.

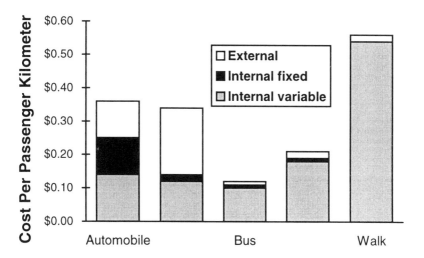

128

However, since internal-variable costs are approximately equal for automobile and bus, automobile owners perceive little incentive for choosing public transit. With current pricing it is socially beneficial but rare for people who own automobiles to leave them at home and ride public transit.

* Walking and bicycling impose minimal external costs. Their internal costs are dominated by travel time, which are sensitive to travel conditions. Their total cost is therefore highly affected by traffic externalities, including accident risk, the barrier effect, noise and air pollution. Encouraging walking and bicycling therefore requires minimizing these impacts.
* Although the magnitude of transport costs differ between developing and developed country conditions, the degree of underpricing is similar, as indicated in Table 3.

IMPACTS OF CURRENT TRANSPORT PRICING

A basic tenet of economic theory is that efficiency is maximized when prices (defined as *perceived, internal, variable costs*) reflect social marginal costs. The estimates cited above indicate that motor vehicle use is significantly underpriced compared with the total costs imposed on society. Major external costs include congestion delay imposed on other road users, road and parking facilities not paid by user fees, uncompensated accident costs, and a number of environmental costs. External costs represent about 28% of average automobile costs in Santiago, and even more during peak periods.

Table 3

Comparison of Santiago and North American Travel Costs
(based on Zegras & Litman, 1997; Litman & Rintoul, 1996.)

	Santiago	North America
Total automobile cost per passenger kilometer	$0.35	$0.55
Total transit costs per passenger kilometer	$0.12	$0.38
Portion of automobile costs that are internal-variable	40%	39%

Note: Although costs are somewhat lower in developing countries, the degree of underpricing is similar. Price (internal-variable costs) is about 40% of total costs in both Santiago and North American urban travel conditions.

External costs are not the only cause of underpricing. About 33% of total automobile costs are internal but fixed. Vehicle owners pay these costs no matter how little or how much they drive. Because of these high fixed costs, average vehicle costs per kilometer decline with increased use, so vehicle owners have an incentive to maximize driving in order to "get their money's worth".

To put this another way, automobile owners receive only a small portion of the total savings they would produce by reducing their driving. For example, under urban peak period travel conditions, automobile driving imposes external costs averaging about $0.17 per kilometer, while bus riders external costs average only $0.01 per kilometer, resulting in external cost savings of $3.20 for a typical 20 kilometer round trip commute shifted from driving to public transit. But these savings are not returned to consumers. Driving often costs an automobile owner less than bus fare, due to the large portion of automobile costs that are either fixed or external. This underpricing reduces the incentive for individuals to use the travel option that is socially most efficient for a particular trip.

Although underpricing may appear beneficial from a narrow perspective (and indeed benefits many individuals in the short term), mispricing reduces overall economic efficiency. External costs are not eliminated. They show up instead as higher prices for commercial goods (for parking subsidies), increased local taxes (to pay for road services), increased injury and illness (from pollution and accidents), and lower residential property values (from urban traffic).

Underpriced driving contributes to a self-reinforcing cycle of increased automobile use, reduced travel options, urban blight, low-density land development and automobile dependency (Kenworthy and Newman, 1989; Moore and Thorsnes, 1994). This underpricing could be justified if automobile use provided external marginal benefits (people benefit if other people increase their travel), but objective studies find that nearly all benefits of driving are internal (Rothengatter, 1994; Sommer, Walter, and Neuenschwander, 1993). It is therefore economically efficient and equitable to charge vehicle users for the full social costs.

Underpriced driving means that other costs, particularly congestion and pollution, are forced to become constraints on further traffic growth. As a result, attempts to eliminate congestion by increasing roadway capacity fail due to "generated" traffic.[4] Transport planning and evaluation that ignores the effects of generated traffic and external costs skew investment and policy decisions toward automobile travel. More comprehensive analyses tend to indicate that it is often more cost effective to implement Transportation Demand Management (TDM) mobility strategies. TDM includes a wide range of strategies for increasing travel choices and encouraging consumers to use the option that is most appropriate for each specific trip.

For example, a combination of transit improvements, congestion pricing and parking restrictions can encourage automobile owners to leave their cars at home and travel by public transit, at least sometimes. Other TDM strategies include flex time, ridesharing, bicycle and pedestrian facility improvements, road pricing, telecommuting, and land use planning that reduces travel requirements. "Least-cost" or "Integrated" transport planning principles can be used to evaluate TDM and compare it with highway capacity expansion options (EcoNorthwest, 1995; Philpott, 1995).

TRANSPORT UNDERPRICING AND ECONOMIC DEVELOPMENT

Underpricing and overinvestment in automobile facilities is often justified for the sake of economic development. Although low transport *costs* increase economic productivity, leading to economic development, transport *underpricing* has the opposite effect because it encourages wasteful use of resources. Most of the economic benefits claimed from underpricing, such as increased employment in vehicle production and bulk transport industries, are really economic transfers, in which one group benefits at another's expense. Recent research (Kenworthy et al., 1997) indicates that past a certain point (approximately 7,500 annual vehicle kilometers per capita) increased urban automobile travel reduces regional economic development and wealth by reducing overall productivity and diverting resources from investment to consumption.

---

[4]Generated (or "induced") traffic is the additional travel that occurs in response to roadway improvements, such as increased capacity on a congested road. Generated traffic tends to reduce the predicted benefits of roadway improvements, and leads to increased external costs. See SACTRA (1994), and Hills (1996).

Increased expenditures on automobiles means fewer expenditures and jobs in other industries. Is there any reason to believe that the automobile industry offers more or better employment than other industries? Generally not, since automobile and petroleum production and sales are relatively capital intensive, while other forms of travel, particularly transit and taxis, are relatively labor intensive. Current international overcapacity in vehicle production capability means that the automobile industry is increasingly less profitable, particularly for new producers that attempt to compete for international markets (Economist, 1997).

Few countries are self-sufficient in both automobile and petroleum production, so increased automobile dependency usually increases import costs. Reducing automobile expenditures stimulates the economy if consumers shift expenditures to goods with more local labour content. Hook (1995) argues that Japan has an economic advantage over the U.S. due to its less automobile oriented transportation system, which increases Japanese productivity and frees funds for capital investment.

APPLICATIONS OF FULL COST PRICING IN DECISION MAKING

Conventional transport investment analysis considers only direct financial expenditures by public agencies as costs, and user travel time savings (and sometimes safety improvements) as benefits. This tends to favor highway investments. Figures 3 and 4 illustrate projected costs and benefits of roadway and transit investments using a conventional analysis.

A more comprehensive analysis incorporates several other factors. It recognizes that over time generated traffic will degrade the congestion reduction benefits of increased highway capacity. It incorporates the social costs of automobile use, including increased parking requirements, congestion on surface streets, accidents, pollution, urban sprawl, and degraded pedestrian and bicycling environment. It accounts for transit benefits such as increased travel choices for non-drivers and more efficient land use. Figures 5 and 6 illustrate a comprehensive estimate of projected costs and benefits of highway and transit improvements.

132

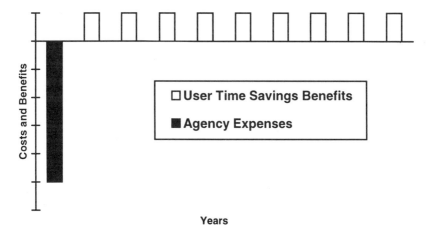

Figure 3. Conventional Highway Investment Analysis.

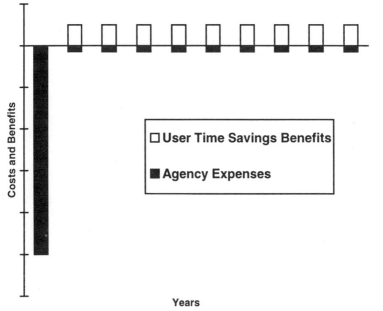

Conventional analysis only considers direct financial public agency expenditures as costs, and congestion reduction (primarily user travel time savings) as benefits. This tends to make highway investments appear most cost effective.

Figure 4. Conventional Transit Investment Analysis.

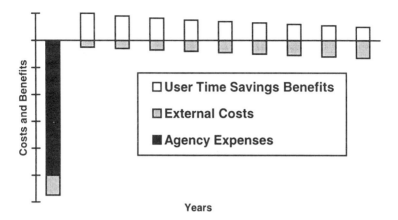

Figure 5. Comprehensive Highway Investment Analysis.

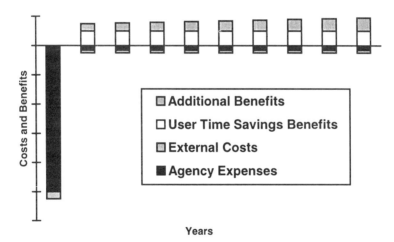

Comprehensive analysis incorporates the impacts of generated traffic, external costs, and mobility benefits provided by transit. This more accurate analysis shows greater costs for highway investments and greater benefits for transit investments.

Figure 6 Comprehensive Transit Investment Analysis.

Similar considerations apply to the analysis of traffic control strategies. For example, urban neighborhoods increasingly request traffic calming measures to reduce vehicle traffic speeds and volumes

(Hass-Klau et al., 1992). This can provide multiple benefits, including increased safety, increased pedestrian and bicycle mobility, increased residential property values, and various environmental benefits (Litman, 1996). A comprehensive analysis of motor vehicle costs provides a broader perspective of traffic reduction benefits, thereby justifying more traffic calming programs.

Full cost analysis has several implications for optimal pricing. Marginal cost pricing means that transportation users should be charged directly for the short term costs they impose, which include congestion, accident risk, pollution, road wear, and traffic management services. In addition, cost effectiveness and equity imply that automobile user charges should provide revenue that is sufficient to compensate society for long-term capital costs, including opportunity costs of land used for road and parking facilities, and any environmental degradation.[5]

An optimal motor vehicle pricing structure is likely to include weight-distance charges to cover roadway use, congestion pricing for peak-period travel on crowded roads, distance based insurance, and pollution charges that take into account vehicle type and distance traveled (Komanoff, 1995). Charging strategies must be realistic for local conditions. For example, distance based charges require accurate odometers on all vehicles, and effective enforcement systems.

CONCLUSIONS

The findings described in this paper have many implications for transport decision making in both developed and developing countries. Recent research indicates that motor vehicles impose a variety of costs, some of which are often overlooked. Analysis techniques are available to estimate many of these costs.

---

[5]Full cost recovery may not be required for transit or other modes that are considered to provide "basic mobility". Underpricing may also be justified for transit because it experiences economies of scale, and as a second-best strategy to reduced underpriced automobile travel. However, as much as possible governments should charge automobile use at marginal cost rather than substituting transit (which is itself economically inefficient) in order to reduce automobile use.

Automobile use is significantly underpriced due to a combination of external costs, which users can ignore altogether, and internal-fixed costs, which users pay regardless of how much they drive. Underpricing increases automobile travel compared with a price structure in which a greater portion of costs are internal and variable. This tends to increase total transportation costs, create automobile-oriented land use patterns, and reduce travel choices. Underpricing is inequitable to the degree that non-drivers are forced to bear the costs of driving, particularly since non-drivers tend to be economically, physically and socially disadvantaged compared with motor vehicle users.

Transportation planners and policy makers must consider the direct and indirect impacts of their decisions on the parking requirements, the environment, accidents, land use, and travel choices for non-drivers. This is not to suggest that automobile use should be prohibited, but rather that consumers should have a variety of travel choices with incentives to use the mode that is most cost effective for each trip. Traffic controls, transit priority, parking management, road pricing, and other demand management strategies are increasingly justified for addressing urban transportation problems in both developed and developing countries.

REFERENCE

Apogee Research (1994). *The Costs of Transportation*, Conservation Law Foundation, Boston.

Birk, M.L. and Zegras, C. (1993) *Moving Toward Integrated Transport Planning: Energy, Environment, and Mobility in Four Asian Cities*, International Institute for Energy Conservation, Washington DC.

Black, W., Munn, D. Black, R. and Xie, J. (1996) *Modal Choices: An Approach to Comparing the Costs of Transportation Alternatives*, Transportation Research Center, Indiana University, Bloomington.

Committee for Study of Public Policy for Surface Freight Transport (1996) *Paying Our Way; Estimating Marginal Social Costs of Freight Transport*, National Academy Press, Washington DC.

Cullinane, S.L. and Cullinane, K.P.B. (1995), 'Increasing Car Ownership and Use in Egypt: The Straw That Breaks the Camel's Back?', *International Journal of Transport Economics*, February, 1995, Vol. XXII, No. 1, pp. 35–63.

136

Delucchi, M. et al. (1996–97) *Annualized Social Cost of Motor Vehicle Use in the United States, Based on 1990–1991 Data*, Reports #1–20, Institute of Transportation Studies, Davis.

Dimitriou, H. (1992) *Urban Transport Planning; A Developmental Approach,* Routledge, London.

Economist, (1977) 'The coming Car Crash; Global Pile-up', 10 May 1977, p. 23.

Eco-Northwest (1995) *Least-Cost Planning: Principles, Applications and Issues,* Office of the Environment and Planning, FHWA, Washington, DC.

Ewing, R. (1996) *Transport and Land Use Innovations; When You Can't Build Your Way Out of Congestion*, Planners Press, Chicago.

Garb, Y. (1997) *The Trans-Israel Highway: Do We Know Enough to Proceed?* Floersheimer Institute (Jerusalem).

Green, K. (1995) *Defending Automobility*, Reason Foundation, Los Angeles.

Haight, F. (1994) 'Problems in Estimating Comparative Costs of Safety and Mobility', *Journal of Transport Economics and Policy*, January, 1994, p. 14–17.

Hass-Klau, C., Nold, I., Bocker, G. Crampton, G. (1992) *Civilized Streets; A Guide to Traffic Calming*, Environmental & Transport Planning, Brighton, UK.

Hau, T. (1992) *Economic Fundamentals of Road Pricing*, Infrastructure and Urban Development Department, World Bank, Washington, DC.

Hills, P. (1996) "What is Induced Traffic?" *Transportation*, February, 1996, Vol. 23, No. 1, pp. 5–16.

Hook, W. (1995) 'Economic Importance of Nonmotorized Transportation', *Transportation Research Record*, #1487, 1995, pp. 14–21.

IBI Group (1995) *Full Cost Transportation Pricing Study*, Transportation and Climate Change Collaborative, Toronto.

James, D. (1994) *The Application of Economic Techniques in Environmental Impact Assessment*, Kluwer, Boston.

Jones, J. and Nix, F. (1996), *Survey of the Use of Highway Cost Allocation in Road Pricing Decisions*, Transportation Association of Canada, Ottawa.

Kageson, P. (1994) *Getting the Prices Right: A European Scheme for Making Transport Pay Its True Costs,* European Federation for Transport and Environment, Bruxelles.

Kenworthy, J. and Newman, P. (1989) *Cities and Automobile Dependency*, Gower, Aldershot.

Kenworthy, J., Laube, L., Newman, P. and Barter, P. (1997) *Indicators of Transport Efficiency in 37 Global Cities*, Sustainable Transport Research Group, Murdoch University (Perth) for the World Bank, Washington DC.

Komanoff, C. (1995) 'Pollution Taxes for Roadway Transport,' *Pace University Law Review*.

Litman, T. (1996) *Evaluating Traffic Calming Benefits, Costs and Equity Impacts*, Victoria Transport Policy Institute, Victoria.

Litman, T. (1997) *Transport Cost Analysis; Techniques, Estimates and Implications*, Victoria Transport Policy Institute, Victoria.

Litman, T. and Rintoul, D. (1996), *Transportation Cost Analyzer*, computer software, Victoria Transport Policy Institute, Victoria.

MacKenzie, J., Dower, R. and Chen, D. (1992) *The Going Rate*, World Resources Institute, Washington, DC.

Maddison, D., Pearce, D., Johansson, O., Calthrop, E., Litman, T., and Verhoef, E. (1996) *The True Costs of Road Transport*, Blueprint #5, Earthscan, London.

Miller, T (1991) *The Costs of Highway Crashes*, publication No. FHWA-RD-055, U.S. Federal Highway Administration, Washington, DC.

Moore, T. and Thorsnes, P. (1994) *The Transport/Land Use Connection*, Report #448/449, American Planning Association, Chicago.

Njoh, A.J. (1997) 'Colonial Spatial Development Policies, economic instability, and urban public transport in Cameroon', *Cities*, Vol. 14, No. 3, June 1997, pp. 133–144.

Nivola, P.S. and Crandall, R.W. (1995) *The Extra Mile; Rethinking Energy Policy for Automotive Transport*, Brookings Institute, Washington, DC.

Pearce, D. (1993) *Economic Values and the Natural World*, MIT Press, Cambridge.

Philpott, J. (1995) *Integrated Transport Management and Development: A Sensible Path to Roads Less Traveled Through Investment Analysis and Strategic Decisionmaking*, International Institute for Energy Conservation, Washington, DC.

Rothengatter, W. (1994) 'Do External Benefits Compensate for External Costs of Transport?', *Transportation Research A*, Vol. 28, pp. 321–328.

SACTRA (1994) *Trunk Roads and the Generation of Traffic*, UKDoT, HMSO, London.

Small, K., Winston, C. and Evans, C. (1989) *Road Work*, Brookings Institute, Washington, DC.

Sommer, H., Walter, F., and Neuenschwander, R. (March 1993) *External Benefits of Transport?*, ECOPLAN, Bern.

The Economist (1997) "The Coming Car Crash; Global Pile-up", 10 May 1997, p. 23.

Transport Concepts (1994) *External Costs of Truck and Train*, Brotherhood of Maintenance of Way Employees, Ottawa.

Vickrey, W. (1969) 'Congestion Theory and Transport Investment', *American Economic Review*, Vol. 59, 1969, pp. 251–260.

138

Works Consultancy Services Ltd. (1993) *Land Transport Externalities*, Transit New Zealand, Wellington.

Zegras, C. and Litman, T. (1997) *An Analysis of the Full Costs and Impacts of Transportation in Santiago de Chile*, International Institute for Energy Conservation, Santiago.

CHAPTER - 8

COST-BENEFIT ANALYSIS AND THE EVALUATION OF NEW TECHNOLOGY AND POLICIES IN NATURAL RESOURCES

David K. Lewis

ABSTRACT

This paper describes the limitations and contributions of cost-benefit analysis in the evaluation of new technology and policies in natural resources. This is achieved through a review of the economic principles of consumer choice and the role of markets in expressing these preferences. Imperfections in these markets are shown to result in limitations on cost-benefit analysis that are primarily due to the valuation of nonmarket goods, irreversible changes, problems of long range forecasts of costs and revenues, and the selection of appropriate discount rates for high technology investments. These are illustrated by examples drawn from generic improvement, forest fertilization, and the preservation of nesting habitat for the northern spotted owl). The utility of cost-benefit analysis is also illustrated with these examples.

INTRODUCTION

The idea of estimating the net benefit of an investment project to society originates in a paper entitled "On the Measurement of the Utility of Public Works," published in 1844 (Dupit, 1844). The earliest work in assessing the value of projects in natural resources comes from the work of Faustman in estimating the value of converting agricultural land to forest in 19th century Austria (Linnard and Gain, 1968). From these 19th century origins, cost-benefit analysis evolved both in concept and practice until the Federal Inter-Agency River Basin Committee of the United States Government proposed procedures for the economic evaluation of river basin projects in 1950 (U.S. Government, 1950). Today cost-benefit analysis is an established part of

[139]

welfare economics and used routinely to evaluate public expenditures. The private sector also applies cost-benefit analysis in the evaluation of investments through net present value and rate of return investment criteria.

The objective of this paper is to describe the limitations and contributions of cost-benefit analysis to the evaluation of new technology and policies in the field of natural resources.

This paper will treat the objective of cost-benefit analysis as supporting the goals being pursued by a decision-maker. This assumes that specific organizational objectives are known and the appraisal of a cost-benefit analysis is based upon these objectives. An alternative approach would be based upon the "potential Pareto improvement criteria." This is to say that a project should be undertaken if and only if the gainers from a project could fully compensate the losers while remaining net gainers (Sugden and Williams, 1978). This objective requires an examination of the distribution of benefits and costs, and is beyond the scope of this paper. The focus of this paper will be on the major limitations in the application of cost-benefit analysis to evaluating the efficiency of implementing new technology and policies in natural resources.

BASIC ECONOMIC PRINCIPLES

Given that cost-benefit analysis is concerned with the evaluation of both public and private expenditures, it is necessary to understand its relationship to the general means used by society to allocate scarce resources to alternative uses. In a largely free-enterprise exchange economy, this is accomplished through voting in the marketplace with money. Under these conditions, the marketplace, through its prices and quantities, reveals the standards of society regarding types of goods and quantities. In the same manner, the market allows producers to evaluate choices among production alternatives. This is accomplished through the interaction of the prices of products and the prices of resources. The social problem of allocating the total product among individuals is also accomplished through the marketplace. This is done through the sale of services by individuals to create their individual purchasing power.

In this way, the market and market prices serve as a guide to society defining what resources are desired and where these resources are to be consumed. Further, the prices serve as an incentive for individuals to follow the collective social guidelines.

These functions of the market deal with the allocation of scarce resources in a static society. In a changing society, making decisions through time, there is also the problem of modifying the volume of resources and changing the way they can be utilized. This is also accomplished by the market through a special price on consumption claims in different time periods, the interest rate.

Through these functions the market place serves as a means by which individuals collectively define guides to the allocation of scarce resources to alternative uses, and encourage individuals to follow the social guidelines defined.

In order to understand some of the limitations of cost-benefit analysis, it is necessary to understand the principles that underlie the relation between exchange, production, consumption, and market prices.

The relationship between exchange, consumption, and market prices is illustrated in Figure 1. In this figure the individual preferences are represented by the lines U U, U' U', and U" U". The individual in this case is indifferent between any of the points on line U U, U' U' or U" U".

However, points on U' U' are preferred to points on U U and points on U" U" are preferred to U' U'. Point Y (y_A, y_B) represents the initial starting point of this individual. The total claims available (wealth) are represented by point W/$_A$ at the intersection of line M M with the A axis. The general principle is that the individual will utilize total wealth available and follow the guidelines of society by exchanging y_A for y_B until point C (c_A, c_B) is reached. The slope of the line M M represents the market price for good B in terms of A or A in terms of B. At point C the individual's marginal rate of substitution along the indifference curve U' U' is equal to the market price defined by the slope of M M. This illustrates how the guidelines expressed by market prices encourage individuals under conditions of simple exchange to adopt the standards of society regarding the ratio of goods consumed and how the distribution of goods in society is apportioned among individuals based upon wealth, which is in turn determined collectively by the price of the goods and services at their disposal. Also note that without the exchange opportunities defined by M M, the individual has no opportunity to move from point Y. The amounts of A and B consumed are determined solely by the amount available and the preferences of the individual.

The principles that underlie the situation where both production and exchange opportunities exist with individual preferences and market prices are illustrated in Figure 2. In this example, the initial endowment, point Y (y_A, y_B), the market line M M, and indifference curves U U and U' U' are identical to Figure 1.

The production possibilities available from initial point Y (y_A, y_B), are represented by curve P P. Under these conditions the general principle is that the individual will engage in productive transformations following the collective guidelines of society until point P* (p^*_A, p^*_B) is achieved. At this point, the marginal rate of transformation is equivalent to society's guidelines expressed by the marginal rate of exchange. This position will then be modified through exchange while following the guidelines established by market prices to a preferred point C* (c_A, c_B), which meets the same conditions as in Figure 1, where the marginal rate of exchange and the marginal rate of substitution are equal. Note that without the guidelines of market prices the individual in Figure 2 would make productive transformations to arrive at CP (c^*_A, c^*_B), which is a totally subjective choice and in this case, not the best choice for either the individual or society.

The principles that apply in a society changing through time are identical to those described in Figures 1 and 2, with the exception that goods A and B become consumption claims in two different time periods and the exchange opportunities represent the special price for intertemporal exchanges, interest.

Up to this point everything has been treated as being completely certain. The principles of choice under uncertainty are described by "State Preference Theory" (Hirshleifer, 1970). This theory treats uncertain events as conditional states, not unlike a parimutual betting ticket in a horse race where a win ticket is purchased for a price with a value being determined by the state resulting from the outcome of the race. In this case, the price is determined by aggregating the preferences of the individual betters to determine the overall price charged to all betters for any conditional claim, and defining an expected probability of occurrences for all claims.

The preceding discussion has been based on perfect markets. The impact of having goods which are not traded in the market place was illustrated in Figures 1 and 2 by the conditions that resulted where the individual choices were totally subjective in the sense that the choice available in Figure 1 without a market is limited to a consume or not decision. In Figure 2, productive transformations are possible; however, they will only be utilized up to the point where the marginal rate of transformation is equal to the subjectively determined marginal rate of substitution.

An example of a second type of market imperfection, divergent prices, is illustrated in Figure 3. In this situation, the individual faces inconsistent guidelines in the form of prices represented by the lines LC_0 and B'B'. Under these conditions, the individual starting at Y could be expected to engage in

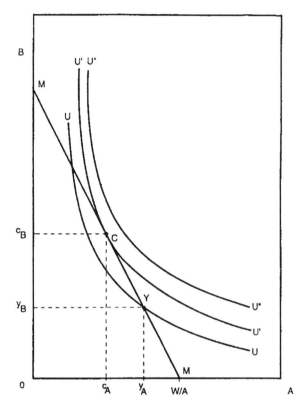

Figure 1. Individual preferences and the marketplace

productive transformations to B* or L*, or some place in between, depending on the nature of their preferences. This is the market condition faced by consumers where they have divergent borrowing and lending rates. It is also similar to the condition in many countries with developing economies where the government set social discount rate is significantly different from the discount rate to individuals. Quite often under this condition it is necessary to protect forest regeneration projects from consumption by private citizens

The objective of this review has been to illustrate the importance of well defined market prices, which represent the accumulated desires of society, as guidelines to individuals in making choices relating to either production

144

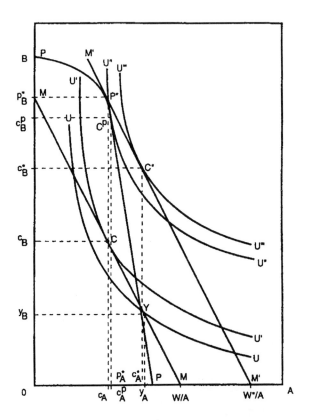

Figure 2. Preferences with production opportunities and marketplace

 or exchange. When these guidelines are absent or confusing, the selection among production and exchange alternatives becomes dependent upon the subjective preferences of individual decision makers (Hirshleifer 1970).

 In their book on "Project Appraisal and Planning for Developing Countries, Little and Mirrlees (1974) argue for the application of cost-benefit as part of project analysis. They also argue for the use of "accounting" or shadow prices to overcome the limitations of nominal market prices in the decision making conditions described above. They further argue that these prices must represent relative prices, i.e., the rates at which real goods and services can be exchanged. These prices must also represent marginal costs.

145

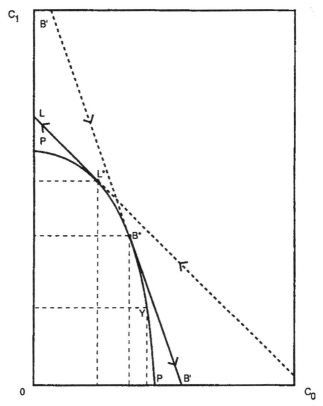

Figure 3. Market imperfection/divergent prices

COST-BENEFIT APPLICATION IN TECHNOLOGY PLANNING & IMPLEMENTATION

How then are these principles reflected the use of cost-benefit analysis in the development and implementation of new technology in natural resources? To illustrate, three examples will be given related to the intensive management of Douglas-fir (Pseudotsuga menziesii (Mirb.) Franco). The first will be drawn from an evaluation of genetic improvement. The second from an evaluation of forest fertilization. And the third will involve the decision to adopt special management practices to preserve the nesting habitat of the northern spotted owl (Strix occidentalis Merriam).

Research is currently underway to develop genetically improved families of Douglas-fir. Offspring from these families when outplanted and grown into genetically improved stands are estimated to produce yields 12% greater than the yields of stands from wild seed. The present value at the beginning of the rotation for this additional yield is estimated at approximately $400 per hectare. The time period over which the present value is calculated averages in excess of 40 years. In addition to the long time period, the yields are based upon information from stands of genetically improved Douglas-fir that have not been grown to final harvest. Therefore, the estimated yields are more uncertain than similar estimates from wild stands.

Any analysis of costs and benefits associated with genetic improvement of Douglas-fir is dependent upon the prices and quantities used in the analysis. Because of the long time horizon and the absence of a perfect futures market there exists no perception of society's preference for wood at the time these stands will be harvested beyond the extrapolation of current and historical prices into the future. Also, because of the uncertainty about the reliability of the estimates of yield and value created by genetically improved Douglas-fir, the lack of value from a long range future market trading in contracts with this degree of uncertainty, there exists no perception of the appropriate rate at which to discount the potential value except the extrapolation of current prices for contracts of similar risk.

Nitrogen fertilization is used to increase the growth and resulting yield at harvest of Douglas-fir. The general practice is to apply nitrogen as urea periodically to stands of Douglas-fir. An analysis of the costs and benefits associated with repeated applications of nitrogen at five-year intervals indicates an average net benefit resulting from the practice of $600 per hectare. The benefit in this case is created over a time period that averages 15 years, which is much shorter than the 40-year period required to capture the benefits of genetic improvement. A characteristic of the benefits of forest fertilization is the increase in size of trees at harvest in addition to the increased yield per hectare. This increase in average tree size requires cost-benefit analyses to estimate the price differences between trees of different sizes in the future in addition to aggregated estimates of wood prices relative to other goods. As in the previous examples, these prices can be extrapolated from current and historic information. However, because of the advances in equipment and methods for handling and manufacturing products from small logs, projections of this type are difficult if not unreliable.

An issue facing natural resource managers is illustrated by the comparison of benefits resulting from the development and implementation of genetically improved Douglas-fir and forest fertilization. A comparison of the estimated benefits from the two programs appears to indicate that forest fertilization should be preferred to genetic improvement. However, because of the imperfect prices incorporated in the analysis, there is no general reason to believe that the differences defined by the comparison are generally consistent with the values of society.

The northern spotted owl is a rare woodland raptor known to occur from southwestern British Columbia south to southern California in the forested areas west of the crests of the Cascade and Sierra Nevada mountains and in the southern Rocky Mountains from New Mexico to Central America. The habitat of this species is the dense old growth timber of the region where nesting sites can be found in cavities of broken-topped trees. The spotted owl also appears to require 100 to 400 hectares for each nesting pair (Jones and Stokes Assoc., Inc., 1980). This species is classed as threatened by the State of Oregon and sensitive by U.S. Forest Service and Bureau of Land Management on a scale of increasing concern that is as follows; no danger-sensitive-threatened-endangered. As a result of this classification, the U.S. Forest Service and Bureau of Land Management has proposed an administrative management plan aimed at preserving the nesting habitat for approximately 594 nesting pairs in Oregon and Washington (Hayword, 1981). Hayword (1981) estimates in a cost-benefit analysis, that when fully implemented this plan will remove approximately 240,000 hectares from production reducing the annual harvest of western Oregon and Washington by over a million cubic meters per year. This loss of production is further estimated to reduce the receipts to federal and county governments by roughly $230 million dollars per year and reduce the number of jobs in the industry by approximately 3,000.

In 1993, in an effort to comply with the legal requirements to preserve the habitat of the northern spotted owl a management team was assembled to develop a regional forest ecosystem management plan that would comply with the law and achieve the highest possible social benefit (Thomas, 1994). The plan developed was subjected to extensive social and economic assessments (Clark & Stankey, 1994 and Greber, 1994). Both of these assessments were criticized illustrating the difficulties of analyzing the costs and benefits of policies related to natural resource systems (Anderson, 1994; Gale, 1994; Long, 1994; McKillop, 1994; and Strong, 1994).

These examples have demonstrated the difficulty of cost-benefit analysis to define a generally best or optimum course of action when planning or implementing new technology or policies in natural resources.
The reason for this limitation is:
*   The failure of the marketplace to define social guides as prices for all the elements involved in the analysis.

The market limitations are due to:
*   Irreversible changes
*   Nonpriced goods
*   Long time periods between costs and benefits
*   Inability to define the influence of external changes in the economic environment over the time periods required for analysis.

These limitations exist in spite of the progress that has been made in the last 30 years in the valuation of natural resources (Johnson and Johnson, 1990). These limitations revolve around the requirement to base the analysis on a complete set of relative prices that reflect the rates at which real goods and services can be exchanged.

CONCLUSION

The current belief that we can decide whether or not to develop genetically improved Douglas-fir, implement forest fertilization, decide the fate of the spotted owl, or any other decision in natural resource management based solely on the results of cost-benefit analysis is predicated on the hypothesis that the analysis is based complete set of prices that represent the real conditions of exchange and marginal costs of production. The difficulty in achieving these conditions in any natural resource analysis is described above. These conditions limit the ability of cost-benefit analysis to define a best or optimum course of action.

The utility of cost-benefit analysis lies in its explicit statement of the environment in which the activity under analysis is to exist, and the estimation of changes introduced to this environment through the implementation of the activity under analysis. In the end, the most important contribution comes through the understanding and insights gained through a detailed examination of the conditions and impact of the proposal under consideration. In the end the value of cost-benefit analysis remains in the analysis itself and not the results.

REFERENCES

Anderson, Michael, (1994), A Prescription for Ecological Disaster, Journal of Forestry 92(4):39.

Clark, Roger N. and George H. Stankey, (1994), FEMAT's Social Assessment: Framework, Key Concepts and Lessons Learned, Journal of Forestry 92(4):32-35.

Dupit, J., (1844), 'On the Measurement of the Utility of Public Works', International Economic Papers No. 2, 1952.

Gale, Richard P., (1994), Not Scientifically Sound, journal of Forestry 92(4):33.

Greber, Brian, (1994), Economic Assessment of FEMAT Options, Journal of Forestry 92(4):36-40.

Hayword, Dennis R., (1981), 'What You Always Needed to Know About the Northern Spotted Owl But Didn't Know to Ask', Northwest Timber Association, Eugene, OR.

Hirshleifer, J., (1970) Investment, Interest, and Capital, Prentice-Hall Inc., Eaglewood Cliffs, New Jersey.

Johnson, Rebecca L. and Gary V. Johnson, Editors, (1990), Economic Valuation of Natural Resources: Issues, Theory, and Applications, Westview Press, Boulder, Colorado.

Jones and Stokes Assoc. Inc., (1980), 'Wildlife Species Accounts - Spotted Owl (Strix occidentalis)', Jones and Stokes Associates, Inc., Sacramento, CA, pp. 105-119.

Linnard, W. and M. Gain, (1968), 'Martin Faustmann and the Evolution of Discounted Cash Flow', Commonwealth Forestry Institute, University of Oxford, Institute Paper No. 42.

150

Little, I. M. D. and J. A. Mirrlees, (1974), Project Appraisal and Planning for Developing Countries, Heinemann Educational Books, London, England.

Long, James N., (1994), More Silviculture Required, Journal of Forestry 92(4):35.

McKillop, William, (1994), Critique of Economic Aspects, Journal of Forestry 92(4):37.

Strong, Ted, (1994), Tribal Right to Fish, Journal of Forestry 92(4):34.

Sugden, Robert and Alan Williams, (1978), The Principles of Practical Cost-Benefit Analysis, Oxford University Press, Oxford, England.

Thomas, Jack Ward, (1994), Forest Ecosystem Management Assessment Team: Objectives, Process and Options, Journal of Forestry 92(4):12-19.

U.S. Government, (1950), 'Proposed Practices for Economic Analysis of River Basin Projects', Federal Inter-Agency River Basin Committee, Sub-committee on Benefits and Costs.

CHAPTER - 9

COST-BENEFIT ANALYSIS AND THE ENVIRONMENT: A CRITICAL ASSESSMENT

Joseph N. Lekakis

ABSTRACT

The use of cost-benefit analysis (CBA) as an instrument of making decisions about environmental resources has been and remains a highly controversial issue. However, as more and more research on both theoretical and empirical grounds is being accumulated, the more distant seems the convergence over an agreement on the validity and usefulness of the relevant technique. CBA today is perplexed into the concept of *sustainability*. While this concept is interpreted differently by ecologists, economists, and other social scientists, it signifies the maintenance of natural capital for current and future generations. Even within the narrower frame of economic theory and practice, CBA is not free of conceptual and technical weaknesses. On the one hand, the estimated consumer surplus through survey techniques on missing resource markets fails to account for existence and bequest values, and, on the other, these techniques meet several problems stemming from elicitation/truncation, information, and embedding effects, as well as from the divergence between WTP and WTA. But, even if these deficiencies could be overcome, the unanswered questions "what is sustainability" and "what are the interests of future generations" cannot be overcome. Therefore, project selection criteria ought to rely on a social theory based on ecology, social sciences, and humanities.

1. INTRODUCTION

The most hotly debated topic in the field of environmental economics is that of "Cost-Benefit Analysis and the Environment". Hanley (1993) and Hanley et al. (1997) provide excellent presentations on this topic. However, as more and more research on both theoretical and empirical grounds is being accumulated, the more distant seems the convergence over an agreement on the validity and usefulness of the relevant technique for decision making purposes concerning the environment.

Cost-Benefit Analysis (CBA) incorporating assessments on the environmental impact of development projects has been termed "extended CBA". But, including such assessments is no longer novel or sufficient. CBA today is perplexed into the concept of *sustainability*, which is interpreted differently by ecologists, economists, and other social scientists (Toman, 1992; Munasinghe and McNeely, 1995; Common, 1995).

Ecologists have broadened the sustainability concept, from its scholarly use referring to the continuous over time harvesting regimen for specific reproducible natural resources (e.g. fisheries), to the survival of entire ecosystems. Ecological sustainability emphasizes the ability of natural systems to withstand stress and adapt to change in response to human intervention. Of particular importance is global stability of the overall ecosystem which depends on the viability of its supporting sybsystems. This implies that society needs to maintain the natural capital stock. Inside the heart of ecological sustainability lies *biodiversity* which characterizes ecosystem complexity more adequately than other terms such as "living environment" etc.

The economic conceptualization of sustainability considers global ecosystem stability as endogenous and dynamic and is less inclined, in contrast to the ecologist's view, to see ecosystem instability as a problem. Thus, maintenance of the natural capital is not essential. What is essential is maintaining the stock of capital in general so that society can enjoy a constant stream of consumption over time, which is fair for both current and future generations. This implies that man-made and natural capital are substitutable inputs. In fact, however, they are complements to each other because of the law of mass conservation. In addition, natural capital is multifunctional and difficult to appraise in monetary terms.

The socio-cultural interpretation of sustainability emphasizes the stability of social and cultural systems, including the reduction of destructive conflict, as well as the attainment of equity between social groups of the current generation and between current and future generations. In this approach intergenerational equity includes the rights of future generations to the natural capital stock, unlike the economic approach which sees it as constant consumption stream over time. An effective decision making framework would require pluralism and grassroots participation for a socially sustainable development.

CBA, which aims to compare the benefits and costs to society from a given project or program, has been the focus of strong criticism, stemming basically from concern that it is a methodology which serves the economic view of sustainability. Sagoff (1993) attacks the theory of welfare economics on which CBA is grounded, charging economists for offering themselves to tell decision makers what the people's preferences would be under hypothetical conditions in missing markets. This amounts to substituting hypothetical choice for actual choice and replacing free markets with centralized planning. The nature of choice itself is in flaw because it is based on 'preference maps' and not on reasons, beliefs, hopes, habits, character traits, principles, promises, and values. Even if preferences did exist as the foundation of economic theory, economists cannot explain why policy makers should satisfy them. Finally, welfare economics is strictly a micro theory leaving out serious macroeconomic matters such as employment, inflation, trade, interest rates, and savings. The specific issue of employment is also brought out by Mechmet (1995) in the context of CBA and sustainable development.

Glynn (1996) introduces some ethical questions which are not limited to the intergenerational environmental problem. In any project aiming to exploit the environment there are qualitative dimensions which cannot be appraised in monetary terms. Such dimensions include self-confidence or anxiety concerning the physical or psychological well being of one's self or the loved ones, the sense of one's self with harmony with or alienation from one's environment, the way one may suffer due to environmental decay, etc. When candidate projects generate the same amount of economic benefits and they need to be compared on the basis of their social costs which stem basically from risk, unpredictability of risk leads to CBA failure. There are also deontological issues concerning the treatment of wholes and parts. For, example, evaluators with strong deontological tendencies may be prepared to trade the risks to some lives against the death of some others, yet the issue of human lives as a whole remains. Even voluntary risk in exchange of compensation is a form of exploitation. Finally, identification of the victims of environmental decay would make CBA analysts rather sceptical.

CBA has also been criticized from inside the profession indirectly, as will be seen in this paper, by working out theoretical inconsistencies or empirical difficulties, as well as directly, e.g. by charging it for failing to deal with questions of equity, etc. Krupnick (1992) maintains that CBA is fraught with uncertainties and gaps in information. For theses reasons it can only be used as an accounting table of the monetary advantages and disadvantages of a candidate policy and not as the only criterion to evaluate its adoption. Some economists seem to judge CBA only as a tool of helping resolve legal battles between the government, interest groups, etc. concerning compensation for damage done by oil spills, chemicals, and other environmental offences (Portney, 1994). From an environmental perspective this view would be considered as short sighted. The role of CBA should be to prevent actions destroying the environment and not resort to monetary estimates of litigation for the victims of such actions.

While much of the above criticism and views can be appreciated, the real issue is whether CBA, an economists' tool, can effectively address the maintenance of natural capital and the achievement of intergenerational fairness, which are both interrelated and integral components of sustainability as seen by non-economists and many economists. The answer appears to be a blunt "No"!

The purpose of this paper is to assess the validity of CBA as a tool of environmental decision making, in light of the need for sustainability. The topic is wide and diverse, so the analysis needs to be selective. For, example, the economics of the greenhouse effect will not be included (see Fankhauser, 1995 on this). Section 2 presents the major problems associated with valuing the environment through the contingent valuation method which remains the focus of the relevant research. Section 3 visits the issue of discounting and intergenerational equity. Section 4 deals with CBA under an ecological sustainability constraint. Section 5 addresses the problem of valuing biodiversity. Section 6 highlights modifications of and alternatives to CBA. Section 7, finally, draws the conclusions of this paper.

2. VALUING THE ENVIRONMENT: THE CONTINGET VALUATION METHOD

The simplest method of assessing the value of the environment is based on the concept of *opportunity costs*, i.e., the economic benefits society will need to forgo in order to leave an ecological good in its natural state. This method, which is independent of people's valuation of nature, continues to be employed today offering valuable input to the debated topic of "CBA and the Environment".

Three methods and their combinations have been proposed to date for eliciting the people's valuation of the environment: The *contingent valuation* method (CVM), the *hedonic valuation* method (HVM), and the *travel-cost* method (TCM). The last two seek the people's valuation indirectly. HVM looks at their behavior in markets where the goods have an environmental dimension while TCM treats travel expenditures for obtaining access to environmental amenities as proxy market prices for these amenities.

CVM seeks to elicit the people's valuation directly by asking them either how much they would be willing to pay (WTP) to improve environmental conditions or how much they would be willing to accept (WTA) for damages inflicted upon them due to environmental decay. Carson et al. (1994) have compiled an invaluable bibliography of works related to CVM which points to the fact that there is no standard approach to the survey instrument used. Nevertheless, this instrument must contain a description of the ecological good to be valued and mechanisms for eliciting the respondents' values or choices as well as socio-economic characteristics. The respondents' values are derived by mechanisms of various forms such as open-ended questions, bidding games, or referendum formats. Socio-economic characteristics including age, sex, marital status, education, income, etc., are used as explanatory variables in WTP or WTA functions.

CVM is liable to several problems and inconsistencies of both conceptual and technical nature. Most of them arise from bias due to the type of questions asked, the respondents' unfamiliarity with the ecological good, the respondents' WTP not for the good in question but for the environment as a whole, and the divergence between WTP and WTA.

2.1. Elicitation-Truncation Effects

Open-ended questions, known as the AU approach, asking "how much would you be willing to pay", may result in true WTP statements but also in understatements ('free riders' or lack of knowledge) or overstatements (when respondents do not really believe in the hypothetical market presented to them and make unfeasible bids). Closed-ended questions, known as the dichotomous choice (DC) approach, asking "are you willing to pay this much", may cause a a 'starting point' or 'anchoring' effect (the proposed bid level becomes a reference-point to the respondent 'leading' him to higher or lower level of an arbitrarily-set-point on his WTP scale. Finally, questions starting with a minimum bid which then doubles or rises anyway if the respondent reply positively, known as iterative bidding (IBC approach), combines elements of both the DC and AU approaches and thus, the possibility for over- or understatement of WTP is still present. In addition, the AU and IBC methods are prone to truncation effects, generally referring to the omission of 'unreasonable' bids, which may represent 'protest' bids from respondents objecting the valuation procedure or refusing to give answers.

Bateman et al. (1995) undertook a CV study with the objective of estimating the WTP for the conservation of Norfolk Broads, a unique wetland in East Anglia, UK, which is threatened by saline flooding from the North Sea. The objective was to examine the differences that actually occur as a result of utilizing different elicitation methods, as well the impact of truncation researchers typically impose on the WTP answers when they apply these methods.

In the case of DC approach, wherein the mean WTP is given by the expected value [E(WTP)] of the cumulative probability distribution (CPD) of a 'no' response, three truncation options were considered: (i) all real numbers; the CPD was integrated in the range $-\infty \leq B_i \leq B_{max}$ (B_i is bid level), (ii) non-negative, truncated; the CPD was integrated in the range $0 \leq B_i \leq B_{max}$, and (iii) non-negative, untruncated wherein the CPD was integrated in the range $0 \leq B_i; \leq \infty$.

The AU approach was applied by considering the regression:

$$LWTP(AU) = a_0 + a_1 LINC + a_2 RELAX + a_3 ENV$$

where $LWTP(AU)$ = natural log of open-ended WTP response; $LINC$ = natural log of respondents income; $RELAX$, ENV = binary variables taking the values 1 or 0 if respondents visit the area to relax (or otherwise) and belong to an environmental group or not, respectively. For the IBC approach, the following regression was used:

$$LWTP(IBC) = b_0 + b_1 LBID + b_2 INC + b_3 BOAT + b_4 ENV + b_5 FIRST$$

where $LWTP$ = natural log of the bid level presented to respondents; $BOAT$ = 1 if respondents participate in boating activities (0 = otherwise); $FIRST$ = 1 if respondent is on his first visit to the area or not (0 = otherwise). Finally, for the DC approach, a logit model was used involving the explanatory variable *LBID, LINC, BOAT, RELAX* and *ENV.*

It was concluded that truncation of response data have a significant impact on mean WTP estimates across all elicitation formats. Also, the general finding, which is wide-spread in the literature, that the DC mean WTP exceeds that from the AU approach is confirmed. The disparity between AU and DC results may be explained by economic theory but also by psychological arguments. The IBC approach can be seen as a hybrid of the DC and AU formats and as such demonstrates a mix of the effects associated with both. Thus, CVM does exhibit elicitation effects and further research is needed in order to refine our understanding of and control for these elicitation effects.

Keith et al. (1996) follow a non-conventional elicitation procedure by looking at opponent and supporting groups among Utah residents to the designation of certain areas as wilderness or open access multiple use areas. Supporters were asked about their willingness to pay to use the areas as wilderness, and opponents about the use of the areas as open-access, multiple-use, land. Mean WTP was estimated for each group (and each proposal) via a logit approach. Additionally, the calculated mean WTP values were weighed by the sample proportions (opponents/ supporters) to obtain a weighted average individual WTP.

This approach was, then, contrasted with the approach most often reported in the literature, that is simply asking all the respondents about their WTP for designating those areas as wilderness. To do that, the two groups of respondents (opponents/supporters) were combined and the logit approach was used in this combined data set. The result shows that the combined sample-WTP estimates differ, in general, from the weighed average estimate. The standard approach to contingent valuation (that is no examination of the opposition) may overstate or understate willingness to pay. Thus, at least in cases wherein there exists evidence of strong opposition to an environmental proposal, CV studies which do not specifically take into account that opposition may generate inaccurate WTP values.

2.2. Information Effects

The very nature of the goods to be valued poses a validity problem for the CV method. Ecological goods must be either described or communicated. Thus respondents have the option of choosing between varying descriptions of an ecological good. To avoid an information overload to survey respondents, researchers usually provide only partial information in their questionnaires by conveying the most important and/or familiar attributes of the examined good. If, however, alternative descriptions of the an ecological good yield different images of the good to respondents, different descriptions may result in significantly different WTP of the same good and render the validity of CV questionable.

Hovenagel and van der Linden (1993) attempt to investigate the validity of this question by applying CV valuation on the ecological good: 'a clean environment around the year 2015'. The good was given three descriptions and via a mail survey was presented to three respondent groups of the Dutch population. The first description (CE 0) simply mentioned the ecological good without any further elaboration. The second description (CE 4) defined the good in terms of 4 attributes: surface water pollution, degradation of the ozone layer, deforestation, and the animal manure problem. The third description (CE 7) defined the good in terms of 7 attributes by adding in the list of the previous four attributes plus three more: greenhouse effect, air pollution in cities, and acid rain.

The hypotheses tested were whether the sample-mean WTP values resulted from the three descriptions were pair-wise equal, i.e.

$$H_0 : WTP_{CE-i} = WTP_{CE-j}$$
$$H_0 : WTP_{CE-i} \neq WTP_{CE-j} \qquad \text{where } i, j = 0, 4, 7 \text{ and } i \neq j$$

Their findings suggest that when extra information on the ecological good is given to respondents this results to significantly different WTP values (the hypothesis $H_0: WTP_{CE-0} = WTP_{CE-7}$ could be rejected) but small refinements may have no impact the hypotheses $H_0 : WTP_{CE-0} = WTP_{CE-4}$ and $H_0 : WTP_{CE-4} = WTP_{CE-7}$ could not be rejected).

Similar hypotheses were also used to test the difference in the number of inadequate bids of the respondents and the response rates as they were presented with extra information on the ecological good. Response rates did not appear to be influenced by the description used while protest bids differed according to the description used implying that provision of extra information to respondents yields data of higher quality. Finally, *information thresholds* beyond which different descriptions of an ecological good result in similar WTP values may exist but they are the subject of additional research.

Hadker et al. (1997), studying the Borivli National Park in India, attempt to adjust stated WTP for hypothetical bias associated with the respondents' unfamiliarity with the valuation process of the ecological good. They define an equation for the stated WTP of the form,

$$\text{WTP} = a + b(x) + c(\text{BID})$$

and derive the actual WTP by setting the BID variable equal to zero. Thus, they subtract an appropriate amount from the stated total WTP for the Park.

2.3. Embedding or Part-Whole Effects

'Embedding' occurs when WTP implies that the amount the respondent is willing to pay for the specific ecological good is not much different from the amount he would pay for the entire environment. Thus, respondents would be willing to pay roughly the same amount to preserve one lake, two lakes or three lakes, etc. These effects constitute the main CVM anomaly because there are 'existence' values which people fail to incorporate in their preferences (Diamond and Hauser, 1994). The only problem with existence values would be that adding them up might be theoretically unjustified for it would ignore possible interrelationships between ecological goods (Bishop and Welsh, 1993).

In their study of the Borivli National Park, Hadker et al. (1997) try to minimize embedding effects by setting the value scale to zero in order to reflect those who said they were willing to pay, yet they did not attribute any value to the assets of the Park. Thus, they subtract an appropriate amount from the stated WTP. The interesting aspect of the Hadker et al study, however, is not in the technique used to adjust for information and embedding effects, but on the fact that even after these adjustments are made, extrapolating through Bombay's population they conclude that WTP in present value terms is incomparably higher than the amounts currently spent by the authorities to preserve the Park.

2.4. WTP vs WTA

People tend to systematically value gains much lower than equivalent losses and forgone gains much lower than reductions in losses. Thus, WTP and WTA tend to diverge rather than converge. This divergence may be attributed to the individuals' loss averting behavior, as well as substitution effects.

Crocker and Shogren (1993) look into the divergence between WTP *vis-a-vis* WTA from a dynamic point of view and attribute it to site-specific and individual specific marginal rates of time preference. In their theoretical model they propose that, at the margin, the individual's marginal WTP to prevent a time loss exceeds his/her WTP to acquire an equal time gain. This, in turn, implies that the marginal rate of time preference (i.e., the time rate of discount) is less for a delay than it is for a time gain (extension). Identical reasoning implies that the reverse is true when time and income are substitutes. Finally, valuation of time delays and extensions at the margin will be equal when income and time are independent in utility.

To test these results, the authors run a CVM survey in winter 1989, of 271 skiers at 9 North Carolina commercial ski areas. Respondents were asked to estimate their WTP for waiting more minutes: 1.2 min, 10.15 min, and 25.30 min in the lift-line. Thereafter they were asked to value the 1.2 min wait when the time interval for this provision is (a) delayed for 2 years or (b) extended for 10 years. The results were in partial accordance with their theoretical propositions. Individual marginal rates of time preference for delayed access were less than the rates for extended access when money and time are complements. Increasing rates were also found as delay increased. This inconsistency was attributed to site-specific and individual specific marginal rates of time preference.

2.5. A Rejoinder

In a recent debate, Hanemann (1994), a devoted supporter of the CBA for the environment, gave the following defensive answers to four deficiencies of CVM surveys he pointed out himself. a) Surveys may be vulnerable to response effects but nobody has stopped using data from the *Current Population Survey, the Consumer Expenditure Survey*, the *Monthly Labor Survey*, etc., b) Surveys may create values that do not exit but testing and re-testing of CVM indicates consistency in value over time and a high correlation at the income level. These levels are compatible with the most stable social attitudes such as political party identification, c) Ordinary people cannot value the environment but whose values should count are questions that economists have no competence to judge, d) Finally, survey responses cannot be verified. Surveys of purchase behavior in market research may not be accurate predictions of purchase behavior but surveys on voting intentions are.

To ease criticism about his position, Hanemann concludes advocating neither a narrow CBA for all environmental policy decisions nor the quantification of everything around us. In addition, to dress his arguments with the 'coat of democracy' he asserts that decisions around environmental issues cannot be made by the 'experts' but by the real experts, the general public.

3. DISCOUNTING AND INTERGENERATIONAL FAIRNESS

Intergenerational fairness is a key element of sustainability. In CBA this could be addressed by adjusting the discount rate to protect the resource/environmental interests of future generations. High social rates of discount would make resource exploitation projects less appealing because they yield lower benefit/cost ratios. However, social rates of discount are usually lower than standard rates of discount. In addition, discounting over time implies that, from the point of view of the decision maker, current benefits are preferred to future benefits and current costs weigh more heavily than future costs, and current revenues are more valuable than future revenues because they could be invested to increase capital and future income. This does not mean that the discount rate should be abandoned as some ecologists have proposed. Rather, so long as CBA continues to control the decision making domain, ecologists argue that it should be used in tandem with safeguards on the integrity of natural systems such as ecological life-support systems (Toman, 1992).

The social rate of discount yields time paths for optimal polices which are time-inconsistent, for it disregards policies made by future generations. This is demonstrated in the context of a simplified framework where pollution and income are discounted at a social and market rate respectively (Horowitz, 1996). In a continuous time, infinite horizon framework with no uncertainty income is denoted by $y(t)$, pollution emissions by $g(y)$ (with $g'(.)$ $g''(.) > 0$) and pollution stock by $z(t)$. Furthermore, this stock evolves as

$$\dot{z}(t) = g\, y(t) - a z(t) \qquad (1)$$

where $a > 0$ is the natural decay of the pollutant and $z(0) = z_0$. The damage caused by pollution (i.e., the social cost of pollution) is $D(z)$ with $D'(z)$, $D''(z) > 0$.

In this setting, the present planner maximizes discounted production minus damages i.e.,

$$\max \int_0^\infty \left[e^{-rt} y(t) - e^{-\gamma t} D(z(t)) \right] dt \tag{2}$$

The critical element of such formulation is the use of the market rate r for the discounting of the pecuniary benefits $y(t)$ and the use of a social (determined outside the market) rate γ for the discounting of environmental costs $D(z)$.

To choose the time paths of income and emissions, the present planner maximizes (2) subject to (1) given initial conditions y_0, z_0 and non-negativity conditions. The first order conditions of this optimization strategy can be combined to yield

$$-\frac{g''}{g'} \dot{y}(t) - (r + a) + e^{(r - \gamma)t} D'(z) g' = 0 \tag{3}$$

It can be immediately noted that the time derivative $\dot{y}(t)$ depends on t (for $r \neq \gamma$) as can be seen from the last term of (3). Thus while the present plans chooses $y(t)$ according to (3), a future planner who will optimize at the actual time t will be faced with the derivative

$$-\frac{g''}{g''} \dot{y}(t) - (r + a) + D'(z) g' = 0 \tag{4}$$

which is different from (3). In other words, the time path suggested by (3) is *time-inconsistent*, it will not be followed by future planners if they revise policy at a future time t. Furthermore the first order conditions can be used to show the path of emissions when (a) the planner commits to future environmental policy, (b) the planner does not commit.

Manipulation of the first order conditions show that for an environmental discount rate $\gamma < r$, emissions fall over time both when the present planner commits and does not commit to the future. However, for $\gamma < r$ emissions are reduced by a smaller amount under no commitment than under commitment;

$$(\text{i. e., both } \left. \frac{dg^*}{d\gamma} \right|_{commitment} f\ 0 \ ; \ \left. \frac{dg}{d\gamma} \right|_{no\ ccommitment} f\ 0$$

but the latter is smaller than the former).

Based on this, if the current value of income is formulated as $y(t) - p(t)\ z(t)$ (rather than $y(t) - D(z)$ as in the initial formulation) where $p(t)$ is the current-value shadow price of pollution, then the present value of this income can be maximized using only the market discount rate and get an identical solution on income and emission paths as in the initial formulation. Thus, time-consistent regulatory policies can be derived when future pollution is valued at its contemporaneous price and then discounted to the present using a market rate. Such an approach might be appealing since the use of the social discount rate essentially disregards the choices of future planners. The use of future environment prices in current valuation can remedy this flaw. However, predicting future prices is an uncertain and controversial task and only if they could be obtained could their use work in the direction of decisions by current planners being consistent with actions and desires of future citizens.

Rabl (1996) suggests a two-step discounting procedure which could be seen as respecting the interests of future generations. According to the conventional approach, the net present value P of a project that yields a benefit B at $t = 0$ and incurs a cost C at $t = N$ is:

$$P = B - \exp(-rN)\ C \text{ and its future value F at time } t = N \text{ is:}$$
$$F = \exp{(rN)}P = \exp{(rN)}B - C$$

where r is the discount rate.

The conventional social discount rate, commonly used in such calculations, is given by, $r = r_{pref} + \eta r_{gro}$, where r_{pref} = pure rate of time preference, r_{gro} = growth rate of real income and η = the elasticity of marginal utility of income (often set equal to 1 under the assumption of a logarithmic function for the utility of consumption). It can be shown that for any rate $r > r_{gro}$, the benefits of any project, eventually, become larger than the entire GNP which is clearly an absurdity. Therefore, conventional discounting breaks down when the time span under consideration is very long. For the present generation, the conventional rate r is justified by the existence of a market of borrowing and lending activities, which expresses preferences between current and future consumption. However, there is no such market between generations and therefore the pure rate of time preference r_{pref} is irrelevant from the point of view of the future generations.

Thus, two types of discount rates might be employed in CBA of intergenerational projects. The conventional rate could be used for the initial period t_{short}; this period is proposed to be about thirty years on the grounds that the market for loans has a time span of up to thirty years and therefore r_{pref} is relevant during this period. Thereafter, the discounting procedure should utilize a reduced rate to account for intergenerational effects. This rate could be r_{grow}, i.e., the average growth rate of GNP.

Let P_{short} denote the net present value of a project calculated over time t_{short} (approximately 30 years) using the discount rate r and excluding any costs beyond t_{short}. The short-term decision criterion should then be: **yes if** $\mathbf{P_{short} > 0}$

Consider this project in the years beyond t_{short}, supposing the cost in year t to be $C(t)$. In the year t the amount P_{short} will have grown to $P_{short}\exp(r_{gro}t)$. The net benefit in the year t is obtained by subtracting from this value the costs incurred after t_{short}. These costs must likewise be corrected because their effect also grows at the rate r_{gro}. The net benefit in the year t is therefore:

$$B(t) = P_{short} \exp(r_{gro}\,t) - \int_{t_{short}}^{t} dt'C(t')\exp(r_{gro}\,(t-t'))$$

where the exponential in the integral reflects the fact that the effect of the cost $C(t')$ grows at rate r_{gro} from t' to t. A generation in year t prefers us to choose the project if and only if $B(t)$ is positive. This is the case if and only if the quantity:

$$P_{long} = \left[P_{short} - \int_{t_{short}}^{t} dt'C(t')\exp(-r_{gro}\,t') \right]$$

is positive. Therefore the criterion for the future generations becomes: **yes if** $\mathbf{P_{long} > 0}$. Combining the discount rate r up to t_{short} and of discount rate r_{gro} for the years beyond intergenerational Pareto-optimality is assured. Regarding the numerical values which r_{gro} assumes, historical data for the major countries indicate that 'values of r_{gro} in the range of 1 to 2% may be a good guess'. Thus, the numbers derived through this discounting procedure might be close to the position of people who are against discounting while still maintaining the framework of cost-benefit approach.

4. CBA AND ECOLOGICAL SUSTAINABILITY

Sustainability needs to be explicitly incorporated into CBA. Barbier at al (1990) attempt to do this by adopting a narrow definition of physical capital (e.g., the stock of environmental assets). Their intent is not to dispute the importance of man-made capital but rather to emphasize the non-substitutability of many natural resource functions by man-made capital (e.g., life support functions via biogeochemical cycles).

The sustainability criterion is then defined as follows: all projects yielding net benefits should be undertaken subject to the requirement that environmental damage (i.e., natural capital depreciation) should be 0 or negative. In most cases, such a criterion is not very useful when applied at the project level (very few projects will be feasible). For a set of projects, however, this criterion is stated as: the sum of individual environmental damages of the program should be 0 or negative, that is, if E_i is the damage caused by the ith project, we require that

$$\sum_i E_i \leq 0 \qquad (1a)$$

This constraint can be operationalized by including in any portfolio of projects, one or more shadow projects, the aim of which is to compensate for the environmental damage caused by the other projects in the port-folio. Conventionally, the 'correct' approach to internalizing environmental damage caused by a project is to simply adjust net benefits, $B_{it} - C_{it}$ to include the costs E_{it} of such damage. This, however, can often be insufficient for overall environmental sustainability. For example, while the net present value calculated via CBA is non negative, there might be cases wherein for some time periods, the total environmental damage costs are greater than 0. In such case, a portfolio may continue as a whole degrading the environment.

Consequently, to ensure that the portfolio of projects does not undermine the sustainability of the resource, an explicit constraint must be adopted. There two possibilities: a 'weak' and a 'strong' sustainability condition. The 'weak' sustainability condition is that the discounted present value of the environmental damage costs across all projects is non-positive, whereas the 'strong' sustainability criterion requires that the net environmental costs across all projects be non positive for each and every time period.

Mathematically, these sustainability criteria are introduced into the standard optimizing framework of a CBA model as follows. Assume a portfolio of projects (a program) consisting of $i = 1,..., n$ projects and $j = 1,..., m$ environmentally mitigating, or shadow, projects. Each project in this portfolio is associated with costs $C_1, C_2, ...,C_T$, benefits $B_1, B_2, ..., B_T$ and net environmental benefits $A_1, A_2, ..., A_T$. Therefore the problem becomes: maximize the sum of returns from all projects subject to the constraint that net environmental damages are non positive, i.e., maximize

$$\sum_t d_t \left[\sum_i (B_{it} - C_{it} - E_{it}) \right] + \sum_t d_t \left[\sum_j (B_{jt} - C_{jt} - A_{jt}) \right] \quad (2a)$$

with respect to Q_{it}, Q_{jt}, subject to the condition that,

$$\sum_t d_t \left(\sum_i E_{it} - \sum_j A_{jt} \right) \le 0, \text{ for 'weak' sustainability,} \quad (3a)$$

and

$$\left(\sum_i E_{it} - \sum_j A_{jt} \right) \le 0, \ \forall t \text{ for 'strong' sustainability} \quad (4a)$$

where d_t is the discount factor, equal to $1/(1 + r)^t$, each ith and jth project is defined by its activity level, Q_{it} and Q_{jt}, respectively, and *the functions B_{it}, C_{it}, E_{it} and A_{it} are differentiable in Q.*

In the case of the 'weak' sustainability criterion (3a), the first order Kuhn-Tucker conditions yield:

$$\sum_i \frac{1}{dQ_{it}} (dB_{it} - dC_{it} - dE_{it} - P_t dE_{it}) = 0, \ \forall t \quad (5a)$$

$$\sum_j \frac{1}{dQ_{jt}} (dB_{jt} - dC_{jt} + dA_{jt} + P_t dA_{jt}) = 0, \ \forall t. \quad (6a)$$

where P_t is the Lagrangean multiplier.

Straight forward manipulation of these first-order conditions yield interesting results: as $(dB_{it} - dC_{it})/dQ_{it}$ is the marginal net benefit $(B_{it}^{m.net})$ of the ith project and dE_{it}/dQ_{it} is its marginal cost of environmental damage $(C_{it}^{m.env})$, equation (5a) can be rearranged as:

$$\sum_i \frac{B_{it}^{m.net}}{C_{it}^{m.env}} = (1+P_t), \quad \forall t \tag{7a}$$

This expression indicates that the total net marginal benefits across the n projects should be equal to their total net marginal cost of environmental damage *plus* a factor $\lambda_t (= P_t \sum B_{it}^{m.env})$ which represents a premium arising from the sustainability criterion.

Similarly by rearranging equation (6a), for the jth environmentally compensating project

$$\sum_j \frac{-B_{jt}^{m.net}}{B_{jt}^{m.env}} = (1+P_t), \quad \forall t. \tag{8a}$$

This expression indicates that sufficient environmentally compensating projects j should be chosen so that their total (negative) marginal net benefits equal their total marginal environmental benefits plus a sustainability premium $\lambda_t (= P_t \sum (B_{jt}^{m.env}))$. This premium is the social value of ensuring that the environmental improvements generated by the m projects compensate for the environmental damages inflicted by the other n projects in the combined portfolio ($m + n$ projects).

Similarly, under the 'strong' sustainability criterion, the first order Kuhn-Tucker conditions can be manipulated to yield:

$$\sum_i \frac{B_{it}^{m.net}}{C_{it}^{m.env}} = \frac{d_t + P_t}{d_t} = 1 + P_t(1+r)^t, \quad \forall t, \tag{9a}$$

$$\sum_j \frac{-B_{jt}^{m.net}}{B_{jt}^{m.env}} = \frac{d_t + P_t}{d_t} = 1 + P_t(1+r)^t, \quad \forall t, \tag{10a}$$

These equations are analogous to those obtained in the case of 'weak' sustainability; here, however, the resulting sustainability premium grows exponentially with time. In concluding, Barbier at al point out that the proposed 'sustainability' constraint approach is a meaningful way of modifying CBA practically. Operationalization, however, requires the proper economic evaluation of environmental impacts, E_{it}, which is the key question in the CBA-Environment debate.

5. CBA AND BIODIVERSITY

Biodiversity is also a key element of ecological sustainability and as a whole is extremely difficult to value in monetary terms. In fact some researchers consider its overall value as being astronomical (Simpson, 1997). In economics, however, the focus is on the exploitation of biodiversity at the margin and not at its entirety. This is exactly the economic justification behind using CBA in this case. The main issues here are 'who is willing to pay for' and 'what is the content of' the biodiversity concept'.

Pearce and Moran (1994) have compiled estimates supplied by numerous biodiversity valuation studies. These studies, however, attempt to value 'biological resources' such as medicinal plants, plant-based drugs, and plant genetic resources for agriculture, rather than biodiversity per se. Thus, the medicinal value per hectare of 'biodiversity' land, $V(L)$, is estimated by,

$$V(L)= p \cdot r \cdot a \; Vi(D)$$

where, p = the probability of success in finding a new drug; r = royalty agreement (%); a = rent capture (1 if a country can capture rent perfectly); $Vi(D)$ = the value of drugs.

Also, WTP of producers, e.g. pharmaceutical companies, to preserve a hectare of land have also been estimated but they are too low even by economists' standards to account for the value of biodiversity (Simpson, 1997). In fact, producers ought to link their WTP to the future scarcity rent which biodiversity withholds as a subject of R&D by those producers (Swanson, 1996). In the context of CBA, valuation of biodiversity requires obtaining monetary estimates not for itemized species but for a range of species to account for biotic ecosystem complexity.

In a CVM study, Spash and Hanley (1995) show that there is a total lack of knowledge of the meaning of biodiversity on behalf of the respondents, a significant proportion of whom refused to make trade-offs which require the substitution of biodiversity for other goods. This implies the prevalence of preferences which Neo-classical economics defines as legicographic and therefore the failure of the CBA as a measure of welfare changes. Therefore, CBA is seriously questioned as a valid method for eliciting the public's valuation of biodiversity.

Echeverria et al. (1995) explore CVM in a third world setting. Studying the Monteverde Cloud Forest Preserve in Costa Rica, they compare the contingent value placed on the Preserve's amenities by Costa Rican visitors with that of non Costa Rican visitors 65 percent of whom came from the United States. The also test if respondents behave identically when faced with a single lump-sum payment or a recurring annual payment.

The visitors' (indirect) utility function is hypothesized to be a function $V = V(M, S, E)$ where M = income, E = education (measured in years of education), and $S = a$ state-of-nature, binary variable ($S = 1$ if Monteverde is available in the future and $S = 0$ is it is lost to other (e.g. agricultural) uses). The respondent is faced with the option of reducing his income M by A so that Monteverde remains available ($S = 1$) or paying nothing so that $S = 0$. The expected (indirect) utility difference denoted by dV is then

$$dV = V(M - A, 1; E) - V(M, 0; E) \qquad (1b)$$

The probability of a respondent to answer YES is equivalent to the probability of the utility difference dV being greater than zero. For the empirical analysis the authors approximate dV as

$$dV = B_1 + B_2 \log A + B_3 \log M + B_4 \log E \qquad (2b)$$

when A is the bid amount in \$, M is annual income in \$ and E education level in years.

The probability that a respondent specified amount A is $G(dV(A))$. Assuming a logistic distribution function for the probability function G, a logit dichotomous choice model was used for the econometric estimation of coefficients B in (2b). The levels of bids (variable A) were predetermined to start at \$10 and proceed in \$10 increments up to \$200 (i.e., twenty bid levels whether the lump-sum or the annual payment was considered). The consumer's willingness to pay to avoid loss of the preserve is then computed as

$$\int_0^{200} G(dV(A)) \, dA \qquad (3b)$$

i.e., by computing the probability of a yes-response for a given bid-amount A and summing across all bid amounts (from \$10 to \$200).

Furthermore, the authors test: (a) the significance of non- Costa Rican visitors and (b) the difference in ways that the contingent value question is asked, by means of the conventional likelihood ratio test. Hypothesis (a) is tested by specifying a full model

$$dV = B_1 + B_2 \log A_{CR} + B_3 \log A_{nonCR} + B_4 \log M + B_5 E \qquad (4b)$$

$$dV = B_1 + B_2 \log A + B_4 \log M + B_5 E \qquad (5b)$$

where A_{CR} = bid variable for Costa Ricans and A_{nonCR} = bid variable for non Costa Ricans.

The likelihood ratio test statistic

$$\lambda_{LR} = 2[L_L - L_{LR}] \qquad (6b)$$

where L_L, $L_{:LR}$ are the log-likelihood function of the full and restricted model respectively, is then used to test the hypothesis $H_0 : B_2 - B_3 = 0$. Hypothesis (b) is tested similarly: a single bid term A is used in the restricted model and two bid terms A_I (denoting lump-sum bid) and A_{II} (denoting recurring annual payments) are used in the full model.

In both cases the likelihood ratio test rejects the null hypothesis. In words, different nationality visitors appear to answer the contingent valuation question differently. Similarly, respondents appear to differentiate between two payment types (lump-sum vs. recurring annual payments). Although statistically the robustness of these results are open to question, they do indicate that additional experimentation is needed on the perception issues of CV questions.

Norton-Giffiths and Southey (1995) return to old yet useful in this context techniques and attempt to estimate the economic value biodiversity conservation in Kenya as foregone economic value of agriculture and livestock production. The net benefits of biodiversity conservation are defined as:

$$NB_{Conservation} = NB_{Direct\ Use} + NB_{Indirect\ Use} + NB_{Non\ Use} - OC_{Conservation}$$

where direct uses are tourism and forestry; indirect uses are soil and watershed protection, pharmaceutical discoveries and carbon sequestration; non uses include various existence values; $OC_{Conservation}$ are the opportunity costs associated with setting land aside for conservation.

Utilizing a variety of land area/data, environmental characteristics (elevation, rainfall, temperature, slope), economic data (from level budgets) and tourist statistics, the authors are able to address only the net benefits of direct uses ($NB_{Direct\ Use}$) and opportunity costs ($OC_{Conservation}$) for a single year. The former are calculated as,

$$NB_{Direct\ Use} = NB_{Tourism} + NB_{Forestry}$$

while the latter as

$$OC_{Conservation} = NB_{Potential\ Development}$$

All Net Benefits (NB) are computed as the difference between the respective gross revenues and costs. The net benefits of potential development are meant as the net benefits from foregone potential agricultural and livestock production within the conservation lands of Kenya.

The respective computations for the year 1989 show that the net benefits from economic activities permissible under conservation are much less than those from economic activities forgone under current conservation status. Living space is also denied to steadily growing Kenyan populations. These largely negative net benefits of conservation might be reversed by improving tourism and forestry revenues as well as by modifying opportunity costs. However improving these revenues is problematic (e.g., increasing tourist number incurs risks of overcrowding while increased revenues might scare away tourists). At the same time, modifying the opportunity cost to land is not likely to happen; as long as Kenyan economy continues to stagnate and rural population grow, dependency on land increases sharply, enlarging rather than reducing the opportunity costs of conservation.

Finally, the chief values from land conservation in Kenya are indirect and external. Very few Kenyans visit parks while existence values, biodiversity values, carbon sequestration, etc. are beneficial for all humanity, i.e., those millions who will probably never visit the country. Kenya constitutes a classical example of conservation wherein the global benefits are substantial yet for the country itself, the benefits under conservation status are for less than opportunity costs. Thus it makes the case that the direct beneficiary of the current situation i.e., the developed world should contribute substantially to these costs that currently the Kenyan state is undertaking alone. Otherwise the increasing magnitude of opportunity costs may in the future provide enough economic incentive for Kenya to convert land to settlement and/or agriculture at the expense of conservation.

Unfortunately, the only method for assessing the global 'existence value' of biodiversity is that of Debt-for-nature swaps (DFNs). In a DNF, an international conservation agency which has purchased debt of a country in a secondary market (at a low price due to the risk involved) offers to give up its debt claim in exchange for action towards nature conservation (Pearce and Moran, 1994).

6. ALTERNATIVES TO CBA

A number alternatives to and modifications of CBA have been proposed. Toman (1992) suggests using instead the safe minimum standard approach, according to which a dividing line should be set between moral imperative to preserve the environment and environmental trade-offs. This line should be based on safe minimum standards, preventing current generations from actions that could cause irreversible damage to such resources as wetlands, wilderness areas, areas of special aesthetic value, global climate, etc. The problem with this approach is how to select such standards and whether some idea of the costs and benefits might help in that direction.

Sagoff proposes a mental model comprised of three intertwined concepts: property rights, knee-of-the-curve thinking, and place. Property rights implies the treatment of environmental offences, such as pollution, not as a social cost but as a legal nuisance or trespass. Once this is secured, knee-of-the-curve thinking calls for the least expensive reductions of these offences. Finally, the concept of place can help in formulating a policy of resources conservation as a policy of protecting places. While modern industrialized states have already introduced in their policy domains legal forms of combating pollution along with cost-effective ways of achieving it, the concept of place may be something new which needs to be made practical for policy.

Unlike the previous two approaches, Multicriteria analysis (MCA) is an alternative technique which places projects and their impacts into a system of broader national objectives and differs from CBA in three aspects (van Pelt, 1993): (i) type of criteria (contrary to CBA focusing on efficiency, equity objectives), (ii) measurement of effects (while CBA requires quantification of all effects including environmental externalities, MCA techniques utilize quantitative data, qualitative data or their combination), (iii) MCA offers the possibility to account for different types of appraisal criteria and to process weak information; if therefore a project has multiple objectives, MCA is more appropriate than CBA. Also, MCA techniques would be more appealing to developing countries wherein there is strong dependency of economic sectors on natural resources and weak data bases.

CBA modifications include the use of "sustainable income" and "shadow or environmentally compensating projects" in the same portfolio, as described by Barbier et al. (1990). 'Shadow projects', provide for substitute environmental services to compensate for the loss of environmental assets under the ongoing projects. Little operational work, however, has been done on this area (Lutz and Munasinghe, 1994). Krupnick (1992) proposes the replacement of WTP in money terms with units of account in terms of time (e.g. WTP in terms of time for reduced risk). For CBA in this case the task would be placing a monetary value on time.

Two more approaches, the choice experiments (C–E) and the generational environmental debt (GED), have close affinity to CBA. C–E uses a set of attributes and levels of specific choice situations to make 'packages' of attributes that reflect different states of the environment. Individuals are asked to choose their preferred alternative from a 'choice set' made up of different packages. C–E and CVM share a common theoretical base namely they are both based on random utility theory which describes discrete choices in a utility maximizing framework (Boxall et al., 1996). While, however, CV methods utilize at most 2 or 3 bids from respondents, choice-experiments, typically, utilize 8 or more choices (depending on the complexity of the situation).

Under the C–E approach, an alternative, say i, in the choice set is assumed to be associated with utility level

$$U_i = \upsilon_i + \varepsilon_i \tag{1c}$$

i.e., utility is comprised of a deterministic component (υ_i) and a random error component ($\varepsilon_{i)}$. Selection of choice i implies that the associated utility U_i is greater than the utility U_j of another alternative j. The probability of choosing alternative i is >

$$\pi(i) = \Pr\{\upsilon_i + \varepsilon_i \geq \upsilon_j + \varepsilon_j ; \forall j \in C\} \tag{2c}$$

174

Assuming that error terms are Gumbel-distributed with a scale parameter, the probability of choosing i is:

$$\pi(i) = \frac{\exp^{\mu\upsilon_i}}{\sum_{j\in C}\exp^{\mu\upsilon_j}} \tag{3c}$$

This formulation can be empirically estimated using the conditioned logit model.

In the CV method, an individual is asked to choose between accepting a particular environmental improvement and a reduction in income or no environmental change with loss in income. In other words, there are two alternatives in the choice set: an improved state i and the status quo j. Given the utility function in (1c), the probabilities that the individual chooses alternatives i or j are:

$$\pi(i) + \Pr(\varepsilon_i - \varepsilon_j \leq \upsilon_j - \upsilon_i)$$
$$\pi(j) + \Pr(\varepsilon_j - \varepsilon_i \leq \upsilon_i - \upsilon_j) \tag{4c}$$

Assuming that the difference between random terms is logistically distributed, the probability that the individual chooses alternative i is given by

$$\pi(i) = \frac{e^{(\upsilon_i - \upsilon_j)}}{1 + e^{(\upsilon_i - \upsilon_j)}} \tag{5c}$$

and this formulation can be estimated by a binary logit model.

An empirical comparison between the two methods is illustrated by studying recreational moose hunting in Alberta-Canada. Under the C–E method, hunters were faced with 16 pairs of alternative descriptions of moose hunting sites. Under CV method, hunters had to choose between hunting in a specific site given an improvement in moose populations or not hunting in that site.

The resulted WTP estimates from the two methods were found to differ, dramatically, in magnitude (by a factor more than 20). This dramatic difference is attributed to the possibility that respondents may have ignored substitution possibilities in CV method; the conditional logit formulation of the C–E model explicitly incorporates substitution possibilities through the denominator of the equation (3c). This was additionally supported by the fact that when the C–E model was restricted to consider only one hunting site, the resulted welfare estimates were similar to the CVM model. Thus, CVM estimates may be decisively affected by the failure of this method to consider possible substitutes in examining the value of an environmental good.

Azar and Holmberg (1995), finally, propose the concept of *generational environmental debt* (GED) which, loosely speaking, is a measure of the total amount of environmental damage that past and present generations have caused but that will affect future generations. GED implies that the present generation should restore a specific damage until the marginal benefit of restoration equals the marginal costs of restoration. Thus, GED, for each specific damage, equals the sum of the restoration cost and the cost of the remaining damage. If the marginal cost of restoration is higher than the marginal benefit of restoration (for every degree of restoration) then, GED is equal to the total damage caused. Total GED is given by summing up GEDs for all specific damages.

Concerning the damages caused by the present generation, these are classified into two types: *identified damages and potential damages.* The former refer to instances wherein the impact of the damages is well understood; while the latter to instances wherein impacts on nature have unknown effects. Both types of damage should be included in the calculation of GED, and only damages caused by human influence should be included (thus damages due to, for example, volcanic activities should be excluded). GED should be calculated as the accumulated debt of the present *and* the past generations while the point in time, which one chooses to start the calculation of GED, is crucial and therefore it is important that is properly highlighted. Alternatively, the problem of choosing the right 'starting year' could be circumvented by focusing on the *change* in the accumulated GED.

The discount rate should be set according to the so called Ramsey rule as,

$$r(t) = \gamma g(t) + \rho(t) = \gamma \frac{c}{c} + \rho(t) \qquad (1d)$$

where γ is the negative of the elasticity of marginal utility of consumption, $c(t)$ is global per capita consumption, $g(t)$ the per capita relative growth rate in consumption and $\rho(t)$ the pure time preference.

On grounds of ethics and other reasons, $\rho = 0$ (e.g., the happiness of future generations cannot be judged as being worth less than the happiness of the present generation). Then, the present value factor in GED calculations can be written as

$$V(t) = \exp\left(-\int_0^t r(t')dt'\right) = \left[\frac{c_0}{c(t)}\right]^\gamma = \left[\frac{C_0}{C(t)}\right]^\gamma \left[\frac{P(t)}{P_0}\right]^\gamma \qquad (2d)$$

where C represents global consumption and $P(t)$ the world population. If we assume that $C_0/C(t) = y_0/y(t)$, where $y(t)$ is the gross world product (GWP), then

$$V(t) = \exp\left(\int_0^t r(t')dt'\right) = \left[\frac{y_0}{y(t)}\right]^\gamma \left[\frac{P(t)}{P_0}\right]^\gamma \qquad (3d)$$

Despite the empirical difficulties associated with this formulation (e.g., GWP is a problematic concept per se), this method of discounting is more comprehensive than just applying the standard constant discount rate.

Limitations of the concept of GED include first, empirical applicability (e.g., GED requires monetary estimates of the value of the environment, there are cases where damages are not yet well understood or a considerable time delay exists between a human influence on nature and the resulting effects). Furthermore, since the method compares restoration cost and the cost of damage, it implicitly assumes full substitutability between natural capital and human-made capital. However, this substitutability is limited; human-made capital cannot substitute forms of natural capital in many cases.

All these limitations are important for the interpretation of GED. Aggregation of GED with other intergenerational transfers should not be made, since such an aggregation, implicitly, assumes that full substitutability is always possible. Instead, GED should only be considered as a monetary estimate of the burden of environmental damage we pass on to the future generations. GED can also be used in deciding appropriate policies for the future. Today, much damage is not avoided or restored since it is considered expensive. Calculation of GED would certainly make the cost that will fall on future generations visible.

7. CONCLUSIONS

For natural scientists and many social scientists including economists, CBA constitutes a questionable tool of environmental decision making for economic theory alone is not sufficient to justify its use for that purpose. Even within the narrower frame of economic theory and practice, CBA is not free of conceptual and technical weaknesses, and for many economists it receives low scores. This was even more evident when attempting to value biodiversity using CVM (Spash and Hanley, 1995) or when dealing with research issues arising from elicitation/truncation, information, and embedding effects, as well as from the divergence between WTP and WTA.

The major conceptual flaw of CBA rests on the very premises it was founded: Consumer surplus which in this case fails to account for existence and bequest values. Ecosystems are interdependent and valuation of one in a way leading to its exploitation may interfere with the stability of another. Furthermore, ecosystems are not divisible across national boundaries. Thus, in an era of continued globalization, CBA studies based on the consumer surplus of the citizens in one nation cannot serve as a proxy for the real economic value of an ecosystem. The Norton-Griffiths and Southey (1995) and the Echeverria et al. (1995) studies point exactly in that direction. But, even if these deficiencies could be overcome, the unanswered questions "what is sustainability" and "what are the interests of future generations" cannot be overcome. Therefore, project selection criteria must rely on a social theory based on ecology, social sciences, and humanities.

CBA studies fail to incorporate an explicit ecological sustainability criterion, and the Barbier et al. (1990) work which attempts to resolve the issue simply returns to the fundamental issue "how do we value the environment?" In addition, efforts to find a suitable discount rate such as those of Rabl (1996) remain mere guesses or hypotheses. Simultaneously, CBA modifications and/or alternative techniques do not appear to be significantly better substitutes. Can then CBA be an acceptable tool of environmental decision making?

The answer is not simple, but there is also little scope in being either too critical or too supportive of CBA, and in accepting or rejecting it unconditionally. The discussion on the meaning of sustainability, the criticism advanced against CBA directly or indirectly, as well as the modifications and alternatives proposed point to a certain direction: The avoidance of environmental risk Thus, when CBA is to be employed by decision makers either to favor 'development projects' which will generate adverse environmental impacts, especially to vulnerable ecosystems, or to reject an environmental program, then CBA is suspect of not meeting sustainability criteria. Whenever CBA is used either to question selection of such projects or in order to point out that private or public programs to protect the environment allocate much less than society would be willing to pay, then CBA is certainly working in the direction of sustainability. This was shown most clearly by Hadker et al. (1997) in their Indian study, where the money spent by the authorities to protect the Borivli National Park is incomparably less than what people would be willing to pay for that purpose.

REFERENCES

Azar, C. and J. Holmberg (1995) 'Defining the generational environmental debt.' *Ecological Economics* 14(1): 7–19.

Barbier, E.B., A. Markandya and D.W. Pearce (1990) 'Environmental sustainability and cost-benefit analysis'. *Environment and Planning A*, 22: 1259–1266.

Bateman, I.J., I.H. Langford, R.K. Turner, K.G. Willis and G.D. Garrod (1995) 'Elicitation and truncation effects in contingent valuation studies'. *Ecological Economics* 12(2): 161–179

Bishop, R.C. and M.P. Welsh (1993) 'Existence Values in Benefit-Cost Analysis and Damage Assessment'. In *Forestry and Environment: Economic Perspectives.* Edited by W.L. Adamowicz, W. White and W.E. Philips. UK: C·A·B International, pp. 135–154.

Boxall, P.C., W.L. Adamowicz, J. Swait, M. Williams and J. Louviere (1996) 'A comparison of stated preference methods for environmental valuation'. *Ecological Economics* 18(3): 243–253.

Bradley, D.P. (1993) 'What Would an Ecological Economics Actually do to Integrate Ecosystem and Social System Health? A Spectrum of Approaches'. In *Forestry and Environment: Economic Perspectives.* Edited by W.L. Adamowicz, W. White and W.E. Philips. UK: C·A·B International. Pages 155–170.

Carson, R. et al. (1994), Bibliography of Contingent Valuation Studies and Papers, La Jola, CA: Natural Resource Damage Assessment, Inc.

Common, M. (1995) *Sustainability and Policy: Limits to Economics.* Cambridge University Press.

Crocker, T.D. and J.F. Shogren (1993) 'Dynamic inconsistency in valuing environmental goods'. *Ecological Economics* 7(3): 239–254.

Diamond, P. A. and T. A. Hausman (1994) 'Contingent Valuation: Is Some Number Better than No Number,' *Journal of Economic Perspectives* 8(4): 45–64.

Echeverria, J., M. Hanrahan and R. Solorzano (1995) 'Valuation of non-priced amenities provided by the biological resources within the Monteverde Cloud Forest Preserve, Costa Rica'. *Ecological Economics* 13(1): 43–53.

Fankhauser, S. (1995) *Valuing Climate Change: The Economics of the Greenhouse.* London: Earthscan.

Glynn, S. (1996) 'Ethical Issues in Environmental Decision making and the Limitations Cost/Benefit Analysis (CBA),' *Ethics and the Environment* 1(1): 27–39.

Hadker, N. et al. (1997), ' Willingness-to-pay for Borivli National Park: Evidence from a Contingent Valuation, *Ecological Economics* 21(2): 105–122.

Hanley, N. and C.L. Spash (1993b) *Cost-Benefit Analysis and the Environment.* Aldershot: Edward Elgar.

Hanley, N., J.F. Shogren and B. White (1997) *Environmental Economics in Theory and Practice.* London: Macmillan Press Ltd.

Hoevenagel, R. and J. W. van der Linden (1993) 'Effects of different descriptions of the ecological good on willingness to pay values'. *Ecological Economics* 7(3): 223–238.

Horowitz, J.K. (1996) 'Environmental policy under a non-market discount rate'. *Ecological Economics* 16(1): 73–78.

Keith, J.E., C. Fawson and V. Johnson (1996) 'Preservation or use: A contingent valuation study of wilderness designation in Utah'. *Ecological Economics* 18(3): 207–214.

Krupnick , A. J. 'Using Benefit-Cost Analysis to Prioritize Environmental Problems,' in J. Darmstadter (ed) *Global Development and the Environment*, Washington, DC.: RFF

Lutz, E. and M. Munasinghe (1994) 'Integration of environmental concerns into economic analyses of projects and policies in an operational context'. *Ecological Economics* 10(1): 37–46.

Mehmet, O. (1995) 'Employment creation and green development strategy'. *Ecological Economics* 15(1): 1 L–19.

Munasinghe, M. and J. McNeely (1995) 'Key Concepts and Terminology of Sustainable Development'. In M. Munasinghe and W. Shearer (eds), *Defining and Measuring Sustainability*, Washington, DC: The World Bank.

Norton-Griffiths, M. and C. Southey (1995) 'The opportunity costs of biodiversity conservation in Kenya'. *Ecological Economics* 12(2): 125–139.

Pearce, D. and D. Moran (1995) *The Economic Value of Biodiversity.* London: Earthscan.

Portney, P.R. (1994) 'The Contingent Valuation Debate: Why Economists Should Care,' *Journal of Economic Perspectives* 8(4): 3–17.

Rabl, A. (1996) 'Discounting long-term costs: What would future generations want us to do', *Ecological Economics* 17(3): 137–145.

Sagoff, M. (1993) 'Environmental Economics: An Epitaph'. *Resources* 111: 3–7

Schulze, P.C. (1994) 'Cost-benefit analyses and environmental policy.' *Ecological Economics* 9(3): 197–199.

Simpson, D.R. (1997) 'Biodiversity Prospecting: Shopping the wilds is not the key to Conservation'. *Resources* 126:12–15.

Spash. C. L. and N. Hanley (1995) 'Preferences, information and biodiversity preservation', *Ecological Economics* 12(3): 191–208.

Swanson, T. (1996) 'The reliance of northern economies on southern biodiversity: Biodiversity as information', *Ecological Economics* 17(1): 1–8.

Toman, M.A. (1992) 'The Difficulty in Defining Sustainability'. in J. Darmstadter (ed) *Global Development and the Environment*, Washington, DC: RFF

van Pelt, M.J.F. (1993) 'Ecologically sustainable development and project appraisal in developing countries'. *Ecological Economics* 7(1): 19–42.

CHAPTER - 10

THE LIMITS OF ECONOMIC RATIONALITY: SOCIAL AND ENVIRONMENTAL IMPACTS OF RECREATIONAL LAND USE

Sabine O'Hara and Susan Mesner

ABSTRACT

During the past twenty years much progress has been made in expanding the traditional instrumentarium of CBA in order to better account for the so called negative externalities of economic development. Despite improved techniques (travel cost, hedonic pricing, continget valuation), however, much is left unconsidered. This is particularly true for such hard to account for social exterbalities as changes in social capital and community well-being. As a result CBA has come under increasing scrutiny. Criticism has questioned not only the ability of CBA to properly account for income inequality but more generally its ability to capture the value of social and environmental functions in monetary terms. A brief discussion of snow making, a prerequisite for the expanding tourism industry in the Northeastern United States illustrates the difficulties in capturing the social and environmental effects of tourism related development. To better account for these effects, an alternative valuation method, discoursive valuation (also termed discoursive ethics) is introduced. This method can help to assess Safe Minimum Standard type restrictions to development strategies as well as lower the enforcement costs commonly associated with such standards.

INTRODUCTION

Economics is generally defined as "the study of how human beings in society coordinate their wants and desires" (Colander, 1994) given the inescapable problem of resource scarcity. This view presumes that all wants and desires are commensurable and all inputs used to generate wanted goods and services can be measured in a common value categories as well. Only then is a rational ranking of alternative resource used and consumer desires possible. Prices, the monetary expression of revealed consumer preferences and production possibilities, take on an key function in this conception of economics. They are not only the allocation and distribution mechanisms coordinating competing wants and resource uses, they are also a fundamental expression of value (O'Hara, 1996a). It is therefore not surprising that Cost Benefit Analysis has taken a central role in applied economics in general and policy-making in particular. CBA reflects the consistent application of the rationality concept of economics whereby a situation is preferable if it results in increased net-benefits expressed in monetary terms. O'Neill writes:

> "Most Cost-benefit analysts assume that rational decisions require strong commensurability. This means that there has to be a particular single property that all objects and states of affairs possess, and that this property is considered to be the source of their value". (O'Neill, 1996, p. 463)

This very consistency of CBA, however, is also the source of growing criticism of this methodology. Two main themes constitute the core of critical voices: first, if money is the decisive measure by which value is assigned and preferences are measured, distributional issues play a key role in the valuation process (Martinez-Alier, 1994). People's revealed preferences are not simply a matter of choice, they are also a matter of opportunity. The greater the budgetary constraint, the lower the potential for expressing one's preferences in the overall societal ranking systems. A low willingness to pay, however, may not at all mean low regard but simply low income. Secondly, not all costs and benefits are easily measurable in monetary terms. Social impacts like the loss of social participation after forced early retirement or job loss, the loss of community as labor follows the movement of jobs, or the loss of social tranquillity in light of rising income disparity are not easily ranked in monetary categories; the same is true for the costs and benefits associated with changes in the environment's many naturalist, recreational, ecological, scientific, aesthetic, utilitarian, cultural, symbolic, moral, and historic services (U.S. EPA, 1993). Wants and desires are more than material and the inability to assign monetary value to some of the myriad things affecting human health and well-being is not necessarily a reflection of their disdain but may well be the opposite–they are so valuable or meaningful that they defy monetary valuation.

Particularly newer, expanded approaches to CBA have tried to take these problems of social and ecological market failure into account by devising a variety of methods to assign 'substitute' monetary value to unpriced goods, services, resources and use options. Estimating travel costs, recreational expenditures, or the replacement costs of a resource itself (Smith and Desvousges, 1993; Chua-Eon, 1993), hedonic pricing (Murdoch and Thayer, 1992, Brookshire et al., 1992), and various types of Contingent Valuation (Eberle and Hayden, 1991; Harris et al., 1989), have all been used to make non-market values commensurate with the monetary value expressed in market exchange. The question, however, remains, whether these methods are suitable to express the diversity of value categories reflective of the complex interactions between economic, social and environmental systems. From a systems perspective, economic activity merely represents one subsystem of a larger nested system of economic, human social and non-human biological, ecological and physical processes (see Figure 1). While each subsystem is characterized by distinct time frames, spatial configurations, behaviors, rules and success measures, all subsystems are interconnected, overlapping and co-equal. Monetary value may be a good reflection of one subsystem's rules, behaviors, and success: that of an economy relying on monetary value as the expression of individual market participants' interests and desires. Yet it can not appropriately express the time frames, spatial characteristics and relational links reflective of the complex social or environmental systems within which all economic activity takes place. As a result, essential information about processes and attributes characterizing the value of ecosystems functions, biodiversity, social cooperation, security, or care are lost (O'Hara, 1995; 1996; O'Hara and Schwendner, 1997).

The following paper explores the question what might constitute a methodology capable of reflecting complex economic, social and ecological systems processes and impacts. It does so by reviewing two areas that prove challenging to CBA. These are: (1) giving expression to the biological, ecological and physical processes of nature – in short referred to as ecosystems functions, and (2) giving expression to social interaction and social context. To illustrate these challenges the example of snow making, a prerequisite for expanding the tourism industry in the North Eastern United States, is discussed. Following the

184

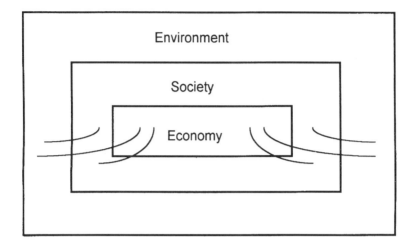

Figure 1. Economy as Contextural System.

empirical discussion of difficulties in assessing the ecological and social impacts of snow making, an alternative valuation method, discourse based valuation, is introduced. A brief discussion of the expanded rationality discourse based methods offer concludes the article.

CHALLENGES IN ECOSYSTEM VALUATION: THE EXAMPLE OF SNOW MAKING

Until recently, the state of Vermont, a small state in the Northeastern United States has avoided the intense conflict over water use commonly seen in the West and Southwest of the United States. Blessed by a large number of rivers, streams, lakes, and ponds, as well as low population density, Vermont's water bodies have in the past amply provided for its residents' diverse needs. But even a state as rural as Vermont has seen increasing pressures on its waterways from residential and commercial development, agriculture, industry, and recreation. Pollution, erosion, stressed aquatic and riparian habitats, reduced stream flows, and diminished aesthetic value and recreational possibilities are the direct and indirect results of these increasing demands. One contributor to the water quality problem in Vermont – artificial snowmaking – is also an important source of private sector incomes particularly in higher elevations where farming is limited. Currently, fourteen alpine ski areas use surface waters for snowmaking, a process by which cold air and water are pumped through compressors to produce artificial "snow" which is then sprayed on ski slopes. Alpine stream flows have been severely depleted in some cases, threatening aquatic biota and habitats. Yet evaluating these external effects of the snowmaking process, that reduce the welfare of other stream users (both individuals and other firms), is a daunting task. The ski industry represents snowmaking as their "lifeblood", a virtual necessity in a market that is intensely competitive and plagued by unpredictable weather patterns. The effects of reduced snow making capabilities are easily translated in revenue losses, reductions in aggregate income, and job losses, all measured in dollars amounts. On the other side of the argument of potential economic impacts are the complex, and uncertain ecosystems effects of reduced stream flow (Lowe, 1990; Environment, 1991).

Reduced stream flow can destroy a stream's ability to sustain aquatic plant and animal species, to supply water for domestic purposes, to support recreational uses, to recharge adjacent wetlands, and to provide for other economically valuable uses, most notably, hydroelectric power generation. The impact of winter withdrawals of stream water on fisheries are especially troublesome because they occur during the crucial spawning and incubation periods that determine future fish stocks. Biologists for the Vermont Agency for Natural Resources (ANR) have testified that ". . . low flow conditions occurring in February may result in the most metabolic stress to aquatic organisms, due to ice impacts and the high physiological stress associated with overwintering". (Conservation Law Foundation, 1995, p. 9). The Agency has produced numerous studies and reports documenting the harmful effects of low flows on the abundance, diversity, and productivity of the aquatic ecosystems. Even fifteen years ago the ANR recognized that "water quality and water quantity cannot be dissociated", and that "... failure to preserve environmentally sound stream flow can cost the public money" by requiring more costly, advanced sewage facilities to meet water quality standards, and by making fisheries and recreational management programs less effective (ANP Report 1980 quoted in CLF 1995, p. 5–6).

Yet evaluating losses of fish stocks, biodiversity, or the ability of aquatic ecosystems to buffer against the impacts of pollution by way of water treatment costs is a poor substitute for the actual losses accrued. This is especially true for irreversible losses that are not simply remedied by subsequent clean up efforts. Comparisons of competing seasonal recreational uses, like fishing and water sports, merely capture human economic benefits. In comparison, contingent valuation based estimates of users' WTA or users' and non-users' WTP can potentially capture the non-economic values of affected stream ecosystems as well. Yet particularly when it comes to expressing the non-human benefits of stream ecosystems, these methods are less than reliable. With species taxonomies lacking far behind estimates of existing species – Wilson estimates that we actually know about 10% of all existing species (Wilson, 1989) – and with our knowledge of species functions and contributions within ecosystems even more scant, our educational basis for assigning monetary value to the complex functions of streams and stream flow levels are questionable at best. More likely, assessments of the benefits of higher stream flow levels are likely to underestimate the contributions of protected freshwater ecosystems.

Recognizing these shortcomings, Vermont has largely relied on regulatory measures to protect stream flow levels from the demands of an economy dependent on seasonal tourism. The ANR is one of several public bodies entrusted with maintaining and improving water quality in the State. It is bound by common law and statutory authority to protect the public trust interests of the state in its public waters and fisheries. Under common law, Vermont is subject to the doctrine of riparianism, which "provides that each owner of land abutting on a stream is entitled both to continuation of stream flow to his land as it flowed in a state of nature and to make reasonable use of that water". (Davis, 1983, p. 47) A riparian right is not one of ownership, but rather one of the usufructory privilege to make reasonable use of the State's waters for private purposes. Generally, the courts have upheld the general principle that a riparian owner may not unreasonably interfere with the riparian interests of others. As a result, the court system has consistently upheld the centrality of water protection for the public good. With respect to stream flows this public right has been translated into aquatic base flow criteria used by the Fish and Wildlife Service (FWS) to establish minimum winter flows limits for water withdrawals for snowmaking. New England flow standard for the fall/winter period is the February median flow of 1.0 cubic feet of water per second per square mile of drainage (csm). The ANR's Flow Procedure prescribes the Vermont statewide average as 0.8 csm. The purpose of the Vermont February median flow (FMF) standard is to foster instream flow releases that "encourage indigenous aquatic organisms". (McLean, 1994) The benefits of maintaining the FMF standard are maintenance, and in some cases considerable improvement, of stream quality by minimizing the harmful effects of low flows to aquatic biota and habitat, riparian habitat, and fisheries. The established flow level standard can thus be compared to Safe Minimum Standards aimed at protecting the long term. health and vitality of ecosystems (Ciriacy-Wantrup, 1968; Bishop, 1978). In addition, the standard also preserves recreational opportunities and the aesthetic value of Vermont's rivers and streams.

Yet all is not well with these regulation based policies. Enforcement of the FMF standard has been lax. In an attempt to solidify non-enforcement, a bill was passed in 1995 which directed the ANR to adopt specific rules governing the withdrawal of water for snowmaking. The bill establishes the precedent of granting one industry (the skiing industry) special treatment, and the proposed rules that were subsequently drafted have come under harsh criticism from FWS, scientists within ANR, and conservation groups. The new rules allow ski areas to continue to draw down water from upland streams to severe levels (below 0.8) indefinitely, with no assurances that the impacts comply with established water quality standards. It further allows for "maximum annual snowmaking volume utilized up to and including the 1994–1995 season" and for the expansion of snow making systems even at water sources with minimum flows below 0.5 csm (ANR 1995, p. 4 & 6). In violation of past priorities to protect the riparian rights of all water users, the burden of proof that private water use will not harm the public has now been shifted from the private user to ANR – the public trustee.[1] In addition, past claims that tensions between various uses are small, and that one activity does not preclude others have been called into question (Dolan and Field, 1995). Increased incidence of drought, which depleted the State's waters and threatened its trout population, have heightened water use conflicts.

---

[1]According to Lewis Milford, senior attorney for the Conservation Law Foundation, last year's Legislature "treated water as if it is an endless resource". Quoted in "Water Rules Could Add to Stream Stress", The Times Argus, July 8, 1995, p. 8.

As competing pressures on water use have increased, ecosystem based standards akin to Safe Minimum standards have come under increased pressure from economic interests. The reason for this seeming change in attitude toward environmental protection are obvious: measurable, human economic interests compete with poorly measurable, human and non-human ecological interests Regulatory standards require complex ecological knowledge that is not easily translated into categories of human usefulness and human welfare.[2] As a result, the uneven appreciation of economic benefits and ecological benefits remains, despite well intentioned regulatory measures. Hard to define, multifaceted and uncertain standards of ecosystems health (Bishop, 1978) do not easily compete with the more readily communicated, seemingly certain value of monetary losses resulting from foregone opportunities for recreational water use. The centrality of monetary value as basis for the assessment of policy measures, evident in the increasing reliance on cost-benefit studies to evaluate policy alternatives, is likely to further disadvantage ecological policy goals over against economic ones. Relying on increasingly elaborate methods to assign monetary value to ecosystems functions may therefore well lead to the opposite of what they set out to achieve: not an increase in recognition and appreciation of complex ecosystems functions may be the result, but rather their decline (O'Hara, 1995b).

CHALLENGES IN EVALUATING SOCIAL CONTEXT: TOURISM AND SOCIAL CAPITAL

While there appears to be an increasing awareness of the need to include the environmental impacts of snow making (as of many other development projects from hydro dams to irrigation mega-projects) in an overall assessment of the effects of increased tourism development, its social impacts are only rarely considered. One reason for this neglect may be a lack of clarity as to what constitutes 'social impacts'. This is particularly true for the United States. Many of the governments of so called

---

[2]According to Cairns and Prate (1995) "Ecosystem services are those functions of natural systems perceived as beneficial to human society", while the term ecosystem functions includes those useful to ecosystems. As ecosystems functions may well sustain ecosystems which constitute human life support systems "the relationship between functions and services is then one of cultural environmental literacy and perception". (p. 67) Even though support services may not be immediately evident the connectedness of human and environmental systems does hardly permit neglect and ignorance.

developed, industrial nations regularly publish documents tracking their nations' social health.[3] The United States does not publish a comparable document either on the national or the state level. This lack of attention to changes in social indicators stands in stark contrast to the vast amount of information about U.S. economic performance. While economic indicators like GDP, inflation, factory orders, inventory stocks or consumer confidence estimates are well publicized, common knowledge, social performance indicators like education, poverty, housing, crime, child abuse, suicide, or infant mortality, are sensationalized at best. It is thus not surprising that public knowledge of such social indicators does not match that of the widely publicized, and accessible economic indicators. Miringoff writes:

"The condition of our economy, or at least those aspects of it that we choose to measure and report, is highly visible and accessible to us. When as a nation, we ask how we are doing, we can only answer in terms of the barometers we have chosen to construct, which reveal to us only the information we have chosen to know. The answer is generally economic". (Miringoff, 1995, p. 462)

As a result, measures of social health and well-being, if considered at all, tend to be couched in economic categories of income or employment. This is certainly true in the case of snow making and its overarching issue – seasonal tourism development. The effects of development strategies aimed at expanding the State's capacity to attract lucrative winter sports business have been generally viewed in terms of their impact on the regions' aggregate income and employment levels. This focus on economic indicators also explains the strong arguments against increased environmental regulations which would force the industry to building water storage ponds or move snow making operations to alternative, downstream water supplies in order to comply with flow standards. Complying with such regulations, the ski industry argues, forces some ski areas out of business and thus poses serious problems to the affected communities' well-being.[4] Particularly small

[3]Social Trends (England), Donnes Sociales (France), Social en Cultureel Report (The Netherlands), Sintesi della vita Sociale Italian (Italy).
[4]The Vermont Ski Area Association's Report, Winter 1992, states that the "percentage of management time devoted to government regulation over the last five years has increased from 12% to 25%". (p. 4) The ski areas' need growing for legal services is even more staggering. It shows a 1,024% increase in lawyers and professional services from 1985 to 1990. (p. 2) At the same time, the number of ski areas has been steadily declining, from 62 in 1975 to 33 in 1990.

communities would be hard hit by the loss of jobs and tax dollars, and the resulting erosion of their financial base. According to the Vermont Ski Area Association 10,000 families and hundreds of businesses in Vermont, a state with only about 1 million residents, depend directly on skiing for their living. Conversely, so the argument, if ski areas expanded or stepped up snow making operations, the effects would be undeniably positive as communities' tourism activities constitute a boost to local economies.[5]

This optimistic assessment of the impact of snow making operations on local communities' social health and well-being may be not so much due to the absence of negative effects as to our inability to properly evaluate them. The proliferation of methods to estimate the monetary value of environmental quality (travel costs, hedonic pricing, contingent valuation) has certainly not been matched by methods to estimate the monetary value a region's or community's social quality or the loss thereof. And if such methods existed, their use would be not only methodologically problematic but morally apprehensible. Establishing the social impacts of snow making thus confronts us head on with the problem of value plurality. Some things can be measured in terms of their monetary value, others can not and require instead a multiplicity of value categories that cannot be easily compared or prioritized according to standard economic procedures of cardinal or ordinal ordering.

Despite these difficulties, attempts have been made to capture the negative social and environmental effects of economic development in non-monetary (or only indirectly monetarily evaluated) quality of life indicators. Taking GDP, the most common measure of economic performance, as their starting point, these alternative measures calculate an aggregate index corrected for defensive expenditures (i.e. expenditures necessary to remedy the damaging effects of environmental pollution and social disintegration), externalities, and the deterioration of public goods (Daly and Cobb, 1989). Others have given a more qualitative, descriptive accounts of the social changes associated with developed industrial societies. Putnam, Coleman and Fukuyama for example have called attention to the loss of social capital prevalent in many communities (Coleman 1988; Fukuyama, 1995; Putnam, 1993; 1995) The term 'social capital' refers to the mutual benefit accrued to a community through its "features of social organization such as networks, norms, and social trust that facilitate coordination and cooperation..." (Putnam, 1995, p.

---

[5]The industry agues that ski areas alone paid $16.5 million in state and local taxes in 1991.

67). It is the degree of civic involvement supported by such social networks and trust of its residents "that a town constantly draws on to ensure its vitality". As evidence of the demise of social capital in United States communities, Putnam cites the alarming decline of citizen involvement in institutions that have traditionally been the breeding ground of the strong social capital associated with U.S. community life: churches, unions, service organizations, and bowling leagues. Strong citizen involvement and community identity form the basis for trust, caring, support, nurturing, networking and communication, qualities which are essential to sustaining healthy and well functioning communities as well as economies. Since these kinds of social support have traditionally been provided outside the realm of the market economy in households and civic organizations, they are simply not considered when it comes to judging what type of economic development is beneficial and what is not. This is not only characteristic for the loss of social capital but for social quality effects in general. Fritsch argues that social quality impacts cannot be assigned a value by the price mechanism because they are indicators of non-market interdependencies (quoted in Beckenbach, 1994). As a result, the demands of making a living in the market economy tend to crowd out the time available for – as well as the value associated with – non-market social interaction (O'Hara, 1997a). Economic development strategies that simply seek to improve economic indicators (like a region's aggregate product, aggregate income, tax revenues, or unemployment rate) without regard for the resulting effects on social quality, networking and provisioning activities in households and communities (Shiva's 'survival economy', 1991) can not be considered development, but merely compensatory development. Such development does not add to, but rather replaces services previously provided outside the market economy in households, civic organizations and community groups.

Some of the more specific changes associated with the increase in winter sports tourism are growing numbers of seasonal residents, pressures on existing infrastructure services due to increased population density, townhouses and condominiums forming entire villages along side historically grown village structures, specialty and outlet stores grouped in strip malls lining country roads, and rising property values that make land and home ownership unaffordable to a growing number of local residents. Increased tourism thus has come at a price – albeit one that is hard to calculate. The erosion of community values, a long established fidelity to place, and small village structures with a functioning provisioning economy that supplies the necessities of life, are not simply a sentimental loss. They simply constitute losses the mainstream of economic theory and method has paid little attention to. Junichi Semitsu a recent honors graduate in economics from the University of California at Berkeley put it succinctly in his commencement address:

> "In our models, the costs of job dislocation, health care insecurities, rising family violence, environmental damage and cultural collapse are all deemed "external". External to what?... We need to change the rules. If we did, we'd see that our country's overall well-being has not improved in 15 years". (Semitsu, 1996)

Assessing the social effects of economic development requires more than slight adjustments to common economic theory and method. It requires innovative approaches to valuation that are capable of moving beyond a single measure of value, monetary or otherwise, and capable of taking the complexities and uncertainties of evolving economic, social and ecological systems into account.

COST-BENEFITS AND BEYOND: THE EXPANDED RATIONALITY OF DISCOURSE

A methodology that is capable of admitting complex, qualitative information to the valuation and decision making process is the open and uncoerced discourse of individuals in a process of mutual acceptance and respect. Such discourse can be viewed as a decentralized coordination of diverse interests akin to the coordination taking place in decentralized markets. Contrary to the coordination mechanism of markets, however, discursive valuation is not limited to monetary value or any other commensurate valuation criteria. Instead, discourse can give expression to the complex life world with all its material constraints, social relationships and normative preferences.[6] The ideal assumption, that a socially optimal market outcome is achieved as individual market participants express their respective preferences in perfectly competitive markets is in principle replicated in the verbally based discourse of participants expressing their interests and preferences. However, in contrast to the common mainstream economic assumption that interest maximizing market participants act in isolation, discourse holds that individual actors are also social beings who form rational decisions not only based on their own interests and preferences but also based on the effects of decision outcomes on

---

[6]The term life world is translated from Habermas 'Lebenswelt', which connotes the life world context of human and non-human interaction, culture, and natural environment.

others. Discourse participants thus cannot simply represent their own preassigned, predetermined values and preferences in the process of coordinating competing individual needs and desires. Instead, each participant is informed in an open discourse process by the contributions of other participants and thus a larger, more informed understanding of the whole decision process is achieved. As individual participants add to their own initial information preferences and values are re-defined in a process of discursive reciprocity. This allows for a more complete expanded rationality of "discursive reason" capable of admitting multiple criteria of "what is" as well as of "what should be" to a fully informed valuation and decision process.

Since multiple valuation criteria, uncertainties, and ambivalences are invariably expressed in the verbal discourse of affected participants, value is not simply reduced to monetary value (the central measure of CBA approaches), nor is value assigned through an 'exclusive', expert driven process of assigning disciplinary based valuation criteria. Instead, discourse admits a broad range of participants' environmental values, social values and individual attitudes to the valuation process. Valuation thus becomes an interactive, social expression of complex contextual information that goes beyond the rational choice based notion of rationality implicit in CBA. A rational ranking of decision alternatives is not dependent on the strong commensurability of value descriptive of all decision alternatives. Moreover, welfare is not simply presumed to be economic welfare. The ability to generate welfare is instead contingent on market transaction as well as the long term health and quality of the social and ecological, material and non-material context within which all economic activity takes place (Biesecker, 1994; O'Hara, 1997b). Context information this is an integral and "internal" to the valuation process and not "external" and in need of being somehow (artificially) internalized. As a result, informed discourse can serve to identify and prioritize valuation criteria reflective of the health and well-being of affected individuals, their social context and the natural environment within which they live. A summary of potential criteria considered in a discourse based valuation process is given in Table 1.

Table 1

Individual, social and ecological quality of life indicators

Individual quality indicators	Social quality indicators	Ecosystem quality indicators

nutrition	income distribution	contamination level
health	quality of infrastructure services	assimilative capacity
education	quality of public goods	resilience
housing	quality of (child and elder) care	biodiversity
transportation	communication & networking	long term productivity
household income	participation in public decisions	generativity

Yet the question might be raised why one should rely on a verbally based discourse process instead of a multi factor quantitative analysis? Georgescu-Roegen gives the rationale for a departure from purely quantitative valuation methods. He writes:

> "To use words, instead of numbers, for truly qualitative changes cannot be represented by an arithmomorphic model. Qualities are not pre-ordered, as numbers are, by their own special nature. The most relevant part of history is a story told in words, even when it is accompanied by some time series that mark the passage of time" (Georgescu-Roegen, 1979, p. 325).

In other words, information about systems linkages, changes and overlaps in complex co-evolving systems can best be expressed through "dialectical approaches", that is through language. The subsystems market exchange, social interaction and environmental quality, for example, are all characterized by distinct time frames, spatial configurations, behaviors and rules even as all subsystems are interconnected, overlapping, co-equal and co-evolving. Attempts to reduce information to its quantitative representation, whether monetary or otherwise, results in a significant loss of differentiated information. Quantification seeks to assign distinctly discrete, numerical value to qualitative differences. Qualitative change, however, may be distinct, but not distinctly discrete. Information about the effects of expanded snow making on tourist related services; working conditions within the winter sports service industry; communities' water supply; the species diversity within affected streams; all these cannot simply be deduced from past relationships and events. Any attempt to compress the infinite properties and endless possibilities of complex human and environmental systems into numerical value must be recognized as what it is: an abstract, reductionist substitution of complex, contextual information.

The expanded rationality of interactive, discursive valuation lies in the method's ability to:[7]

(1) make the life world, that is the larger social and environmental context of development decisions visible and admit it explicitly to the valuation process rather than relying on the implicit (generally positive) value assumptions contained in criteria like income, revenues, or jobs;

(2) view individual actors not in isolation but as acting within a network of social relationships and interactions (Apel, 1973; Habermas, 1983). As research in behavioral economics and game theory shows, the social rationality attributable to the verbal interaction of decision makers is distinctly different from that established by individual decision makers acting in isolation (Caporael et al., 1989; Dawes et al., 1990; Bohnet and Frey, 1995).

(3) define rationality much more broadly than as instrumental rationality of the individual interest maximizing economic agent seeking to attain predetermined goals or interests. Discourse gives expression to both consequentialist and non-consequentialist values as participants bring their own preconceived priorities and preferences to the discourse process but also seeks to increase their own understanding of the complex issues through discursive interaction;

(4) allow for an integrated valuation process instead of a compartmentalized one in which various criteria are considered separately. Such multifaceted considerations may lead to quite unexpected results in the overall decision process particularly as a wide variety of views are considered;

(5) introduce an applied understanding of ethics as the commitment of discourse participants to not simply pursue pre-contemplated norms, but to allow norms to be questioned and redefined by the discourse process itself; generally unaccounted for, marginalized voices are not considered 'outliers' but central to a fully informed, open valuation process (O'Hara, 1996b).

Table 2

Comparison of monetary versus discourse based valuation

Monetary valuation	Discursive valuation

---

[7]For a more extensive discussion of the methodological advantages and limits of discourse based valuation see also Biesecker, 1994; O'Hara, 1996a and 1996b.

– market exchange reflects values	– communication reflects value
– individual act in isolation	– individual act in life world contexts
– actors seek success (maximize self interest)	– actors seek understanding (discursive reciprocity)
– rationality means instrumental reason (consequentialist)	– rationality means communicative reason (consequentialist and non-consequentialist)
– norms based on utilitarian ethic	– norms based on discursive ethic

Table 2 summarizes the above characteristics of discursive valuation and compares them to the familiar valuation framework of market economics (see also Biesecker, 1996; O'Hara, 1996a).

Since discourse based valuation is at its core participatory, it cannot simply be contemplated but. must be practiced. Empirical examples of discourse include mediation in environmental policy or land use conflicts (Gaßner et al., 1992), cooperative approaches to land use and resources management (Renn, 1996), corporate discourse between producers and users on product quality or product safety, vertical discourse between intermediate producers and their various sub-contractors on who carries the costs of policies affecting production processes or product specifications, and broader based discourse on environmental policy guidelines (O'Hara, 1996b) or long term planning. An example of discourse based valuation involving stream flow levels can be found in Hall, et al. This particular example made extensive use of computer models to simulate stream flow levels associated with alternative strategies of water flow regulation of a hydroelectric dam in Montana (Hall et al., 1994). Each alternative flow regulation strategy had varying positive or negative effects on different types of wild life (i.e. fish, birds) and vegetation. Different groups and proponents of particular wild life and conservation agendas thus favored alternative strategies of water flow regulation. Recognizing the affects on other ecosystems components, however, broadened the narrow, special interest view or participants, and agreement on a particular strategy was reached.

In the case of Vermont's snow making issues, past attempts of negotiated mediation have been less successful. In 1994 an Agency Flow Procedure specifically laid out conservation flows for snow-making projects. These flow levels were the result of a negotiated rulemaking process involving the Agency, the Vermont Ski Areas Association, and several environmental groups. Despite efforts to bring all concerned parties to the table, the resulting policy governing stream flows generated only further controversy and renewed charges by the ski industry that ANR and FWS standards were too stringent and without biological justification. Further study is necessary to determine what caused Vermont's mediation efforts to fail. The example illustrates, however, that not all negotiation processes bare the characteristics necessary for successful discourse based valuation. At its best, discourse can make hidden normative assumptions, limited motivations shaped by a narrow special interest agendas, and socially irrational behavior, visible. At its worst, discourse is reduced to a manipulative process that simply seeks to reinforce well established knowledge patterns and segmented interests. Seven conditions distinguish a manipulative, static discourse process from open, ethical discourse (Source: O'Hara, 1996a; see also Biesecker, 1996):

1. Inclusion – all potentially affected parties must be given access to the discourse table;
2. Mutual acceptance – participants must be willing, and held accountable to mutually accept all discourse participants and their contributions;
3. Equal rights – all participants' contributions must be given equal weight in the discourse process and every participant must have the opportunity to influence the whole;
4. Equal access to information – participants must have equal access to information and be willing to share information;
5. Procedural flexibility – all participants must have the opportunity to revise their positions as well as preliminary results of the discourse process;
6. Open enededness – the process must be open ended and can neither insist on permanent solutions nor on permanent procedural constraints;
7. Absence of power – formal equality between discourse participants must assure that no one party can assert power over others.

These conditions make it clear that discourse based valuation is quite different from a manipulative process intent on pushing a predetermined agenda. Open discourse requires that preconceived notions of decision outcomes are suspended and critically reflected. A broad based heterogeneous group of discourse participants alone does not guarantee mutual openness and a willingness to increasing intersubjective understanding. What is also needed is the willingness to uncover hidden value biases and to expose them to the scrutiny of the conflicting cognition of different participants: long time year round residents versus new seasonal residents; those involved exclusively in the market economy and those also active in the subsistence economy of intentionally local production and land use patterns; those living seemingly independent of nature's economy and those making their living in close interaction with it. Discourse thus takes time, mutual acceptance and trust, and willingness to create institutional venues to honor and implement negotiated results.

CONCLUSIONS

Much progress has been made over the past twenty years in expanding the traditional instrumentarium of CBA. This expansion has made it possible to better evaluate the so called external effects of economic development, most especially its environmental effects. Yet past neglects of the negative environmental impacts of economic development have not been the only source of criticism directed against traditional CBA based assessments. More recently, unaccounted for social effects have come under scrutiny as well. As the brief discussion of snow making, an increasingly controversial procedure affecting water use and water quality in Vermont and other Northeastern States of the United States, shows, addressing the complex environmental and social results of development is a challenging task. The possibility of conducting a full scale cost-benefit study of snowmaking has so far been abdicated as too difficult and open to criticism since the necessarily simplified assumptions and incomplete information about the long term effects of snow making are likely to generate more controversy rather than agreement.

An alternative approach to CBA is discursive valuation. This method does not presume it necessary to meet the criterion of strong commensurability as a prerequisite for comparing alternative development strategies. Instead, discourse based valuation considering multiple economic, social and environmental criteria brought to the discourse table by affected participants. Yet this is merely where discourse based valuation takes its starting point. The process of seeking understanding in a mutual, reciprocal process of discursive valuation forms in fact the basis for a broadened rationality of discursive reason that draws upon social valuation criteria rather than solely individual ones. In addition, discourse offers a venue for admitting diverse local knowledge and affectedness to the valuation process.

The consequence of successful broad based valuation outcome are significantly reduced transaction and enforcement costs. Given the fact that high enforcement costs (or lax enforcement) have often accompanied regulatory safe minimum standard (SMS) type policies. In the case of snow making, the SMS has been deemed 0.8 square mile of drainage (csm) of February median stream flow levels. These standards have been under repeated attack by ski areas are being unreasonable and unachievable despite the fact that it has not yet been demonstrated that with better water efficiency practices by ski areas and utilization of state-of-the-art snowmaking technology, which wastes less water, FMF standards cannot be met. At the same time, unpredictable weather conditions, droughts and increased population density have raised concerns about the future of Vermont's surface water quality even in areas where water has previously seemed unlimited. Snow making thus exemplifies the water use conflicts many rural areas increasingly face.

As rapid tourism related development continues to replace traditional land use of agriculture and forestry regional economies' linkages to the so called informal 'survival economy' (Shiva, 1991) are increasingly replaced by linkages to the market economy. Participatory, discourse based valuation offers the possibility to account for the often neglected impacts of expanding tourism development on the provisioning relationships of households, communities and the natural environment. Allowing the range of social and environmental concerns to become explicit in the valuation process of development alternatives is all the more important as a stable social environments and a high quality natural environment are important assets, essential to future survival and prosperity of rural communities.

REFERENCES

Agency for Natural Resources (1995) Water Withdrawals for Snowmaking. Chapter 16 in: Environmental Protection Rules. Draft 6/23/95. Montpelier, Vermont.

Agency for Natural Resources. (1980) Vermont's Need for Streamflow Protection. Annual Report. Montpelier, Vermont.

Apel, K.-O. (1973) Diskurs und Verantwortung. Das Problem des Übergangs zur postkonventionellen Moral. Surkamp Verlag. Frankfurt am Main.

Beckenbach, F. (1994) Social Costs in Modern Capitalism. in: O'Conner, M. (editor), Is Capitalism Sustainable: Political Economy and the Politics of Ecology. Guilford Press. New York.

Biesecker, A. (1994) Ökonomie als Raum sozialen Handelns – ein grundbegrifflicher Rahmen. in: A. Biesecker, K. Grenzdörfer (eds) *Ökonomie als Raum sozialen Handelns*. Donat Verlag. Bremen. pp. 7–15.

Biesecker, A. (1996) Power and Discourse. Some Theoretical Remarks and Empirical Observations. *Bremer Diskussionspapiere zur Sozialoekonomie.* A. Biesecker, W. Elsner, K. Grenzdörfer, H. Heide (eds.) Nr. 14, October.

Bishop, R.C. (1978) Endangered Species and Uncertainty: The economics of a safe Minimum Standard. *American Journal of Agricultural Economics*, no. 60, 10–18.

Bohnet, I., Frey, B. (1995) Ist Reden Silber und Schweigen Gold? Eine oekonomische Analyse. *Zeitschrift fuer Wirtschafts- und Sozialwissenschaften.* 2, 169–209.

Brookshire, D.S., Thayer, M.A., Schulz, W. D'Arge, R. (1993) Valuing public goods: a comparison of survey and hedonic approaches. in: Mardandya, A., Richardson, J. (editors) *Environmental Economics: A Reader.* St. Martin's Press, New York. pp 204–19.

Cairns, J., Pratt, J.R. (1995) The Relationship between Ecosystem Health and Delivery of Ecosystem Services. in: D.J. Rapport, C.L. Gaudet and P. Calow (eds.) *Evaluating and Monitoring the Health of Large-Scale Ecosystems.* NATO ASI series, vol. I 28. Springer Verlag, Berlin, Heidelberg.

Caporael, L., Dawes, R., Orbel, J., van de Kragt, A. (1989) Selfishness Examined: Cooperation in the Absence of Egoistic Incentives. *Behavioral and Brain Science.* 4, 683–98.

Ciriacy-Wantrup, S.V. (1968) *Resource Conservation: Economics and Policies.* 3rd edition. University of California, Berkeley

Colander, M. (1994) *Economics.* IRWIN. Boston, New York.

Coleman, J. (1988) Social Capital and the Creation of Human Capital. American Journal of Sociology. 97 (suppl.): S 95–S 120.

Conservation Law Foundation (1995) Comments of Conservation Law Foundation on the Proposed Rules for Water Withdrawals for Snowmaking. September 22. Montpelier, Vermont.

Daly, H., Cobb, J. (1989) For the Common Good. Beacon Press, Boston.

Davis, P. (1983) The Riparian Right of Streamflow Protection in the Eastern States. *Arkansas Law Review* 47, 47–8.

Dawes, R., Alphons, J. Van de Kragt, A., Orbel, J. (1990) Cooperation for the Benefit of Us: Not me, or my conscience. In: Mansbridge, J. (ed.) *Beyond Self-Interest.* The University of Chicago Press. Chicago and London.

Dolan, K., Field, P. (1995) Fishing for Values: A Primer for River Protection Activists in the Use of Contingent Valuation as an Economic Tool for Conserving Anadromous Fisheries. *NE Natural Resource Center of the National Wildlife Federation & River Watch Network.* Montpelier, VT.

Eberle, D., Hayden, F.G. (1991) Critique of Contingent Valuation and Travel Cost Methods for Valuing Natural Resources and Ecosystems. *Journal of Economic Issues.* XXV: 649–87.

Environmnet 1991 (1991) Alteration of Vermont's Terrestrial and Aquatic Ecosystems. Technical Appendix to: *Environment 1991: Risks to Vermont and Vermonters.* Montpelier, Vermont.

Fukuyama, F. (1995) Trust: The Social Virtues and the Creation of Prosperity. The Free Press. New York.

Gaßner, H., Holznagel, E., Lahl, U. (1992) Mediation. Verhandlungen als Mittel der Konsensfindung bei Umweltstreitigkeiten. *Planung und Praxis in Umweltschutz.* Band 5. Economica. Bonn.

Georgescu-Roegen, N. (1979) Methods in Economics Science. *Journal of Economics Issues.* Vol. XIII No.2: 317–328.

Habermas, J. (1983) *Theory des kommunikativen Handelns.* Vol. 2. Surkamp Verlag. Frankfurt am Main.

Harris, C., Driver, B., McLaughlin, W. (1989) Improving the Contingent Valuation Method: A Psychological Perspective. *Journal of Environmental Economics and Management* 17, 217–229

Lowe, S. (1990) Okemo Denied Permit to Take River Water. *Rutland Daily Herald*. January 31.

Martinez-Alier, J. (1994) Distributional Conflicts and International Environmental Policy on Carbon Dioxide Emissions and Agricultural Biodiversity; in: Van den Bergh, J. And J. Van de Straaten. *Toward Sustainable Development*. Island Press. Washington DC.

McLean, S. (1994) Streamflow Policy in Vermont: Manging Conflicting Demands on the State's Waters. *Vermont Law Review*, Vol. 19, #1, Fall. pp. 216–217

Miringoff, M. (1995) Toward a National Standard of Social Health: The Need for Progress in Social Indicators. *American Journal of Orthopsychiatry*. 65(4): 462–467.

Murdoch, J.C., Thayer, M.A. (1993) Hedonic price estimation of variable urban air quality. in: Markandya, A., Richardson, J. (editors) *Environmental Economics: A Reader*. St. Martin's Press, New York, pp. 167–174

O'Hara, S. (1997a) Toward a Sustaining Production Theory. *Ecological Economics*. 20, 141–154

O'Hara, S. (1997b) Internalizing Economics: Sustainability Between Matter and Meaning. Essays in Honor of Clement Allen Tisdell, Part IV, John C. O'Brien (ed.), *International Journal of Social Economics*, MCB University Press. Forthcoming.

O'Hara, S. (1996a) The Challenges of Valuation: Ecological Economics Between Matter and Meaning. Plenary lecture. 4th Biannual Meeting of the International Society for Ecological Economics, Boston University, Boston, August 4–7.

O'Hara, S. (1996b) Discursive ethics in ecosystems valuation and environmental policy. *Ecological Economics*. 16 (1996): 95–107.

O'Hara, S. (1995a) Valuing Socio-Diversity. *International Journal of Social Economics*. Vol. 22, No. 5: 31–49.

O'Hara, S. (1995b) From Production to Sustainability: Considering the Whole Household. *Journal of Consumer Policy*. 18: 1–24.

O'Hara, S., Schwendner, R. (1997) Ecological Economics: A Framework for Developing Social and Ecological Intelligence. *Rostocker Beiträge zur Regional- und Strukturforschung*. Forthcoming.

O'Neill, J. (1996) Cost-benefit analysis, rationality and the plurality of values. *The Ecologist*. Vol. 26. May/June. pp 98–103.

Putnam, R. (1995) Bowling Alone: America's Declining Social Capital. *Journal of Democracy*. Vol. 6, no.1:65–78.

Putnam, R. (1993) The Prosperous Community: Social Capital and Economic Growth. Current no. 356: 4–9.

Renn, O. (1996) Möglichkeiten und Grenzen Diskurssiver Verfahren bei umweltrelevanten Planungen. In: A. Biesecker und K. Grensdörffer (ed.) *Kooperation, Netzwerk, Selbstorganisation. Elemente demokratischen Wirtschaftens*. Pfaffenweiler: Centaurys. pp 161–197

Sesitsu, J. (1996) It's time for a new breed of economists. *Albany Times Union*. Sunday, May 26.

Shiva, V. (1991) *Ecology and the Politics of Survival*. United Nations University Press. New Delhi.

Smith, V.K., Desvousges, W. (1993) The generalized travel cost model and water quality benefits: a reconsideration. in: Markandya, A., Richardson, J. (editors) *Environmental Economics: A Reader*. St. Martin's Press,. New York. pp. 184–93.

Stirling, A. (1993) Environmental Valuation: How Much Is the Emperor Wearing? *The Ecologist* 23, May/June: 97–100.

The Times Argus (1995) "Water Rules Could Add to Stream Stress", July 8. p. 8.

U.S. EPA Ecosystems Valuation Forum (1993) Report to the U.S. Environmental Protection Agency. Issues in Ecosystem Valuation – Improving Information for Decision Making. (Unpublished Manuscript) Washington, DC.

Vermont Ski Area Association (1992) Annual Report. Montpelier, Vermont.

Wilson, E.O. (1989) *Biodiversity*. National Academy Press, Washington, DC.

CHAPTER 11

COST-BENEFIT ANALYSIS AND WILDLIFE CONSERVATION: A SUSTAINABLE APPLICATION?

By Peter Clough

ABSTRACT:

This paper examines how cost-benefit analysis can assist or hinder formulation of policy towards wildlife conservation, drawing on the experience of English Nature, the statutory body advising the UK government on matters affecting England's natural environment. In the context of recent policy evolution to encompass national goals on biodiversity and sustainable development, cost-benefit analysis is applied to a range of projects and policies with environmental consequences, but formulating such procedures has not proved compatible with many of the aims of conservation policy. The paper examines these applications with examples of the imputation of monetary values for non-market goods. The various techniques of non-market valuation are found wanting and the paper outlines an approach to the valuation of habitats through a set of environmental inventory accounts, encompassing the natural capital - air, water, space, soils, landforms and biological resources - whose contribution to productive sectors and community well-being may be fundamentally transformed by adverse environmental effects. It links these accounts to project appraisal and other environmental economics issues, such as the use of incentives and instruments in implementing policy.

1. INTRODUCTION

The drive for fiscal restraint and efficient public expenditure have combined with increasingly sophisticated computing power to make cost-

---

The author, at the time of writing this paper was an Economic Adviser at 'English Nature' based in Peterborough, UK. Any errors of omission or commission in this article remain his responsibility, and the opinions expressed should not be taken as necessarily representing those of 'English Nature'.

benefit analysis (CBA) more apparently feasible than it has been hitherto, but doubts have also arisen about the technique's limitations. In the field of environmental policy, in particular, questions remain about the ability of CBA to represent the complexity of natural systems, with their characteristics of irreversibility, uniqueness and uncertainty about the long-term consequences of change (Hanley, 1992). A more immediately pressing problem for environmental management arises where CBA undertaken for a non-environmental purpose supports activities which are environmentally damaging.

This paper examines CBA implications for conservation of wildlife and protected natural areas, drawing on the experience of English Nature, the statutory body advising the United Kingdom government on matters affecting England's natural environment. It surveys the institutional framework for UK environmental policy, the prescriptions of environmental economics for dealing with wildlife, and the practical implementation of CBA in three public expenditure fields. It concludes by outlining amendments to current appraisal procedures to take more account of wildlife conservation, with implications for future directions in applied economics research.

2. BACKGROUND TO WILDLIFE CONSERVATION IN THE UNITED KINGDOM

With its dense settlement and long history of private land ownership and management, England has evolved a form of nature conservation not based on recreating pristine naturalness. The cost of creating adequate reserves would be prohibitive, and wildlife both co-exists with, and depends upon, human activity, since some habitats are joint products of particular land uses. Rather conservation aims to maintain and enhance biodiversity by setting aside sufficient special areas for wildlife to flourish and creating conditions across the wider countryside that allow species movements and prevent isolation of habitats, through a gradual attenuation of private property rights in favour of wider public interests such as wildlife and landscape.

The UK's current structure of statutory environmental administration dates from the 1947 Town and Country Planning Act, which made conversion of rural land to urban uses conditional on permission from locally-elected authorities. The 1949 National Parks and Access to the Countryside Act created national parks as a special form of planning designation, and established a Nature Conservancy empowered to designate other areas of privately-owned land as Sites of Special Scientific Interest (SSSIs), on grounds of their biological or geological characteristics. The 1981 Wildlife and Countryside Act required the then Nature Conservancy Council to review and re-notify SSSIs, and enter into management agreements with landowners to control "potentially damaging operations", compensating them for net profits forgone. UK policy is increasingly adapting to European influences, such as the Birds Directive (79/409/EEC) and the Habitats and Species Directive (92/43/EEC) which require demarcation of further areas for conservation purposes.

This structure remains broadly unchanged since 1990, when the NCC was divided into separate bodies for England, Scotland and Wales. Following the 1992 Earth Summit in Rio de Janeiro, the UK government expressed public commitment to "conserve and enhance biological diversity within the UK and to contribute to the conservation of global biodiversity through all appropriate mechanisms" (Department of Environment 1994a, 1994b). Such an objective reflects biodiversity's contribution to distinct human uses, including commodity values, where traded products or services depend on wildlife or natural settings (such as sporting rights, eco-tourism); indirect support of other productive processes such as soil conservation and watershed protection; the options and potential for future uses of genetic variability in improved products, cultivars and pharmaceutical feedstocks; and the social well-being derived from knowing that wildlife exists (Dixon & Sherman 1991). These correspond to the components of total economic value in neo-classical economics (Randall 1987), commonly described as current use values of conserved areas; option values in retaining biodiversity for possible future use; and existence (non-use) value, or the appreciative loss people would feel if a species or habitat were irrevocably destroyed.

3. THE PRACTICE OF COST-BENEFIT ANALYSIS AND THE NATURAL ENVIRONMENT

Since CBA is commonly described as applied welfare economics, it needs to reflect environmental effects which impact on human well-being. These include biodiversity status, whose consumption is largely non-rival and non-excludable, and which is prone to damage from externalities, making it a prime contender for government intervention on market failure grounds and a necessary consideration in public sector expenditure assessments.

3.1   The prescriptions of environmental economics

Environmental economists seek to extend the scope of CBA to account for environmental effects, by quantifying them and assigning them an economic value consistent with public expressed preferences (Pearce et al 1989). Valuation of environmental goods and services employs various methods, ranging from market prices for traded items, to non-market valuation techniques, including indirect "revealed preference" methods such as travel cost analysis and hedonic pricing, and direct "stated preference methods" such as contingent valuation and conjoint analysis.

Recent academic interest has focused on stated preference methods which in theory elicit the full range of current use, future use and non-use values held for the environment. In the USA such non-market valuations have been accepted as evidence in litigation, but in the UK non-market valuation studies are viewed as too costly, too few and too issue-specific to transfer the individual empirical results to other contexts, and have yet to overcome the credibility threshold in practical policy applications. The hypothetical nature of contingent valuation surveys raises questions about their representation of realisable economic choices, reinforced by empirical evidence that respondents express larger values the more information they are given, and baulk at paying their stated willingness to pay when sent a real bill. Do respondents fully allow for their income constraints; and do they confuse values for the individual assets being studied with values held for environment in general, which become conflated as the results of successive studies are extrapolated across the population at large? There is also philosophical questioning of whether values for collective public goods should be assessed as if they are simply accumulations of individual trades, or whether there are citizen values distinct from individualistic consumer values (Jacobs 1997).

Most studies undertaken to date value biological resources rather than biodiversity as such (Pearce and Moran 1994), and the valuation literature is dominated by "charismatic mega-fauna" rather than less spectacular species filling critical ecological niches. In site valuations, preferences for public access, open space and landscape often prevail over considerations of scientific importance. Even large values generated by contingent valuation are not always sufficient to secure the conservation interest.

An example is given by lowland heathlands, a species-rich habitat covering about 16,000 of England's total of 13 million hectares, which in the early 1990s were threatened by urban encroachment. Had the local authorities concerned considered broad social costs and benefits and the precautionary principle in the face of uncertain future effects, they might have concluded that the nationally scarce heathland required greater protection from urban expansion than nearby areas of productive farmland, whose major outputs are readily transportable and available elsewhere. But planning statutes still retain from post-war austerity a presumption against building over farmland, directing development onto less productive heathland.

However, even a quantified CBA need not protect the heathland. A 1991 contingent valuation study of a 250-hectare heathland found its users' aggregate annual willingness to pay for protection rose with information provided, from ú44,000 to ú92,000, but was still far below its realisable market value for housing development (Bilsborough & Heap 1991). Larger aggregate values could be obtained by extrapolating across a wider population, but the extent of the relevant population is indeterminate in such local site studies, since other sites will be more valued by distant residents.

In practice the non-market valuations needed for CBA are not widely used in promoting conservation, where the emphasis is more on cost-effectiveness analysis, in which conservation targets are taken as given without attachment of explicit values. Conservation encounters CBA more often in the case of projects for non-environmental purposes, where the treatment of environment varies widely with distinct implications for conservation and public expenditure decisions.

3.2   The application of economic appraisal to road projects

Road building has become a touchstone of environmentalist concern in Britain, following substantial expansion of the motorway network in the 1980s and several instances of large schemes damaging sites of conservation interest. With few exceptions, roads in Britain are provided as if they were public goods, with improvement schemes funded by government expenditures channelled through either a national Highways Agency or local authorities. All proposals above a low expenditure threshold are subjected to a CBA, formalised in a computer programme known as COBA.

In common with appraisal methods used in other countries, COBA compares conventionally defined construction and maintenance costs against a narrow range of road user benefits in the form of savings in vehicle operating costs, travel time and accident costs. Values are variously based on avoided costs, in the case of vehicle operation and accident damage, and non-market estimates of willingness to pay for reduced delay and casualty risk. A separate Environmental Impact Assessment (EIA), sweeping up all the effects which cannot readily be assigned a monetary value, is conducted for each scheme option parallel to COBA. Environmental values do not enter explicitly into COBA, except where design features included for environmental protection or remediation are included in the scheme's costs, enlarging the denominator in the benefit:cost ratio and making options with high environmental design standards look less desirable than those delivering the same user benefits with lower design standards.

More serious for conservation is the treatment of land taken for proposed schemes, which enters COBA at an acquisition value. For SSSIs, the value used is the market price of similar land adjusted downwards to reflect the use restrictions caused by the conservation designation. Ostensibly this practice is to avoid double-counting of site damage in COBA and the EIA, but it contradicts the purpose of designation in signalling a social value for the site not reflected in market price, and creates a perverse incentive to favour route options across SSSIs. Although supposed to ensure economic efficiency, COBA's use of land market prices incorporates the capitalised value of farmland subsidies and effectively makes it more of a private appraisal for the highway authorities than an economic appraisal of social net benefit.

Since traffic delays detract from a scheme's benefit stream, in comparing options for a proposed road improvement those which work on the existing corridor will appear less favourable than those minimising delays by constructing on new land-take, exacerbating pressures on conservation land. There is no remedy for this within the COBA methodology, other than ensuring that the new land take has a significantly higher value where its use would damage conservation, for instance by valuing damaged habitats at a full replacement cost, or valuing undesignated farmland at its true opportunity cost of lost production stripped of all subsidy component. Aside from these structural biases against conservation, other details of current COBA procedures, such as the assumptions of traffic growth, or the initial choice of options for comparison, can adversely affect conservation outcomes (SACTRA 1992).

3.3. The application of economic appraisal to flood and coastal defence schemes

Land drainage and flood embankments have major implications for conservation, transforming wetlands and destroying fringe habitats along canalised watercourses. Given the natural tendency for river channels to change course, and for the relative levels of sea and land to change over time, the long term sustainability of maintaining the substantial investments in flood defences made around England over centuries is coming under increasing scrutiny in the face of climate change and global warming.

The Ministry of Agriculture, Fisheries and Food over-sees public expenditure on flood protection and coastal defence, and requires proposals seeking funding to include a cost-benefit analysis as specified in MAFF's Project Appraisal Guidance Notes (1993). These define a scheme's objectives in terms of national benefit of reducing the probability and severity of inundation or erosion of land and property, and use incremental benefit:cost ratios to compare successive levels of investment for a particular scheme. The benefits are the avoided costs of physical damage to stock, lost industrial production, loss of land and agricultural output, and cost savings for emergency services and disruption of infrastructure. These are valued primarily with market or cost-based methods, but with recourse to non-market valuation for some recreation and amenity effects. To avoid over-stating the value of farmland relative to less intensive land uses, farm output and land values are adjusted to counteract subsidies, and disruption losses are confined to physical stock and property damage, in recognition that flood disruption is localised and much "lost production" is simply diverted to other locations, with no net national loss.

The guidelines recommend that "impacts not quantified in money terms should be set out and in a way which assists the process of discriminating between options", as an annex to the appraisal. But the relative weighting given to non-monetised effects is unclear, and it is common for reports in practice to omit these non-monetary effects and to provide little in the way of sensitivity analysis on their results.

For nature conservation the primary drawbacks with these procedures are their omissions. The appraisals have no way to value some habitat consequences, - such as the squeezing of food-rich mudflats against hard defence structures as sea level rises - and give little recognition to the cumulative and consequent effects which may be far removed from the scheme site itself, such as sediment and energy dispersion along channels and coasts. Their valuation basis is more justifiable where the environmental benefit is related to terrestrial habitats - for instance, protection of an area of wet grazing marsh with recreation or landscape value - than in the maritime zone where the conservation preferences have no obvious human benefit, such as retaining natural erosion processes rather than deflecting them onto other habitats. Uncertainties over cause and environmental effect are greater in the maritime zone, and imply the need for more recognition of the precautionary principle built into the analysis structure.

3.4   The application of economic appraisal to water quality improvements

Recent European Community directives on Drinking Water, Bathing Water and Urban Waste Water Treatment impose new requirements for water quality at a time when the water supply industry in the UK has been recently privatised and under pressure from the regulator, the Office of Water Services, to reverse the under-investment of previous years without excessive rises in water charges.   This impetus for assessing value for money in water quality investment was reinforced in 1996 by creation of the Environment Agency which has broad functions over rivers management and pollution, and a statutory requirement to "take into account the likely costs and benefits of the exercise or non-exercise of its powers".

While the legislation does not specify the methodology of cost-benefit analysis, the Environment Agency is encouraging a CBA framework for use by those whose activities affect the UK's freshwater resources. In December 1996 a manual on Assessing the Benefits of Surface Water Quality Improvements was issued which, although not yet mandatory, is likely to be influential on how water quality improvements are assessed in future.

The manual.values raw water quality improvements on the basis of avoided treatment costs for extraction uses such as irrigation, industry or potable supply purposes. It also uses non-market valuations of willingness to pay for quality improvements by anglers, boaters, informal recreation users and general amenity for adjacent property owners. A similar approach is applied to non-use benefits which are expected to capture public preferences for wildlife conservation. Household willingness to pay for improvements through three quality levels is estimated across the relevant population of households served by the water company which would be expected to pay for delivery of any quality improvement. But the manual recognises the contentiousness of the valuation method and appears ambivalent about whether to include non-use values in the benefit calculation. It has a short section on assessing non-monetary benefits in terms of how big they would have to be to turn a negative

Net Present Value into a positive one. It also describes a weighting and scoring exercise on these non-monetised effects, but offers little guidance on how to use this and ensure consistency between applications, or how the resulting scores would be compared against the CBA results in any final decision.

This procedure has specific limitations for assessing nature conservation benefits, since the water quality index used for non-use benefits is based on the conditions for fish life, and omits some parameters required for broader ecological management, such as sediment and phosphate loadings. Moreover, by combining this index's five levels into three levels for valuation purposes, the manual obscures the public willingness to pay for the crucial incremental improvement to the top quality level which most closely fulfills the requirements for river-based SSSIs.

4. DISCUSSION

Although the methods described above all acknowledge the same government guidelines and aim for efficient public spending (HM Treasury 1993), their treatment of environment differs widely. Road project appraisals compare narrowly focused costs and benefits, handling environmental effects through a separate non-monetised assessment, but this disguises rather than avoids the environmental valuation problem: it emerges again in the implicit weighting between the CBA and EIA results in the final decisions which, on past record, have rarely seen an EIA overturn the options preferred by CBA. The flood defence appraisals admit a broader range of benefits and costs, but are largely restricted to cost-based valuations, with impacts not quantifiable in money terms consigned to annexes. The water quality manual ambitiously assigns non-market values to a wide range of effects, but recommends results be presented with non-use benefits both included and excluded.

The inconsistencies in these approaches make it hard to compare investments in the different expenditure categories or to assess the optimality of investment across them. Adopting a project- or site-specific approach risks missing regional or national effects, the role of habitats and species within wider ecosystems and minimum viable habitat or population sizes. Natural habitats such as estuaries and river systems have been transformed by the cumulative effect of individual schemes, with consequences which were never foreseen in the original scheme assessments. Without this wider view of environmental consequences, it is difficult to conclude that appraisal processes are contributing positively to environmental sustainability.

Faced with implementing sustainability which is vaguely defined by statute, agencies such as English Nature are developing means of managing environment as if it were a stock of assets or infrastructure, drawing distinction between Critical Natural Capital (CNC), whose natural attributes are non-substitutable, non-recreatable, and require the greatest protection; and Constant Natural Assets (CNA) for which the individual components may be changed, as long as the aggregate total is maintained with offsetting or compensatory measures. They have divided the country into localities sharing common characteristics of geology and land cover for setting baseline ecological integrity conditions, within which national targets for habitat or species recovery can be guided by cost-effectiveness considerations. In practice identifying CNC through criteria such as non-recreatability is difficult, but the broader notion of CNA has more ready application to CBA.

Where a proposed scheme detracts from existing natural stocks, the damage is a form of economic depreciation which can be valued as the expenditure required to maintain the stock in a constant condition, or restore it. Such depreciation can be internalised by the activity causing it, by including it as the resource cost of habitat deterioration within CBA, and using it as a basis for economic instruments such as impact fees or damage liability (OECD 1996). In economic terms such valuations are incomplete in excluding elements of willingness to pay, and environmentalists doubt that some habitats can be restored within an economically meaningful time-frame. But such an approach does provide readily understood non-zero values and indicate one dimension of society's loss if the scheme goes ahead, addressing a common omission from current appraisals. If depreciation value includes the opportunity cost of land and other resources used in restoring a habitat over a substantial period, it will give greater weight to protecting conservation land than current valuation procedures.

For project appraisals the values may be purely hypothetical. They can reflect the wider context and be varied the more nearly habitat depletion approaches critical local or national thresholds by linking them to environmental accounts, such as inventories showing the combination of soil, water and biological attributes of different habitats. They also provide a basis for computing "genuine savings", an aggregate indicator of weak sustainability obtained by dividing the hypothetical depreciation on natural capital by the investments in natural capital enhancement (Pearce et al 1996). Extending the links between aggregate accounts and individual appraisals promises to further Solow's (1992) "almost practical step towards sustainability".

5. CONCLUSIONS

The increasing use of cost-benefit analysis in public expenditure assessment means it will frequently be used to analyse environmental effects, creating an urgent need to recognise environmental consequences in CBA. To date practical appraisal procedures either relegate environmental impacts to a separate non-monetised assessment, whose weighting against CBA results in final decisions is often slight and arrived at by far from transparent means, or else prescribe procedures involving complexity, analyst discretion and contentious valuations which undermine the comparability of the results for competing projects. The outcome of such processes is frequently dubious for both the natural environment and the efficiency of government expenditure. But increasing empirical research into the development of environmental stock accounts and the depreciation and restoration costs of particular habitats provides the opportunity to incorporate environmental values more widely and consistently into economic analyses, alleviating some of their unfortunate consequences for wildlife conservation.

REFERENCES

Bilsborough, S. and Heap, J. (1991) "Environmental economics and nature conservation: a compilation of work undertaken in 1990/91 for the NCC"; Nature Conservancy Council, Peterborough

Department of the Environment (1991) Policy appraisal and the environment; HMSO, London

Department of the Environment (1994a) Sustainable Development - the UK Strategy; HMSO, London

Department of the Environment (1994b) UK Biodiversity Action Plan HMSO, London

Dixon. J.A. and Sherman P.B. (1991) "Economics of protected areas"; Ambio 20(2). 68-74

Foundation for Water Research, (1996) Assessing the benefits of surface water quality improvements; Henley-on-Thames

Hanley, N. (1992) "Are there environmental limits to cost-benefit analysis?"; Environmental and Resource Economics 2; 33-59

Treasury, H.M. (1991) Economic appraisal in central government - a technical guide for government departments; HMSO, London

Jacob. M. (1997) "Environmental valuation, deliberative democracy, and public decision making institutions"; Chapter 13 in Foster J. (Ed) Valuing nature? Ethics, economy and environment; Routledge, London

Ministry of Agriculture, Fisheries and Food, (1993) Project appraisal guidance notes: flood and coastal defence; HMSO, London

OECD (1996) Saving biological diversity - economic incentives; Organisation for Economic Co-operation and Development, Paris

Pearce, D.W. and Moran. D. (1994) The economic value of biodiversity; Earthscan Books, London

Pearce D, Hamilton K. and Atkinson G. (1996) "Measuring sustainable development - progress on indicators"; Environment and Development Economics 1; 85-101

Pearce D.W. Markandya.A. & Barbier. E.B. (1989) Blueprint for a green economy; Earthscan Books, London

Randall.A. (1987) "Total economic value as a basis for policy"; Transactions of the American Fisheries Society 116; 325-335

Solow R. (1992) An almost practical step towards sustainability; Resources for the Future, Washington DC

Standing Advisory Committee on Trunk Road Assessment (SACTRA, 1992), Assessing the environmental impacts of road schemes; HMSO, London

COST BENEFIT ANALYSIS OF CLIMATE CHANGE: TOWARDS AN OPERATIONAL DECISION MAKING RULE FOR CLIMATE CHANGE POLICY

Sardar M.N.Islam, Jim Gigas, Peter Sheehan

ABSTRACT

This paper discusses the suitability of cost-benefit analysis as an operational method for policy making to address the issue of climate change. This paper reports the results generated from an integrated dynamic optimisation model of climate change and the economy and shows that the benefits of climate change abatement are greater than the costs incurred in climate change abatement. The paper concludes that the cost-benefit framework is a consistent and superior decision making tool for climate change.

1.0 INTRODUCTION

Much of the work in the analysis of the climate change and its impacts on economies through out the world has been focused on the issues determining the effects and costs of climate change. Generally the issues have been addressed in a cost-effective framework and some major such studies have been conducted to address the issue. Several principal cost-effectiveness models are presented in OECD (1993), while Gigas and Islam (1995) survey the Australian models. However, such models neglect the benefits side of the climate change abatement and thus only present one side of the issue. The number of integrated assessments of costs and benefits is also on the rise, either in a partial equilibrium framework as in Cline (1992) and Fankhauser (1995) or in a general equilibrium framework are Nordhaus (1994), and Manne, Mendelsohn and Richale (1995). While the need for a cost benefit analysis of climate change in Australia has been stressed (IC, 1991), no systematic work was done until Islam (1995). The purpose of this paper is to apply the integrated approach of assessing the climate change economic interaction to Australia based on Islam (1995) and to make an assessment of the integrated modelling of the costs and benefits of climate change.

The paper will give a brief introduction to cost benefit analysis in section 2.0. Section 3.0 follows with the synthesis of cost-benefit analysis into the climate change policy formulation. Section 4.0 presents the integrated model of climate change and the economy. Section 5.0 presents the results from the integrated assessment model of climate change. Section 6.0 provides an evaluation of cost-benefit analysis as an operational tool for climate change policy making in general and for the Australian perspective. The paper finishes with conclusions and suggestions for future research in the area of general equilibrium modelling of costs and benefits of climate change.

2.0 COST BENEFIT ANALYSIS: AN INTRODUCTION

Cost-Benefit Analysis (CBA) as a methodology was developed in the United States in the 1930s when the federal government had to decide upon the viability of large publicly funded projects, such as publicly funded irrigation, water supply and hydroelectric schemes. The theory and practice of cost-benefit analysis has evolved from the works of Little and Mirrlees (1969, 1974), Daspupta, Marglin and Sen (UNIDO, 1972), Harberger (1972), Corden (1974), and Squires and van der Tak (1975). The method is widely used and involves a financial, economic and social analysis of the costs and benefits of a project to determine the best course of action for a policy or decision maker with various alterations for the specific circumstances faced by the project.

3.0 COST-BENEFIT SYNTHESIS IN CLIMATE CHANGE POLICY FORMULATION

Several early methods of integrating costs and benefits in the modelling of climate change are Cline (1992) and Nordhaus (1991). The integration of the costs and benefits into a study methodology has progressed towards providing a robust methodology for decision making. The integrated approach brings the cost and benefits together in one modelling exercise and the integration of the physical process and the economic sector as well as the conversion from physical effects to monetary values have been of great significant in policy development and formulation. Further development of integrating the costs and benefits in a modelling methodology can be found in Kaya (1993, 1994).

The policy debate surrounding the issue of global climate change concerns the changed status of the goods in question, from public goods to private goods and determining the market price for these goods. For example, the atmosphere has the attributes of a pure public good (air to breath, or other life support systems, amenity value, and so on) it also has the attribute of a common-property resource (receptacle for wastes, provider of natural resources such as water and fish). In the past, many goods were free public goods and common property goods. The increased scarcity of these goods and the externality impacts associated with free goods have caused a gravitation towards consideration of these goods as private goods with attached property rights. This would require an establishment of a market for these goods and an imputation of market value of these goods with the associated legislative infrastructure to support that market. Siebert (1992) suggests that cost benefit analysis can be used to overcome the possible biased allocations of public goods in other methods of resource allocation, where the market for these resources is imputed rather that allowed to manifestly operate.

The further integration of the cost-benefit methodology within a dynamic optimisation framework allows the feedbacks from the process to interact dynamically to determine the paths of economic and climate variables and thus provides a more realistic modelling approach. The ADICE model of Islam (1995), the DICE model of Nordhaus (1994), the CETA model of Peck and Tiesberg (1995), and the MERGE model of Manne et al. (1995) are just such integrated models and more are being developed.

3.1 Australian Studies

Although there have been various Australian studies that have assessed the economic effects of climate change using a cost effectiveness framework (see Gigas and Islam, 1995 for a survey), only two studies address climate change from cost-benefit framework. The IC (1991) study highlights the difficulties associated with the estimation of the costs and the benefits of climate change and has not estimated the benefits of climate change. Islam (1995) using Nordhaus's (1994) estimate of costs and benefits estimates the costs and benefits of climate change for Australia.

4.0 ADICE MODEL

The ADICE (Nordhaus, 1994 and Islam, 1994) model is an integrated model that incorporates the dynamic greenhouse gas (GHG) emissions and economic variable impacts as well as the economic costs of implementing GHG abatement policies. The ADICE model extends the standard neoclassical optimal economic growth model by incorporating a linkage between a climate sector and the economic sector, hence, the economic effects of climate change due to GHG emissions can be analysed. The model incorporates a full valuation submodel to evaluate the impacts of costs and benefits and hence integrate the cost-benefit analysis in the model framework. The model optimises social utility over a given time horizon subject to the usual economic constraints with the additional environmental constraints. Social utility is defined as the sum of individual utilities and is based on a broad concept of consumption.

The economic sector produces one composite good, assumed to be produced competitively and to be perfectly substitutable with other composite goods. The composite output is optimally allocated by the social planner between consumption and investment to maximise social utility, while population growth and technological progress are assumed to be exogenous. The social planner allocates resources from the economic sector to the climate sector to reduce GHG emissions and to lower the detrimental effects of climate change to the economy. An abstract version of the ADICE model is show below

$$\text{Maximise} \quad \int \quad (1+p)-ptU(c(t),L(t))\,dt$$

Subject to:

(1) Production function $\quad Y(t)=F[O(t),A(t),K(t),L(t)]$
(2) Per capita Consumption $\quad c(t)=C(t)/L(t)$

(3) Output composition Equation $\quad Y(t)=C(t)+I(t)$

(4)	Capital Balance Equation	$K(t+1)=(1-dk)K(t)+I(t)$
(5)	Emissions Equation	$E(t)=[1-m(t)]s(t)Y(t)$
(6)	Emissions Accumulation Equation	$M(t+1)=(1-dm)M(t)+\_[Ew(t)-Ea(t)]$
(7)	Radiative Forcing Equation	$f(t)=4.1[\log(M(t)/590)/\log(2)]+O(t)$
(8)	Climate Change Equation	$T(t+1)=F[M(t),T(t),O(t)]$
(8)	Deep Ocean Temperature	$O(t+1)=F[T(t),O(t)]$
(9)	Damage Function	$D(t)=F[Y(t),T(t)]$
(10)	Cost Function	$TC(t)=F[Y(t),E(t)]$
(12)	Tax on emissions	$Ctax=F[ee(t),kk(t)]$

Where

I	= investment (control)
Ew	= world greenhouse gas emissions (exogenous)
Ea	= Australian greenhouse gas emissions (control)
K	= capital Stock
M	= stock of greenhouse gases
T	= mean atmospheric temperature
O	= mean deep ocean temperature
c	= per capita consumption
D	= climate damage
Y	= GDP
ee	= shadow price of emissions
kk	= shadow price of capital
p	= pure time preference
L	= population (labour supply)
t	= time
δM	= greenhouse gas decay rate
δK	= capital depreciation rate
$Ctax$	= rate of tax on GHG emissions

Source: Islam (1994)

5.0 AUSTRALIAN COST-BENEFIT ESTIMATES FROM ADICE

The aforementioned model was applied to the Australian situation to determine the optimal economic and climate change variables. The two models reported here optimise the emission control rate under two different growth rates of uncontrolled emissions. Model 1 represents an accelerated decrease in GHG emissions while model 2 use an estimate of the true growth rate of GHG emissions.

In the ADICE model it is also assumed that the global warming abatement will induce a cost given by $TC(t)$ and the avoided damage for abatement is given by $D(t)$. The form of the model functions are shown below:

$$\text{Costs} = TC(t) = Y(t).b_r.\mu(t)^{b2}$$
$$\text{Damage Avoided/Benefit} = D(t) = Y(t).\Theta1.T(t)^{\Theta2}$$

where $b1$, $b2$ are the parameters for emission reduction costs function and $TC(t)$ is the total cost of reducing GHG emissions. $\Theta1$, $\Theta2$ are parameters of the damage function and $D(t)$ is the damage from greenhouse warming. The parameters have been calibrated and estimated using previous studies and expert opinion. Fankhauser (1995), Nordhaus (1994) and Cline (1992) have a discussion on the derivation of the cost and damage functions which are based on previous empirical studies and findings.

The cost benefit results of these model are shown in Table I. Model 1 has a 3% discount rate, a GRUE of -0.2168 and the emission control rate is (ECR) is optimised. Model 2 has a 0% discount rate, a GRUE of -0.1168 and the ECR is also optimised.

In model 1 the damage avoided is less than in model 2 this suggests that the benefits of abatement are smaller due to a slower growth in global warming. Model 2 presents the option of a rapidly increasing technology however there is no discounting. Suggesting a symmetry in intergenerational equity exists. If such are the condition with the economy the results suggest that a far greater expenditure in abatement would increase the benefits accruing to climate change. The results show that a zero discount rate would in effect increase the damage caused, disproving the notion that a zero discount rate is required to preserve our natural resources for future generations. What is unclear from the results is what is the effect of the discount rate singularly without the confounding factor of the decrease in the ratio of uncontrolled emissions.

From Table 1 it is evident that the cost of climate change abatement are swamped by the benefit of avoiding climate change. The loss in income due to climate change is exceeded by the expenditure on mitigation of climate change.

Table 1

Costs and benefits of the two models

	Model	1	Period 10	20	30
Damage Avoided	1	0.0	4000	45000	176000
($A Million)	2	0.0	5000	58000	227000
Cost of abatement	1	0.0132	0.0489	0.1839	0.4909
($A Million	2	0.3707	1.916	6.698	8.219

6.0 MERITS AND LIMITATIONS OF COST BENEFIT ANALYSIS: THE OPERATIONAL RULE

Although the applications of cost-benefit analysis to climate change policy formulation have increased recently, its limitations have also been widely argued. The limited applicability of cost-benefit analysis to climate change policy formulation due to the risk and uncertainty of climate change has been stressed in the literature (Clarke, 1991). The problem of non substitutability of different forms of capital, limited availability of required information giving rise to a quasi option value and irreversibility justify the preservation of environmental resource and restrict the use of cost-beneft analysis. In this conditions decisions are in favour of preserving the natural resources if the foregone benefit is significantly evident.

Brown (1993) summarises some arguments for not using cost benefits analysis in climate change as follows: (1) cost-benefit analysis was not developed to analyse projects that have a duration of centuries, (2) it cannot address the uncertainties in the cost and benefit curves and the general uncertainty adequately. (3) discounting is inappropriate for long term concerns of global warming. (4) the use of money in the valuation tool of CBA is not appropriate. (5) it does not address the distributive issues, (6) it includes costs and benefits only to humans.

The merits of cost benefit analysis include the possibility of an integration of the costs and benefits and thus a complete view of the problem is considered. The integenerational equity of the solution is easily determined with its consequent effects. A greater degree of flexibility is provided in determining alternative policy options and decision strategies. As a methodology it allows a unified treatment of the issues that can be used in decision making. Under the same set of assumptions the effects of policy options and other factors can be assessed. Most of the limitations as an operational rule of cost-benefit analysis as highlighted by Brown (1995) can be addressed in the cost-benefit framework and work is progressing to address these modelling limitations (IC, 1991). Most of these criticisms of the CBA approach are valid but they apply to other methods such as expert opinion survey, qualititative analysis, cost effective analysis etc. and as discussed above the limitations of the cost benefit method are being resolved.

The lack of cost-benefit analysis studies in the Australian literature suggests that there is a greater need for undertaking such studies. The IC (1991) has acknowledged the difficulties in using the cost-benefit approach to analyse the effects of climate change, given the reason associated with uncertainty as to the effects of benefits in Australian. However, such cost-benefit approaches have been used and are in use in other parts of the world to investigate the climate change issue. In fact the integration of costs and benefits to address the issue of acid rain in Europe facilititated a solution to the acid rain problem. This suggests that the cost-benefit approach to the climate change issue may also facilitate a solution. The operational rule proposed and implemented in this study is that of valuing all the costs and benefits associated with climate change (not an inconsequential task, and full of uncertainty) and integrating this approach into a dynamic optimisation procedure to provide a basis for decision making for a policy maker. The ADICE results suggest that ADICE study has made a systematic cost-benefit study of climate change in Australia which is operational and provides plausible cost benefit estimates resulting in a development of an improved methodology for Australia.

7.0 CONCLUSIONS

The abatement policies suggested by the model indicate that the costs associated with climate change abatement are smaller than the benefits achieved by the abatement of climate change, although no fixed target of abatement was included in this study. The expenditure of resources to abate climate change will generate less economic damage to the Australian economy than allowing climate change and global warming to occur. The number of cost-benefit studies of climate change around the world has grown rapidly, which suggests that this methodology will provide greater scope for addressing the policy and developmental issues inherent in the climate change literature for Australia.

REFERENCES

Arrow, K., and Anthony, F., (1974), "Environmental Preservation Uncertainty and Irreversibility", Quarterly Journal of Economics, vol. 88, pp. 312-19.

Brown, L.R.,(1993), State of the World 1993, Earthscan, London.

Clarke, H., (1991), "Risk, Uncertainty and Irreversibility: Implications for Sustainable Development", Paper to ESD Intersectoral Workshop, June.

Cline, W.R.,(1992),The Economics of Global Warming, Institute for International Economics, Washington, DC, USA.

Corden, W.M., (1974), Trade Policy and Economic Welfare, Oxford University Press, London.

Fankhauser, S.,(1995),"The Social Cost of Greenhouse Gas Emissions:An Expected Value Approach",The Energy Journal,15(2),157-184.

Fankhauser, S., (1993), "The Economic Costs of Global Warming: Some Monetary Estimates", In Kaya, Y., Nakicenovic, N., Nordhaus, N.D.,and Toth, F.L.,(eds), (1993), Cost, Impacts, and Benefits of CO2 Mitigation, CP-93-2,IIASA, Laxenburg, Austria.

Gigas, J., and Islam, S.N.M., (1995), "Modelling of Climate Change and Economic Growth in Australia: Issues, Models and Implications - How Far Have the Modelling Exercise Been Successful in the Formulation of Optimal Policy", Seminar Paper, CSES, Victoria University, Melbourne.

Harris, S., (1996), "Economics of the Environment: A Survey", The Economic Record, vol. 72, no. 217, June.

Industry Commission (IC) (1991), Costs and Benefits of Reducing Greenhouse Gas Emissions, 2 vols., Report No. 15, AGPS, Canberra.

Islam, S.M.N.,(1994), "Australian Dynamic Integrated Model of Climate and the Economy (ADICE)", CSES, Victoria University, Melbourne.

Islam, S.M.N., (1995), Australian Dynamic Integrated Model of Climate and the Economy (ADICE): Model Specification, Numerical Implementation and Policy Implications, Seminar Paper presented on 7 December 1995, Centre for Strategic Economic Studies, Victoria University of Technology, Melbourne.

Little, I.M.D., Mirrlees, J.A.,(1969), Manual for Industrial Analysis in Developing Countries, II, Social Cost Benefit Analysis, OECD, Paris.

Little, I.M.D., Mirrlees, J.A.,(1974),Project Appraisal and Planning for Developing Countries, Heinemann Educational Books, London.

Little, I.M.D., Mirrlees, J.A.,(1990), "Project Appraisal and Planning Twenty Years On", Proceedings of the World Bank Annual Conference on Development Economics.

Kaya, Y, Nakicenovic, N., Nordhaus, N.D.,and Toth, F.L.,eds, (1993), Cost, Impacts, and Benefits of CO2 Mitigation, CP-93-2,IIASA, Laxenburg, Austria.

Manne A., Mendelsohn, R., Richels, R.,(1995),"MERGE: A Model for Evaluating Regional and Global Effects of GHG Reduction Policies", Energy Policy,23(1),17-34.

Nordhaus, W., (1994), Managing the Global Commons: The Economics of Climate Change, MIT Press. London.

Nordhaus, W.D.,(1991), "A Survey of the Costs of Reduction of Greenhouse Gases", The Energy Journal,12(1):37-65.

226

OECD, (1993), The Economic Costs of Reducing CO2 Emissions, OECD, Paris.

Peck, S.C., Teisberg, T.J.,(1995), "International CO2 emissions Control: An Analysis using CETA", Energy Policy,23(4/5),297-308.

Siebert, H.,(1992), Economics of the Environment, Springer-Verlag, London.

Squire, L., (1989), "Project Evaluation in Theory and Practice", in H.Chenery and T.N. Srinivasan (eds), Handbook of Development Economics,Vol 2, North Holland, Amsterdam.

Squire, L., van dar Tak, H.G. (1975), Economic Analysis of Projects, John Hopkins University Press, London.

UNIDO, (1972), Guidelines for Project Evaluation, United Nations, New York.

CHAPTER - 13

THE EFFECT OF SOCIAL TIME PREFERENCE ON THE FUTURE OF THE AUSTRALIAN ECONOMY AND ENVIRONMENT: FINDINGS FROM THE AUSTRALIAN DYNAMIC INTEGRATED CLIMATE AND ECONOMY MODEL (ADICE)[1]

Sardar M.N. Islam and Jim Gigas

ABSTRACT

A dynamic integrated climate and environmental model of Australia (ADICE), which is a dynamic optimization model of the Australian economy, is used to investigate the economic, environmental and intergenerational equity issues facing Australia. A shift in the value used for the Social Time Preference has a major impact on economic thought and these changes will foster new approaches to policy issues. This paper outlines the model and the economic, environmental and policy implications for sustainable development under various Social Time Preference scenarios. It is found that a lower Social Time Preference implies intergenerational equity in Australian society requires higher efforts for environmental management or higher rates of emission controls.

1. INTRODUCTION

The industrialisation process has brought the world prosperity and wealth and it has also brought the world environmental degradation and higher atmospheric concentrations of greenhouse gases (GHG). The IPCC (1990)

---

[1]A summary version of this paper was presented at the ANZEE Society Ecological Economics Conference, Coffs Harbour, Australia on November 19–23, 1995.

has confirmed that GHG concentration in the atmosphere will increase and thus average global temperature will rise. The effect of a temperature rise of the order of 1.5–4.5°C (IPCC, 1990) will have significant effects on the Australian Economy. Australia's severe climate variability, when combined with land, air and water degradation, has fed the effects of global warming. The changing patterns of climatic conditions will cause restructuring of sectors in the economy with consequent costs and benefits. However, attitude changes to intergenerational issues can cause a shift in optimal policy paths for Australian economic sustainability and growth. The choice of an appropriate social time preference is thwart with enormous difficulties and controversy. An understanding of the implications of the social time preference in sustainable environmental management is imperative.

The objective of this paper is to investigate the implications of alternative social time preference rates in sustainable environmental management and global warming policy formulation in Australia. This study adopts the ADICE model developed by Islam (Islam, 1994) by adapting DICE (Nordhaus, 1994). The structure of the paper is as follows; section (2) will discuss the social time preference rate and its use in global warming and sustainable economic growth, section (3) will outline the ADICE model and its features, section (4) will discuss the results of three ADICE optimisation runs this will be followed with section (5) the conclusion drawn from the three simulation runs.

2. SOCIAL TIME PREFERENCE, GLOBAL WARMING AND SUSTAINABLE ECONOMIC GROWTH AND MANAGEMENT

The social rate of time preference is the intertemporal preference of social wants between current consumption and future consumption. The STPR determines the pattern of intertemporal and thus intratemporal allocations of resources. The STPR is composed of the pure rate of time preference arising from myopia or impatience and the second component represents declining marginal utility due to the increase in consumption. The STPR is given by:

$$STPR = p + ng \qquad (1)$$

where p is the rate of pure time preference, g is the growth rate of consumption and n is the income elasticity of marginal utility. In the ADICE model the value of n is assumed to be one.

The relationship between output and environmental quality (global warming) and sustainable development is linked therefore by the social discount rate through the effects of intertemporal allocations of economic and environmental resources. Output produced today also uses environmental inputs, and generates global warming that will limit the possibilities for future output and sustainable development. Theory suggests a higher discount rate will increase the rate of resource extraction and will increase global warming. Nordhaus (1994) suggests and uses a pure time preference rate of 3% while Cline (1992) suggest a pure time preference rate of 0% and a discount rate on goods and services of 1.5% per annum. However, as Nordhaus (1995) points out the approach is inconsistent with the actual saving and investment decisions. Manne (1995), in an empirical study also suggests that a discount rate of less than 5% is unrealizable and unsustainable for similar reasons given to Nordhaus (1994); the level of investment is higher than expected or which actually occurs and the return on capital is too low.

3. OUTLINE OF ADICE MODEL

There are numerous models used to investigate the economic impact of climate change. An OECD (1993) report surveys several global models, while BIE (1995) and Gigas and Islam (1995), highlight a series of Australian studies. Most of these models have assumptions and constraints that do not allow the exposition of the Australian situation. World models focus on the world GHG emissions and policies and do not model the Australian situation explicitly. The Australian models are limited by the comparative static and/or partial equilibrium framework employed and do not consider the full costs and benefits associated with climate change. DICE and ADICE are part of an emerging modelling trend to encompass the full costs and benefits of climate change and these models are able to provide greater insights into the issues possible solutions and policy problems that will need to be faced.

The ADICE model is an extension of the standard Ramsey-type economic growth model and is essentially a neoclassical growth model (Koopmans, 1967; Nordhaus, 1994 and Ramsey, 1928). It incorporates the linkages between GHG emissions and output. This allows the economic effects of climate change to be analysed. The model contains two sectors. In the economic sector, only one good is produced and is assumed to be perfectly substitutable and to be produced competitively. Population growth and technological change are modelled as exogenous variables. The social planner withdraws resources from the economic sector and allocates them to the environmental sector in order to reduce GHG emissions and thus reduce the climate change effect. The social planner maximises utility by choosing the optimal trajectory of consumption, investment and emission control variables. A dynamic growth model with the above features is developed within the structure of optimal control theory to investigate the path of the Australian economy.

The data for the model were obtained from published sources (Australian (RBA, 1991) or International) or calibrated from similar studies (Nordhaus, 1994). The ADICE model is fully specified and shown in Appendix 1.

4. DISCUSSION OF RESULTS

ADICE is solved for three different pure time preference rates. In the following sections the results of the three runs are reported. Each run spans a time frame of 40 periods with each period spanning 10 years. The three runs are based on the previously described ADICE model specification detailed in Appendix 1. Models 1, 2 and 3 are simulation with pure time preference rates of 3%, 0% and –3% respectively. Some of the results generated by the three models are shown in Table 1.

The relationship between the PTPR and the STPR is shown in the previous section and the PTPR is positively related to the STPR. Any alteration of the PTPR will induce a similar change in the social time preference rate. The results are discussed with reference to the model parameter used, the PTPR. However, the results can be attributed to the STPR. The model sequence 1 to 3, represents an intertemporal shift in consumption from current consumption to future consumption.

4.1. Climate and Economic Variables

The model results show that under a decreasing pure time preference rate (PTPR) the level of output increases for all periods. This result suggests a lower PTPR generates growth and increases utility for current and future generations. Although the growth rates for output and consumption

Table 1
Australian Climate/Emission variables under Models

	Model	Period Growth#	1	10	20	30	40
Output	1	1.320	0.114	0.423	1.593	4.252	7.095
($A trillion)	2	1.825	0.107	0.653	2.737	7.311	9.576
	3	1.825	0.107	0.653	2.737	7.311	9.576
Per capita	1	0.587	6.689	12.005	27.351	53.838	74.702
Income	2	0.824	6.689	15.272	34.901	68.829	92.469
(A$000)	3	1.085	6.293	18.521	46.990	92.510	100.815
Per Capita	1	0.530	5.334	9.047	20.889	41.456	69.416
Consumption	2	0.843	4.051	9.376	21.918	43.880	92.469
(A$000)	3	1.232	1.876	6.343	16.241	35.300	88.482
Saving rate	1	–	0.201	0.246	0.231	0.230	0.070
	2	−0.015	0.391	0.305	0.372	0.363	0.112**
	3	0.053	0.693	0.657	0.654	0.619	0.112
Interest rate	1	3.230	0.002	0.048	0.045	0.043	0.093
	2	1.620	0.002	0.010	0.008	0.007	0.044
	3	2.163	−0.002	−0.017	−0.020	−0.020	0.029
*Temp.	1	2.565	0.200	2.517	4.375	5.307	5.921
Atmosphere C	2	2.565	0.200	2.518	4.377	5.310	5.925
	3	2.562	0.200	2.511	4.370	5.307	5.928

#percentage growth per annum from period 1 to period 10
*Variable represents world value
**Period 39 result

have increased under the lower PTPR (1.320% and 1.262% to 1.825% and 2.052% respectively from period 1 to 10), per capita consumption has fallen drastically over all periods (A$5,334 to A$1,876 in period 1), and the saving rate has increased across all periods (20.1% to 69.3%, in period 1) under a lower PTPR. This effect of a lower STPR is to increase future consumption at the expense of current consumption. The increase in capital stock formation is part of this scenario and so is the general rise in the saving rate as investment is the only alternative to current consumption. The penalty for generating greater growth by affecting the STPR will dampen current consumption and utility.

The CO_2 Emissions due to the choices of PTPR also vary. In general, the lower the PTPR the higher is the growth rate of CO_2 emissions. The effect is caused by the temporal distribution of the costs and benefits of emission abatement. The lower discount rate will cause greater accumulation of current costs and less of future costs. It should be noted, that while the CO_2 emissions for Australia show dramatic changes over the three scenarios, the effect on the world atmospheric temperature is very minor. The Australian policies and emissions have very little effect on the lower ocean temperature, radiative forcing, CO_2 atmospheric concentration and atmospheric temperature. This suggests that Australian emissions seem to have relevance only for Australia and the relevance appears to be an economic relevance.

The policy variables of saving rate and the emission control rate vary significantly under the three models. Figure 1 shows the time path of the mission control rate over the span of th eoptimisation run. With a lower PTPR, higher rates of saving and higher emission controls (0.010 to 0.990, in period 1) are needed to maximise the utility of society. The mechanism used to accomplish the reduction in GHG emissions is a tax charged on emissions, with higher levels of tax being charged with the increase in emission controls required.

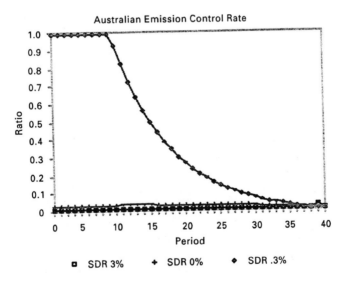

Figure 1. Emission Control Rate.

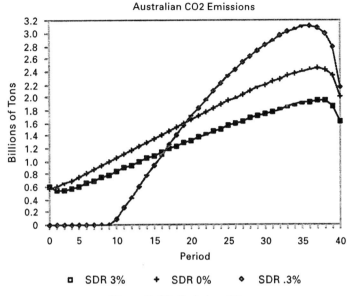

Figure 2. CO_2 Emissions *B/t*.

Given the PTPR for a society, Figure 1 and Figure 2 suggest that an optimal policy would be to strictly reduce CO_2 emissions for a negative PTPR while policy would be to delay the costs of CO_2 abatement if the PTPR was positive.

The issues surrounding policy formulation concerning the determination of the best policy to address global warming and social welfare is vested in the situation the society faces and in the pure time preference and social time preference that exists in the society.

4.2. Policies

Under a PTPR of 3% the optimum saving rate and emission control rate are 20% and 1% respectively. This policy regime is based on current and historical practice and consistent with the observed behaviour (Nordhaus, 1994). The shift to a 0% PTPR (no time discounting) alters the optimal path of the policy variables. The rate of saving increases to 39% and the rate of emission reduction increase to 3.2%. A further shift of the PTPR to −3% causes the paths of saving to increase to 69% and the emission control rate to increase further to 99%, and unsustainable levels. As the social time preference rate decreases the optimal policy measure is to increase the savings rate and emission control rate. The tax required to bring about these levels of emission control grows and becomes excessive when the PTPR is decreases (A\$0.026 for a PTPR of 3%, A\$0.568 for a PTPR of 0%, and A\$2,846.30 for a PTPR of –3%).

The results suggest that policies that assume a lower PTPR and thus a lower social discount rate would cause per capita consumption to decline initially. As a policy option for government and the community at large, this may not be desirable or acceptable. The argument that would need to be made is the drop in per capita consumption is for the good of future generations. Associated with falling PTPR is the decline is the marginal utility of capital (interest rate). Under a –3% PTPR the return on capital assets is negative suggesting that returns on capital will incur losses or there is abundance of project funding.

4.3. Intertemporal Allocation

The modelling approach taken suggests that the policy planner has the leavers of policy (Emission Control rate and saving rate) at his/her disposal. The policy planner exercises these policy leavers and determines that, as the PTPR decreases, the intertemporal allocation of resources increases towards future generations, the levels of savings/investment increase and the levels of emission reduction via the emission control rate increase. The decrease in the PTPR from 3% to –3% decrease the level of consumption available for the current generation. The level of output produced is largely unaffected, but the allocation of resources is. Initially, the per capita consumption is reduced from A\$5,334 for a PTPR of 3% to A\$1,876 for a PTPR of –3%. The smaller PTPR benefits future generations by increasing current capital formation and savings, while the current generation has higher emission reductions to achieve via larger GHG taxes and less consumption. The policy conditions mentioned in section 4.2 above, remain valid and consistent across all 40 periods of the three models.

The policy planner's choice variable of the emission control rate would be set such that emission abatement is achieved (High emission control rate) when discounted future costs are increased or lower emission control rates when the future costs of abatement are expected to be smaller. If the policy planner takes the view that, as Ramsey (1928) has, "That time discounting is ethical indefensible and is caused by a weakness of imagination" and causes a weighting of the current generation over the future generation. Then intergenerational equity requires more effort be expended to abate CO2 emissions or greater environmental management efforts to reduce the effects of CO_2 emissions.

The policy planner will need to weigh the distribution of benefits and cost across the several generations and then decide of the policy option that is desirable. The ADICE model gives a quantified assessment of the value for such a temporal decision by the policy planner.

4.4. Sustainability of the economy

Sustainable economic development falls into several categories. Strong sustainability requires that the rate of change of a vector of desirable social objectives (D) be non decreasing over time, while weak sustainability requires the trend in the rate of change of desirable social objective (vector D), be positive (Pearce et al., 1994). The rate of change in per capita consumption, income and saving for the three models presented is positive. The growth rates for output over the first 10 periods under decreasing PTPR range from 1.32% for a PTPR of 3% to 1.825% for a PTPR of 0% and −3%. This suggests that the models are all sustainable. One aspect of concern in the modelling is the effect of a lower PTPR is to increase the rate at which resources and emissions are used. This effect is disconcerting as it suggests that although, the sustainability of the economy may be achieved with a lower discount rate the higher discount rate is preferable since it flattens the growth of emissions and taxes. In fact the rate of resource use and consumption will be greater as is evident from Figure 1 and Figure 2.

If sustainability of the economy and the environment are desirable, then the best option would be to use the current settings as described by Nordhaus (1994). A removal of time discounting as suggested by Ramsey (1928) and others would lower current consumption and increase the speed of consumption towards unsustainability.

4.5. Choice of STPR and Environmental Management

A nonzero PTPR biases the intertemporal allocation of resources by valuing the distribution of costs and benefits with a discounted weight.

The results in Table 1 show that the emission control rate has risen sharply when a zero and unbiased weighting of utility (and thus intergenerational equity) is considered. Greater emission reductions or more environmental management will be required to curtail GHG emissions. A PTPR of −3% causes emissions to be reduced sharply, but causes the emission control rate to increase beyond sustainable levels (0.990, this is unrealisable). A PTPR of 3% provides a smaller growth path of emissions while starting at a higher and more environmentally and economically sustainable emission level.

If the policy planner is of a mind to reduce the level of CO_2 emission released into the atmosphere this would require a lower PTPR and thus a lower STPR. The effects of such a lower STPR would be to increase the costs to the current generation of emission abatement taxation and suppress the level of per capita consumption and income. The benefits of such a proposal would be to cause the growth rate to increase generally and thus provide for future generations. A balance between these competing desirable outcomes must be reached by the policy planner.

4.6. Formulation of the STPR for sustainable economic growth

While all three models are sustainable when per capita consumption and per capita income is considered, models 2 and 3 are unsustainable when other variables are considered. The optimal paths of the policy variables (savings and the emission control rate) under the STPR of 0% and −3% are unrealisable and unsustainable, Nordhaus (1994) and Manne (1995) comes to a similar conclusion. The carbon tax level under model 3 is also very high and may not be palatable, if implemented. This leaves the most effective model and policy formulation for sustainable economic growth as a 3% PTPR with 20% savings and 1% emission reduction rate with a small carbon tax.

5. CONCLUSION

The model results of a climate-economic system suggest the PTPR and thus the STPR have a large effect on the path and conditions of sustainability of the Australian economy. A decrease in the STPR will cause greater levels of savings and emission control while maintaining current levels of output and reducing per capita consumption. With all three social discount rates, the change in per capita consumption and income is positive implying economic sustainability. However, the effects of lower STPR (0% and –3%) on the policy variables of emissions control rate, and saving are unrealisable and thus unsustainable. This leads to the conclusion that a lower STPR that implies more intergenerational equity in Australian society requires higher efforts for environmental management or higher rates of emission controls. The conclusion reached is the best STPR (from those used) for environmental as well as economic sustainability is the 3% STPR.

APPENDIX 1. ADICE MODEL SPECIFICATIONS

Equations of the model

The optimization model with exogenous technical progress.

(0) Objective Function:
$$\text{Max} \sum_{\substack{i=1 \\ \{c(t)\}}}^{t_T} U[c(t), L(t)](1+p)^{-t}$$

Definition of Utility
$$U[c(t), L(t)] = L(t)\frac{c(t)^{1-a}-1}{1-a}$$

Subject to

1. Per capita consumption $c(t) = C(t)/L(t)$
2. Production Function $Q(t) = \Omega(t)A(t)K(t)^t L(t)^{1-t}$
3. Output Composition Equation $Q(t) = C(t) + I(t)$
4. Capital Balance Equation $K(t) = (1 - d_K)K(t-1) + I(t-1)$
5. Emissions Equation $E(t) = [1 - m(t)]s(t)Q(t)$
6. Emissions Accumulation Equation $M(t) - 590 = \beta[E(t-1) + \text{Erow}(t)] +$
    $(1 - d_M)[M(t-1) - 590]$
7. Radioactive Forcing Equation $F(t) = 4.1\{\log[M(t)/590]/\log(2)\} + O(t)$
8. Climate Change Equation:

$T(t) = T(t-1) + (1/R_1)\{F(t) - fT(t-1) - (R_2/t_{12})[T(t-1) - T^*(t-1)]\}$
$T^*(t) = T^*(t-1) + (1/R_2)\{(R_2/t_{12})[T(t-1) - T^*(t-1)]\}$

9. Damage Function $D(t) = Q(t)Q_1 T(t)Q_2$
10. Emissions Reducing Cost Function $TC(t) = Q(t)b_1 m(t)b_2$
11. Relationship showing the impact $\Omega(t) = (1 - b_1 m(t)b_2)/[1 + Q_1 T(t)Q_2]$
of emissions reduction and
climate change on output

Initial values of parameters in the ADICE model

$a = 1$ [elasticity of marginal utility with respect to consumption]
$b_1 = 0.0686$ [fraction of output per unit emissions control]
$b_2 = 2.887$ [exponent of control cost]
$\beta = 0.64$ [pure number]
$t = 0.35$ [elasticity of output with respect to capital]
$d_K = 0.08$ [per year]
$d_M = 0.0833$ [per decade]
$d_A = 0.02$ [per decade]
dpop= 0.050 [per decade]
$f = 1.41$ [degrees $C/W - m^2$]
$Q_1 = 0.00148$ [fraction of output per degrees C squared]
$Q_2 = 2$ [exponent of damage function]
$p = 0.03$ [per year]
gpop (1990) = 0.100 [per decade]
g_A (1990) = 0.0206 [per year]
g_s (1990) = $- 0.1168$ [per decade]
K (1990) = 0.687107 [trillion Australian dollars, 1990prices]
M (1990) = 727 [billion tons CO_2 equivalent, carbon weight]
L (1990) = 17.068 [million persons]
$1/R_1 = 0.226$ [degrees cm^2/watt-decades]
$R_2/_{112} = 0.44$ [watts/degrees cm^2]
Q (1990) = 0.266047 [trillion Australian dollars, 1990 prices]
s (1990) = 0.519 [billion tons CO_2 equivalent per trillion dollars, 1990 prices]
T (1990) = 0.2 [degrees C]
T^*(1990) = 0.1 [degrees C]

Major variables in the model
Exogenous Variables

$A(t)$ = level of technology
$L(t)$ = labor inputs
$O(t)$ = forcings of exogenous greenhouse gases
Erow(t) = rest of world emissions (World(t) = Erow(t) + $E(t)$)
t = time

Parameters

a = elasticity of marginal utility of consumption
b_1, b_2 = parameters of emissions-reduction costs function
β = marginal atmospheric retention ratio of GHGs (w)
t = elasticity of output with respect to capital
d_K = rate of depreciation of the capital stock
d_M = rate of transfer of GHGs from upper to lower reservoir (w)
f = feedback parameter in climate model (w)
p = pure rate of social time preference
R_1 = thermal capacity of the upper layer (w)
R_2 = thermal capacity of deep oceans (w)
$s(t)$ = GHG emissions/output ratio

n_2 = transfer rate from upper to lower reservoir (w)

Q_1, Q_2 = parameters of damage function

Endogenous Variables

$C(t)$	= total consumption
$c(t)$	= per capita consumption
$D(t)$	= damage from greenhouse warming
$E(t)$	= emissions of greenhouse gases (CO_2 and CFCs only)
$F(t)$	= radiative forcing from GHGs (w)
$\Omega(t)$	= output scaling factor due to emissions controls and to damages from climate change
$K(t)$	= capital stock
$M(t)$	= mass of greenhouse gases in atmosphere (w)
$Q(t)$	= gross domestic product
$T(t)$	= atmospheric temperature relative to base period (w)
$T^*(t)$	= deep-ocean temperature relative to base period (w)
$TC(t)$	= total cost of reducing GHG emissions
$u(t)$	= $u[c(t)]$ = utility of per capita consumption

Policy Variables

$I(t)$	= investment
$m(t)$	= rate of emissions reduction

Source: Nordhaus (1994) and Islam (1994)

REFERENCES

Barnes, D.W., Edmonds, J.A. and Reilly, J.M. (1992). Use of the Edmonds-Reilly Model to model energy-related greenhouse gas emissions. OECD Economics Department Working Papers, No.113 (April).

BIE, 1995. Greenhouse gas abatement and burden Sharing: An analysis of efficiency and equity issues for Australia. Research Report 66, AGPS, Canberra, Australia.

Cline, W. (1992). The Economics of Global Warming, Institute of International Economics. Washington.

Gigas, J. and Islam, S.N.M. (1995). Modelling of Climate Change and Economic Growth in Australia: Issues, Models and Implications – How Far Have the Modelling Exercise Been Successful in the Formulation of Optimal Policy. Seminar Paper, CSES, Victoria University, Melbourne.

Hanslow, K., Hinchy, M. and Fisher, B. (1994). International Greenhouse Economic Modelling, ABARE paper presented at the 'Greenhouse 94: An Australian – New Zealand Conference on Climate Change'. Wellington, New Zealand, 10–14 October.

Intergovernmental Panel on Climate Change (IPCC), 1990. Climate Change: The IPCC scientific assessment. Houghton, J., Jenkins, G. and Ephraums, J., Cambridge University Press, New York.

Industry Commission (IC), 1991. Costs and Benefits of Reducing Greenhouse Gas Emissions. 2 vols., Report No. 15, AGPS, Canberra.

Islam, S.N. (1994). Australian Dynamic Integrated Climate-Economy Model (ADICE). CSES, Victoria University, Melbourne.

Kaya, Y. Nakicenovic, N., Nordhaus, W.D., Toth, F.L. (Editors), 1993. The Costs, Impacts, and Benefits of CO_2 Mitigation. Proceedings of a Workshop Held on 28–30 September 1992 at IIASA, Laxenburg, Austria.

Koopmans, T. (1967). Objectives, constraints and outcomes in optimal growth models. Econometrica 35: 1–15.

Lind, R.C., 1995. Intergenerational equity, discounting and the role of cost-benefit analysis in evaluating global climate policy. In: Nakicenovic, N., Nordhaus, W.D., Richels, R. and Toth, F.L., (Editors). Energy Policy. 23 (4/5): pp 379–390.

Manne A.S. (1995). The rate of time preference: Implications for the greenhouse debate. In: Nakicenovic, N., Nordhaus, W.D., Richels, R. and Toth, F.L. (Editors). Energy Policy. 23 (4/5): pp 391–394.

Manne, A.S. (1992). Global 2100: Alternative scenarios for reducing carbon emissions. OECD Economics Department Working Papers, No.111 (April).

McKibbin, W. (1994). New developments in multi-country modelling: Evaluating the Uruguay Round and Carbon Tax in Australia. Paper presented at the 1994 Conference of Economists, Gold Coast, 25–29 September.

Nordhaus, W. (1994). Managing the Global Commons: The Economics of Climate Change, MIT Press. London.

OECD, 1993. The Economic Costs of Reducing CO_2 Emissions. OECD, Paris.

Ramsey, F.P. (1928). The Mathematical Theory of Saving. The Economic Journal, Dec, 543–59.

Reserve Bank of Australia (RBA), (1991). Australian Economic Statistics: 1949–50 to 1989–90, Occasional Paper no. 8, Ambassador Press.

CHAPTER - 14

AN ECONOMIC AND ENVIRONMENTAL ASSESSMENT OF HERBICIDE-RESISTANT AND INSECT/PEST-RESISTANT CROPS

David Pimentel and Madinah S. Ali

ABSTRACT

The use of biotechnology to develop insect/pest-resistant crops has the potential to increase crop yields while at the same reducing the use of insecticides and environmental pollution. However, the development and use of herbicide-resistant crops has limited potential and, in most cases, will result in increased herbicide use without any increase in crop yields. The end result will be increased pesticide use and pollution and high production costs for the farmer.

1. INTRODUCTION

"I believe it is far better for mankind to be struggling with new problems caused by abundance rather than the old problem of famine". Norman Borlaug, *"the father of the Green Revolution"* made this statement when he accepted the 1970 Nobel Peace Prize (Borlaug, 1972). The Green Revolution took place in the 1960's and 1970's were new varieties of rice and wheat were developed that substantially increased crop yields through the use of improved irrigation, fertilizers, and chemical pesticides (Hyami, 1981).[1]

---

[1]It mainly took place in Asia, and it is commonly referred to as the new seed-fertilizer technology period in agricultural development (Ruttan, 1982). Chemical pesticides include insecticides, fungicides, and herbicides which control insects, viruses, and weeds respectively.

242

The purpose of the Green Revolution was to increase food production in the United States and world that would eventually eradicate world hunger. In 1965, U.S. farmers were able to increase their yields, and supply 100 million people with needed cereal grains in developing countries. Between 1965 and 1969, new varieties of wheat and rice plantings increased from 800,000 ha to 14 million ha in Asia, accounting for one-tenth of total grain acreage worldwide (Brown, 1970). However, that abundance of food provided by the Green Revolution did not help to alleviate the hunger in the world, but it did help reduce some malnutrition and poverty (Eicher & Staatz, 1990). Furthermore, it caused several environmental problems which continue to plague modern society today. These problems caused by the heavy use of fertilizers, chemical pesticides, and irrigation during the Green Revolution lead to significant environmental pollution. However, in 1978, per capita irrigated lands for major agronomic crops in the United States., Asia, and the Middle East started to decline (FAO Fertilizer year book, 1992 & Postel, 1996).[2]

During the 1970's and 1980's in Asia, 75% of total yield increases in rice and wheat varieties was due to improved irrigation systems and heavy fertilize use. Since the late 1980's there is evidence of a steady decline in total cereal yields in both Pakistan and India (Byerlee, 1989). Furthermore, environmental problems such as the contamination of groundwater by pesticides has increased human and animal health problems; reduced the numbers of wild animals and plants (i.e. biodiversity); and increased green house gases which contribute to global warming (GREAN Report, 1995).

Because of these environmental problems, a transition is taking place in the agricultural and food industries. The trend now is to reduce dependence on pesticides and utilize biointensive integrated pest management systems (IPM) (Benbrook and Groth, 1997). Biointensive IPM promotes the reduction in the use of chemical pesticides by 50% on major agronomic crops, and advocates the use of genetically altered crops (i.e. transgenic crops), biopesticides, and natural products (Benbrook and Groth, 1997, Agra Quest, 1997 and Pimentel, 1997)[3] Furthermore, Pimentel et al.

---

[2]Major agronomic crops are soybeans, corn, wheat, and cotton.
[3]Genetically altered crops are crops that have been changed through insertion of DNA which makes the crop resistant to weeds, pests, or viruses – the most widely used are herbicide resistant crops (HRCs) and pest-virus resistant crops.

(1991) confirmed that by substituting nonchemical alternatives for pesticides it would be possible to reduce the total usage of U.S. agricultural pesticides by about 50% while maintaining crop yields and cosmetic standards. This change or transition is due to three main social, environmental, and economic forces which are: 1) the current threat to global food security; 2) the need for environmentally sound sustainable agriculture; and 3) the private sector's role in marketing genetically-altered crops such as herbicide-resistant crops and pest resistant crops (i.e. modern agricultural biotechnology).[4]

Global Food Security: By the year 2025, the world population will be more than 8 billion, and 85% of the population will be in developing countries. The world food supply would have doubled and the number of malnourished people would increase from the current 2 billion to possibly 3 billion people. Scientists, economists, and sociologists claim that the global food supply must increase annually by 2% to 3% in order to maintain food security. Furthermore, it is believed that modern agricultural biotechnology techniques such as genetically altered herbicide-resistant crops are essential to increase agricultural and food production (Leisinger, 1995).

Recently, the Global Research on the Environmental and Agricultural Nexus for the 21st Century (GREAN) which is an initiative by researchers among U.S. universities, Consultative Group on International Agricultural Research Centers (CGIAR), and developing country institutions have collaborated to transfer herbicide-resistant crops and other genetically engineered crops from the United States to developing countries, hoping to increase food production and reduce malnutrition and hunger. This hopefully would be accomplished, while lessening environmental degradation caused by the heavy use of insecticides, fungicides, herbicides (GREAN Report, 1995).

Environmental Movement for Sustainable Agriculture: Scientists argue that insecticides, fungicides and herbicides have lead to increased

---

Biopesticides use living organisms such as microorganisms and fatty acid compounds, the most common microorganism is Bacillus thuringiensis (Bt) which combats pests (Agra Quest, 1997, Biotechnology Industry Organization, 1997). Natural Products are substances produced by microbes, plants, and other organisms which kill pests (Agra Quest, 1997).

[4]Modern agricultural biotechnology refers to the use of technological innovation in agricultural and related products by utilizing scientific techniques such as recombinant deoxyribonucleic acid (rDNA) (i.e. genetic engineering),which has lead to the creation of herbicide, viral, and insect resistant plants (Caswell et al., 1994, Krimsky & Wrubel, 1996).

244

resistance among weeds, insects, pests, and plant pathogens. The heavy use of pesticides has contributed to a loss of diversity in plant and animal species (Pimentel et al., 1996). According to Ian Heap's report, *the International Survey of Herbicide Resistant Weeds*, a total of 185 weed species have evolved herbicide resistance worldwide. Most of the weed species are resistant to more than one herbicide chemical (Heap, 1996, Benbrook & Groth, 1996).[5] Herbicide-resistance glyphosate, been reported in a few weed species, including the rye grass in Australia (Gressel, 1997). When weed species becomes resistant to herbicides, it results in abundant weed growth, which often leads to reduced crop production. Furthermore, this resistance and increased herbicide use has had negative effects on the soil biota and environment in general.

Recently, the U.S. Congress passed the Food Quality Protection Act of 1996 which would reduce the use of old type pesticides like atrazine, known to cause environmental problems (Benbrook & Groth, 1997). This was a major legal achievement to reduce some of the problems caused by these hazardous pesticides. Even though, the U.S. Environmental Protection Agency (EPA) has prohibited the use of some of the worst pesticides in the market place, it still approves for use approximately 10 new pesticides for each one it takes off the market place (Brenbrook et al., 1996). This is occuring at a time when pesticide residues are being found increasingly in the food and water supplies (Goldburg et al., 1990). The private sector feels pressure from environmental groups and the high costs of regulations for the development of new pesticides. Chemical companies appear to be changing their approach and plan to incorporate biotechnology pest control in their development programs.

Private Sector's Role in Biotechnology

Companies have invested heavily in the field testing of genetically engineered crops either through in-house agricultural biotechnology research programs or obtaining licenses from scientists of their technological inventions. Their strategy is to sell the farmer genetically-altered seed of herbicide-resistant crops along with needed pesticides. Thus, they will profit from both the sale of seed and the herbicide

---

[5]Herbicide resistant weeds are weeds that have the ability to survive herbicide treatment (Heap, 1996).

chemical. For instance, the agrochemical company Monsanto markets and distributes "Roundup Ready", the herbicide-resistant soybean seed along with chemical herbicide glyphosate to the farmer. This combination of the resistant crop and herbicide may reduce the use of herbicide per hectare.

The economic reasons behind the development of herbicide-resistant crops are: 1) high costs involved in developing new herbicides; 2) public pressure from environmental groups to reduce the use of pesticides in agriculture; and 3) the lower regulatory costs involved in developing herbicide-resistant technology compared to developing a new herbicide (Ollinger and Pope, 1996).

Furthermore, U.S. companies, such as Monsanto, are now forming alliances with international research institutions to transfer biotechnology to developing countries. To date, Monsanto has formed collaborations with Mexico's public Center of Research and Advanced Studies (CINVESTAV) to develop transgenic potatoes with virus resistance in potatoes (Raman, 1996). These public-private collaborations have implications for the future transfer of genetically-engineered crops to developing countries.

Currently, there are two major types of genetically-altered crops being introduced in the marketplace, they are herbicide-resistant crops and insect pest-resistant crops. This paper will focus on the costs and benefits of these two types of genetically-engineered crops.

HERBICIDE-RESISTANT CROPS

Herbicides are synthetic chemicals used to control weeds in specific crops. Herbicides in some cases have contributed to an increase in crop yields, which have decreased farm populations (Duke, 1996). Currently, herbicides account for 60% to 70% of pesticides sold in the United States (Kirshner, 1994, & Duke, 1996). Major agronomic crops such as corn, cotton, and soybeans have 90 to 95% their acreage treated (Caswell et al., 1995, Krimsky et al., 1996, Ollinger & Pope, 1996), while only 50% of wheat acreage is treated (Krimsky et al., 1996).

Despite the continuous industrial support to produce new herbicides, there is a trend now for agrochemical companies such as Monsanto to reduce their pesticide business and move into developing genetically-altered crops that are resistant to weeds, insect-pests, and plant pathogens (Duvick, 1996 & Duke, 1996). Currently, 40% of genetic-engineering research in agriculture is focused on herbicide-resistant crop technology (Paoletti & Pimentel, 1996). Robert Shapiro, CEO of Monsanto announced in December 1996, that the corporation plans to disperse and divide its $3 billion chemical sales division amongst their shareholders in 1997 (Lenzer & Upjohn, 1997). Currently, the company is positioning itself as the leading agricultural-biotechnology firm in the world by acquiring 54% share in Calgene, 40% in Dekalb Genetics, 10% in Ecogen, and 100% in Agracetus (Lenzer & Upjohn, 1997).

Monsanto and other agricultural biotechnology companies have developed herbicide-resistant crops in corn, soybeans, and cotton crops. Economic reasons for this trend were discussed earlier. The National Agricultural Chemical Association (NACA) suggests that the development cost for a new pesticide is $50–70 million, and one-fourth goes to environmental and health testing to meet EPA regulations (Ollinger and Pope, 1996). Furthermore, Charles Benbrook (1996) claims that total regulation expenses of all pesticides are estimated to cost U.S. industry and tax payers $1 billion annually. However, a genetically altered crop costs about $10 million to develop and the regulatory expenses totals only $1 million (Ollinger & Pope, 1996). Therefore, it is cheaper for a company to invest in developing new herbicide-resistant crops than a new herbicide. Companies also report that by using the herbicide-resistant crop technology, the farmer can reduce his/her use of actual herbicides, and weed control costs. However, this report is generally not accurate (Paoletti and Pimentel, 1996).

Monsanto's soybean herbicide-resistant seed is reported to increase soybean yields, and their herbicide-resistant cotton is reported to increase cotton yields (James and Krattinger, 1996). By the year 2000, the estimated market value for herbicide-resistant crops for soybeans, cotton, and corn are projected to be worth $500 million per year, and the majority of the market will be controlled by the private sector (Goss & Mazur, 1989). Agricultural economists and scientists tend to believe that benefits from genetic-engineered crops are overstated.

According to agricultural economists Tauer and Love (1989), the adoption of herbicide-resistant technology in the Cornbelt (Midwestern states) may slightly increase corn yields about 251 kg/hectare (or 2% to 4%) on average. However, Tauer (1996) recommends that it may be best to use the technology where fertile lands are seriously weed infested, and use this technology only as an alternative method because of the cost.

The use of pesticides, including herbicides, return approximately \$4 for every dollar invested in benefits from reduced pest losses (Pimentel et al., 1991). Currently, about 3 kg/ha of herbicides are applied to corn at a cost of about \$50/ha. Despite the application of herbicides and mechanical cultivation for weed control, corn losses due to the impact of weeds are estimated to be 10% (Pimentel et al., 1991). The added costs of using herbicide-resistant corn total \$50/ha for the new corn seed (Tauer and Love, 1989).

To use the herbicide-resistant corn requires a more expensive herbicide (glyphosate).Total cost of the glyphosate herbicide treatment is \$93/ha for the glyphosate herbicide treatment (Wiese et al., 1994). Therefore, the \$50/ha for the high priced herbicide-resistant corn seed plus the \$93/ha for glyphosate herbicide totals \$143/ha for weed control using biotechnology. Although Tauer and Love (1989) suggested that by using the herbicide-resistant corn system would improve weed control and increase corn yields, they presented no experimental evidence to support their proposition. Based on experimental published results using various weed control technologies, there is no evidence to suggest that the herbicide-resistant corn technology will reduce corn losses to weeds by the current level of 10% (Pimentel et al., 1991). Therefore, based on the limited data that are available, it appears that employing herbicide-resistant corn will increase costs by \$143/ha but will not provide any benefits in weed control over the current weed control technology.

Scientists argue that herbicide resistant crops are bound to increase the environmental problems caused by herbicides. They feel it will not increase yields, but intensify current environmental problems already associated with herbicides (Goldburg, 1992, Mellon and Rissler, 1995, Paoletti and Pimentel, 1996; Gressel, 1997).[6]

Ronnie Cummins (1996) of the Pure Food Campaign claims that herbicide-tolerant soybean genes could be transmitted to some weeds in the ecosystems, this could worsen the weed-control problems.

The Euro Commerce which is a trade association that represents one-third of European Union food wholesalers and retailers refused to accept Monsantoes Roundup Ready soybean-seeds unless they are labeled as a genetically altered crop. Currently, U.S. farmers export 40% of their soybean crop to Europe (Cummins, 1996). While U.S. agribusiness firms

---

[6]Currently, glyphosophate, the toxic chemical in Roundup is the number one pesticide poisoning among California's farm workers (Cummins, 1996).

248

are not requiring labeling of Roundup Ready soybean products sold in America, they have to label their products sold in Europe (Cummins, 1996).

INSECT/PEST-RESISTANT CROPS[7]

In 1996, Monsanto's insect resistant cotton, *Bollgard* is suppose to combat the cotton ballroom and budworm which are supposed to reduce significantly cotton yields (James and Krattinger, 1996). Monsanto predicts that resistant cotton could result in a two million kilogram reduction or more than 35 percent reduction in insecticide use in cotton. Earlier reports indicated that resistant cotton yields in Texas would increase. However, Gary Barton of Monsanto reports that since the introduction of *Bollgard*, the bollworm presence is 40 times greater compared to the recommended insecticide treatments. He also indicated that if *Bollgard* fails, it will not be a major loss for Monsanto, since the majority of their business is in herbicides (Cummins, 1996).

Another genetically-engineered crop that is causing much debate among the scientific community is insect/pest-resistant crops. Insect/pest-resistance in plants enable them to resist the attack of insects. The approach has been to introduce the toxic gene of Bacillus thuringiensis (B*t*) into the crop thus making it resistant to caterpillars (James, 1996, Krimsky and Wrubel, 1996).

The use insecticides return approximately $4 for every dollar invested in benefits from reduced insect pest losses (Pimentel et al., 1991). In cotton, about $120/ha is invested in insecticides to control insect pests. Therefore, based on the $4:$1 ratio, the $120 investment should return $480 in increased cotton yields. If *Bt* sprays were substituted for chemical insecticides, the cost of insect control would increase to $180/ha. However, the return would remain at about $480/ha because insect control would not be improved.

We assume that *Bollgard* cotton seed costs about $40 more per hectare than normal cotton seed. The *Bollgard* cotton is assumed to provide effective control of the bollworm and budworm. The *Bollgard* cotton would probably reduce total insecticide costs by one half or about

[7]Their is no actual estimates on the cost of pest/virus resistant technologies. We can only assume that is the same as herbicide tolerance based on information told to Ollinger (1996) by the EPA.

$60/ha. Therefore, the *Bollgard* cotton pest control system would cost a total of about $100/ha. Thus, this would reduce pest control costs by about $20/ha.

It had been our hope that the effectiveness of the *Bollgard* cotton for insect pest control would remain for at least three years before the bollworm and budworm evolved resistance to the *Bt* toxin. However, as noted above, the *Bollgard* cotton has not proven as effective as we had hoped. This then makes the return on the investment much less than that obtained when using the regular insecticide treatment.

Scientists Krimsky and Wrubel (1996) suggested early on that it may be economically beneficial to use *Bt* resistant cotton and insecticides simultaneously to reduce crop losses. Furthermore, the environmental costs of *Bt* toxin in cotton and other major crops was not known at the time *Bollgard* was introduced (Paoletti and Pimentel, 1996). However, Rebecca Goldburg, Chair of the Environmental Defense Fund suggests that over a period of time, insects like the bollworm and budworm will become resistant to the *Bt* toxin in transgenic crops. The Union of Concerned Scientists (UCS) and the Environmental Defense Fund has urged the EPA to evaluate the *Bt* resistance failure in cotton (Rissler, 1996).

In addition, farmers were upset with Monsanto for charging a $79/ha technology fee on *Bollgard* when they only received 60% of the bollworm and budworm control. This was in contrast to Randy Deaton of Monsanto claim that the product would give farmers 90 to 95% control of bollworms and budworms in cotton (Demaske, 1996).

Scientists believe that genetic-engineering techniques, if used responsibly may lead to an increase in crop productivity because of improved control of insects and plant pathogens (Pimentel et al., 1996). In terms of transgenic crops which are used to replace chemical fungicides. Krimsky, Wrubel (1996) and Paoletti and Pimentel (1996) state that transgenic crops have the potential to be both economically and environmentally beneficial. The benefits would stem from the reduced fungicide use, improved crop yields, and reduced environmental problems in agriculture.

It is estimated that disease losses in corn, wheat, cotton, and soybeans total $1.3 billion annually and losses in fruits and vegetables total $500 million annually in the United States (James, Teng and Nutter, 1991). Transgenic crops resistant to plant pathogens would reduce yield losses which may result in fewer hectares being planted which would lead to a

250

reduction in soil erosion and other environmental problems (Krimsky and Wrubel, 1996). In addition, developing disease-resistance crops would reduce the use of toxic fungicides (Paoletti and Pimentel, 1996).

CONCLUSION

Biotechnology may help increase food production. However, precise estimates of actual yield increases both aggregated and disaggregated in the United States and developing countries are needed. These data will help reveal the roles that these "new technologies" are playing in solving the global food security problem and possibly alleviating environmental degradation.

Furthermore, the private sector may need to rethink its strategy in terms of which are the best alternative methods to increase yields and control pests. Corporations should shift from developing genetically engineered crops that enhance the use of pesticides like herbicides to biointensive Integrated Pest Management techniques (Benbrook & Groth, 1997), such as host-plant resistance (HPR) crops which help to improve pest control (Pimentel et al., 1996). In terms of controlling weeds, farmers need to assess the costs and benefits of non-chemical weed control techniques as well as herbicide weed control techniques (Pimentel, 1997).

Finally, policy makers both from the industrialized and the developing world should collectively decide which agricultural biotechnologies are most beneficial to their respective farmers in improving food production, and at the same time protecting the environment. These decisions should include inputs from the farmer, consumer, business, and environmental groups.

REFERENCES

Biotechnology Industry Organization, "Agricultural Biotechnology: The Future of the World's Food Supply" www.bio.org/bio/foodrep8.html.

Borlaug, Norman. *The Green Revolution, Peace, and Humanity Speech.* delivered upon receipt of the 1970 Nobel Peace Prize, Olso, Norway, 1970, 1972.

Brenbrook, Charles and Groth III, Edward, "Indicators of the Sustainability and Impacts of Pest Management Systems", presented at the AAAS 1997 Annual Meeting, February 16, 1997.

Brenbrook, C., Groth, E., Halloran, J., Hansen, M. and S. Marquardt. 1996. *Pest Management at the Crossroads*, Consumers Union, Yonkers, New York. See also *PMAC* website at http://www.pmac.net.

Brown, Lester, *Seeds of Change – The Green Revolution and the Development in the 1970s* (1970).

Byerlee, Derek, "Technological Challenges in Asian Agriculture in the 1900s", p. 424–433, in *Agricultural Development in the Third World* (2nd Edition), Editor Carl Eicher ad John Staatz, 1990.

Caswell, M., Fugile, Keith O. and Klotz C., *Agricultural Biotechnology: An Economic Perspective,* ERS Report 687, May 1994.

Demaske, Chris, "Bollgard/Bollworm Debate", *Cotton Grower*, Fall 1996.

Duke, Stephen O. (Editor) *Herbicide Resistant Crops: Agricultural, Environmental, Economic, Regulatory, and Technical Aspects* , (1996), Chapter 1

Eicher, Carl K. and Staatz, J.M., *Agricultural Development in the Third World* (2nd Edition), pp. 3–41, 1990.

Goldburg, R.J., 1992. Environmental Concerns with the development of herbicide-tolerant plants. *Weed Technology*. 6: 647–652.

Goldburg, R.J., Risser, J. and Shand, H., Hassebrook, 1990b. *Biotechnology's Bitter Harvest*. A Report of the Biotechnology Working Organization.

Gressel, J., 1997 Review of Glyphosphate Resistance in *Resistant Pest Management*, Volume 8, Number 2, Winter 1996.

GREAN, *Global Research on the Environmental and Agricultural Nexus for the 21s Century.* The Report of the Task force on Research Innovative for the Productivity and Sustainablity, Univ. of Florida and Cornell University, 1995.

Hayami, Yujiro, "Assessment of the Green Revolution", in *Agricultural Development in the Third World,* pp. 416–423, 1990.

Heap, Ian, *International Survey of Herbicide Resistant Weeds,* 1996, www:pioneer.net/~heapian/index.html.

Islam, Nural (Editor), *Population and Food in the Early Twenty-First Century: Meeting Food Demand of And Increasing Population,* IFPRI, 1995.

Krimsky, Sheldon, and Wrubel, Roger P., "Agricultural Biotechnology: An Environmental Outlook", Department of Urban and Environmental Policy, Tufts University, Medford, Mass. 1993.

Krimsky, Sheldon, *Bioecthics and Society,* pp. 59–80, 1991.

Krimsky, Sheldon and Wrubel, Roger P., *Agricultural Biotechnology and the Environment: Science, Policy, and Social Issues*, pp. 29–191, 1996.

Lenzner, R. and Upbin, R., "Monsanto vs. Malthus" in *Forbes*, March 10, 1997, pp. 58–64.

James, C., Teng, P. and Nutter, F., "Estimated Losses of Crops from Plant Pathogens", In *CRC Handbook of Pest Management.* pp. 15–50, 1991.

James, Clive "Agricultural Research and Development: The Need for Public-Private Sector Partnerships", *CGIAR,* June 1996.

James, Clive and Krattinger, Anatole F., *Global Review of the Field Testing and Commercialization of Transgenic Plants, 1986 to 1995: The First Decade of Crop Biotechnology, ISAAA,* 1996.

Mellon, M. and Rissler, J., 1995, Transgenic crops USDA data o small-scaletests contribute little to commercial risk assessment. *Bio/Technology* 13 (1): 96.

Ollinger, M. and Pope, L., "Strategic Research Interests, Organizational Behavior, and Emerging Market for the Products of Plant Biotechnology," Resource and Technology Division-USDAERS, pp. 1–22, 1996.

252

Paoletti, Maurizio, G. and Pimentel, David, "Genetic Engineering in Agriculture and the Environment: Assessing the Risks and Benefits." *Bioscience* Vol. 46, No. 9, October 1996.

Pimentel, D., Wilson, C., McCullum, C., Huang, R., Dwen, P., Flack, J. Tran, Q., Saltman, T., Cliff, B, "Environmental and Economic Benefits of Biodiversity", April 12, 1996. In Press.

Pimentel, D., L., McLaughlin, Zepp, A., Lakian, B., Kraus, T., Kleinman,P., Vancini, F., Roach, W.J., Graap, E., Keeton, W.S., and Selig,G., Environmental and economic impacts of reducing U.S. agricultural pesticide use. In *Handbook on Pest Management inAgriculture*, Ed. D. Pimmentel, pp. 679–718. Boca Raton, FL: CRC Press.

Postel, S., 1996. *Dividing the Waters: Food Security, Ecosystem Health, and the New Politics of Scarcity.* Vol. 132. Washington, DC: World Watch Institute.

Raman, K.V, (Personal Communication, 1996).

Raman, K.V., "Public and Private Research Promoting Synergies", Paper presented at the 2nd International Crop Science Congress, Nov. 17–24, 1996 in New Delhi, India.

Rissler, Jane, "Urge EPA to Hold Scientific Advisory Panel Meeting on Bt Cotton Failure, December 9, 1996, www:pmac.net/bt3.htm.

Ruttan, Vernon, *Agricultural Research Policy*, 1982.

Tauer, Loren W. and Love, John M., "The Potential Economic Impact of Herbicide Resistant Corn in the USA," *The Journal of Production Agriculture*, Vol. 2, No. 3, July-Sept 1989, pp. 202–207.

Tauer, Loren W., "Farmer and Public Perspectives of Herbicide-Resistant Crops" (Chapter 18) in *Herbicide Resistant Crops Agricultural, Environmental,   Economic, Regulatory, and Technical Aspects* ,(1996).

Wiese, A.F., W.L. Harmon, and C. Reiger. 1994. Economic evaluation of conservation tillage systems for dry land and irrigated cotton (*Gossypium hirsutum*) in the southern great plains. *Weed Science* 42(2): 316–321.

Woodfin, Max, "Bt Cotton Creating Resistance to Bt?", Southern Sustainable Farming # 12, September 1996, www:pmac.net/bt2.htm.

CHAPTER - 15

SPATIAL DISCOUNTING AND THE ENVIRONMENT: AN EMPIRICAL INVESTIGATION INTO HUMAN PREFERENCES

Karl Steininger

Economic decisions frequently involve impacts on persons distant in time and place. While time discounting has a long tradition in economics, spatial discounting is of more recent concern. For environmental impacts the socially optimal spatial discount rate is motivated by the diffusion of emissions in space. In this paper we look into the presence of spatial discounting in human preferences, i.e. the private spatial discount rate. In particular we investigate into its empirical basis; we test whether or to what degree a discounting is present in the concern about environmental impacts on people distant in space. We use a contingent valuation approach to quantify the benefits arising from air quality change due to waste incineration, which may occur either locally or at a distance. Two distinct groups at one location, but with different information on the site of the new plant, are surveyed for that purpose. We find that even within the same cultural context the empirical basis for spatial discounting is a strong one, encouraging the further expansion of this newly developing theoretical field into the empirical domain.

The author would like to thank Birgit Friedl, Susanne Hasenhüttl, Katharina Sammer, Brigitte Gebetsroither and Andrea Stocker for inspiring research cooperation in data preparation and discusion, Charles Perrings for the triggering momentum in the development of the analytical structure, Hans Kellerer for statistical advice, and Henk Folmer and the participants of the 1997 Annual Meeting of European Environmental and Resource Economists at Tilburg for their helpful comments on an earlier version of this paper. The usual disclaimer applies.

[253]

254

1. INTRODUCTION

Many economic actions and decisions taken at one point in time and space do have non-negligable impacts on persons living distant in time and/or distant in place. Economics – and environmental economics in particular – thus is asked to supply the conceptual framework to make current and local impacts commensurable with impacts distant in time or place. While there is a long tradition in the analysis of impacts that involve a time lag (i.e. the rich literature on discounting), the concentration on spatially dispersed effects (the evaluation of "spatial lags") is of much younger concern. In theoretical terms the two concepts of time discounting and spatial discounting are close, as Perrings and Hannon (1996) make explicit. Even more so, one may wonder why the focus on the latter is of such recent date only.

Empirical findings in the "growth and environment" field seem to have been one of the triggering mechanisms for the discussion of the spatial dimension in discounting. In analyzing the environmental impacts of trade liberalization Grossman and Krueger (1993) sought to shed light on the combined scale and technique impact of (trade-triggered) growth on the environment. In a cross-section analysis of urban pollution in 23 countries they found a relationship that later has become labeled environmental Kuznets curve, i.e. an inverted-U shaped relationship between environmental quality and per capita income. As per capita income rises, environmental quality first deteriorates and then, after some point, improves. In both the mentioned study and later refinements in Grossman (1995) and Grossman and Krueger (1995), however, the inverted-U shape holds for local pollution, but not for pollution with effects distant in space. Considering the most relevant greenhouse gas, for example, with effects distant in both space and time, CO_2 emissions to date continuously rise with income. One important explanation may be found in spatial discounting. People seem to be more concerned with environmental impacts in their neighbourhood than with those distant in space. Among others, a group of economists and environmental scientists does point out this relationship in Arrow et al. (1995).

As it is the case with time discounting, we are concerned with two different types of discount rates in spatial discounting, the private and the social one. The basis for the private spatial discount rate are peoples' preferences. The basis for the social environmental spatial discount rate is primarily found in the fact of spatial dispersion of pollutants. The impact of pollution thus is less severe at distant places where concentration has declined. Transfering the time related definition by Mäler (1995) the level of the spatial discount rate can be considered "ethically neutral" if it does not exceed the dispersion factor, which implies that the carrying capacity of all affected ecosystems, close and distant, is not exceeded. Given dispersion, the spatial discount rate in the public decision process will be positive, i.e. pollution impacts for optimal allocation decisions need to be discounted the more distant the respective population lives. The choice of the optimal social discount rate in the area of environment thus mainly is a matter of natural scientific evaluation, based on dispersion models and dose-response functions. The larger the uncertainty, the more the risk and the precautionary aspect need to be additionally included.

In the empirical analysis two approaches can be taken. One can determine either the social spatial discount rate, or the private one. Further, one may compare the two to point out policy deficiencies if the effective social one (determined e.g. by voter models from the private ones) differs from the socially optimal one.

Economics in our view supplies rich methodology, particularly contingent valuation methods, to trigger the empirical research on spatial discounting with a focus on the *private* spatial discount rate. This is the approach chosen in this paper. What difference do people make in evaluating an adverse environmental impact with respect to the distance at which it occurs?

One first recalls studies on the valuation of (a) sites that grant benefits (e.g. parks) or (b) land uses that are connected to local rejection (e.g. toxic waste sites). In both areas the impact that distance to the site has on the valuation has been determined in various studies (e.g. Pate and Loomis (1994) on the former and Howe (1986) on the latter). In this type of studies, however, the framing is one in which the net benefit of one site is evaluated from the perspectives present at different sites at various distances. For example, a national park at location i is evaluated by people living at this same location i, by those at a slightly more distant location j, and by those at an even more distant site k etc. The question with spatial discounting is a different one. Here, it is the evaluation expressed at one site only, i.e. the net benefits of one project at site i to people at locations i, j, and k etc. are taken into account, but they are evaluated under the preferences (and knowledge)

256

given at location*i* only.[1] The relevance of the concept is with the many projects that do have distant impacts, but are decided at the local level only. To what degree do location *i* individuals discount the impacts their project exerts on the population at localities *j* or *k*?

The field of spatial discounting begins to rank prominently in theoretical research. The focus of this study thus is to investigate the empirical (quantitative) basis for spatial discounting. Emphasis is on the private spatial discount rate. Empirical research on spatial discounting is considered not only an important complement to the development of the theoretical concept, its quantitative results may also be directly used in project evaluation.

The structure of the paper is the following. The next section will focus on the analytical structure in spatial discounting. Section 3 then describes the details of the empirical analysis undertaken. The results are presented in section 4 before a final section summarizes the main conclusions.

2. THE STRUCTURE IN SPATIAL DISCOUNTING

We may – at this place in a mere intuitive way – explicate the basic concept of geographical preference (and spatial discounting) when thinking of consumption. We are familiar with the concept of time preference in consumption. Consumption now is preferred over consumption later (our own consumption or analogously consumption by later generations) by a rate which can be measured by the respective partial derivatives. In the most simple production model a necessary condition for the intertemporally optimal rate of time preference is that it equals the rate of return on investment. Similarly, we may prefer consumption at our immediate location to consumption at a distant location (again, either consumption by ourselves or by other people at this distant location). A local consumption increase may be connected to (environmental) costs at a distance. Due to absorption by the natural system these costs are somewhat lowered by the fact that they become relevant only at a distance. Thus, the costs at the distance can be considered as investment connected to a positive rate of return in terms of local consumption. Consequently, in optimally evaluating distant costs locally we need to employ a spatial discount factor. For the fully detailed

[1] The author wishes to express his thanks to Charles Perrings, who emphasized this aspect in personal communication. Equation (1) in section 2 explicates this issue in analytical terms, which was supplied in the course of this communication.

description and a nice analytical representation of spatial discounting see Perrings and Hannon (1996).

Our interest in this study is the quantification of the spatial discount rate present in the preferences of the individual. We will focus on the most simple model possible. Let us take an investment project at site i. It will supply both costs and benefits to people at site i; people might have to pay for its construction but they also will benefit from its services; they might also suffer from pollution created in operating this new capital good. Their net benefit is B_i. People at different sites will be affected as well. For matters of simplicity, we assume that this project at location i only affects people at i and at one second location j, one unit of distance away. People at j enjoy some benefits of the services of this investement, as well, as they are also affected by pollution arising from operation. Their net benefit is B_j.

At location i people consider the net discounted benefit DB_i for the project

$$DB_i = B_i + \frac{B_j}{(1+s_i)},$$ (1)

employing their spatial discount rate s_i.

The quantitative value of DB_i can be obtained empirically in the course of a contingent valuation experiment; for example for an improvement in environmental quality the willingness to pay (WTP) for the realization of this project can be measured.

For the determination of the quantitative value of s_i we can start with the WTP-quantification of DB_i but then would need to disentangle the influence of B_i and B_j on the WTP. This might turn out a complicated task indeed.

We thus go one step further in simplifying matters. We will look at an investment example the explicit benefit of which is only *local*. In particular we will look at the potential installment of a scrubber in a waste incineration plant that is far enough from the second site, such that emissions do not affect the other site and consequently the installation of the scrubber does not improve air quality at the distant site. Now we can think of two alternatives to locate this waste incineration itself in the first place, namely at i or j. For both scenarios we ask the population at i (two distinct subgroups 1 and 2) on their willingness to pay for a scrubber, i.e. we measure;

$$wtp_1 = WTP_i(B_i) \text{ and } wtp_2 = WTP_i\left(\frac{B_j}{1+s_i}\right).$$

If the setting is one where we look at exactly the same value of explicit benefits, i.e. $B_i = B_j$, then

$$WTP_i(B_i) = WTP_i\left(\frac{B_j}{1+s_i}\right)(1+s_i) \iff wtp_1 = wtp_2 \times (1+s_i). \qquad (2)$$

Our setting, however, also involves a benefit other than air quality improvement, a benefit which is arising beyond the borders of a single location. While such further links will be present in most settings, we actually need this link to motivate why we ask people at i for their WTP for an improvement in environmental quality at j. It is simply the fact that the waste of *both* locations is incinerated in the plant, irrespective of its location. Thus, wherever the plant is built, there is an additional benefit AB_i and AB_j for each of the respective sites due to the fact that they can get rid of their waste.

The net discounted value of these additional benefits evaluated at one location, however, is the same irrespective of where the plant is located. The net discounted additional benefit at i (DAB_i) for both scenarios is

$$DAB_i = AB_i + \frac{AB_j}{(1+s_i)}. \qquad (3)$$

In the survey we ask for the evaluation of the *explicit* (environmental) benefit. Respondents in expressing their willingness to pay may acknowledge the *implicit* benefit DAB_i as well. If they do, DAB_i enters at both sides of equ. (2):

$$wtp_1' = WTP_i(B_i + DAB_i) = WTP_i(B_i) + WTP_i(DAB_i) \text{ and}$$

$$(4)$$

$$wtp_2' = WTP_i\left(\frac{B_j}{1+s_i}\right) + WTP_i(DAB_i)$$

This implies $\underline{s}_i$ to represent a lower bound for the spatial discount rate s_i

$$wtp_1' = wtp_2'(1+\underline{s}_i) \qquad (5)$$

In the following we will focus on the difference $wtp'_1 - wtp'_2$, where the additional term cancels out. However, the additional benefit does increase the variance: $VAR(wtp'_1) > VAR(wtp_1)$ and $VAR(wtp'_2) > VAR(wtp_2)$. Thus, when respondents in their answers do acknowledge also the implicit benefit we will continue to determine a lower bound for the spatial discount rate.

3. THE EMPIRICAL INVESTIGATION

The first task was to select a relevant issue that enables a test for the presence of concern on spatially distant impacts. In this selection we focused on the criteria "current political relevance" and "public awareness" in order to ensure both answers based on informed evaluation and sufficient return rates.

In 1996 the Austrian parliament passed a waste management law that requires all provinces and larger communities to incinerate waste that exceeds a certain heat content level. No province but Vienna to date has the necessary equipment in place to fulfill this law. Thus the discussion was begun in the rest of Austria. The second largest Austrian city, Graz, took a time lead in discussing the issue. In the province of Styria, the capital of which Graz is, four different potential sites for waste incineration are discussed at the moment, one of which is located in Graz itself.

The issue of waste incineration was thus perfectly available to be used to study the question of spatial preferences of environmental impacts. A questionnaire was sent to 1,100 households in the city of Graz, which were selected on a random basis. Half of them were given the information that the waste incineration in discussion is the one in the city of Graz itself, thus the environmental impact is local (poll "local impact"; also poll LI). The other half were given the information that the waste incineration in discussion is to be located at a linear distance of 40 kilometers (within the town of Niklasdorf), however, with two mountain ranges hindering the exchange of air between this site and the city of Graz (poll "distant impact"; poll DI). Both groups were told that the waste incineration plants will be equipped with technology ensuring emission cleaning at the legally required level. However, there is the possibility of installing an additional scrubber for a further cleaning of plant emissions. Both groups were asked (a) whether they would vote for such an additional scrubber and (b) whether they would be willing to give a personal one-time financial contribution to finance this additional scrubber and if so, how much they would be willing to contribute (categorised answer).

To introduce people to the problem, in a fifteen-question-block, they were first asked on air quality, types of emissions, health effects, and the relative impact of waste incineration emissions on air quality. After the willingness-to-pay question-block the final block of questions concerned social characteristics.

The questionnaire was sent such that people received it two to three days ahead of a special meeting of the Graz city council on waste incineration. One reminding letter was sent after a two-week period.

The rate of return was 33.7%, i.e. 371 questionnaires, of which 178 concerned poll LI and 193 were out of poll DI. Table 1 shows that the age distribution in each of the polls indeed can be considered representative for the population of the city of Graz. In terms of income, there is no information on the population of Graz; comparing the poll data with the Austrian data we find that the median income of both polls is in the category 15,001 to 20,000 ATS per month and thus in correspondence with the Austrian overall median at ATS 18,101.

Table 1

Age distribution of respondents

	Scenario LI	Scenario DI	City of Graz average
	[% of respective poll]		
18–30	26.4	23.83	25.97
31–40	20.79	18.65	17.62
41–50	12.36	17.62	16.62
51–65	20.79	19.69	18.66
above 65	17.98	19.69	21.13

Table 2

WTP for additional scrubber, Wilcoxen-Test

WTP	Poll LI	Poll DI	Wilcoxen-Test H_0 and H_1 as specified	
	[number of respondents]			
more than 5000	2	1		
up to 5000	5	3	w_0	6729
up to 3000	3	4	E(W)	7339
up to 1000	27	24	VAR(W)	117422
up to 700	5	3		
up to 500	14	21	test-value	−1.78
up to 300	11	20		
up to 100	15	20		
	82	96		

4. RESULTS

4.1. The difference in concern with the close and the distant

Our first interest is in the significance of the difference between the willingness to contribute to an improvement in air quality expressed by the subgroup considering the local impact (poll LI) on one hand and the subgroup considering the distant impact only (poll DI) on the other hand. We test whether the difference is significant (specifically whether wtp_1', the willingness to pay expressed in poll LI is on average significantly larger than wtp_2', the willingness to pay expressed in poll DI). If the difference is significant, then from equ. (5) it follows that the lower bound of the spatial discount rate at location i, $\underline{s}_i$, is positive.

$$H_0: wtp_1' \leq wtp_2'$$

$$H_1: wtp_1' > wtp_2'$$

The wtp-values obtained in our polls LI and DI clearly show a multiple peak density function. We thus use a distribution-free test procedure, the Wilcoxen-Test (also: Mann-Whitney-U-Test) out of the class of rank tests.

The questionnaire first asks whether people opt for a private contribution at all. In poll LI 82 do (46%), in poll DI 96 do (49%). While the difference of shares is insignificant, the deviation is at least in an unexpected direction. While this does make a rejection of H_0 less likely, it also strengthens the meaning of such a rejection, if it can be established.

Applying the Wilcoxen-Test we have to reject H_0 at the 95%-level of significance. We thus find that even the lower bound of the spatial discount rate, $\underline{s}_i$, is strictly positive. The two subgroups in our case study, when asked to evaluate an identical explicit environmental benefit, are found to statisitcally significantly evaluate the distant less than the close.

4.2. A level estimate of the spatial discount rate

On the basis of a significant difference between the wtp-values expressed in the two samples we can proceed to test for the absolute size of the difference D.

$$H_0: wtp_1' - wtp_2' \leq D$$

$$H_1: wtp_1' - wtp_2' > D.$$

We thus again correct for the potential level-distortion by DAB_i, as specified in section 2.

We obtain the lower bound of the difference, as variances are increased by DAB_i. This minimum absolute difference D can be related to the significance interval of wtp_1', $[\underline{wtp_1'}, \ldots, \overline{wtp_1'}]$, which binds the range for $\underline{s}_i$:

$$\frac{\overline{wtp_1'}}{wtp_1' - D} - 1 < \underline{s}_i < \frac{\overline{wtp_1'}}{wtp_1' - D} - 1 \tag{6}$$

We first need to determine D. As long as we are bound to remain with a rank test in a setting of categorised answers we will not be able to narrow down a minimum difference below the smallest of the category step sizes. To be more accurate on D, knowledge of the class and parameters of the wtp density function would be required. This turns out to be difficult for the overall polls. But subgroups along specific social charactersitics within the polls are more homogenous and thus may result in wtp-value distribution subject to a particular density function which can be easier specified. Among other cases, for the subgroup of the employed a normal distribution of wtp-values for both samples is approved at the 95%-significance level in the two according χ^2-adjustment tests. We choose this example on the basis of its weight: the fraction of the employed accounts for 49.4% in poll LI and 54.4% in poll DI. We obtain

$$MEAN(wtp_{1,employed}') = 1260.044 \,, \quad \sigma_{wtp_{1,employed}'} = 1455.264 \text{ and}$$

$$MEAN(wtp_{2,employed}') = 789.361 \quad \sigma_{wtp_{2,employed}'} = 870.091 \,.$$

For a distance D up to $D_{employed} = 57.311$ H_0 is rejected at the 95%-level.

The 95%-confidence interval of $MEAN(wtp_{1,employed}')$ is determined with [777.534, 1627.932].

Using (6), for the lower bound of the employees spatial discount rate we specify the range

$$.52\% < \underline{s}_{employed} < 7.37\%.$$

4.3. Robustness and further aspects

In analysing further characteristics of the survey we can qualitatively interpret the robustness of the results obtained.

The responsibility of financing the improvement
While roughly 80% of the respondents of both polls state their preferences in favour of an additional scrubber for the waste incineration plant, only 40% state that they are prepared for a personal one-time financial contribution. Table 3 gives the exact levels for the two polls. This combination leads to the conclusion that there is wide distribution of the opinion that responsibility for installation and financing of this scrubber is with the public, not with private individuals. This finding holds equally for both polls as Table 3 shows, and thus is independent of the distance to the environmental impact.

The consequence is mean values of willingness to pay to turn out low. Looking at the medians of the two polls, they are indeed both zero. Also, for many subgroups defined by social characteristics the median is zero.

While this impact equally is present in both polls – and thus does not distort the analysis – it pushes the values for WTP to lower levels. This also reduces the absolute value of D, and thus does not change the estimate of the spatial discount rate.

The lower bound characteristic once more

In addition to the analytical link establishing the lower bound characteristic as specified in section 2 above, we need to consider a cultural link. In our case study on spatial discounting we looked at two locations within the same province. Thus responsibility for a population of the cultural parameters

Table 3
Wish for additional scrubber and personal WTP

	Scenario LI	Scenario DI
	[% of respective poll]	
Wish for additional scrubber	82.02	80.83
Personal willingness to contribute	40.45	41.45

same culture, here even of the same province, can be expected to be experienced at a level higher than for a population "more distant" in both cultural parameters and actual geographical distance. This consideration strengthens the fact that we do focus on a lower bound for the spatial discount rate in our empirical investigation.

However, there is also a tendency present that may be considered to run counter to the above distortion. The initial air quality in both localities is not considered the same by the population living at i. Thus, the population at i may not consider B_i to be equal to B_j, an assumption upon which we draw in section 2. The difference is a small one, though. Table 4 states the location i evaluation of pre-investement air quality for both locations. The distant location is considered to have slightly better air quality, and correspondingly the additional emissions are considered to be of more impact to reduce air quality (Table 5). The negative impacts on health are also seen slightly different: 37.1% of poll LI expect a negative health impact, while 46.1% of poll DI do expect one for people living at the distant location. How does this affect our result? In the literature generally WTP for an improvement in environmental quality is found to rise with the deterioration of the initial quality (though this direction is not established unambigously, see Mäntymaa (1991)). This causation would bias the WTP in poll LI in the upward direction, and thus also bias upward the spatial discount rate that we establish in our study (cf. equ. (2) or (2′)). In this case it would run counter to the distortions mentioned above. However, this link only holds when we consider an equal improvement at different levels of initial quality. In the scenario we give to respondents we specify an equal improvement in emission reduction, which is not resulting in equal air quality impacts and thus health impacts. On the contrary, the same emission reduction causes a stronger improvement of air quality at the distant site. One Schilling of personal contribution spent on the distant site on average is considered to be connected to a higher marginal benefit in health improvement than one Schilling spent when the plant is at the local site. This biases the WTP upwards in the poll DI and lowers the spatial discount rate we determine. It thus reinforces the conclusion that we find a lower bound.

The contribution of waste incineration to air quality change is small

We found the respondents well informed on both the different relevant types of emission originating from waste incineration and their relative

Table 4
Current air quality (reference level: other province capitals)

Air quality	At location	
	Local	Distant
	Evaluated by the local population	
	(Poll LI)	(Poll DI)
	[% of respective poll]	
Much better	0.00	1.04
better	3.93	5.18
Somewhat better	19.10	20.73
Somewhat worse	27.53	26.42
Worse	37.08	33.68
Much worse	10.67	10.36

Table 5
Estimated impact of plant operation on air quality

Quality impact	At location	
	Local	Distant
	Evaluated by the local population	
	(Poll LI)	(Poll DI)
	[% of respective poll]	
Strong improvement	0.00	1.04
Improvement	3.93	5.18
Small improvement	19.10	20.73
Small decline	27.53	26.42
Decline	37.08	33.68
Strong decline	10.67	10.36

share in overall air pollution. 75% and 89%, respectively, turn out to be well informed about (a) the types of emissions and (b) the comparatively low contribution of waste incineration to air pollution. Public awareness of the issue had caused better informed population. The low values of WTP are consistent with this knowledge.

Income dependency

Finally, we will point out the link between WTP in the two polls and income, as income is considered one of the main explaining parameters for WTP. The link is depicted in Figure 1. The diagram reveals the interesting fact that the mean WTP for reducing the distant impact is roughly

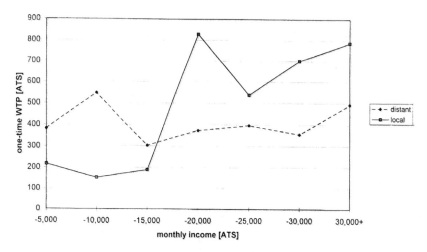

Figure 1. WTP for local and distant impact, by income class.

constant across income categories, whereas for reducing the local impact
it rises with income. This relationship leads to the hypothesis that low
income classes are relatively more concerned with the distant than high
income classes are, or, specified more exactly, that high income classes
discount spatially distant effects at a higher rate. When we apply the
Wilcoxen-test within each income class, in fact we find that
$H_0: wtp_1' \leq wtp_2'$ is rejected for each of the three lower income classes at
the 95%-significance level, whereas $H_0: wtp_2' \leq wtp_1'$ is rejected for the
remaining four higher income classes. Thus, for the low income classes,
the wtp values for an improvement in the distance are significantly above
those for a local improvement. This, inter alia, may be due to the upward
bias of the wtp in poll DI, which is arising from the difference in initial
air quality conceived, as was pointed out above. It is not so much the fact
that for low income classes the wtp for the distance outweighs the one for
the local impact, that is important, but the fact that there is reversal of this
relationship with rising income. This means that the preference for "the
close" is rising with income, the concern for "the distant" is declining
with income.

Note that this finding is an – *intra*temporal – cross section result. It
does not necessarily imply a corollary in the *inter*temporal context that in
the course of development ("when people get richer") they are concerned

increasingly with their own neighbourhood, at the cost of the distance. Both an analysis to test this intertemporal hypothesis within one nation and an expansion of the cross-section-aspect to nations at different states of development constitute important topics that future research may focus on.

<h2>5. CONCLUSIONS</h2>

The purpose of this study was to establish a result on whether there is an empirical basis for research on the rate of spatial discounting. Using the example of air quality improvement for a newly to be constructed waste incineration plant we undertake a questionnaire survey distinguishing two representative groups at one location each of which we supply with information on one of two locations for this plant, one of which is local, the other distant. To specify the most simple structure, we focus on a problem that has only local environmental impacts and compare the two subgroups willingness to pay for an improvement in air quality (by installation of an additional scrubber) at the local site and the distant site respectively.

Our finding is that indeed there is a significant difference between the two subgroups in their willingness to pay. Independent of any natural system emission absorption due to dispersion (as we restrict ourselves to local environmental effects) we find that people do assign less concern to impacts on their neighbours in 40 kilometers distance than to their immediate ones or to themselves. For the fraction of the employed we quantify the private spatial discount rate, with a range for its lower bound between 3.5 and 7.4%. Further, we find that the private spatial discount rate changes with income. A discount rate rising with income implies the poor to be most concerned with the distant.

Our case study is one on preferences with respect to spatially dispersed impacts. We analyse a distant impact that affetcs neither the respondent nor his immediate neighbourhood. However, in our study the "spatially distant" impact affects people of the same culture, even within the same province. The most interesting extension to the research along the lines presented in this paper in our opinion would be to investigate the strength of the empirical basis for spatial discounting when the impact is more distant in both geographical and cultural terms. What this study does establish to date is that it is worth the effort to consider spatial

268

discounting in both political decision making and empirical research even at the scope of distance where cultural proximity is given. It is also meant to define one starting point for empirical research in this new field of spatial discounting in environmental economics.

Arrow, K., B. Bolin, R. Costanza, P. Dasgupta, C. Folke, C .S. Holling, B.-O. Jansson, S. Levin, K.-G. Maler, C. Perrings and D. Pimentel (1995) Economic Growth, Carrying Capacity, and the Environment, *Science* 268: 520–521.
Grossman, G.M. (1995) Pollution and Growth: What do we know?, in: Goldin, I., and L.A. Winters (ed.), *The Economics of Sustainable Development*, Cambridge: Cambridge University Press: 19–82.
Grossman, G.M. and A.B. Krueger (1993) 'Environmental Impacts of a North American Free Trade Agreement', in P. Garber (ed.), *The U.S.-Mexico free trade agreement*, Cambridge: MIT Press, pp. 13–56.
Grossman, G.M. and A.B. Krueger (1995) Economic Growth and the Environment, The Quarterly Journal of Economics, May: 353–377.
Howe, H.L. (1988) A Comparison of Actual and Perceived Residential Proximity to Toxic Waste Sites, Archives of Environmental Health 43/6: 415–419.
Mäler, K.-G. (1995) Sustainable Development, in: Perrings, Ch. et al. (eds.) *Biodiversity Loss: Ecological and Economic Issues*, Cambridge: Cambridge University Press.
Mäntymaa, E. (1991) Some new ideas and preliminary results for using the CVM in measuring the environmental benefits of a lake, presented to the EAERE Autumn workshop in Environmental Economics, Venice.
Pate J. and J. Loomis (1994) The Effect of Distance on Willingness to Pay Values: A Case Study of Wetlands and Salmon in California, mimeo, College of Natural resources, Colorado State University.
Perrings, Ch. and B. Hannon (1996) A sense of time and place: An introduction to spatial discounting, Proceedings of the *Conference Ecology, Society, Economy*, Universitè de Versailles, May 1996, Plenary Session Papers.

CHAPTER - 16

THE FREE-RIDING BEHAVIOUR IN CULATRA ISLAND CASE STUDY: DETECTION AND CORRECTION

Vitor Santos and Fernando Perna

ABSTRACT

This work is about an island (Culatra) placed in the south of Portugal, in the "heart" of Ria Formosa, a Natural Park since 1987. The island constitutes a public place for sustainable production of recreation benefits based on sun & beach. The hypothetical benefit user value estimated with "open-ended format", promotes an understanding and powerful argument for regional decision making. In this evaluation process one has to take into account the free-riding behaviour of some individuals. This behaviour introduces a distortion in the evaluation of the individuals real willingness to pay for and is one of the main causes of inaccuracy in the results obtained with this type of analysis. In this paper we estimate the probability of an individual to have a free-riding behaviour as a function of several individual characteristics and we reevaluate the individuals real capability to pay for based on their fitted probabilities of having a free-riding behaviour.

1. INTRODUCTION

The market paradox between use and environmental preservation arose in the last two decades as a central issue in economic theory and practice. Several development efforts have faced real and hypothetical damage phenomenon, highly potentiated when the focus area is a natural reserve or park with strong public recreational use, among others. The social characteristic of these resources and the inexistence of an efficient strategic local and regional planning, tend to promote over exploration and congestion, including irreversible effects.

[269]

Unfortunately, there are several examples of these circumstances along the portuguese coast. The Island we intend to study is placed in the Algarve, the southest region of Portugal, and is one of the five sand islands that divide Ria Formosa Natural Park from Atlantic Ocean waters. Culatra Island is growing as a recreational and tourist destination, with benefits resulting mainly from sun&beach activities, however, the inexistence of a monetarized environmental argument associated with the public characteristic and the quality of the resource, tend to transform this natural island into an over explored resource.

We argue for the use of Contingent Valuation as a method to produce an important set of arguments to clarify the paradox, particularly adapted to this kind of resources and values. Monetarized environmental benefits can be measured, and their values consist of a reality that can not be put apart in any local/regional sustainable development choice-decision process.

As we can see on Figure 1.1, Culatra Island geographic limits are clearly identified. This feature togheter with the uniqueness of access, are essential to the operacionality of Contingent Valuation Method (Freeman, 1986). In this case, the access is made almost exclusively by a small ferry through the channel that links the island to the city of Olhão. Culatra

Figure 1.1. Culatra Island.

Island has an area approximately of 300 hectares with almost 5500 meters of beach continuously, with nothing in between, although its utilisation can be centred on two specific points (centre and west), being the utilisation of the other remaining areas a residual characteristic.

Longitudinally we can identify 3 distinct areas of occupation: the first (east) it is a place with very difficult access conditions, almost wild; the second (centre) is composed basically by a fishermen community with 700 habitants, and a vast zone for restricted use by the portuguese navy; the third (occidental) is compose by summer houses, people are there only in the summer and at the weekends, having the majority of the houses a court order for demolition since 1991. The population floats between 17 residents during the winter and around 1500 in summerseason.

The ferry is the main means of transport between Olhão and the Island and it works in a regular basis. In 1992, a total of 220 137 passengers used the mentioned boat to visit the island, paying each one 135$00 as an entrance fee. The existence of this fee is very important to familiarise the users with a certain payment for access the service.

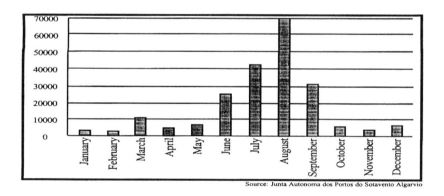

Source: Junta Autonoma dos Portos do Sotavento Algarvio

Graph 1.1. Culatra Total Visits/1992.

A special remark for the summer season, on which the number of visitors reached 1409 per day; this fact, occurring in an island with a dimension of approximately 300 hectares and with the permanent

272

occupations described before, brings out the importance of its demand as a public natural resource, specially for watering recreational activities.

Assuming the adequacy and supremacy of Contingent Valuation Method for assessing the benefits of environmental regulations when choice data are limited or unavailable (Mitchell and Carson, 1989), the next step of research was the choice between different survey-instrument designs, including differences in question format.

2. SURVEY RESEARCH

2.1. The open-ended format

The ultimate objective of a Contingent Valuation research is to obtain the individual consumer surplus for the environmental benefit, which is the maximum amount the good/service is worth to the individual before he prefers not to use or preserve it. A number of different formats have been used to ask contingent valuation questions. These formats are generally classified into two main categories: simple question and interacted series of questions approach.

The simple question category thinks the best way to estimate the consumer surplus is to ask the respondent the maximum price he is willing to pay for the good/service, record the answer and, as we are at the presence of a non-rival and non-exclusive benefit, aggregate the individuals values. One of the earliest attempts is the *open-ended format* (Hammack and Brown, 1974), but other relevant formats have been discussed and applied, as *dichotomous-choice* (Bishop and Heberlein, 1979, 1980), *payment-card* (Mitchell and Carson, 1981, 1984) and *sealed bid auction* (Bishop and Heberlein, 1986).

Interated approach argues that individuals often have strong difficulty to determine or pick a value that represented their maximum willingness to pay, as a consequence the elicitation techniques attempts to simplifying the choice process by offering a context in which the good/service is valued. The oldest interated technique is the *bidding game* (Davis, 1964); other methodological efforts have been materialised on *oral-auction* (Bohm, 1972) and *take-it-or-leave-it-with-follow-up* (Carson, Hanemann and Mitchell, 1986).

Besides the efforts and results of the last referred interated practices, where an initial amount is proposed and bid up or down, this type of dialogue tends to induce different forms of compliance bias: the individual gives higher values for an amenity, not because this value represents his maximum willingness to pay, but because he feels pressured by the follow up questions to give more than he really is willing to pay for (Mitchell and Carson, 1989).

Currently, the open-ended and dichotomous-choice simple question formats appear to be the most popular formats, with open-ended response distributions being used to generate dichotomous-choice bids.

The actual research presents a first step of this kind of join valuation technique approach, where in a second round it will be used the di-chotomous-choice format on Culatra case study (Perna, forthcoming). Generally, the empirical results suggest that the open-ended format under estimates actual willingness to pay and dichotomous choice format over estimates, but there is no agreement about the reason for the difference or about which format estimate the most accurate estimation of actual willingness to pay (McFadden, 1994).

Our option for open-ended format results from strong concern about precision and bias in willingness to pay estimates. First, the continuous open-ended data elicit more information about each individual's willingness to pay; second, the common criticism about individual's non-experience with an open-ended environmental choice decision, falls down with the generalised relation between Culatra recreational users and the ferry fee to access the Island; finally, if we use dichotomous choice on the first evaluation approach, we will need to impose strong assumptions about distribution of willingness to pay across individuals to estimate values from discrete data (Ready, Buzby and Hu, 1996).

Assuming the adequacy of open-ended format for estimating the maximum amount the good is worth to the users, where the respondents are familiar with the concept of paying for using the good with quality (Mitchell and Carson, 1986), the collecting of hyphotetical data through a questionnaire will lead us to the central scientific question of identification free-riding behaviour and efforts to respective bias correction in the total user value calculated for the population.

2.2. Data retrieval

With the objective of collecting all the necessary information to enable
the use of the evaluation technique, perceiving the purpose on making an
estimate of the user value of the island directly for recreation proposes,
majority sun&beach, it was made a questionnaire to the visitors of the
island during the year in study.

Calculated the population in 220137 annual visits, the sample was
collected by a random way, on a total of 450 visitors. This dimension is
due to framing between the dimensions considered usual in this kind of
surveys (Mitchell and Carson, 1989). The questionnaire was given and
fulfilled on the ferry during the trip, in the presence of the researcher,
who spoke only when was required to do so, mostly to explain the goal of
this study.

From the initial sample of 450 questionnaires, 100 were eliminated
due to formal incorrections, mainly the non-response to "net monthly
income" question, and other 18 because they mentioned "work" as their
main occupation in the island. As a result, we began with a valid sample
of 322 questionnaires for recreational proposes, having all of them less
one recreational visit during the year of 1992.

The use of an open-ended/direct question format will tend to produce a
large number of nonresponses or protest zero responses to the willingness
to pay question, which is a widely recognized problem on contingent
valuation discussion (Desvouges, 1983). Meanwhile, the mentioned
presence of the researcher and the previous experience of payment of an
entrance fee by the visitors, reduced a lot this tendency, having on the
final only 69 non or zero protests responses, on the total of the valid
sample; this means 79% of the inquired indicated their hypothetical
willingness to pay.

During the interrogation of the visitors, the scenery that was proposed
to them through the questionnaire, and always when requested a verbal
support, include four ordinay character information:

a) Establish the reference utility level through what the individuals are
    actually paying for the good (ferry fee);
b) The goods nature is explained, being considered all the island, this
    means that the visitor has or doesn't have access to the island
    recreational uses (sun&beach) and consequent benefits;

c) The possible variation of the demand's island does not affect much the price of the others goods (Mitchell and Carson, 1989);

d) The visitor is informed about the way in which the entrance fee is collected (in local and in cash), for how long their payment will allow them the access to the island (1 year), and that the other visitors also contribute obligatorily.

The questionnaire includes beyond the framing questions easier to answer, others directly connected with information capture to allow operationally of the evaluation: age, job, number of visits during the summer season, number of visits during the rest of the year, how he/she will fulfill his/her time on the island (main occupation), monthly income, willingness to pay to ensure the total of visits during all the year.

Afterwards we will show the potential biases and respective control attempt on *ex-ante*, specially the compliance and strategic behaviour, visible on the open-ended format question used in the questionnaire.

3. POTENTIAL BIASES

3.1. Compliance behaviour

Any benefits evaluation is subject to bias, even those based in real markets where the consumer behaviour is not free but compulsive (Rhoades, 1985), until the hypothetical markets where the inexistence of a traditional valorisation introduces more challenges to the investigation, namely the necessity of joining more incentives to true revelation (Cummings, Brookshire and Schulze, 1986), matter that is being subject of intensive analysis in contingent literatute and practice.

Confronted with this challenge, the main objective of contingent valuation consists on the obtention of a monetary value the most correct as possible. By correct we mean the most approximatly between the amounts of Revealed Willingness To Pay (RWTP) represented by each individual in the questionnaire and True Willingness To Pay (TWTP), that would exist in case the good or service was regulated by the traditional market laws.

In practice, the moment when open-ended questionnaire is being fulfilled, a relation between research and respondent is established and an emergent bias issue arises before econometric approach: can we trust the answers that people give us? If we can not, two situations could

276

happen, or their misstatements are honest ones, or they represent an option to strategic behaviour trying to influence the future social decision in his own advantage.

According to the most generalized classification (Mitchell and Carson, 1987), the first situation corresponds to named compliance behaviour, which attempts (consciously or unconsciously) to fulfill what the respondent perceives as the expectations of the interviewer. This includes design, hypothetical and operational bias.

3.1.1. Design Bias

The potential design bias is an outcome of several sources, with prominence for starting point bias, present in all the techniques of bidding game and take-it-or-leave-it-with follow-up, when the interwier chooses a first order offer. Several empirical studies have come to reassure the tendency to obtain a higher RWTP when the initial offer is higher than TWTP, and vice-versa, showing the existence of a correlation between the starting point and the average willingness obtained (Boyle, 1985).

A second source of design bias results from the payment vehicle adopted (Brookshire and Crocker, 1981). The election of a payment instrument used on collecting amounts of RWTP, can have some influence on the final result. The effectiveness of payments can be realised through governmental taxes, local taxes, entrance fees, loans, charitable donation, among others. The RWTP can float between the several payment vehicles, not because a change of good values, but, as an example, according to the individuals trust on the behaviour of the government (governmental taxes) or in the local administration (local taxes). The ideal is the adoption of a neutral payment vehicle, realistic and understandable by everyone.

Finally, the third source of this type of bias, consists on the so called information bias, those results from the information perception explicit in the questionnaire. It should contain relevant data for the evaluation and characterisation of the good, as well as neutral data that promotes prominence marks and incentives the individuals to answer. The scenario situations must be explained objectively and by the most natural order as possible (Mitchell and Carson, 1986b), otherwise they can influence the evelution result.

On the questionnaire made in Culatra Island, we consider that we had the *ex-ante* potential sources of the design bias under control. It was not considered any starting point offer as we use the open-ended format, although there is one that every individual is used to, which is the ferry's fee. The payment vehicle adopted is realistic and familiar: we suggest the total paralization of the ferry – and as a consequence the non-access into the island – that will end up with certain payment (bribe) to the ferry owner. This is an action fulfilled every day when visitors pay the ticket. The information bias is not present since every individual is concerned with what is being evaluated, because all of them know the island for recreation proposes and there is only a unique good under evaluation, the island on it self.

3.1.2. Hypothetical Bias
An initial difficulty in any contingential evaluation technique consists on its reducionist characteristic, because any good with various characteristics, such as Culatra Island, has to be identified and classified in a unique evaluation scale (monetary), that can cause or lead us to an underevaluation of some characteristics and overevaluate others. The presence and acknowledgement of detailed information about the island is essential to explain the several possible alternatives.

It adds that the RWTP for a good that until a certain time was free accessible or with a very low price, might not give a correct image of TWTP, in cases where the hypothesis on which the study is sustained remains confused. In those cases of misunderstanding, the individuals with the habit of a reduced entrance fee to use the good, tend to consider it part of their nature rights, which will increase their possibility of evaluation insurrection (Cummings, 1984). Due to this reason it is necessary to explain very well the hypothesis that sustains the study, namely the concretization or not of RWTP.

In Culatra Island case, we consider that this kind of bias was controlled successfully *ex-ante*, by the visitor's habit on paying for Island access. So, they are acquainted with confront the island use with a monetary scale. This payment familiarisation, and still according to Cummings (1984), is essential to avoid hypothetical bias, because it introduces a greater approach to real market conditions, so that potential estimates can be the most realistic as possible. Finally, on the questionnaire fulfil moment, any misunderstandings about the hypothesis that sustains the study were explained *in loco* by the interviewer and in the most clearly way.

278

3.1.3. Operational Bias

We have constantly pointed to several operational conditions of reference, essential for the correct operationally of contingent technique and specifically for open-ended format. The operational bias analysis concludes that it will be as minor as bigger is the individual's familiarity with the good (Cummings, Brookshire and Schulze, 1986). It is also important to have some previous experience concerning the use of different quantities of the good. However, those conditions of operationally if applied with severity, stipulate a lot the technique used, due to that we should add or allow the presence of a certain margin of freedom concerning to these conditions.

On the present evaluation the use of open-ended question reveals operational. The individuals are familiar with the good (1 or more visits during 1992), still being possible that they have some previous experience about variation on good use, this is, in previous years they might have done more or none visits, and due to that, they can feel the utility change assembles with this variation.

3.2. Strategic Behaviour

The preoccupation with strategic behaviour results from the presumption problem of making the individual reveal their true preferences, in contexts where if he does not say the truth, it still ensures a superior benefit according to the cost that he will support. This is the free-riding problem, very pertinent on the evaluation of recreational services based on public natural resources, because the inexistence of market unables the exclusion and rivality of consumption, leading the users (consumers) to act as free-riders through the distortion of RWTP.

The distortion can be on the ascendant way, in cases where the individual feels that a possible indication of an RWTP < TWTP can originate their future exclusion from good consumption, or in situations where the payment of RWTP is meanly hypothetical. In extreme cases the individuals can indicate an infinite value of RWTP, showing the total refusal to this kind of evaluation. This kind of distortion is less common and usually negligent.

The usual distortion will be on descendent way, when individuals consider not right the attempts of adopting a price (RWTP) bigger than what they are paying actually, namely the entrance fee. The users also tend to reveal a minor RWTP as a disavowal of any Island property rights.

In extreme cases they can deny to indicate any RWTP, that is the common situation of nonresponses.

The presence of free-riding behaviour has been object of numerous control efforts. Distinguish the Clarke-Groves mechanism, in which the individuals benefit is bigger if he indicates RWTP = TWTP, independently from the other individual's strategies (Clarke, 1971) and (Groves and Loeb, 1975).

Another type of control consists on the hypothesis tested by Rowe et al. (1980), that ask the RWTP on two user groups, and then inform one from the average RWTP of the other group, expecting a RWTP readjustment as function of this new information.

The control technique adopted in Culatra evaluation to control free-riding behaviour, is based on a third hypothesis, known as decision socialisation, actually successfully utilized in local portuguese scenarios (Figueira, 1994). On the question relationed with the RWTP, we suggest the total ferry paralization as scenario, which will end with an obligatory payment of a certain amount by each visitant to the ferry owner. After the payment by all individuals, the ferry re-establishes the visits for all year. Notice the fact that the ferry only stops the paralization if the sum of all individuals RWTP amounts is superior than to given quantity, which is not known.

In this way, the participation of all individuals implies that no one will benefit from the Island reopening without having contributed with a certain RWTP. The possibility of collective exclusion works as an incentive to no subevaluation of RWTP; the unpossibility of paying alone the total amount necessary to reopen the ferry or to assure a bigger benefit than he or she actually has, works as an incentive to no overevaluation of RWTP; also the individuals do not have any reference point for the average contribution, once they do not know the exact total amount necessary to reopen the access to Island. Together, these three factors may contribute to the desired RWTP = TWTP, with the consequent ex-ante free-rider control behaviour.

4. CALCULATING REVEALED USER VALUE

To estimate the Culatra Island user value for recreational proposes during 1992, from now on referred to as *V*, we realised a first simplified approach. More detailed analysis and calculus can be carried out in Perna (1994), inclusively an estimation of the demand curve and a confrontation with Travel Cost Method estimates.

Through the questionnaire fulfils, each individual i of the valid sample reveals his/her willingness to pay, $RWTP_i$, and the number of visits performed during 1992, k_i. Adding all the $RWTP_i$ and the k_i, we obtain the following amounts

$$\sum_{i=1} RWTP_i = 3361 \times 10^3 \text{ esc.}$$

$$\sum_{i=1} k_i = K = 9404 \text{ visits.}$$

Also, based on this sample data, we can calculate the average RWTP for each visit to Culatra Island

$$\sum_{i=1} RWTP_i \Big/ \sum_{i=1} k_i = 357 \text{ esc.} \tag{4.1}$$

We consider that the user value, V, is calculated based on the RWTP for all the individuals. We can define V as

$$V = (T/K) \left(\sum_{i=1} RWTP_i \right) \tag{4.2}$$

Knowing Culatra Island total visits during 1992, $T = 220137$, we estimate the user value given in equation above, through the substitution of $RWTP_i$ by the observed values in the sample. Calculating we have

$$V = 7868 \times 10^3 \text{ esc.}$$

as the total user value of Culatra Island for recretional proposes during the year of 1992. Assuming the control of design, hypothetical and operational bias, we have now to ask about the presence of strategic behaviour, after all, the mainly source of bias in this type of analysis.

5. DETECTION FREE-RIDING BEHAVIOUR

Culatra Island has an approximated market price for access, based on the ferry fare (135$00). This is, we know the minimum amount that each individual I spends to visit the Island during the year, S_i, results from

$$S_i = (k_i) (135\$00) \qquad (5.1)$$

Now, we can establish an hegemony criteria for free-riding behaviour detection based on the comparison for each individual i

$$RWTP_i < S_i, \text{ individual } i \text{ is a free-rider} \qquad (5.2)$$

$$RWTP_i = S_i, \text{ individual } i \text{ is not a free-rider} \qquad (5.3)$$

Observing the sample data collection we conclude that 47% of individuals have potential free-riding behaviour, with a strong tendency for distortion on descendent way. So, if we validate the above estimate of V, we assume a great risk for underestimating the real Island use value, with all the problems that can rise in a future cost-benefit analysis.

6. ESTIMATING TRUE USER VALUE

6.1. Correction of Free-Riding Bias

The true willingness to pay for from individual i, $TWTP_i$, can be considered a random variable which assumes one among two possible values according to

$$TWTP_i = RWTP_i \text{ if individual } i \text{ is not a free-rider} \qquad (6.1)$$

$$TWTP_i = RWTP_i + b_i \text{ if individual } i \text{ is a free-rider} \qquad (6.2)$$

where b_i is a positive quantity measuring the bias for individual i occurring from a free-riding behaviour. $TWTP_i$ can be considered a Bernoulli random variable equal to $RWTP_i + b_i$ with probability p_i, the probability that individual i is a free-rider, and to $RWTP_i$ with probability $(1 - p_i)$, that is the probability that individual i is not a free-rider. Therefore the expected value of an individual true willingness to pay for is

$$E\,[TWTP_i\,] = RWTP_i + b_i\,p_i \qquad (6.3)$$

We consider now that the user value is calculated based on the true willingness to pay for all individuals instead of the revealed willingness to pay for as before. We call it V^* to distinguish from the later identified as V in equation (4.2), and define it as

$$V^* = (T/K)\left(\sum_{i=1} \text{TWTP}_i\right) \qquad (6.4)$$

The expected user value is obtained substituting in the equation above TWTP_i by its expectation leading to the following expression,

$$
\begin{aligned}
E[V^*] &= (T/K)\left(\sum_{i=1} \text{RWTP}_i\right) + (T/K)\left(\sum_{i=1} b_i p_i\right) \\
&= V + (T/K)\left(\sum_{i=1} b_i p_i\right)
\end{aligned} \qquad (6.5)
$$

where the first term in the second hand-side is equal to the usual user value and the second term gives the bias correction for the free-riding effect. This correction is always greater than zero if there is at least one individual with a non null probability of having a free-riding behaviour.

To estimate the expected user value given in equation above, RWTP_i can be substituted by the observed values in the sample. However quantities b_i and p_i are not observable. They have to be substituted by accurate estimates. In the following we show how these quantities can be estimated for the particular example under study in this paper.

6.2. Estimation of individual probability to be a free-rider

For each i individual consider the random variable Y_i such that, $Y_i = 1$ if the individual has a free-riding behaviour and $Y_i = 0$ otherwise. We assume that the probability that individual I has a free-riding behaviour can be explained by a logit model according to:

$$P(Y_i = 1|X_i = x_i) = 1/(1 + \exp(-x_i'\beta)) \qquad (6.6)$$

where x_i is a vector of explanatory variables characterizing the individual and β is a vector of unknown coefficients. The variables used in the regressions performed within this application are identified and described in the table below.

Table 6.1
Description of the variables used in the application

Variable	Definition/Comments
Age	Age of the respondent
Sex	Dummy, is equal to 1 if the respondent is male
Student	Dummy; is equal to 1 if the respondent is a student
District	Dummy, is equal to 1 if the respondent has residence in the Algarve
Income	Logarithm of the income declared by the respondent
Winter trips	Dummy, is equal to 1 if the respondent visits the island in winter
Total trips	Total trips made within the year by the respondent
Safety	Dummy, is equal to 1 if the respondent has a positive opinion about the Island safety
RWTP	Logarithm of the willingness to pay for declared by the respondent

6.3. Results of the logit fit

Among the variables available in the sample, we have considered as explanatory variables that characterize the individual and may influence his behaviour as free-riding the following: the age of the individual; the sex of the individual; a dummy that indicates if the individual is a student given the high percentage of students in the sample (32%); a dummy indicating if the individual has residence in the Algarve given the high percentage of locals in the sample (53%); the individual income; a dummy indicating if the individual visits the island in winter because the use and utility that the individual gets from the winter visits have different characteristics than those he gets in general from summer visits and consequently individuals with winter visits may have a distinguished behaviour; the total number of visits which gives an indicator of how much the individual enjoys the use of the public good; the individual opinion about the Island safety (for recreational purposes); and finally, the amount of willingness to pay for declared by individual.

The logit fit was obtained using the Multinomial Logit Estimation module of the package TSP Version 4.2A. The *t*-values are shown in Table 6.2, below.

The amount of willingness to pay for, island safety, total number of visits, income, student condition and sex, seems not to be statistically significant to explain the individual probability of being a free-rider given that the respective coefficient estimate has a *t*-statistic with value out of confidence interval. Therefore, all these variables were dropped

Table 6.2
Results of the logit fit – full model

Variables	Coeffic. Estimates	*t*-Statistics
Intercept	−0,8962	−2,1052
Age	0,0158	1,5888
Sex	0,0282	0,4856
Student	−0,3309	−1,1733
District	−0,1590	−1,5646
Income	−19,1065	−0,8627
Winter trips	1,0939	3,6660
Total trips	−0,0086	−0,1621
Safety	−3,0121	−0,2592
RWTP	−265,9930	−0,1490

Table 6.3
Results of the logit fit – restricted model

Variables	Coeffic. Estimates	*t*-Statistics
Intercept	−1,0627	−3,1893
Age	0,0220	2,4910
District	−1,1689	−1,6902
Winter trips	1,0638	4,3240

and a logit regression was run for the remain variables. We call to this regression the restricted model. The results are shown in Table 6.3.

The sign of the coefficient estimates leads to significant conclusions. Let us emphasize the age results: the older a person is the greater the probability of having free-riding behaviour. We think this situation results from two main reasons. First, older visitors tend to deny this type of hypothetical evaluation, typically they are more close-minded and tend to refuse unexpected changes; second, older people have a strong memory of island access with no rules (economic or other), it is not easy to accept a change of this *status quo* after years and years of practice.

Also the tendency for free-riding behaviour is a fact associated to winter visitors. As well as older visitors motives, we think this situation is developed by a more prominent property right winter, people who go there in that season are almost alone in the Island.

Finally, visitors with residence in the Algarve show a disposition not to assume a free-riding behaviour. Presumably this happens as a consequence of their bigger island closeness and familiarity, together with a crescent sensibility to environment user problems, common to the Algarve population, after some natural resources like water and clean beaches became scarce in the name of "development". As consequence they are skilled to transmit a close RWTP = TWTP, and do not deny a payment for what they positively use.

6.4. Estimation of Free-Riding Bias

To calculate the expected user value it is needed the quantity b_i, that is the bias resulting from the strategic behaviour of the individual as free-rider. In other words, the quantity he or she would have declared additionally if the free-riding behaviour is absent. Given that this quantity is not observable makes it harder to estimate. We use an heuristic procedure to obtain this estimate (Perna and Proença, 1996). This approach is open to criticism. We intend to contribute to improve it, being the subject of further research. The subsequent paragraphs explain the mentioned procedure.

We expect that if the individuals with a free-riding behaviour had not chosen that option then they would have a behaviour similar to the non free-rider individuals. Therefore, if a model is found that explains reasonably the willingness to pay of the individuals with non free-riding behaviour it can be used to forecast the willingness to pay for for the other individuals, that is, to simulate this quantity if the free-riding behaviour was not present. An estimate of the bias for each individual is then calculated by the difference of this adjusted willingness to pay for with the declared willingness to pay for.

Based on the idea expressed above we have considered a linear model to adjust the declared willingness to pay for the individuals in the sample which were classified as non free-riders. Recall that the correction term for the expected user value is the addition for all individuals of the possible bias as free-rider, times the respective probability of having a free-riding behaviour. Therefore, we need for all individuals in the sample an estimate of the bias. This estimate will be important in the correction term for the individuals with free-riding effect because it is expected that their estimated probability of being free-rider is high while for the others the estimated bias is multiplied by a small quantity, the probability of being a free-rider.

Table 6.4
Results of the linear fit for RWTP

Variable	Coef. Estimates	t-Statistics
Intercept	−4,443	−2,481
Expenses	0,612	10,588
Income	−0,814	5,491

For each individual the estimated bias is equal to the maximum among zero and the difference between the adjusted willingness to pay for given by the linear regression and the declared willingness to pay for by the individual. Note that for individuals classified in the sample as having no free-riding effect the bias is just the residual of the linear regression and consequently may be negative which theoretically is not possible. Thus, negative values should be assigned equal to zero instead.

One alternative approach would be to run a regression for the individuals in the sample with free-riding effect and use this model to calculate an estimate of the possible bias for those with no free-riding behaviour. This procedure assumes that the free-riding behaviour would have the same structure in all individuals. This may not be the case and if so, introduces some distortions in the calculation of the expected user value.

For the individuals in the sample classified as having no free-riding behaviour, a linear regression was run for the logarithm of their declared willingness to pay for having as explanatories the logarithm of the individual expenses to visit the island and the logarithm of the individual income. Other variables were previously included in the linear regression but they have shown to be statistically not significant. The results are shown in Table 6.4. They were obtained using the package SPSS.

7. THE UNBIASED EXPECTED USER VALUE ESTIMATION

We can now calculate the corrected expected user value for Culatra Island, based on TWTP$_i$ with the conditions assumed in equations (6.1) and (6.2). Adding all the TWTP$_i$ we have now

$$\sum_{i=1} \text{TWPI}_i = 5036 \times 10^3 \text{ esc.}$$

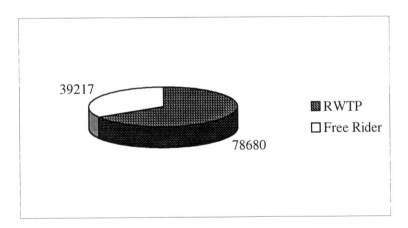

Graph 7.1. True User Value for Culatra Island.

Once again, based on sample data but assuming the bias correction on reformulating equation (4.1), we can calculate the average TWTP for each visit to Culatra Island

$$\sum_{i=1} \text{TWTP}_i / \sum_{i=1} k_i = 536 \text{ esu.} \tag{7.1}$$

We have the necessary conditions to estimate the corrected user value based on equations (6.4) and (6.5)

$$V^* = (T/K)\left(\sum_{i=1} \text{TWTP}_i\right) = 117897 \times 10^3 \text{ esu.}$$

Concluding, when we correct the strategic behaviour in Culatra Island recreational benefit evaluation, the user value estimation for recreational proposes based on RWTP suffers a real increment of almost 50%, that is the dimension of free-riding behaviour. The implications on a cost-benefit analysis are obvious. This is enough to argue for the urgent necessity to utilize the TWTP as preferential benefit measure, even in those special hypohetical cases when this quantity is not observable.

REFERENCES

Bishop, R.C. and T.A. Heberlein (1979) "Measuring Values of Extra-Market Goods: Are Indirect Methods Biased?", *American Journal of Agricultural Economics*, vol. 19, n.4, pp. 926–930.

Bishop, R.C. and T.A. Heberlein (1986) "Does Contingent Valuation Work?", in Ronald Cummings, David Brookshire and William Schulze eds., *Valuing Environmental Goods*, Totawa N.J., Rowman and Allanheld.

Bohm, P. (1972) "Estimating Demand for Public Goods: An Experiment", *European Economic Review*, vol. 3, pp. 111–130.

Boyle, K.J. (1996) "Valuing Public Goods: Discrete versus Continuous Contingent-Valuation Responses", *Land Economics*, vol. 72, n.3, pp. 381–96.

Brookshire, D.S. and T.D. Crocker (1981) "The Advantages of Contingent Valuation Methods For Cost Benefit Analysis", *Public Choice*, vol. 36, pp. 235–252.

Brown, T.C. et al., (1996) "Which Response Format Reveals the Truth about Donations to a Public Good", *Land Economics*, vol. 72, n. 2, pp. 152–166.

Carson, R.T., W.M. Hanemann, R.C. Mitchell (1986) "Determining the Demand for Public Goods by Simulating Referendums at Different Tax Prices", manuscript, University of California, San Diego.

Clarke, E.D. (1971) "Multipart Pricing of Public Goods", *Public Choice*, vol. 11, pp. 19–33.

Cummings, R.G., D.S. Brookshire, W.D. Schulze, eds (1986) *Valuing Environmental Goods, A state of the Art Assessment of Contingent Valuation Method*, Totowa N.J., Rowman and Allanheld.

Davis, R.K. (1964) "The Value of Big Game Hunting in a Private Forest", in *Transactions of the 29th North American Wildlife and Natural Resources Conference*, Washington DC, Wildlife Management Institute.

Desvouges, W. (1983) *A comparison of alternative approaches for estimating recreation and related benefits of water quality improvements*, U.S. Environmental Protection Agency.

Groves, T. and M. Loeb (1975) "Incentives and Public Inputs", *Journal of Public Economics*, vol. 4, pp. 211–226.

Figueira, D. (1994) *Contingent Valuation Method Applied to Public Water Services: The Case of Vila do Sardoal*, Master Dissertation, Technical University of Lisbon, Lisboa.

Freeman, A.M. (1986) "On Assessing the State of the Arts of the Contingent Valuation Method of Valuing Environmental Changes", in Ronald Cummings, David Brookshire, and William Schulze eds., *Valuing Environmental Goods*, Totawa, N.J., Rowman and Allanheld.

Hammack, Judd and Gardner Brown Jr. (1974) *Waterfowl and Wetlands: Towards Bioeconomic Analysis*, Baltimore, Johns Hopkins University Press.

McFadden, D. (1994) "Contingent Valuation and Social Choice", *American Journal of Agricultural Economics*, n. 76 (Nov,) pp. 689–708.

Mitchell, R.C. and Richard T.C. (1981) "An Experiment in Determining Willingness to Pay for National Water Quality Improvments", draf report to the U.S. Environmental Agency, Washington DC.

Mitchell, R.C. and R.T. Carson (1984) *A Contingent Valuation Estimate of National Freshwater Benefits: Technical Report to the US Environmental Agency*, Washington DC, Resources for the Future.

Mitchell, R.C. and R.T. Carson (1986) "Some Comments on the State of the Arts Report", in Ronald Cummings, David Brookshire and William Schultze eds., Valuing Environmental Goods, Totawa N.J., Rowman and Allanheld.

Mitchell, R. and R.T. Carson (1986b) "Property Rights, Protest, and the Siting of Hazardous Waste Facilities", *American Economic Review*, vol. 76, n. 2, pp. 285–290.

Mitchell, R.C. and R.T. Carson (1987) "Evaluating the Validity of Contingent Valuation Studies", Discussion Paper QE87-06, Quality of the Environment Division, Washington DC, Resources for the Future.

Mitchell, R.C. and R.T. Carson (1989) *Using Surveys to Value Public Goods: The Contingent Valuation Method*, Washington, DC, Resources for the Future.

Perna, F. (1994) *Environmental Benefits Evaluation: The Culatra Island Case Study*, Master Dissertation, Technical University of Lisbon, Lisboa.

Perna, F. (forthcoming) "Contingent Valuation Techniques Applied to Environment: Alternative Scenarios to Ilha da Culatra", University of Algarve, Faro.

Perna, F. and I. Proença (1996) "The Free-Riding Behaviour in Applications With the Contingent Technique of Open-Ended/ Direct Question", Andrea Baranzini and

Fabrizio Carlevaro eds., *Econometrics of Environment and Transdisciplinarity*, pp. 260–261, Applied Econometrics Association, Lisbon.

Rhoads, S.E. (1985) *The Economist's View of the World: Goverment, Markets and Public Policy*, New York, Cambridge University Press.

CHAPTER - 17

THE COST OF WEALTHY MODERN CITIES

Peter Seidel

ABSTRACT

Affluent cities in developed nations impose a rapidly increasing burden on the earth that cannot be sustained. Yet people elsewhere desire to copy many of these cities' features. Cities do offer benefits. However, nature, those who live in them, those who live elsewhere, and future generations pay a high price for the earth's affluent cities. These costs are discussed. Inhabitants derive most of the benefits from wealthy cities and make the decisions involving them. Nature and most of those who bear the burden are powerless. This is dangerous. To do better, we must look at cities in new ways and deal with them as systems that are part of the world system. In doing so, we need to protect nature and divide the planet's resources more equitably between all people, including future generations.

INTRODUCTION

Today we are changing the face of our planet at an explosive rate. Our rapidly expanding urban areas, particularly affluent ones in "developed nations", and how people live in them play an important role in this. These cities have an impact that reach around the world. Their high levels of consumption and waste affect people far beyond their borders, future generations, and the earth itself. Many people see features of these cities as models to emulate. And the inevitable forces of the modern world drive other cities to adopt many of their characteristics. We would be wise to examine the benefits offered by these urban areas and compare them with their costs.

North American metropolitan areas, which are surrounded by reasonably priced farm land and have roots reaching back into the mid-nineteenth century or before, are good models to examine. They are technically advanced, wealthy, and have plenty of room to grow. They also have districts which predate modern transportation that present problems similar to those many other cities are experiencing. I shall call these conurbations "technorich cities".

Cities have always attracted people because they provide a wide variety of jobs, educational opportunities, social contacts, cultural experiences, entertainment, and shopping. They offer businesses skilled employees, easily procured materials, energy, and access to markets. Vital, energetic cities are economic and cultural assets to regions, nations, and sometimes the world.

In technorich cities streetcars (and later buses), rapid transit, and commuter railroads enabled people to escape congested central urban areas and move to low density suburbs or nearby communities. This caused cities to expand along these routes. Later, automobiles, trucks, and electronic communication permitted people, businesses, and institutions to move anywhere people were willing to commute. This spurred cities to expand over nearby countryside. Safe water distribution systems (sometimes bringing water from hundreds of miles away) and sanitation systems made it practical and safe for large numbers of people to live in urban areas.

Modern modes of transportation and communication have put these cities in close contact with both the region right around them and remote places on the earth. This has enabled them to become large, wealthy, and to provide a high standard of living to their inhabitants. However, there are costs related to the physical aspects of these cities – some obvious, some not. They are paid not only by those who live in them, but also by those who do not, and by nature.

TECHNORICH CITIES ARE BAD FOR NATURE

The energetic technorich city is ever greedy for more land and is a high metabolizer, consuming large amounts of energy and raw materials from which it produces products and services. In doing so, following the laws of physics, it produces waste materials in the form of pollution, and waste energy in the form of heat.

According to the Farm Land Trust, the United States lost four million acres of prime farm land to urbanization between 1982 and 1992. As American population grows, its food surplus will disappear and, if present trends continue, will neither be available for export nor to meet America's own needs. Considering the deterioration of the earth's soils, for countries grown dependent on American exports, this will be tragic.

Land that once supported oxygen producing, water retaining vegetation has been stripped of topsoil, built upon, paved, or replaced with thin layers of sod. Now instead of replenishing aquifers, water is quickly shed into waterways, increasing the danger of flooding, and causing water levels to be low in streams, lakes, and reservoirs when moisture is needed during dry seasons. Chemicals used on pavement and lawns pollute runoff. Pavement absorbs radiation from the sun and retains heat, significantly increasing local temperature in cities. This raises the demand for air-conditioning – which produces still more heat. Streets and parking lots also require energy to produce, maintain, and illuminate them. Still more pavement is needed to carry traffic past parking lots.

Traditional communities obtained food from the surrounding countryside and returned organic waste to it to help maintain its fertility. Now, large cities need more food than can be produced nearby and demand exotic varieties in both summer and winter. To meet these demands, in the United States large food distribution companies desiring a steady, year-round supply of fruits and vegetables buy from producers thousands of miles away. Meat, poultry and eggs are increasingly obtained from agribusinesses that concentrate animals and poultry in huge complexes. This makes it uneconomical to return organic wastes to the soil. Instead, precious nutrients are deposited in landfills or find their way into waterways and aquifers which they pollute.

Chemicals are used to replace nutrients necessary to produce marketable crops, but there are few incentives to replace others that are needed for human health. Soils deprived of humus and compacted by heavy farming equipment deteriorate over time. To maximize profits, farms in many distant producing areas grow a single crop, year after year. This requires the administration of ever-increasing levels of polluting fertilizers, herbicides, and pesticides. For a while this is profitable, but in essence, it is mining the soil of its productivity.

This practice is not limited to affluent nations. To profit from the wants of technorich cities, land in poor countries that was once farmed by peasants to feed themselves has been accumulated by rich landowners to produce cash crops for export. These landowners grow richer while many former peasants are left without work and little to eat. Sometimes the well-to-do in poor countries gain at the expense of the citizenry and environment by accepting garbage and hazardous waste from wealthy cities.

By causing us to reshape and expand our cities, the automobile has made itself indispensable. We cannot buy food, get to our job, see a doctor, or visit friends without one. Autos are a drug we have been lured into taking and now cannot get along without. Ordinary trips, which once consumed no more than human energy, now require the utilization of huge quantities of petroleum, steel, and concrete.

In the United States, people used to walk to grocery stores which had offices or apartments above them. Today, these same facilities, separated from each other and with all necessary parking, may cover from ten to fifty times as much land. Additional streets covering more land are needed to bring people to them. Over the years grocery stores have been replaced by supermarkets of ever larger size that continue to become fewer and more remote. We have no choice but to drive farther and farther to shop for food and other necessities.

This works well for businesses which save on labor costs and fuel by delivering to a few major locations. However, the total amount of time spent and miles driven by shoppers to reach these large stores dwarfs the merchants' savings. The store owners are very aware of their costs, but the shoppers largely ignore theirs. Municipalities do no better. They react by building the roads needed to handle the additional traffic but do nothing to reduce it. In fact, zoning regulations, tax structures, lending practices, and public concepts of what is desirable dictate the consolidation of functions, such as retail outlets, at a low densities.

BAD FOR PEOPLE, COMMUNITIES, AND DEMOCRACY

Without doubt automobiles are attractive – to those who are in them. They take us where we want to go, when we want to go, in comfort and privacy. When there are few of them, they get us to our destination quickly, can be fun to drive, and make us feel important. However they are a menace to everyone else, are destructive to the urban and natural environment, mutilate and kill millions of people and countless animals, consume irreplaceable resources, and pollute. And when there are many automobiles, they make urban life close to unbearable as in Los Angeles and Bangkok.

In the United States the automobile offers those who wish to, and can afford to, the potential to escape the social and economic problems, noise, pollution, and congestion (largely caused by motor vehicles) in central cities by moving out to independent legal entities called suburbs. This way affluent people can ensure that their property taxes will be used to benefit themselves and not be used to support services such as city public schools, parks, libraries, and social services. Undesirable land uses, such as housing for low income people and many types of businesses, can be kept out – although inoffensive businesses that pay high taxes may be actively solicited. This creates what may now have become a non-ending process of people leaving problems, moving away, and erecting new fences (sometimes physical ones with guarded gates) around enclaves in order to avoid facing up to communal problems. Nearly all cities in the United States are now collections of self-governing districts trying to disengage themselves from shared responsibility.

The people who escaped central cities also left much that was good and created an environment for themselves that is neither city nor country. Modern homogeneous suburbs isolate homemakers, children, the aged, and the handicapped. They lack the stimulation and educational experiences for children that farms, small towns, and older neighborhoods provide. Once children could watch their father at his trade, observe the blacksmith and the weaver, visit school friends, and go to the public library and city museum on their own. Lacking these possibilities, they may be left with activities such as passively watching television or getting into trouble. Streets, often without safety-providing sidewalks, lead past houses belonging to people with similar incomes and tastes to more of the same. To make up for their lack of exercise, some of the inhabitants drive to health spas to walk on specially designed walking machines.

For a democracy to work well, people need to communicate with each other, especially with people who have needs and views different than their own. Suburbs, the automobile, and the electronic media have reduced such contact. Shopping malls owned by large corporations and filled with strangers and national chain-stores do not belong to the community, as "Main Street" with shops owned by one's neighbors did. Most people, for that matter, shop in malls that are outside of the community they live in. The only way to participate in a mall is to spend.

TECHNORICH CITIES ARE UNECONOMICAL

It costs more to run a business requiring a parking lot with a brightly lit sign than one where a lettered front door suffices. Reliance on the automobile and the infrastructure of pavement, sewers, lighting, signage, and policing needed to support it is expensive. In addition, much time is wasted moving people and goods about. This dependence siphons money out of local economies to pay for fuel, parts, and the vehicles themselves. In calculating the cost of cities, the health risks, damage to people and goods resulting from pollution and traffic accidents, and social problems arising from abandoning the poor in central cities and from the boredom in the suburbs should not be ignored.

TECHNORICH CITIES ARE VULNERABLE

In the United States our euphoria based on a long period of prosperity, economic growth, and developing new technologies has lulled us into ignoring lessons of the past and our increasing dependence on things beyond our control.

Cities need regular supplies of food, materials, and energy from remote locations. If their supplies of clean water, energy, and medicine are interupted, epidemics can start and spread rapidly. Without energy, water cannot be pumped, waste cannot be removed, people are immobile, food and medical supplies cannot be transported and communication systems do not work. In high-rise buildings, electricity is needed to operate elevators, provide light, pump water to upper floors, remove waste, heat, cool, and supply fresh air to rooms with inoperable windows. In the suburbs, electricity is essential to run furnaces, pumps, and refrigerators. Gasoline is needed to go almost anyplace, to obtain food, and bring food to markets.

L.F. Ivanhoe, geologist, geophysicist, engineer, oceanographer, and sponsor and coordinator of the M. King Hubbert Center for Petroleum Supply Studies, predicts that world demand will likely catch up with crude oil supply around the year 2010, with sharp increases in retail prices. Unless some yet unknown technology comes to the rescue, if Mr. Ivanhoe is right, we in technorich cities are in for a terrible shock around 2010 AD. If his estimate of when this event will occur is too early, the shock will come later, but the consequences will be worse.

A prolonged economic downturn with moderate unemployment could make the affluent lifestyle now prevalent in some countries unaffordable for many people, creating instability. Under such circumstances, societies dependent on energy and other necessities imported from afar will find it difficult to compete economically with those that have small material demands and are not dependent on an infrastructure that is costly to maintain. North American cities' complex water, energy, communication, information, and transport systems are susceptible to disruption and are easy targets for terrorists. They rely on a dependable supply of intelligent, responsible, trained personnel to run them. As time passes, finding people capable of maintaining increasingly complex systems will become more difficult and the likelihood of breakdowns more likely.

Referring to technorich cities as "developed" is a misnomer. They are in a state of flux, changing more rapidly each day, exploding outwardly, remaking themselves inwardly, and are often eroding at the core. We have no idea what they will be like in fifty years or how they will react under stress. They are poor models to emulate.

CONVOLUTED FEEDBACK SYSTEMS

Stable dynamic systems, whether they be steam engines or beehives, have feedback loops that maintain equilibrium – the right speed or population.

Technorich cities have feedback mechanisms, but they are incomplete and may actually promote instability.

While many benefits of these cities are obvious to their citizens, many of their costs are not. Consequently, decisions are often made without considering the cost. Sometimes important choices are made by people with political or economic power who base decisions on what is good for them, disregarding negative effects on less influential people. Those who live in other places, future generations, and the planet itself have no say at all. Without their input, these cities are pursuing a dangerous path.

The automobile presents a similar situation. While driving may benefit drivers and passengers, everyone else and nature are hurt but have little influence over their use. But even for their owners the choice of whether to drive is not a balanced one. Once the car and its insurance are paid for, it is relatively inexpensive to operate, it seems to be almost free. Many of its costs, such as roads and caring for those permanently injured by it, may be paid for by property taxes. The automobile has established a positive feedback loop for itself. The more of them there are, the more they change our cities and the more difficult it is to get along without one.

These harmful feedback loops are strengthened by how we who live in these affluent cities view reality. In our minds, our artificial environment is more real to us than the soils, waters, and atmosphere that support our life. We see food as coming from supermarkets in plastic packages instead of from the soil. Airplanes and automobiles make Florida's beaches and Disneyland more familiar to us than the countryside around our cities. Television makes us more familiar with the names of soaps, beers, and breakfast foods than the plants in our gardens. We feel freed from the constraints and discomforts of nature, to the necessity of enduring hot, humid days, for example. Consequently, our concept of how we and our urban environment fit into nature is illusionary. By our demands and lack of understanding, we inadvertently do great harm to nature.

WE FIX SYMPTOMS, NOT CAUSES

Cities have many complex social and economic problems, and governments make many detailed studies of them. These studies normally approach things as phenomena having limited relationships to other things.

They then try to solve these difficulties by fixing their symptoms. To relieve traffic, we widen roads or build more of them. To reduce pollution and save petroleum, we require manufacturers to build more efficient cars with pollution reducing (but fuel consuming) catalytic converters and encourage people to use public transit. To encourage "desirable" uncongested growth, municipalities require homes, factories, and shopping centers to be placed on large lots. This necessitates moving people and goods over greater distances – increasing the amount of traffic on roads.

Rarely do we see a city's problems as parts of an integrated whole interacting with all aspects of its inhabitants' lives and the biosphere. We would do well to begin solving problems by standing back not ignoring, but looking beyond detailed data, and like the little boy who noted that the emperor was naked, seeing cities in a very simple way and considering what they basically are.

MACRO VIEW NEEDED

We should see a city for what it is, a collection of connected places. The places contain people, activities, goods, and what they need such as buildings, water, clean air, and information. The connections are means for moving people, goods, energy, and information. By viewing cities holistically, we will discover how to achieve our goals in ways that work well for people and are also efficient, economical, and much more compatible with nature.

We should not regard transportation as a means to move as many cars as possible from point A to point B, but rather as a connecting structure – transferring people and goods from one *function* to another. Distance and means then become irrelevant. What matters is getting to work, to shopping, or a secure place to play, quickly, comfortably, safely, and economically; and moving goods unobtrusively at minimum cost. By locating places people want to go as near to each other as possible, and where this cannot be done, arranging them so that they have easy access to good public transportation, the automobile is no longer a necessity. By using transportation routes as a structure to place functions along, rather than as a repair tool for existing problems, a very different form of city with less traffic, pollution, noise, and wasted energy will emerge.

Status and the ease of division and salability of land should not determine lot shapes and sizes. Equal or even better access to light and air, privacy, and improved aesthetics can be provided on much smaller parcels than those on the edges of technorich cities. We can save energy and materials by reducing the building surface these cities present to the weather, and by proper orientation, gain much energy from the sun.

People living in pedestrian-oriented communities strung along a rapid transit route would have better access to each other, their jobs, and needs than people in similar size technorich cities have today. The land beyond these communities, within easy walking distance of everyone, could provide locally grown food, accept treated organic wastes, and provide recreation. Solving problems in an integrated way enables the solution of one problem to contribute to the solution of others, not to the creation of others as is now so often the case. Actually, almost all of our human-made problems today are the results of past efforts to better our lives.

CITIES FOLLOW NATURAL LAWS

Cities are governed by natural laws like those of physics, chemistry, and biology. Some of their features can be described by mathematical equations. The maxims of psychology, sociology, economics, and politics, by acting through us, also affect what cities are and how they work as well. All of these factors interact with each other and cannot be considered alone. Cities are systems made up of interacting subsystems and are themselves subsystems of the world about them.

Although new on Earth, cities are governed by the laws of evolution and ecology just like every thing else. Ants, bees and beavers have evolved community structures that have found stable places in nature. Many indigenous peoples have done the same. What is different about our cities is that they have not been around long enough to receive significant feedback from nature. To avoid evolution's and ecology's unpleasant ways of eliminating misfits, we must foresee the dangers we are creating, and alleviate them before we suffer the consequences.

We really have not considered what level of damage to most of the world's people, future generations, and our planet is fair and an acceptable cost for the way we build and live in our cities. This is an ethical question that goes beyond the scope of this article. However, we can look at some of its implications.

We really do not know how much abuse our planet can take and still provide a viable environment for people. Nor do we know how long the world's present population and levels of consumption and pollution can be sustained. It is clear our environment has deteriorated from that of twenty-five years ago and it is continuing to do so. High as it already is, the living standard of the people in technorich cities continues to grow. And the swelling population of the rest of the world would like to catch up. We are not all going to get what we want, nor be able to sustain what we have.

It is not easy to ask people to reduce their standard of living, nor is it fair to expect others to forgo what people in the technorich cities enjoy. But for everyone to pursue their goals of an ever higher standard of living would be certain disaster for our planet, future generations, and in time, even for some of us alive today.

Without confronting difficult ethical questions, there are several things that can help. We can find more efficient ways to achieve our goals. I have suggested how that we can do that by restructuring our cities. We should also examine what really contributes to human happiness and fulfillment. My observations of people as a child during the depression, when I was in the Navy, and in less affluent parts of the world, is that, if one is healthy, free, not deprived of necessities, and has challenging tasks to do, additional possessions do not increase one's happiness. I think most people know this, but do not live accordingly. We need to stress this point in education. While we cannot directly measure happiness, several suggestions have been made which would bring us closer to it.

In its Human Development Report 1990, the United Nations Development Program proposed establishing a "human development index" combining gross national product (GNP) per capita with life expectancy at birth, adult literacy rate, and purchasing power which could be used to

302

measure the economic well-being of a country. Economist Herman Daly and theologian John Cobb have gone further. They developed an "Index of Sustainable Economic Welfare". It incorporates a wide range of factors: air and water pollution, cropland losses, income inequality, and the total costs related to automobile use. Economists could do the world a great service by moving in this direction.

REFERENCES

Farming on the Edge, American Farmland Trust, Washington, DC, 1997, p. 18.

L.F. Ivanhoe, "Get Ready for Another Oil Shock," *The Futurist*, vol. 31, no. 1, January–February '97, pp. 20–3.

Herman E. Daly and John B. Cobb Jr., *For the Common Good*, Boston, Beacon Press, 1989, pp. 401–455.

CHAPTER - 18

VALUING MULTIPLE HEALTH RISKS FROM LONG-TERM LOW DOSAGE EXPOSURE TO HAZARDOUS CHEMICALS

Susan B. Kask, Jason F. Shogren and Todd L. Cherry

ABSTRACT

The abundance of low dosage chemicals prevalent in the environment and recent research raising issues about the health effects from these chemicals, have increased concern over risks to public health. What are the benefits of reducing the health risks from long-term low dosage exposure to hazardous chemicals? The characteristics of this class of health risks pose several challenges for benefits estimation including the difficulties involved when valuing a complex package of goods, embedding, potential for individuals to modify researcher defined goods, choice of risk reduction mechanism, and the low baseline risk level of these health effects. This paper examines these issues using a CVM study on Dioxin exposure and health risks. We find several interesting results, such as willingness to pay does not vary across risk types, although perceived baseline risks do vary. This result is explained by the broad range of risk reduction estimates given by respondents.

1. INTRODUCTION

In 1995, 150 billion kilograms of synthetic organic chemicals were produced in the United States, a thousand fold increase from 1935

Acknowledgments: Appreciation is extended to the summer grants program at Western Carolina University for partial funding of this research. Thanks to Bengt Kristrom for helpful comments on the Dichotomous choice model and to Elizabeth Barnhart, formally with the Center for Disease Control, for assistance with the survey information sheet. The authors accept sole responsibility for all remaining errors in this work.

[303]

(Mitchell, 1997). The abundance of low dosage chemicals prevalent in the environment and recent research (enviro-news: 1, 1997) raising issues about the health effects from these chemicals, have increased public officials' concern over risks to public health. Policy makers are currently reviewing the clean air act (enviro-news: 2, 1997), drinking water standards (enviro-news: 3, 1997) and pesticide risks (enviro-news: 4, 1997) looking for ways to reduce risks to public health. Given the current policy of cost-benefit analysis for all regulatory activities we must ask: what are the benefits of reducing the health risks from long-term low dosage exposure to hazardous chemicals?

Dioxins, on of the toxins raising concern, are a group of by-products that come primarily from agricultural herbicides, chemical production, pulp and paper manufacturing, and waste incineration. There are 75 different chlorinated compounds called dioxins. Two examples include 2,3,7,8-Tetrachlorodi-benzo-p-dioxin (TCDD) and the fully chlorinated dioxin, Octochlorodi-benzo-p-dioxin (OCDD). TCDD is considered the most toxic of the 75 compounds. While OCDD is only 1/1000 as toxic as TCDD, it is 1000 times more prevalent than TCDD in the environment.

Dioxin can be absorbed, ingested and inhaled from contaminated air, water, soil, wastes and consumer products. The average level of dioxins in the bloodstream is 30 parts per trillion (ppt) with 7 ppt of TCDD. As a reference, a part per trillion can be related to a grain of sand on the surface of Daytona beach or 1 second in 32,000 years. Present estimated daily exposure levels range from 0.3 to 1.0 parts per quadrillion (ppq) which is 50 to 166 times the present acceptable level of .006 ppq set by the EPA. A part per quadrillion is like a grain of sand on 1000 Daytona beaches, or 1 second in 32,000,000 years. European and Canadian regulators have argued that acceptable levels can be 100 to 1000 times higher than present U.S. levels

The health impacts from dioxins include both risk of mortality from various types of skin and organ cancer and increased risk of many non-life threatening diseases from the reduction in immune response from exposure (Schmidt, 1992). The combined mortality-morbidity impacts and the multi-attribute nature of the health impact provide an opportunity to study economic values for these types of health risks. In the study of these health risks we address four issues surrounding estimation of benefits for this class of health risks: the complex nature of the good, embedding, perceptions versus objective data, and choice of reduction mechanism.

Section 2 of this paper discusses the benefits estimation problem in more detail. The methodology is explained in section 3. Section 4 presents the results and section 5 concludes the paper.

2. CHALLENGES FOR BENEFITS ESTIMATION

The characteristics of this class of health risks pose several challenges for benefits estimation including the difficulties involved when valuing a complex package of goods, embedding, potential for individuals to modify researcher defined goods, choice of risk reduction mechanism, and the low baseline risk level of these health effects.

The potential health risks from dioxin are numerous, including both acute and long-term morbidity and mortality effects, which are not easily untangled. As a result, consumers are faced with a complex package of health problems from exposure to the environmental hazard. This raises a problem with the ability of individuals to value the complex packages of goods. However, if we do untangle the good, such as looking at mortality or specific symptoms as opposed to a package, then the potential for an embedding effect occurs. Both are discussed below.

Dickie and Gerking (1991) suggest that individuals may be able to better value bundled health problems when independent risk reduction options do not exist for each health problem. Since risk reduction options are not symptom specific in our study, bundled health problems may be more easily valued than unbundled problems. Thus, this valuation problem may not be as difficult to tackle as first expected. Furthermore, allowing individuals a choice of risk reduction option may assist this valuation process.

Valuing a single health problem as opposed to a package of health problems may result in what has been called by Kahneman and Knetsch (1992) an embedding effect, where consumers place higher values on environmental goods when given single goods than when given those same goods in a package. They suggest this problem negates the potential for contingent valuation methods (CV) to provide valid estimates of non-market goods. Randall and Hoehn (1996) show this effect is to be expected for market goods due to scarcity, availability of substitutes, and / or multi-stage budgeting, and can be expected for non-market goods as well. They emphasize, however, the potential for survey design in CV to exacerbate this effect and thus recommend care in study design. Viscusi, Magat and Huber (1987) also note the theoretical potential for an embedding effect with respect to valuing multiple health risks finding that if a nonincremental risk reduction occurs, the sum of willingness to pay (hereafter WTP) for reduction of the risks separately may be greater than, less than or equal to the simultaneous reduction of the risks.

We take several precautions to reduce the potential for embedding in this study. We use a split sample which reduces the potential impact of sequencing on value estimates and we use respondent perceptions of the good valued to reduce the potential for respondent modification of a researcher defined good. The latter is discussed in more detail below. Our study finds embedding effects between the broad category of morbidity risk, mortality risk, and combined risk, similar to results found in other studies (Randall and Hoehn, 1996).

Given the literature suggests individuals may be able to more easily value a package of goods due to the non-independence of risk reduction options and that we may get over estimates of WTP in the case of single goods, this study evaluates the complex package of health problems as well as the single goods separated into morbidity and mortality using a split sample. Note the morbidity package itself is a complex package of health problems.

Another significant challenge for CV studies is the potential for respondents to modify a researcher defined CV scenario based on their own perceptions of the environmental good (Randall and Hoehn, 1996). In this study the potential is exacerbated since risk reduction is the good valued and we know individuals have difficulty transforming objective risks accurately, thus risk perceptions can over or underestimate risks (e.g. Lichtenstein et al., 1978; Kunreuther et al., 1978). Furthermore, the human health risks from long-term low dosage exposure to dioxin are not fully understood. Although respondents may be given information on baseline risks and risk reduction from an environmental hazard and policy approach, they may perceive a different level of risk and a different level of potential risk reduction. When values are elicited, individuals may value their perceived levels rather than the actual level. As a result, perceptions are often used in value estimation and studies suggest perception data better explains individual behavior. Gegax and Gerking (1991) found risk perceptions achieve better valuation estimates for risks from job related fatalities and Adamowicz et al. (1997) found models using perceptions data provided more robust predictions of recreation behavior. To address this issue our study uses information based respondent perceptions on two variables, baseline risks and potential risk reductions. Our results show there is significant variation in perceptions across respondents.

A fourth challenge for benefits estimation is the potential impact of risk reduction mechanism choice on valuation. Shogren (1990) showed that the reduction mechanism matters and that all alternative reduction mechanisms should be used to get a more comprehensive view of value. Our study introduces flexibility for individuals to select their most preferred mechanism. We found that the expected risk reduction across mechanisms did not vary significantly, however, there are clear preferences for different mechanisms with community self-insurance as the least preferred and community self-protection as most preferred and that values differ across risk reduction groups.

Finally, the potential health effects from dioxin may not occur for many years after a long period of exposure to low dosages, thus the lifetime health risks are expected to be small. Research finds that individuals can overestimate risks from low risk hazards, (see Lichtenstein et al., 1978; Viscusi and Magat, 1987) or can underestimate risks when objective risk levels are below some threshold (Kunreuther et al., 1978), thus benefit estimates for these health risks may be considered upper or lower bounds, depending on the risk behavior expected or observed (Kask and Maani, 1992).

3. METHODOLOGY

Study Site

The sample was derived from counties in western North Carolina and eastern Tennessee. This area provided a unique opportunity to analyze the previously mentioned issues. Dioxin is a primary contaminant in the Pigeon River (USEPA, 1989a, b), and the population in the region has been aware of the pollution for many years. The 80+ year presence of a paper mill and the various EPA hearings and activities provide us with a base information set greater than zero, but certainly less than full information, therefore priors exist in the population. The survey design elicited both prior and posterior risk perceptions.

Table 1
Survey Categories

	Mortality	Morbidity	Combined
Dioxin	A	B	C

Study and Survey Design

We use a block design to elicit the economic values of a reduction in lifetime risk of health problems from dioxin in the environment. The block design included the three blocks shown in Table 1.[1] Blocks A and B test for variation between mortality and morbidity bids, and block C and A, and C and B test the variation between these bids and the combined value.

The survey contained three parts: the introduction with warm up and background questions, the risk reduction mechanism and valuation questions, and the demographic questions.[2] The warm up questions established the initial pre-information perceptions of a respondent toward awareness, information levels, exposure, concern, existence of dioxin related health problems, chances, control, seriousness of health problems, and their prior subjective probabilities. The probability question asked "What do you think your household's chance is in one million of having health problems from dioxin in any given year?" The question was adjusted for the various design blocks and was tested by four focus groups to ensure clarity and ability to respond.

In part 2 respondents were given information on dioxin. The information was presented in a format that addressed five fundamental questions. What is it? Where does it come from? How can I be exposed? What are the health problems? What is the risk? The information provided in the survey was reviewed by scientists at the Center for Disease Control in Atlanta to ensure accuracy, and reviewed in four focus groups to ensure clarity, readability, and understanding. The information section was adjusted for the different design blocks, for example the mortality survey only provided information on the cancer risks from dioxins. Following the information, respondents were asked if they wanted to change their initial probability, and if so, to give their new

---

[1] A fourth block was included that used an alternative causal agent, PCB, however, this data is not included in this study.

[2] The survey and information set were tested using four focus groups with residents of Canton NC, Sylva NC, Cullowhee NC and Newport TN. Focus group participants were self-selected from invitations sent to civic groups in each location. A total of 40 persons participated.

estimate. The survey reminded respondents that although actual risks are unknown, policy makers must make decisions regarding risks for the general public.

Respondents were then asked to select a risk reduction mechanism, estimate their perceived risk reduction from that mechanism, and finally, state their WTP to implement that mechanism. The selection of the risk reduction mechanism followed a modified decision pathways survey approach (see Gregory et al., 1997). Four risk reduction pathways were offered (private protection, private insurance, collective protection, and collective insurance) each with a description of what actions may be taken and the possible payment vehicles. Three key objectives were provided to aid in the choice process: effectiveness, expense, and implementation. Respondents were asked to rank the four options using each objective to assist them in their selection of their most preferred choice. Finally, respondents were asked to rank the four options based on their own and their household's preferences. Given their most preferred choice, respondents were then asked their perception of the percentage risk reduction their preferred option would bring.

The valuation questions were presented as a series of three dichotomous choice questions with a subsequent open-ended maximum valuation question. Zero bidders were asked their reasons for a zero bid. Demographic questions concluded the survey. In addition to the standard demographic questions, specific questions related to factors that might potentially influence dioxin risk reduction values were included such as type of employment (e.g. pulp and paper or chemical industries), veteran status (Vietnam), or outdoor and/or environmental hobbies.

Mail surveys were sent to a randomly selected sample of 2000 households from seven counties in western North Carolina and five counties in eastern Tennessee. A modified Dillman method was used with four sequential mailings: survey-postcard-survey-postcard (Dillman, 1978). A three week period separated the two survey mailings.

The Sample
Given our overall response rate of 17 percent we consider this a pilot study. A comparison of the two respondent groups (first mailing and second mailing) suggests we did broaden the sample with respect to the level of interest (an environmental/outdoor hobby question) and level of information with the second mailing; thus pooling the two groups

provides a pilot sample for exploratory analysis of benefits from risk reduction for long-term low dosage chemicals such as dioxin.

The pilot sample was cleaned by removing zero protest bids and inconsistent willingness to pay responses (13.88% and 5% percent of the full sample, respectively). Item non-responses (15.77%) remained in the clean sample as they are automatically dropped during the analysis process. Valid zeros (7.57% of the full sample) also remained in the sample. Zero protests comprised 64 percent of all zero responses in the full sample. As Table 2 shows the zero and zero protest bidders were older, less educated, and had lower incomes than the consistent non-zero bidders. The final sample included 192 observations.[3] Table 3 gives the

Table 2

Status of all survey responses (n = 256) using maximum WTP

Response status full sample	Number of responses	Mean age**	Mean education**	Mean income*
Consistent non-zero				
Responses	182	44	14.2	3.9
Valid zeros	24	65	11.8	2.8
Zero protests	44	55	12.3	3.3

*significant difference at 03% level; **significant difference at 01% level.

Table 3

Demographics of final sample as compared to region and nation

Demographic characteristic	Sample n = 192	Region sampled	Nation
Median education	13	12	12
Racial distribution			
%White/%Black	na	94/3	80/12
Age distribution			
(% pop>65)	21	15.7	12.56
Median age	50*	36.7	32.9
Mean household income	34470	30,524	29,943
Gender distribution			
%M/%F	55/45	48/52	49/51

*Mean age for sample. Note sample minimum age is 18, as required by law.

demographics for the sample as compared to the region and nation. Observations in the sample are evenly distributed across the study

---

[3]This excludes the PCB sample data.

categories and bid sets. Demographics for the sample are similar across the risk types except for number of Vietnam veterans (99% significant difference) and the number of respondents who were married (98% significant difference). However a t-test shows there is no significant difference in WTP responses between vets and other respondents and between married and unmarried respondents. Therefore this sampling variation across risk types should not affect the results in section 4.

4. RESULTS

Evaluation of complex package of goods: risk perception, risk reduction, and choice of reduction options

An important issue for this study is the ability of respondents to evaluate the complex package of health problems. As discussed previously, if risk reduction options are not symptom specific, respondents may be able to better evaluate a package of goods rather than singular goods. From Table 4 we see that respondents appear to have differentiated between

Table 4

Comparison across risk types for reduction level, post information household lifetime risk level, and most preferred reduction option. (*mean values, +percent selected as most preferred risk reduction mechanism)

	Mortality $n = 63$	Morbidity $n = 69$	Combined $n = 60$
% Risk reduction*	54.5	55	54.9
min/max.	0/95	5/100	0/95
Posterior baseline risk*			
#/1,000,000	10443	54800	60261
%	1.04	5.5%	6%
%min/max	0/50	0/84	0/100
Income*	34955	37745	30188
% Private protection+ (%risk reduction)	27 (49)	26 (52)	27 (54)
% Private insurance+ (%risk reduction)	27 (58)	12 (39)	17 (53)
% Collective protection+ (%risk reduction)	40 (57)	53 (63)	48 (59)
% Collective insurance+ (%risk reduction)	6 (38)	9 (44)	8 (33)
% All collective action+	46	62	56
% All insurance action+	33	21	25

types of risks. Evidence from the mean baseline risk estimates for mortality, morbidity and the combined risk shows respondents did evaluate the risk differently with the risk from mortality at 1.04 percent or 10443 persons per 1,000,000 as compared to morbidity which was significantly higher at 5.5 percent or 54800 persons per 1,000,000 with a p-value of 0.07. Interestingly, the combined value is very close to the sum of the two values at 6 percent or 60261 persons per 1,000,000, however, this value is not significantly different ($p = 0.11$) from the morbidity risk. These results suggest respondents may differentiate between the types of complex goods.

Are sample information levels driving this result? From table 5 we find the percent of respondents choosing 'well informed' or 'somewhat informed' is similar across the mortality, morbidity and combined samples at 23 percent, 33 percent, and 30 percent, respectively. Comparisons across the other pre-information variables such as awareness, concern, chance, and exposure are also all similar across the samples. Thus, we may conclude that the respondents appear to have evaluated the risks in a manner consistent with expectations, e.g., that mortality risks would be lower than morbidity risks and that the combined risks would be greater than each separately.

In addition to the perceived risk, the perceived risk reduction from the individual's preferred risk reduction mechanism provides insight into respondent behavior. From table 4 we see the means for risk reduction across each risk type are not significantly different, nor are the minimum and maximum values. These results show the very wide range of perceptions regarding potential risk reduction. Thus, although respondents appeared to differentiate between types of risks, their perceptions for risk reduction (ultimately the good they are buying) are similar across the mortality, morbidity and combined samples.

Is this a result of the choice of risk reduction mechanism? The mean percent reduction across risk reduction options, presented in Table 5, are similar across risk types ranging from 33 percent to 63 percent. However, none of these means are significantly different due to the broad range of values given and the high standard deviations.

The broad range of estimates and lack of variation across samples suggest respondents in the sample possess variation in their perceptions of the effectiveness of risk reduction mechanisms, but the variation is consistent across reduction mechanisms. Thus, for this sample, no

Table 5

Comparison across risk types for sample characteristics of pre-information factors that may influence baseline risk perceptions.

Question	Full sample	Mortality	Morbidity	Combined
%Aware of toxins in area	35	33	33	38
% Well or somewhat informed	28	33	23	30
% Very concerned or concerned about exposure	59	61	68	48
Exposure:				
%Don't know	63	65	57	68
%Yes/%No	20/17	19/16	29/14	12/20
Control over exposure				
%Comm/%Home: Complete	1/3	2/3	2/3	0/2
Partial	6/14	5/19	6/13	7/10
Little	18/17	21/16	15/18	17/17
None	32/21	30/15	32/18	34/32
chances of health problems and/or cancer:				
%Don't know	47	46	45	53
%not very likely/ not likely	28	29	28	27
%very/some what likely	24	25	27	20
mean level of seriousness of health problems and/or cancer (index 1–10)	5.59	5.80	5.62	5.36
% Vietnam vet	7	17	3	0
% Outdoor/environmental recreation activities	43	41	45	40
% Employed in related industry	8	9	9	5

approach is generally perceived as providing more risk reduction than another approach, nor do they consider risk reduction more likely for one type of risk over another (e.g., mortality, morbidity or the combine risks).

Finally, the respondents were able to state their preference for reduction mechanisms. Across all samples there is a clear avoidance of the community insurance approach with only 6–9% of respondents selecting this option, and there is a preference for the community protection approach over all others with 40–43% of respondents selecting this option. However, in the mortality sample, private approaches were slightly more preferred to community approaches with only 46% selecting community action. Again further investigation into the risk reduction mechanism choice is

314

suggested given the distinct preferences apparent in the data. The differences found in the data with respect to the risk estimates and the selection of reduction mechanisms are suggestive that respondents in this sample were able to evaluate the complex health problems and make estimates of risk consistent with expectations.

Willingness to pay for risk reduction

Potential health problems from long-term low dosage exposure to highly toxic environmental hazards, such as dioxins, range from non-life threatening skin disease to cancers resulting in death. These problems can impact our quality of life and potentially cause premature death. The probability of one or more of the possible health problems depends on our exposure levels and our actions taken to reduce the probability of exposure or health effects. Our willingness to pay to reduce the risk of these health problems, premature death, or the combination of these risks likely depends upon our perception of the risk, expected potential risk reduction, income, and other demographic variables that may influence our tastes and preferences.

The WTP question followed a one way up format with an initial bid (b_1) and two possible follow up bids (b_2 and b_3). Each respondent was asked if they were willing to pay an initial bid. If the answer was yes, a higher bid was offered. If the answer to the second bid was yes, an even higher bid was offered. A final open-ended maximum WTP question was asked after the third bid, or if any answer was negative. Five sets of 3 bids ($s = 1, 2,..., 5$) varied across the sample to avoid a starting point bias.[4]

In our analysis of willingness to pay we estimate a valuation function using Ordinary Least Squares (OLS) with the maximum willingness to pay value from the final open-ended question. In the application of this model we assume there is independence between the choice of baseline risk, risk reduction and willingness to pay.

The OLS model estimates the natural log of willingness to pay, as a function of perceived baseline risk, perceived risk reduction, choice of risk reduction mechanism, income, age, number of children, education, perceived exposure, perceived level of control in both home and

---

[4]The bid values included in each are: Set 1 - $5, $25, $250; Set 2 - $10, $50, $500; Set 3 - $25, $100, $1000; Set 4 - $50, $250, $2000; Set 5 - $75, $400, $2500.

Table 6

OLS Results with ln(maxWTP) as dependent variable and full sample (n = 120)

Variable	Model 1
Constant	−1.0908
	(1.149)
Risk Variables:	
Baseline Risk	0.1365
	(0.769)
Baseline risk*Mortality	−99.328
	(101.88)
Risk Reduction	0.1349***
	(0.034)
Risk Reduction Squared	−0.0011***
	(0.3E−03)
Collective Action	−0.247
	(0.282)
Insurance Action	0.676**
	(0.322)
Exposed	1.581***
	(0.439)
Exposed*Mortality	−1.298
	(0.856)
Exposed*Morbidity	−2.088***
	(0.602)
Complete Control	0.051***
	(0.0015)
Complete Control*Morbidity	−4.297***
	(0.675)
Partial Control	0.532
Partial Control*Mortality	(0.687)
	(0.909)*
Demographic Variables:	
Income	0.244***
	(0.062)
Male	−0.764***
	(0.254)
Age	0.0667*
	(0.0408)
Age Squared	−0.0009**
	(0.0004)
Number of Children	−0.292***
	(0.119)
Control Variables:	
Bid Set	0.10
	(0.096)
Morbidity	0.609*
	(0.335)
Mortality	0.474
	(0.365)
F statistic	4.71
(*p*-value)	(0.0000)
Adj R^2	0.395

*statistically significant at the 10% level; **at the 5% level; ***at the 1% level standard errors in parentheses community, and type of risk. The natural log form is used to reduce the skewness and kurtosis of the distribution of the WTP variable. The results are given in Table 6 below.

In Table 6 a pooled sample[5] provides some intuitively appealing results for income and risk reduction, showing respondents demonstrate diminishing marginal utility in risk reduction and that they are willing to pay more as income increases. Both variables are significant at the 1 percent level. The result for the age variable, a proxy for current health, is also as expected with older persons willing to pay more, but at a decreasing rate.

Although surprising, the insignificance of the baseline risk is consistent with other studies (Johansson, 1995) and is discussed in more detail below. It is interesting to note that, although insignificant, the sign on the interactive baseline risk variable for mortality has the correct sign where lower risk levels bring higher WTP as compared to morbidity and the combined sample. Additional variables capturing risk behavior also give interesting results that vary across risk types. In our sample we find that respondents who believe they have been exposed to dioxin are willing to pay more for the combined risk, but less for morbidity and mortality risks. Respondents who believe they have complete control over their risks in their home and community were WTP more for combined and mortality risks, but less for the morbidity risk. Respondents who believe they have partial control over their risks in their home and community were willing to pay more for mortality risks, but not for morbidity or combined risks.

Other demographic results suggest men are willing to pay less while the number of children has an unexpected inverse relationship with willingness to pay. Finally, there is no starting point bias as is evident by the insignificance of the bid set variable and the adjusted R^2 of 39.5 percent is significant at the 1 percent level.

---

[5]If we expect respondents to respond in a similar fashion when given a mortality, morbidity, or combined survey, a pooled sample is appropriate. Using a chow test with the OLS results we reject the null hypothesis of similar samples at the 1 percent significance level (Gujarati, 1988). However, due to the small sample size of each of the split samples, we use a pooled model with interactive binary variables to capture the sample differences.

Table 7 summarizes the mean WTP values across risk types for the sample and model estimates. A *t*-test of difference in means suggests there is no significant difference between the sample mean willingness to

Table 7

Mean WTP comparisons across risk type

	Morbidity	Mortality	Combined
Sample Means	$178	$300	$158
(standard deviation)	(370)	(717)	(210)
OLS	113	118	84
(99% confidence band)	(6-1995)	(7-2094)	(5-1487)

pay across the risk types or the mean WTP estimates from the OLS model. Therefore, although respondents differentiated between types of risk in their evaluation of the risk, they do not differentiate in terms of willingness to pay in this pilot sample. Given that respondents did not differentiate between their perceptions for risk reduction across the risk types, this may explain the lack of variation in values across risk types. This may also be caused by an embedding effect.

Embedding

The results in table 7 suggest embedding exists in this sample population, since we observe the combined good is valued lower than the summed individual goods. Recall there is no significant difference between the WTP across risk types, thus the $158 and $84 mean WTP values for the combined risk are not actually lower or higher than the individual values presented for mortality and morbidity.

The combined survey results may be a characteristic of how the combined health problems are presented in the survey. Throughout the survey respondents are asked about their knowledge, awareness, preferences and values for health problems from dioxin. Only in the information sheet, where health problems are discussed, are they presented with the combination of

318

cancer and health problems. On this sheet, cancer is presented first in the list of health problems. In the mortality survey, respondents are asked about their awareness, knowledge, preference and values for cancer from dioxin. Thus, this embedding result may be exacerbated by survey design. However, given the differences found in baseline risk across the samples, it appears respondents did differentiate between the different risk types when evaluating their baseline risk levels despite the survey design, thus why not in WTP values? This may result from the lack of difference in respondents' expectations of potential risk reduction across the risk types and that they are focusing on this level of risk reduction instead of baseline risks. These results suggest further exploration into the valuation process by respondents is needed.

Finally, is the choice of risk reduction mechanism (RRM) driving the valuation process rather than risk type? As mentioned above there is little difference between choice of RRM across the risk types, however, as discussed below, our results suggest that a variation in value does occur with RRM selection.

Risk reduction mechanism and WTP

Using the pooled sample we compare the sample mean WTP values between respondents who selected insurance or protection actions and between community or private actions. We find respondents selecting insurance have a mean WTP of $405 where those selecting protection have a substantially lower mean WTP of $163.64. These are significantly different at between 10 and 20 percent level with a t value[6] of -1.589. Respondents

---

[6]Approximate t values are estimated since we expect the samples to have unequal variances. The following formulas were used for estimating the t-value and degrees of freedom.

$$t = \frac{(x_1 - x_2) - (\mu_1 - \mu_2)}{\sqrt{\frac{s_1^2}{n_1} + \frac{s_2^2}{n_2}}} \qquad df = \frac{\left(\frac{s_1^2}{n_1} + \frac{s_2^2}{n_2}\right)^2}{\frac{\left(\frac{s_1^2}{n_1}\right)^2}{n_1 - 1} + \frac{\left(\frac{s_2^2}{n_2}\right)}{n_2 - 1}}$$

choosing private (household) action for risk reduction have a mean WTP of $327.50 compared to the much lower $144.61 mean WTP for those selecting collective (community) action, which are signi-ficantly different at the 10 percent level. The OLS results also provide evidence of variation of WTP across RRM choice with a positive and significant coefficient on the insurance variable, but there is no difference found between private and collective action.

These results suggest the choice of mechanism may influence WTP values. Allowing this choice in the survey design may better capture respondent values since it reduces the potential for respondents to modify the non-market good given by researcher. In this case respondents defined their perceived good by choosing the risk reduction mechanism and the level of risk reduction they expected from the mechanism chosen.

6. SUMMARY AND CONCLUSIONS

In this study we find several interesting results. First, that willingness to pay does not vary across risk types (mortality, morbidity, and combined) in our pilot sample. Second, respondents in our sample appear to differentiate between risk types in their determination of perceived baseline risks, but they do not distinguish between risks or risk reduction mechanisms with respect to their perception of risk reduction. Third, the influence of various risk factors on willingness to pay, such as control and exposure, varies across risk types and fourth, the choice of risk reduction mechanism may influence willingness to pay values.

Although, our results suggest that respondents do differentiate between individual risks and combined risks when stating risk perceptions, they do not distinguish between these risk types when determining willingness to pay. This may be a result of their perceptions of risk reduction, which was not dependent on risk type or reduction mechanism selected, and may also be an embedding effect. The apparent ability of respondents to differentiate between risk types when stating baseline perceptions appears promising for future valuation studies. In addition the

320

variable impacts of risk factors across risk types provide further insight into valuation behavior. However, to ensure these results are not anomalies to this sample, further research is needed.

The broad range of perceived risk reduction estimates stated by respondents in this study suggest that the potential for respondent modification of researcher defined study scenarios may be significant and thus may exacerbate the embedding problem often cited in CV studies. However, it is important to note that using respondent perceptions has not removed embedding. Finally, evidence suggesting that the risk reduction mechanism may influence WTP values suggests researcher defined scenarios may generate biased benefit estimates when policy options are flexible. The implication from these results is that the gains from flexibility in scenario design may be worth the costs of difficulty for survey respondents. Further research on using flexible survey scenarios is needed.

REFERENCES

Adamowicz W., J. Swait, P. Boxall, J. Louviere and M. Williams (1997) "Perceptions versus Objective Measures of Environmental Quality in Combined Revealed and Stated Preference Models of Environmental Valuation", *Journal Of Environmental Economics and Management* 32(1): 65–84.

Boyle, K. and R.C. Bishop (1988) "Welfare Measures Using Contingent Valuation: A Comparison of Techniques". *American Journal of Agricultural Economics* 70(Feb.): 20–28.

Carson, Richard T. (1991) "Constructed Markets", in J.B. Braden and C.K. Kolstad (eds.), *Measuring the Demand for Environmental Quality*, Amsterdam, North-Holland.

Dickie, M. and S. Gerking (1991) "Valuing Reduced Morbidity: A Household Production Approach", *Southern Economic Journal* 57(3): 690–702.

Dillman, D.A., 1978. Mail and telephone surveys: The Total Design Method. John Wiley and Sons, New York.

enviro-news@nal.usda.gov. (1997) EPA holds meeting to review pesticide risk assessment issues" news release, March 7.

enviro-news@nal.usda.gov. (1997) "Statement of Carol M. Browner, Administrator, EPA, news release, March 12.

enviro-news@nal.usda.gov. (1997) "EPA releases interim report on current research about endocrine disrupting chemicals" news release, March 13.

enviro-news@nal.usda.gov. (1997) "EPA Solicits research proposals on health effects of arsenic" news release, April 21.

Gegax, D., S. Gerking and W. Schulze (1991) "Perceived Risk and the Marginal Value of Safety", *The Review of Economics and Statistics,* 73(4): 589–596.

Gregory, R.J. Flynn, S.M. Johnson, T.A. Satterfield, P. Slovic and R. Wagner. 1997. "Decision-Pathway Surveys: A Tool for Resource Managers", *Land Economics* 73(2): 240–254. May 1997.

Gujarati, D.N. (1988) Basic Econometrics. New York: McGraw-Hill.

Harrison, Glenn W. and Kristrom, Bengt (1995) "On the Interpretation if Responses in Contingent Valuation Surveys" in P. Johansson, B. Kristrom and K. Maler (eds.), *Current Issues in Environmental Economics,* Manchester University Press.

Johansson, P.O. (1995) Evaluating Health Risks: An Economic Approach. Cambridge: Cambridge University Press.

Kahneman, D. and J.L. Knetsch. (1992) "Valuing Public Goods: The Purchase of Moral Satisfaction". *Journal of Environmental Economics and Management* 22(?): 57–70.

Kask, S.B. and S. Maani (1992) "Uncertainty, Information, and Hedonic Pricing". *Land Economics* 68(2): 170–184.

Kunreuther, H., R. Ginsberg, L. Miller, S. Phillip, P. Slovic, B. Borkan and N. Katz. (1978) Disaster Insurance Protection: Public Policy Lessons. John Wiley and Sons. New York.

Lichtenstein, S., P. Slovic, B. Fischoff, M. Laymen and B. Combs (1978) "Judged Frequency of Lethal Events." *Journal of Experimental Psychology: Human Learning and Memory* 4(6): 551–578.

Loomis, J.B. (1987) "Balancing Public Trust Resources of Mono Lake and Los Angeles Water Right: An Economic Approach." *Water Resources Research* 23 (Aug.): 1449–1456.

Mitchell, J.D. "Nowhere to Hide: The Global Spread of High-Risk Synthetic Chemicals" World Watch, Vol. 10, No. 2, March/April 1997.

Randall, A. and J.P. Hoehn (1996) "Embedding in Market Demand Systems". *Journal of Environmental Economics and Management* 30(3): 369–380.

Schmidt, K.F. (1992) "Dioxin's other face: Portrait of an environmental "hormone". *Science News* 141,: 24–27, Jan 11, 1992.

Shogren, J.F. (1990) "The Impact of Self-Protection and Self-Insurance on Individual Response to Risk". *Journal of Risk and Uncertainty* 3(?): 191–204.

Smith, V.K. and W.H. Desvousages. (1987) "An Empirical Analysis of the economic Value of Risk Changes". 95(1): 89–114.

U.S. Environmental Protection agency (USEPA) Region IV, Fact Sheet: Application for National Pollution Discharge Elimination System permit to discharge treated waste water to U.S. waters, Appl NC0000272, July 1989a.

322

USEPA Region IV, Fact Sheet amendment based on comments received July 12, 1985–August 25, 1989, Sept. 1989b.

Viscusi, W.K. and W.A. Magat (1987) Learning About Risk: Consumer And Worker Responses To Hazard Information. Cambridge: Harvard University Press, 1987.

Viscusi, W.K., W.A. Magat and J. Huber. (1987) "An investigation of the rationality of consumer valuations of multiple health risks". *RAND Journal of Economics* 18(4): 465–479.

CHAPTER - 19

CHALLENGES AND PITFALLS OF COST-BENEFIT ANALYSIS IN ENVIRONMENTAL ISSUES

Jan van der Straaten

ABSTRACT

When environmental issues are at stake, there is an urgent need for economic information, since environmental goods often do not have a market price. CBA can provide insight into this complex problem to a limited degree. For example, the environment does often not react in a linear way which makes the quantification of environmental costs difficult. Environmental uncertainty is not similar to the type of uncertainty used in economic models. Furthermore, in environmental policy there is a strong tendency to have sufficient information about the costs connected to the implementation of strict norms, while the benefits of environmental policy are difficult to calculate and therefore not available. Contingent Valuation Method, Travel Cost Method, and Hedonic Pricing can be evaluated as an attempt to overcome these problem. These methods, however, are not without problems. The implementation of a critical load, limiting the stress on the environment to a certain acceptable degree, can be seen as another option to overcome these evaluation problems.

1.   INTRODUCTION

Public policy decisions have to be made using certain elements which are appropriate in that they provide sufficient information for that type of decision. In most cases, these elements include physical information, for example, the number of cars that will probably use a proposed road. On the other hand, decision makers want to be informed about the costs of the

324

construction of the road. These costs can be calculated between rather well-defined margins. But what are the benefits of the future use of that road? The simple answer is that it is the number of cars that will use the road. But this information is in physical terms, which differ from the monetary terms in which the costs of the road are expressed and must therefore be 'translated' into monetary terms. These procedures are common practice in cost-benefit analysis (CBA). The crucial question is, however, whether we really know *all* the costs and benefits of the road project including the environmental aspects, as they are an integral part of the project and thus connected with economic costs and benefits. In that case, we are faced with a number of questions such as: What are the costs of acid rain resulting from the emissions of acidifying substances by motor cars when they use the road? What are the costs of the global climate change resulting from the increased emissions of CO_2 by these cars? Do we know the costs of the depletion of the stocks of fossil fuel resulting from the increased use of gasoline?

From this example, we may conclude that crucial theoretical and practical question arise as soon as environmental issues are a substantial part of the project in question. As long as environmental questions and problems were not considered more than an insignificant side-effect of economic activities as was the case many decades ago, these problems could be ignored without it seriously effecting the outcome of traditional CBA. Currently, however, environmental problems are no longer be seen as a marginal part of the decision-making process. On the contrary, many authorities argue that they are in urgent need of sufficient information regarding the societal costs and benefits in all decisions in which environmental issues are at stake, which is quite often the case.

This implies that there is a great pressure to expand CBA in the field of environmental problems. In this paper, the extent to which such an expansion is possible will be investigated. In other words, what are the possibilities and pitfalls of the application of CBA in environmental issues? In the second section, attention will be given to the concept of 'the environment'. What do we mean by this term? We will discuss in detail the extent to which the concept of the environment can influence the outcome of CBAs. In the third section, we will concentrate on the possibility of finding a market price based on the discussion of the environmental concept in the previous section. Finally, conclusions will be presented, indicating in which situations CBA can contribute to the decision-making process when environmental problems are at issue. Finally, some methods and concepts will be suggested which can be used in the decision-making process in cases when CBA is not the most appropriate instrument.

2. THE 'ENVIRONMENT'

In most economics textbooks, it is argued in the first chapter that labour, capital, and natural resources are the three production factors necessary for the production of economic goods consumers want. Most of these textbooks, however, provide more information about labour and capital than about these natural resources. What labour and capital are or how they can be used in the economic process is relatively clear, something which cannot be said of the concept of natural resources.

Therefore, we need to clearly define these environmental production factors. In our view, we have to come to conclusions in all cases where natural resources are used in the production or consumption process, regardless of whether or not they have a price. The crucial point is whether or not they are scarce, as this places them in the realm of economics. Scarcity can influence prices, as is the case, for example, with agricultural products or fossil fuels. In many cases, however, there is no price, not because these products are not scarce but owing to the absence of markets for these scarce goods. This is true of landscapes, wilderness areas, clean water, and clean air. They are scarce, but do not have, in many cases, a real price. Therefore, attention must be given to all scarce environmental inputs in the production and consumption process regardless of whether or not they have a price.

Strictly speaking, the environment is restricted to all situations in which abiotic elements can be defined. When biotic elements are dominant, we define it as nature. This implies that when we are dealing with tropical rain forests to be cut by international timber companies, we will define this as a destruction of nature. However, if acid rain, which is abiotic, destroys the same forest, this is defined as an environmental problem. Such a division can be arbitrary and somewhat confusing. Nevertheless, we need this distinction to avoid semantic discussions which are detrimental to the understanding of environmental problems.

Here the lines of Hueting (1980) and De Groot (1992) are followed, who argued that it is the functions of nature and the environment to be used by mankind in the production and consumption processes. These functions, therefore, have an economic value. The following distinction can be made.

2.1. Nature

The economic value of nature is quite complex. Nature is used in the economic process in may ways. Tourists prefer to visit unspoiled landscapes; mountain climbers enjoy mountains which are not overloaded with human infrastructure such as parking places, ski lifts, and cable cars. Furthermore, environmental groups such as Greenpeace argue that nature has a value in it-self, regardless of its use in economic processes. Pearce (1993, p. 17) argues that the total economic value of nature is identical to the direct value + the indirect value + the option value + the existence value. The sum of direct, indirect, and optional values seen as the use value, while the existence value can be regarded as the non-use value. The sum of use value and non-use value is the total economic value. Pearce gives the example of a tropical rain forest, where the direct value includes sustainable timber products, plant genetics, medicine, non-timber products, education, human habitat, and recreation. The indirect value is based on elements such as watershed protection, air pollution reduction, nutrient recycling, and microclimate. The option value is based on the idea that, even in the absence of current direct and indirect value, the asset can be relevant in the future. The existence value includes intrinsic values and heritage and cultural values. The concept of biodiversity, which has been used recently in documents of the United Nations Conference in Rio de Janeiro of 1992, deals with use values as well as non-use values. Biodiversity is relevant in agriculture and forestry, so it has a direct use value which is to a certain extent articulated in the price of the product on the market. On the other hand, biodiversity is related to the rich variety of ecosystems all over the world, regardless of their use in market processes (Pearce and Moran, 1994; Barbier et al., 1994).

Some of these values can be measured on a market and others not. A tropical rain forest will only have a recreational value if the forest is visited, which is not the case for many very important, isolated rain forests of high ecological value. Nature areas located in the vicinity of significant human settlements in Western countries will have a higher number of visitors living in the neighbourhood than Arctic destinations in the North of Russia.

The ecosystem, which is in principle the same concept as nature, is used in economic processes in many different ways. The agricultural sector, fisheries, and forestry all use the yields of the ecosystem as a product which can be sold on a market. However, the main parts of the value of the ecosystem such as the availability of sufficient water, the level of sunlight, and the fertility of the soil do not have a price. This use of the ecosystem is based on the ability of the ecosystem to create new life.

Furthermore, fossil parts of ecosystems that functioned in the past can be used in current economic processes. This holds for the use of fossil fuels, which consist of the cumulations of carbons in the geological past, and minerals which are taken from the earth's crust for construction purposes. The use of these materials will lead to the depletion of fossil stocks, and additionally, when its rests are emitted, result in serious environmental problems.

2.2. Environment

As argued previously, the concept of the environment is based on abiotic elements. Air pollution, water pollution, and pollution of the soil are the main factors. It is not pollution alone which connects nature and the environment; it is also the so-called cleaning capacity of nature. Pollution can to a certain extent be absorbed by the ecocycles in the ecosystem. As far as pollution can be absorbed or neutralised, the capacity can be regarded as 'a free gift of nature', which has no price.

As soon as the level of discharge exceeds the amount that can be absorbed and neutralised by the ecosystem, the current ecocycles will be damaged with materials which are normally not found in the ecocycles. Pollution with organic materials is different from that with anorganic (in most cases fossil) materials. Non-organic elements are seldom found in ecocycles, which implies that the emission of these materials are alien to the ecosystem and therefore will cause serious damage with which the ecosystem cannot cope. These environmental types of pollution are summarised in Figure 1.

328

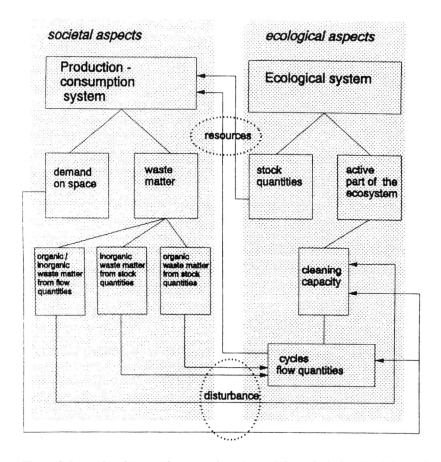

Figure 1. Interactions between the economic system and the ecological system (Dietz and Van der Straaten, 1992)

The previous discussion leads to the conclusion that nature and the environment interfere strongly with the process of production and consumption in many, and often complex, ways. We can also conclude that when CBA is being applied in the case of damage to nature and the environment, we often do not have sufficient information regarding costs and benefits. That means that we have to look for alternative methods and instruments to solve the problem. However, before we can do that, we need to pay attention to fundamental and principal problems occurring in the event of damage to nature and the environment.

3. BARRIERS AND PITFALLS

Pitfalls and barriers in the application of CBA are quite diverse. Some of them can be found in the functioning of the ecosystem itself; others have to do with difficulties in economic theory. Furthermore, the way in which institutions in society work has a significant effect on the outcome of estimations of costs and benefits in environmental policy. A short overview of these frictions are given. We will only mention those problems and frictions which will or can hinder the appropriate functioning of CBA in the field of nature and the environment.

3.1. Problems in the Ecosystem

The way in which CBA functions is based on the characteristics of the market process. However, the ecosystem has its own characteristics and its own way of functioning. It is necessary to determine to what extent these two systems can work in combination when CBA is applied in the field of nature and the environment. In this section, we will discuss the frictions which may occur as a result of the characteristics of the ecosystem itself.

A major problem is the difficulty of *predicting the effects of human actions* on ecosystems. Monetary costs and benefits have to be related to certain levels of damage or pollution. In other words, in economic modelling, we need to define a strict dose-effect relationship, which means that we know *ex ante* that a certain level of emission or the use of the ecosystem will lead to a certain level of damage which can be translated into monetary costs and/or benefits. However, this is often not the case. We do not know what the effect is of certain emissions on the ecosystem. A striking example is the dying off of forests in Northern and Central Europe, as a result of the emissions of acidifying substances leading to acid rain. These problems were first noticed in Western Germany at the beginning of the 1980s. At that time, however, nobody could explain what the causes of these problems were. It took some years of discussion and research before it became clear that acid rain was the cause.

These unexpected effects of human activities on the ecosystem means that we are often not able to quantify the damage in physical terms *ex ante*. Translation into monetary terms is blocked in that situation.

A difficult factor is the problem of *accumulation, thresholds, and synergetic effects*. When there is already a certain level of pollution in the water of a lake and other sources of pollution enter this ecosystem, the effect is often more serious than could be expected on the basis of the separate levels of all the polluting substances. In particular, when ecological damage is the result of a mix of polluting substances, the effect can be very substantial. For example, laboratory experiments made it clear that the combined effect of acid rain components SO_2, NO_x, and NH_3 on plant vegetation is much more serious than would have been expected on the basis of the linear addition of the impact of each of these components alone. (Tonneijck, 1981). This implies that we are not able to define a clear dose-effect relationship between the levels of the emissions and the level of ecological damage in physical terms. This means that we do not have the physical basis which is necessary to translate the ecological damage into monetary terms.

The same problem arises when thresholds are apparent. The Dutch government, for example, took the critical load of 2,400 acid equivalents to be reached in the short term as a guiding principle in Dutch environmental policies (Minister of Housing, Physical Planning and the Environment, 1989). At that moment, the emissions were considerably higher. Polluting sectors were ordered to reduce their emissions in such a way that the combined efforts would lead to the desired emission level. The most significant sectors in this type of pollution are oil refineries, motor cars, electric power plants, and intensive cattle breeding. All of them recently reduced their emissions considerably with the exception of the intensive cattle breeding sector (Rijksinstituut voor Volksgezondheid en Milieuhygiëne, 1993). The result is that the intensive cattle breeding sector is currently using more than 100 per cent of the 'free' situation of 2,400 acid equivalents. The crucial question, of course, is which sector is allowed to use the 'free' environmental space (Opschoor, 1994). In such a situation, it is impossible to relate the level of the societal costs resulting from acid rain to any level of emission by any sector. The translation from physical terms into monetary terms proved to be impossible in this case.

An additional problem can be found in the *concept of nature*. In many parts of the world, the quality and quantity of nature is deteriorating rapidly. Tropical rain forests are cut for timber; wetlands are used for housing, industry, agriculture, and recreation; mountain slopes are often used for skiing, resulting in erosion; intensive agriculture, particularly in western countries is having a detrimental effect on ecosystems, etc.

Based on these experiences, many organisations and citizens are trying to protect the remaining parts of nature. But they are dependent on the policies of states and such international bodies as the European Union. Many countries want to protect parts of the nature areas of their territory. Plans are developed for that purpose (Stanners and Bourdeau, 1995; European Commission, 1992). But the crucial question is to what extent should nature be protected. There is no scientific answer possible to that question. That means that economic sectors such as agriculture, which benefit considerably from the use of nature free of charge, put pressure on the decision-making process, arguing that the use of the environment is essential for their own sector and thus for the economy of the country. This means that the societal benefits resulting from the protection of nature cannot be balanced against the costs resulting from the use of nature. Again, a situation where costs and benefits cannot be defined.

3.2. Problems in Economic Theory

The protection of nature and the environment is strongly related to *intrinsic values* as defined previously. It is often argued that conservation and protection is necessary for the sake of *future generations*. However, this concept cannot be translated into economic theory. Market prices do not reflect the opinions of future generations regarding problems in the field of nature and the environment, which implies that, in traditional economic theory, no categories are defined which can cope with these problems.

It is often claimed that these problems are, in principle, dealt with by the use of the discount rate. However, as early as 1928, Ramsey argued that the use of a discount rate in these cases could be considered as "ethically wrong"; furthermore, Harrod (1948) said that the use of a discount rate could be seen as "a polite expression of rapacity". Since then, many arguments have been used to express the use of the 'right' level of a discount rate. Baier (1984), for example, asserted that current generations can have more than a vague idea about the biological and social needs of future generations. Consequently, current generations are able to incorporate these ideas in their current behaviour in such a way that they can secure these basic future needs. For a sound overview of this discussion, see *inter alia* Parfit, 1983; Norton, 1982; Mäler, 1974; Norgaard and Howarth, 1990; Hanley and Spash, 1993).

Another theoretical problem is strongly related to the *uncertainty issues* discussed in the previous paragraphs dealing with problems in the ecosystem itself. It is not correct to say that economic theory cannot deal with uncertainty. However, the type of uncertainty which is normal to ecosystems is different from those in normal market processes. In the latter, it is possible to make calculations resulting in a certain level of uncertainty which can be expressed in a probability figure. These types of uncertainties can, therefore, be used in traditional economic models. However, when ecosystems are at stake, the type of uncertainty is different. The examples in the section on ecosystems makes it clear that our knowledge of ecosystems is insufficient to predict a change in the ecosystem with a certain degree of probability, of, let us say, 30 per cent.

Additionally, we need to pay attention to the problem of *irreversibility*, which is a phenomenon not known in market processes and which is not found in traditional economic theories. However, ecosystems can be damaged in such a way that an irreversible change takes place. Krutilla and Fisher (1975) were the first authors to recognise the difficulties in this field. They developed a model in which the main point is that asymmetric growth rates are recognised in development and conservation benefits of a certain project to be developed as not being beneficial to nature and the environment. The model has been used in the case of mineral extraction and the building of hydroelectric power dams (Krutilla and Fischer, 1985). An overview of the possibilities and problems of this model is given by Porter (1982) and Hanley and Spash (1993).

Arrow and Fisher (1974) brought an additional element in the debate on irreversibility by introducing the concept of *quasi-option value*. In this line of reasoning it is recognised that, in the future, new information can become available regarding the irreversible damage of a certain project. Henry (1974) argued that such a quasi-option value could be seen as a type of insurance premium and thus as an extra cost of the project. In fact, such reasoning would, in many cases, lead to repeatedly postponing the project as there will always be the possibility of new and relevant information in the future. It can be concluded that the concept of quasi-option value is quite similar to the idea of protecting natural capital as an important source for mankind now and in the future (Spash and Clayton, 1992).

Nonetheless, one should not ignore the empirical problem of making an estimation of this quasi-option value in monetary terms. To make a CBA, we need monetary values for the most relevant cost and benefits items in the project in question.

A crucial problem in this field is the use of market prices when there is a societal problem is at stake. Traditional neoclassical theory is based on *individual methodologism*. It is the consumer and the producer who are the relevant actors in the market process. Of course, it has been accepted since Pigou (1920) that the government has the task of correcting market failures leading to societal costs, but this does not neutralise the problem of private prices to be used in a societal problem. Can we aggregate the individual wants expressed in the market to come to a societally acceptable decision? This is a complex problem which we cannot discuss here in detail. An overview of these problems is given by Dietz and Van der Straaten (1992).

Related to this issue is the problem of the definition of the *property right* of common properties which is quite often found in the field of nature and the environment. The problem is that the monetary damage to nature and the environment resulting from human activities is closely related to the definition of property right. This damage is easier to calculate in the case of private property than of a common property. The property right issue led Hardin (1968) to wrote his article 'The Tragedy of the Commons' in which he argued that common properties would always suffer from overuse and overexploitation. It is common property, in his view, which will lead to environmental damage. Bromley (1991) made it clear that common property right is not the problem, but uncontrolled open access which is different from common property to which access is, by definition, regulated. For an overview of this discussion, see Nelissen, Van der Straaten, and Klinkers, 1997.

Perhaps the main problem is the *lack of prices* resulting from the fact that nature and the environment are only traded to a limited degree. This issue is, of course, related to previous ones such as individual methodologism and the common property issue, as only private needs and wants can be articulated on markets. This implies that societal needs do not, in principle, have a price which can be derived from a market transaction. The only way out is the 'construction', in one way or another, of values which are taken from market transactions.

3.3. Problems in Environmental Policy

Although we are dealing with conceptual and theoretical problems, we cannot overlook the problems Stemming from the policy process. They are often related to theoretical starting points and, additionally, they have strong connections with the role of modern states. Some of these issues will be discussed.

Environmental and economic policies are, or should be, based on economic theories. Economic theories reflect to a certain extent *societal developments*. This means that problems in the field of nature and the environment are only incorporated in economic theories in so far as they are recognised in society. One could argue that these problems have been recognised as serious ones only in the last few decades. One of the main challenges of current economic theories is to incorporate these issues. This has not been done so far. In the opinion of many economists and political leaders, economics deals with market transactions, labour and capital, the growth rate of 'the economy', and public deficits, but not with the extinction of species, the destruction of tropical rain forests, the global climate change, or the hole in the ozone layer. It is insufficiently recognised that these problems can result in very high future societal costs. This type of development has significant effects on CBA. If costs in the field of nature and the environment are insufficiently recognised, and if the costs of environmental policies are given a high profile because they are detrimental to 'the economy', it will become clear there is a strong bias in society regarding a lack of knowledge about the monetary costs and benefits of problems in the field of nature and the environment. Costs which affect 'the economy' in a negative way will be calculated rapidly, while the benefits of environmental policies are viewed as a soft issue. The reaction of the society in the field of nature and environmental policies cannot be seen as separated from standard economic thinking.

The previous argument is connected with the role of *vested economic interests* in societal plans and decisions. Polluting industries and sectors have used nature and the environment for a long period without paying for it. This means that they have been able to build up a strong competitive position in the course of time. When new policies are formulated to protect nature and the environment better than before, they will not give up their favourable position without any discussion. This position is, in many cases, exacerbated by the fact that many of these industries have a strong position in national states. For example, the intensive agriculture in the Netherlands is not only a significant contributor to surpluses in the balance of trade and the balance of payment, it is also one of the main polluters. The position of the motor car industry in Germany, Britain and France is similar to that of agriculture in the Netherlands. None of them have ever been a great advocate of reducing the mileage of private motor cars to reduce the global climate change problem. Furthermore, the low price of energy in the USA has given a comfortable international competitive position to American producers using a lot of energy. This situation is certainly connected with the position of the USA regarding the use of energy in the global climate change debate, in which they indicate a reluctance to cooperate.

These issues are not only interesting in the field of nature and environment policies, they have a significant influence on CBA issues. The crucial point is that nearly all policies in this field have a great influence on the costs and benefits of polluting and non-polluting industries. Furthermore, some policies will hurt certain countries more (intensive agriculture or restrictions in the use of motor cars) than others. This implies that environmental policies have strong distributional effects. This has had, and will have, the effect that the costs of measures to be taken to protect nature and the environment are very well known, even when many difficulties have to be overcome. On the other hand, the benefits of these policy measures are nearly always underestimated owing to the fact that these benefits are not so well concentrated in society. Furthermore, these benefits are very often related to future situations: there are no economically powerful groups in society who will make these calculations of future benefits known, leading to the situation that, in many cases, insufficient knowledge about these costs is available. If a CBA is made in this situation, there is a strong bias to give the costs a higher practical relevance than the benefits.

The role of the state has been an important issue for discussion recently. It is often said that modern states should not interfere with the functioning of market processes. However, the state will be held responsible for the results of the market process. When governments are confronted with decreases in the growth of the GNP and with rising unemployment figures, it is the government that will be blamed. In particular, when elections are nearby, the voters and the government are quite keen on the development of these issues. When strict environmental policies with detrimental effects on traditional economic parameters have to be implemented, governments are in a weak position. Therefore, governments are not much inclined to develop plans that include strict environmental norms. Generally speaking, plans for the expansion of the Dutch airport Schiphol are more quickly and more accurately made than plans to decrease the number of pigs and cows in intensive livestock breeding. This implies that more figures related to traditional economic parameters are available than figures concerning nature and the environment. If CBAs have to be made, the government has, in most cases, more data about the traditional economic parameters available than about nature and the environment. Here again we see a bias in the use of cost and benefits regarding the conflict between traditional economic parameters and those in the field of nature and the environment.

4. ATTEMPTS TO OVERCOME THE PROBLEMS

From the previous sections, it can be concluded that the problems and barriers regarding the use and application of CBA in the field of nature and the environment have attracted significant attention and have been widely discussed. Several methods and refinements of existing methods have been proposed. The validity and the applicability differs widely regarding the problem in question. The main ones will be discussed.

One reaction is to abandon the CBA approach when issues in the field of nature and the environment are at stake. This option should be selected in cases where CBA cannot give a correct solution to the problem. Ciriacy-Wantrup (1952) suggested implementing a policy in which *certain limits* would be taken as the starting point in environmental and economic policies. In that case, the carrying capacity of the ecosystem is taken as the starting point for policies. The same option is given by Baumol and Oates (1988) who argued that, in all cases where a principal lack of information of environmental costs and benefits can be recognised, a limit proposed by the natural sciences has to be taken as a second-best solution in economic policies.

This approach was used by the Dutch government in their acid-rain policies (Minister of Housing, Physical Planning and the Environment, 1983–1984), in which they propagated the use of a critical load regarding the deposits of acidifying substances of 1,800 acid equivalents per ha per year as a guiding principle for their policies. They argued in this document

that the costs and benefits of acid rain and acid rain policies could not be provided. However, they had to define a certain level of pollution as acceptable. They took the correct functioning of the ecosystem as the starting point in acid rain policies and, based on scientific research, came to the conclusion that 1,800 acid equivalents would meet these aims. Later on, in the National Environmental Policy Plan (Minister of Housing, Physical Planning and the Environment, 1989), they refined the acceptable level to 1,400 acid equivalents in the long run and 2,400 in the short run. In the latter document, they said that they would take the principle of sustainable development, as defined by the World Commission on Environment and Development (1987), as a guiding principle for all their policies. In fact, the European Union did the same when they accepted a new policy plan entitled Towards Sustainability (1992).

This does not mean that CBA is not an appropriate instrument in the field of nature and the environment when a critical load is taken as a starting point for policy implementation. Even in that case, there is still the question of how this political aim can be met in *the most efficient way*, and CBA is particularly relevant in that matter. A good example can be found in the negotiations about acid rain reductions. Sweden put the acid rain problem on the international agenda at the United Nations meeting in Stockholm in 1972 (Royal Ministry of Foreign Affairs and Royal Ministry of Agriculture, 1971). Generally speaking, the other countries did not recognise this issue as a pressing problem. They claimed that additional research had to be done.

In 1977, the OECD published a report making it clear acid rain was, indeed, an international problem, which implied that international measures had to be taken. As the costs and benefits of acid rain and of acid rain abatement policies are unevenly distributed in Europe, different countries had different interests in this field. Therefore, it took eight years before an international agreement could be reached (United Nations, 1985). The disputes and debates about these costs and benefits were so intensive that only a flat rate reduction of 30 per cent of SO_2 emission could be agreed upon. Of course, this was a solution, far removed from efficiency, as the efficiency argument could not be used because of the high controversies. As this reduction was seen as insufficient, further reductions became necessary. New negotiations started in which the so-called RAINS model (Alcamo, Shaw and Hordijk, 1990) was taken as a starting point. In this model, sub-models were included describing the level of emissions, the dispersion process of emissions, the level of deposits, the costs of bringing down emissions in different production processes, and the environmental costs of acid rain in certain areas. Using this model, made it possible to define the industries in which countries had to reduce their emissions to guarantee the most beneficial effects on the reduction of deposits in vulnerable areas at the lowest costs. In fact, this approach made it possible to apply CBA intentions, namely, the efficiency criterion, in the complex field of acid rain abatement. Finally, the different countries accepted the general outcome of this model, with some modifications, as it could realise acid rain abatement at the lowest costs.

This positive example of the use of CBA in a complex policy field should not lead us to conclude that the problems of CBA can be overcome in all cases. The Nordhaus articles on global climate change (1991a and b) can make this clear. In these articles, calculations of the costs and benefits of global climate change are made. The result of the study is rather positive. Global climate change will not create high costs in the future. However, in these articles, the most relevant elements in the whole debate, such as the ecological effects on the world ecosystem, are included as PM. The effects on the ecosystem of the world are unknown and can, therefore, not be calculated. This means that these CBA calculations cannot give the desired and needed information. It is better to take the precautionary principle as the starting point. This approach is mainly based on the application of the quasi-option value mentioned in one of the previous sections.

In cases where insufficient knowledge about the value of nature and the environment is available, it can make sense to construct values using some type of market behaviour. *The hedonic pricing method* was developed in the 1960s and 1970s (Lancaster, 1966; Grilliches, 1971; Rosen (1974). In this method, it is assumed that the prices of houses reflect in one way or another the characteristics of the location. A house located in a national park will have a higher value and price than the same house located near a garbage belt. The difference in price is caused by the value people give to nature. The method can be applied in situations where the values of houses and amenities plays a role. These types of study have been realised in fields such as noise pollution in the neighbourhood of airports (O'Byrne et al., 1985), urban air quality (Brookshire et al., 1982), earthquake risks (Brookshire et al., 1985), and amenity values of woodlands (Willis and Garrod, 1991). The method is quite limited in scope: the application is only possible when consumers have made a decision, so there is no possibility of predicting the specific damage that would occur if a particular project would be realised. Additionally, it can only be used when houses or other amenities are at stake. It cannot answer questions related to such matters as the decrease in biodiversity and global climate change. An overview of this method is given by Hanly and Spash (1993).

People are willing to spend time and money to visit certain areas of outstanding natural beauty, they are willing to spend *travel time and travel costs* to visit the area in question. This is evaluated as a revealed preference. The method was introduced by Wood and Trice (1958) and Clawson and Knetsch (1966). It is often used in cases of outdoor recreation such as hunting, boating, mountain climbing, and visits to beaches and forests. The travel costs are taken as a proxy for the value given by tourists to nature areas.

One of the main problems of this method is the valuation of the number of hours spent by respondents. Tourists often like it to drive to a destination they are going to visit. What value should these travel hours be given in the calculation? Cesario (1976) suggested, based on empirical evidence, taking one third of the hourly wage rate. McConnel and Strand (1981) and Common (1973) used a simulation process to make an evaluation possible. Other approaches have been suggested by Chevas et al. (1989) and Hanley and Ruffel (1992).

A serious problem, not often mentioned in the literature, is the bias which can be recognised in the choices made by tourists. Tourists can only visit a certain site when they have adequate information about that site and when there is an infrastructure which can be used by tourists. For example, the tropical rain forests in Costa-Rica are visited by a great number of tourists from abroad, mainly because of the good tourist infrastructure which can be identified in that country. But does this mean that the economic value of rain forests in Columbia, Guatemala, or Amazonia is lower, as they do not receive that number of overseas visitors? Indeed, there is not the same revealed preference to visit these rain forests. When the autonomy of the choices made by tourist is taken as the basis for economic evaluation, one can easily argue that many shortcomings are inherent to this method.

Nature and the environment can have many *functions* for human beings. A loss of these functions due to disruption or degradation of nature and the environment can be seen as an economic loss. Hueting (1980) was the first author to focus on this approach. He argued that environmental disruption, accompanied by serious losses in the functions nature can provide to mankind, will result in considerable economic losses and that consequently, prices can no longer be seen as adequate signals indicating economic scarcity. Consumers and producers receive the 'wrong' signals; the price signals stimulate them to use the environment free of charge, as they are not confronted with the real social costs. Corrections have to be made. In this study, in which he tried to arrive at the correct price of water pollution with organic materials, he could not achieve the result he wanted, mainly owing to a lack of prices and insufficient information about the preferences of consumers regarding nature and the environment.

Nevertheless, Hueting held firm that market prices include so many elements of pollution and degradation that these prices cannot reflect economic scarcity. Additionally, Hueting argued that the calculation of GNP is based on the same incorrect market prices. So, society also receives the 'wrong' signals in the economic process. When the concept of sustainable development was accepted by most countries and international organisations, Hueting concluded that this could be seen as a revealed preference for a certain level of protection (1991). When the standards for sustainable development are taken as a type of revealed preference, we can correct the prices. A CBA on nature and the environment is, in this view, again possible. The main problem in this approach is that there is, in many cases, not a fixed set of Sustainability standards. Sustainable development is a container concept; it has to be filled with certain standards, which are again a result of political debate and decision (Van den Bergh and Van der Straaten, 1996; Latesteijn et al., 1994).

This concept of functions nature and the environment has for mankind has been elaborated on by authors such as De Groot (1994). He tried to expand the argument in all possible fields. Also a recent publication (Costanza et al., 1997) tried to calculate the total value of the ecosystem Earth. One can ask what the relevance of this information is. What can we do with it? What more do we know after we have read these calculations? The crucial question, of course, is whether we are able to monetarise all the different functions of nature? Or are the assumptions which have to be made so rigid that we may have many doubts regarding the outcome of this calculation process?

An overview of the pitfalls which can be confronted when functions of nature are used for economic evaluation can be found in Hanley and Spash (1993). They use the concept of averting expenditure and dose-response models which describe the relationship between several levels of environmental pollution and the yield of products dependable on a certain environmental quality.

The Contingent Valuation Method (TVM) is probably the best known method to estimate the preferences of consumers regarding nature and the environment. The starting point of the approach is that people have a certain preference, but that this preference will often not result in market behaviour. In that case, it can make sense to ask people what their willingness to pay (WTP) or their willingness to accept (WTA) financial compensation for a change in a certain level of the functions nature or the environment can provide. The method was propagated by Davis (1963). In the 1970s and 1980s, the method attracted the attention of many economists. Many pitfalls have since been identified. One of the main problems is the difference between WTA and WTP. In principle, these values measure the same thing. However, a serious difference is often found. Other problems are related to insufficient information regarding the topic in question. A sound overview of many of these shortcomings are given by Hoevenagel (1994) and by Hanley and Spash (1993).

There are some serious problems which do not receive much attention in the literature. The first one is that CVM takes the current distribution of income as a starting point. Of course, this is completely in line with traditional neoclassical assumptions; however, in this case, this has serious effects on the results. This can be demonstrated with the oil spill of the Exxon Valdez on the coast of Alaska some years ago. CVM played an important role when ESSO was brought to court. The population of the USA was taken as a reference group to calculate the damage to the existence value caused by this incident. Owing to the relatively high income of American citizens and their great number, a considerable amount of monetary damage was calculated. However, if the same ecological damage had been realised by an oil spill on the coast of Denmark, the Gambia, Costa Rica, or El Salvador, the result of the calculation would have been a small segment of the CVM result on the coast of Alaska. This difference is not caused by a difference in ecological damage, but by the low number of inhabitants in these countries or due to the low income level. Of course, one could argue, in line with traditional economic approaches, that these differences in outcome have to be accepted as a result of the definition of the property rights of the ecosystems in question. Nonetheless, it also makes it clear that these approaches cannot result in monetary calculations which will protect nature and the environment adequately.

Another serious point is the type of problem we want to discuss. Small isolated problems in the field of nature and the environment can be recognised by many respondents, and we may assume that the WTP or the WTA can reflect the preferences of individuals quite satisfactorial. However, when serious problems such as the global climate change, the hole in the ozone layer, nuclear pollution, the pollution of the high seas, acid rain, a considerable loss in biodiversity, and the destruction of tropical rain forests come up for discussion, one cannot assume that the vast majority of respondents have the slightest idea about the scale and the seriousness of the problems. Additionally, in many of these cases, experts differ seriously regarding the relevance of these issues. How is a normal consumer able to give information to express his or her willingness to pay when these issues are at stake? The level of uncertainty is too high. On the other hand, one should not overlook that this uncertainty is particularly high in the case of serious and often global environmental problems.

5. CONCLUSIONS

Some conclusions can be drawn:

- The possibilities regarding the application of CBA in the field of nature and the environment are strongly connected with the definition of the value of these issues. The main point is that the value of nature and the environment cannot be given precisely because many of its elements are not traded on a market. It is sometimes said that, in that case, energy or the ecosystem has to be taken as a proxy for that value. However, as has been made clear by Martinez Allier (1987), this argument is not valid. This is a subjective choice which cannot be made without making many political decisions. This leads to the conclusion that the value of nature and the environment is based on political ideas and decisions.
- This being the case, we cannot overlook the point that CBA is based on the assumption that we know the economic value *ex ante*, otherwise we cannot calculate the costs and benefits of environmental damage and environmental regulation. This leads us to the conclusion that the concept of CBA is strongly related to political decisions.
- This does not mean, however, that CBA is always value loaded. As soon as political decisions are taken, as has been demonstrated by the RAINS model, CBA can be a good instrument to achieve the political aims in the most efficient way.
- In general, economic theories do not pay sufficient attention to the problems of nature and the environment. Labour and capital issues attract

much more attention; choices to be made in economic and environmental policies reflect this situation.

- Many methods to define costs and benefits in nature and environmental issues have been developed. All of them have their limitations. Some of them, such as travel cost method and hedonic pricing, cannot cope with future situations; others such as CVM can do this, but are quite hypothetical. Additionally, this method can only be used for well-defined and limited problems.

- The use of the discount rate in CBA is, in fact, a problem which has still not been solved. Every choice of any rate is based on ethical and political opinions about the relevance of future generations and the seriousness of the problems in the field of nature and the environment.

- When the choice is made to use a CBA approach, the best attitude is a pragmatic one. Researchers have to realise what the limitations are, given the problem at hand. It is the type of problem which facilitates the choice of the most appropriate instrument, including a CBA approach. Other instruments such an environmental impact assessment or a multi-criteria analysis can give additional and sometimes better information in the decision-making process.

REFERENCES

Alcamo, J., R. Shaw and L. Hordijk (1990) *The RAINS Model*, Kluwer Academic Publishers, Dordrecht, The Netherlands.

Arrow, K. and A. Fisher (1974) Environmental Preservation, Uncertainty and Irreversibility. *Quarterly Journal of Economics*, 88: 312–319.

Baier, A. (1984) 'For the Sake of Future Generations'. In: T. Regan (Ed.), *Earthbound: New Introductory Essays in Environmental Ethics*. Temple University Press,Philadelphia.

Barbier, Edward B., Joanne C. Burgess and Carl Folke (1994) *Paradise Lost? The Ecological Economics of Biodiversity*. Earthscan, London.

Baumol, W.J. and W.E. Oates (1988) The Theory of Environmental Policy, second edition. Cambridge University Press, Cambridge.

Bromley, D.W. (1991) *Environment and Economy; Property Rights and Public Policy*. Basil Blackwell, Oxford.

Brookshire, D.S., M.A. Thayer, W.D. Schulze and R.C. d'Arge (1985) Valuing Public Goods: a Comparison of Survey and Hedonic Approaches. *American Economic Review* 72: 165–178.

Brookshire, D.S., M.A. Thayer, J. Tischirhart and W.D. Schulze (1985) A Test of the Expected Utility Model: Evidence from Earthquake Risk. *Journal of Political Economy* 93: 369–389.

Cesario, F., Value of Time in Recreation Benefit Studies. *Land Economics* 52: 32–41.

Chevas, J.P., J. Stoll and C. Sellar (1989) On the Commodity Value of Travel Time in Recreational Activities. *Applied Economics* 21: 711–722.

344

Ciriacy-Wantrup, S.V. (1952) *Resource Conservation: Economics and Policies..* Division of Agricultural Sciences. University of California, Berkeley.

Clawson, M., and J. Knetsch (1966) *Economics of Outdoor Recreation.* Johns Hopkins University Press, Baltimore.

Common, M. (1973) A Note on the Use of the Clawson Method. *Regional Studies* 7: 401–406.

Costanza, R., R. d'Arge, R. de Groot, S. Farber, M. Grasso, B. Hannon, K. Limburg, S. Naeem, R.V. O'Neill, J. Paruelo, R.G. Raskin, P. Sutton and M. van den Belt. (1997) The Value of the World's Ecosystem Services and Natural Capital. *Nature,* Volume 387, 15 May 1997: 253–260.

Davis, R. (1963) Recreation Planning as an Economic Problem. *Natural Resources Journal.* 3 (2): 239–249.

de Groot, R.S. (1992) *Functions of Nature: Evalutaion of Nature in Environmental Planning, Management and Decision Making,* Wolters Noordhoff, Goningen, The Netherlands.

Dietz, F.J. and J. van der Straaten (1992) Rethinking Environmental Economics: the Missing Link between Economic Theory and Environmental Policy. *Journal of Economic Issues,* Vol. XXVI, Nr. March 1992: 27–51.

European Commission (1992) *Fifth Environmental Action Plan: Towards Sustainability,* European Union, Brussels.

Griliches, Z. (1971) *Price Indexes and Quality Change.* Harvard University Press, Cambridge, MA.

Hanley, N. and R. Ruffel (1992) *The Valuation of Forest Characteristics.* Discussion Paper 849, Institute for Economic Research, Queens University.

Hanley, N. and C.L. Spash (1993) *Cost-Benefit Analysis and the Environment.* Edward Elgar, Aldershot.

Hardin, G. (1968) The Tragedy of the Commons. *Science* 162: 1243–1248.

Harrod, R. (1948) *Towards a Dynamic Economy.* St. Martin's Press, London.

Henry, C. (1974) Option Values in the Economics of Irreplacable Assets. *Review of Economic Studies:* 89–104.

Hoevenagel, R. (1994) *The Contingent Valuation Method: Scope and Validity.* Institute for Environmental Studies, Free University, Amsterdam.

Hueting, R. (1984) *New Scarcity and Economic Growth.* North-Holland, Amsterdam.

Hueting, R. (1991) 'Correcting National Income for Environmental Losses: a Practical Solution for a Theoretical Dilemma. In: R. Costanza (Ed.), *Ecological Economics. The Science and Management of Sustainability.* Columbia University Press,New York: 194–213.

Krutilla, J. and A. Fisher (1975 and 1985) *The Economics of Natural Environments,* Resources for the Future, Johns Hopkins Press, Baltimore.

Lancaster, K.J. (1966) A New Approach to Consumer Theory. *Journal of Political Economy.*74: 132–157.

Mäler, K. (1974) *Environmental Economics: a Theoretical Inquiry.* Resources for the Future, Johns Hopkins Press, Baltimore.

Martinez Alier, Juan (1987) *Ecological Economics,* Basil Blackwel, Oxford.

McConnel, K. and I. Strand (1981). Measuring the Cost of Time in Recreation Demand Analysis. *American Journal of Agricultural Economics:* 153–156.

Minister of Housing, Physical Planning and the Environment. (1983–1984). *De Problematiek van de Verzuring (Problems of Acidification),* 18225, nrs. 1–2.

345

Minister of Housing, Physical Planning and the Environment (1989) *National Environmental Policy Plan: To Choose or to Lose.* Second Chamber of the States General, SDU, The Hague.

Nelissen, N.J., van der Straaten and L. Klinkers (1997) *Classics in Environmental Studies: An Overview of ClassicTexts in Environmental Studies.* International Books, Utrecht. The Netherlands.

Nordhaus, W. (1991a) To Slow or not to Slow : the Economics of the Greenhouse Effect. *Economic Journal* 101: 920–938.

Nordhaus, W. (1991b) A Sketch of the Economics of the Greenhouse Effect. *American Economic Review* 81(2): 146–150.

Norgaard, R.B. and R.B. Howarth (1990) *Sustainability and Discounting the Future.* Paper presented at the Conference of the International Society for Ecological Economics, May 1990. Washington, DC.

Norton, B.G. (1982) Environmental Ethics and the Rights for Future Generations. *Environmental Ethics* 4: 319–337.

O'Byrne, P., J. Nelson and J. Seneca (1985) Housing Values, Census Estimates, Disequilibrium and the Environmental Cost of Airport Noise. *Journal of Environmental Economics and Management* 12: 169–178.

Opschoor, J.B. and R. Weterings (1994) Environmental Utilization Space: an Introduction. *Milieu,* Volume 9, 1994/5:198–205.

Parfit, D. (1983) 'Energy Policy and the Further Future: the Identity Problem. In: D. Maclean and P.G. Brownd (Eds.), *Energy and the Future.* Rowan and Allanheld, Totowa, NJ.

Pearce, D. (1993) Economic Values and the Natural World, Earthscan, London.

Pearce D. and D. Moran (1994) *The Economic Value of Biodiversity.* Earthscan, London.

Pigou, A.C. (1920/1952) *The Economics of Welfare,* MacMillan, London.

Porter, R. (1982) The New Approach to Wilderness Appraisal through Cost-benefit Analysis. *Journal of Environmental Economics and Management,* 9: 59–80.

Ramsey, F. (1928) A Mathematical Theory of Saving, *Economic Journal,* 38, December 1928.

Rijksinstituut voor Volksgezondheid en Miluehygiëne (1993) *Nationale Milieuverkenning 3* (National Environmental Inquiry) 1993-2015. Samson H.D. Tjeenk Willink, Alphen aan den Rijn.

Rosen, S. (1974) Hedonic Prioces and Implicit Markets: Product Differentiation in Pure Competition. *Journal of Political Economy* 82: 34–55.

Royal Minister for Foreign Affairs and Royal Minister of Agriculture (1971) *Air pollution across National Boundaries. The Impact on the Environment of Sulfur in Air and Precipitation. Sweden's Case Study for the United Nations Conference on the Human Environment,* Stockholm.

Spash, C.L. and A.M.D. Clayton (1992) *Strategies for the Maintenance of Natural Capital.* Paper presented at the Conference of the International Society for Ecological Economics, Stockholm, August 1992.

Stanners, D. and P. Bourdeau (1995) *Europe's Environment. The Dobříš Assessment.* European Environment Agency, Copenhagen.

Tonneijk, A.E.G. (1981) *Research on the Influence of Different Air Pollutants Separately and in Combination in Agriculture, Horticulture and Forestry Crops.* IPO Report R 262, Wageningen, The Netherlands.

United Nations (1985) *Protocol to the 1979 Convention on Long-range Transboundary Air Pollution of Sulphur Emissions or their Transboundary Fluxes by at least 30 per cent.*

van den Bergh, J.C.J.M. and J. van der Straaten (1996) 'Historic and Future Models of Economic Development and Natural Environment', in: J.C.J.M. van den Bergh and J. van der Straaten (Eds.), *Toward Sustainable Development: Concepts, Methods, and Policy.* Island Press, Wshington, DC, 209–234.

Van Latesteijn, H.C., D. Scheele and I.J. Schooneboom (1994) Paradigms of Sustainability and Perceptions of Environmental Utilisation Space. *Milieu,* 1994/5: 244–252.

Willis K. and G. Garrod (1991) *The Hedonic Price Method and the Valuation of Countryside Characteristics.* Countryside Change Centre working paper No. 14, University of Newcastle-upon-Tyne, Newcastle-upon-Tyne, UK.

Wood S. and A. Trice (1958) Measurements of Recreation Benefits. *Land Economics* 34: 195–207.

World Commission on Environment and Development (1987) *Our Common Future,* Oxford University Press, Oxford.

CHAPTER - 20

CHALLENGES IN VALUATION: THE HEALTH BENEFITS OF REDUCING AIR POLLUTANTS

Jane V. Hall and Victor Brajer

ABSTRACT

Economic valuation of environmental improvements is an important tool to assess how limited social resources can best be used. There are many empirical and conceptual challenges to the process of estimating value. This paper identifies and discusses some of these challenges for the case of valuing health benefits that result from better air quality.

1. INTRODUCTION

An extensive and growing health science literature associates numerous adverse health effects with levels of ozone or fine particles found in urban regions worldwide. These effects range in severity from minor respiratory symptoms to premature death. Controlling emissions from industry and transportation is necessary to reduce unhealthful levels of pollution, but this control is also costly. Consequently, policy-makers – typically governments – need to know what the gains from pollution control might be in economic terms. In essence, what value does society place on cleaner air?

Obviously, for many items that improve the quality of life, one can determine what they are worth from the actual prices paid in the market. A newspaper is worth at least 25 cents, because consumers are willing to pay that much for it. An automobile is worth much more, because it adds more to the quality of life. However, there is no market, and therefore no market price, for better health. Clean air is a nonmarket good, perhaps the quintessential public good.[1] There is no commodity exchange or department store where air quality can be purchased. Consequently, economists have been forced to develop a variety of techniques to approximate what the price might be if there were a market.

In order to estimate the "price" we would be willing to pay for cleaner air, benefit estimation requires reliable data on current and future air pollution concentrations, population size, and the specific quantitative relationships between different levels of pollution and frequency of adverse effects (Hall et al., 1992). While the basic approach to estimating health benefits is well established, each aspect of assessing benefits presents challenges (Hall, 1996a,b). In this paper, we provide background on how benefit estimation is typically assessed and then present and discuss some empirical and conceptual challenges. Finally, we offer some observations about the current state of the art.

2. VALUING HEALTH BENEFITS

What a decision-maker needs to know, from a policy perspective, is how much the overall well-being of society increases when the adverse effects of unhealthful air are reduced. Ideally, value measurements would represent all of the loss in quality of life that results from adverse health effects. People value avoiding these adverse health effects to reduce: medical costs; school, work, or leisure time loss that results from avoiding or responding to the adverse health condition; discomfort, inconvenience and fear resulting from the adverse effects, or effort to avoid or treat them; and impacts on others as a result of the adverse health effects experienced. In this section, we briefly explain the methods that economists have developed to calculate these values. The methods are based on finding values analogous to price in a competitive market. It is important to bear in mind that other considerations, such as income distribution and equity, may also be important, and that market price may not accurately reflect society's values.

The two general economic methods for measuring the value of changes in health-related well being are the *cost of illness (COI)* method and the *willingness to pay (WTP)* or *willingness to accept (WTA)* methods.

---

[1] A public good is non-rival in consumption (one person's consumption does not diminish anoether's) and non-paying users cannot be excluded. Consequently, markets l supply less than an efficient amount of such goods.

While actual data on health care costs and wages measure COI, WTP and WTA estimates are provided by hedonic or contingent valuation (CV) studies. A review of each of these methods is offered below. Economists believe that, taken together, a group of studies using these methods provides what is the best currently available range of measures for evaluating the benefits of improvements in air quality.

Cost of Illness Method

The COI method was the first economic valuation method to be developed in the health and safety literature, and involves the calculation of the dollar value of direct medical costs and lost wages due to illness. Some recent studies have still utilized this method to value hospital admissions and other medical treatments. (See, for example, Krupnick and Cropper, 1989). The COI method has the advantage of being based on real dollars spent to treat specific health effects or the actual market value of work time. Since it includes only direct monetary losses, however, and does not include losses associated with the value of leisure time, of school or unpaid work time, or of general misery and, therefore, does not capture all of the benefits of better health, the COI method is generally viewed as somewhat limited. It basically defines a measure of the *financial* impact of illness, not the *change in well being* due to illness, since financial loss is only part of the effect on well being.

Most economists support the use of WTP or WTA measures as alternatives or adjuncts to COI because they more completely account for loss of quality of life. A number of valuation studies indicate that only about one-half of an individual's WTP is typically captured by the COI approach (Chestnut et al., 1988, Rowe and Neithercut, 1987). Other studies have provided evidence that the difference between COI and WTP is much wider for more serious health endpoints, such as hospital admissions or development of chronic disease. For example, commonly accepted WTP values to *avoid* chronic bronchitis are 10 to 20 times higher than the cost of *treating* the illness. Clearly, COI measures represent an incomplete picture of the losses caused by deteriorating air quality; they are useful, at the very least, in providing lower-bound value estimates.

Market-Based Measures

In certain situations, individuals facing changes in environmentally related health risks actually take part in related market transactions. By studying the differences in payments (prices or wages) related to differences in risk, one can estimate the value to members of the exposed group of avoiding or reducing the risk. Studies using this *hedonic* approach can determine the implicit value for a nonmarket characteristic, such as the air quality in a neighborhood, or the risk associated with a job. For example, a statistical analysis of many different homes, with varying characteristics (including cleaner and dirtier air) can be used to estimate the value of a specific characteristic – cleaner air. The compensation that people require to bear the risk of higher pollution levels can be used to infer the value of a safer, or cleaner, environment when poor environmental quality presents a health risk. In the case of job-related risk, if people require higher pay to accept a higher probability of injury on the job, a related wage differential indicates what reducing that risk is worth to them. The results of these hedonic studies must be carefully interpreted, however. For the wage risk approach, in particular, problems may arise from the presence of job attributes not directly related to the probability of harm. More recent studies control for such factors. In addition, the values of employee groups may not be the same as those of the general population, making the extrapolation of results somewhat problematic.

Contingent Valuation

The CV approach estimates the value of nonmarket goods (such as cleaner air) by surveying groups to determine personal preferences and the corresponding WTP or WTA for changes in environmental quality. Interest in this approach has increased significantly over the last two decades. Again, the CV approach is conceptually preferable to the COI method because COI measures omit all but direct medical costs and lost income. In contrast, the value of other things given up, but not readily measurable, including loss of enjoyment and life experience, can be included in CV survey responses. It should be noted, however, that even CV studies might not completely measure the benefit to society of harm avoided, since they do not capture the value to others of avoiding harm to the individual surveyed and assume that the sum of individual values represents social value.

Method Comparison

Several criteria are typically considered in determining which measures of value are most appropriate for estimating health benefits. First, the measure should be appropriate for the type of risk being studied. Risk can be differentiated by a number of characteristics: its size and direction (that is, whether the risk is increasing or decreasing); whether the risk is voluntary or involuntary; and whether the harm can be prevented or has already occurred. Second, the value measure should provide the most comprehensive estimate possible, capturing complete gains or losses in well being. Third, when similar values are derived from more than one type of study (from both wage-risk and CV studies, for example), such value measures are generally viewed as having a greater presumption of validity than those values obtained solely from one method.

Of course, there will always be some uncertainty regarding the closeness of value estimates, from any method, to the "real" value of avoiding some health effects. The ability (or lack thereof) of people to perceive small environmental risks, and the fact that environmental improvements are really "bundles" of goods, and not changes in isolated effects, are both relevant, and important issues here. For example, the environmental improvement that will reduce risk of bronchitis also reduces risk of asthma attacks, and improves visibility. Nonetheless, economists, government agencies and the courts have concluded that values derived from CV studies and estimates based on wage-risk studies constitute an appropriate basis for valuing a variety of health risks, whether mortality or morbidity (see Viscusi, 1993 and the references therein).

Valuing Mortality

Increased risk of premature death is one of the health effects that has been long associated with exposure to fine particulate matter (and now in recent studies, also with ozone), and one of the effects that can be quantified. Obviously, this is a very significant effect and serious attention must be given to how it should be valued; in most valuation studies to date, mortality effects (in dollar terms) tend to dominate the economic benefits of improving air quality. It is important to remember that value is not being ascribed to the life of any individual, but instead to reducing the annual probability of death for a large population by a small amount. The value of reducing pollutant-related mortality is really the value of reducing small risks to many individuals, where it is anticipated that fewer will die prematurely if the air is cleaner. Of course, we do not know exactly which individuals these are, and herein lies one of the controversies inherent in this valuation process.

Clearly, the COI approach can only provide a partial measure of the loss to the individual, or to society, of reduced life expectancy. Consequently, economists have turned to the more comprehensive WTA and WTA measures, which assess the aggregate value to individuals of reducing the probability of some (unidentified) individuals in a group giving up life earlier than would otherwise be expected. The value of averted death, or reduced annual risk of death, is a more accurate term for what is measured, but the expression "value of life" (VOL), or "value of a statistical life" (VSL), has become the more commonly used term.

One mathematically straightforward method of calculating the VSL is the widely used CV, or survey, approach. For example, suppose that each individual in a group of 1,000 people is asked what he/she would pay to reduce the probability of their death in a given time period by, say, 0.5 percent. If, on average, each person responds $25,000, then the total WTP to reduce risk to that group can be determined to be: $1000 \times \$25,000 = \$25,000,000$. Moreover, since the expected number of deaths in this situation is 5 (the probability of death multiplied by the population at risk, or 0.005×1000), the value of avoiding *one* additional death is $25,000,000/5 expected deaths = $5,000,000. In effect, then, the VSL equals the total amount that all of the members of a group are willing to pay to reduce risk enough to avert one death in the group. What makes this methodology so appealing to many economists is the fact that this is precisely the *social* question raised by programs designed to reduce small environmental health risks, including particulate and ozone exposure, to a large population.

The hedonic method may also be used to obtain measures of the value of life. In hedonic studies, the VSL is deduced from the costs people actually incur to reduce risk or the compensation they require to accept greater risk. Behavior can be observed either in situations involving on-the-job risk or consumer purchases of risky products. The value of life is then inferred by identifying different risk levels and accounting for the consumer cost or wage differential between them. In the workplace, for example, suppose that for a group of 100,000 workers, there are 15 more job-related deaths each year in one industry than another, and that the higher risk jobs pay $1,000 more per year. The value of a statistical life can then be calculated to be $(100,000 \times \$1,000)/15 = \$6.7$ million. Dividing the income foregone on the part of the group of lower-risk workers by the expected number of deaths avoided in that group reveals what those workers are "willing to pay", and actually sacrifice in income, for less risk.

Consumer behavior studies are based on the same basic principles. However, consumers choose products for multiple reasons, making it more difficult (but still possible) to sort out the specific characteristics, such as safety, that persuade a consumer to pay more for one product than for another. In one such study, Atkinson and Halvorsen (1990) evaluated the behavior of car buyers to determine their WTP for lower risk of death in automobile accidents. Price differences for different models were adjusted for factors other than safety, and the value of safer cars inferred from the price differentials paid for safer models. Since fatality risks are known for various models, it was then possible to directly associate prices and risk to estimate the value of life. This study produced an estimate of $4.2 million. Because this figure is based on actual expenditures by the general public, it provides an important indicator of how society values risk to life.

Based on a recent assessment of virtually all available estimates from published studies, including contingent valuation, wage-risk, and consumer behavior studies, most VOL estimates fall in the range of $3 million to $7 million (Viscusi, 1993). Recognizing that the value of reduced risk varies across circumstances helps to explain the wide range in monetary values. For example, the voluntary or involuntary nature of the risk, the kind of death being considered (sudden, or slow and painful), and the magnitude of the risk are all important factors in influencing peoples' perceptions of, and subsequent valuation of, the risk being considered. Viscusi (1986) concluded that for involuntary risk or smaller risks (averaging less than a 1 in 10,000 probability of a job-related death in one year), the value of a statistical life for a "representative" worker ranged from about $2.9 million to $4.3 million. An important caveat to this figure concerned a possible "income bias", in so far as lower income groups are disproportionately represented in most wage-risk studies. When an adjustment was made to account for this income bias, the value of life increased to $5.7 million (Viscusi, 1993).

Contingent valuation studies have also produced a wide range of estimates. Viscusi et al. (1991), for example, found a mean value of $9.8 million to avoid an automobile-related death. The median value, however, was closer to $3 million, near the average of all studies.

Valuing morbidity

The reduction in acute or chronic illness or symptoms, apart from premature mortality, is another important component of the welfare gain resulting from cleaner air. "Morbidity" has been classified (by the National Health Survey, for example) in a number of specific ways. These include: "restricted activity days" (RADs), during which a person is able to undertake some, but not all, normal activities; and "work loss days", on which a person is unable to engage in his or her ordinary employment. In addition, many health studies offer evidence of morbidity effects by reporting the actual occurrence of specific health conditions (asthma attacks and respiratory infections) or specific symptoms (sore throat, eye irritation, and chest tightness), as well as higher rates of hospital admissions and emergency room visits.

In the economics literature, considerably less empirical work has been done to estimate dollar values associated with reduced morbidity than has been performed for premature mortality. In addition, the concept of morbidity covers a wide range of health conditions of differing severity and duration. A wide range of value estimates for different types of morbidity therefore exists, which makes comparisons and judgments of validity difficult.

The earliest, and most commonly used, method of valuing morbidity is the cost of illness method, which considers both direct and indirect costs. Direct costs cover all medical and illness-related medical expenditures made by patients, insurance companies and government agencies, and typically include: hospital care (inpatient and outpatient), services of physicians and other health professionals, and drugs and drug sundries. Indirect costs typically measure lost productivity due to illness and disability for employed individuals, and are calculated as some variant of the wage rate multiplied by the time lost from work. A problem with this method is the omission of value for lost time at school, leisure time, and unpaid work.

Since many types of morbidity effects are well within the range of the experience of most people, however, the contingent valuation method of eliciting WTP may be especially appropriate here. Respondents can be given information about levels of morbidity, or factors that may affect morbidity. They are then presented with a hypothetical market through which payments may be made, say through increased taxes, to reduce expected health effects. Finally, the respondents are asked their maximum bid for a specific change in morbidity, thus revealing their willingness to pay for the improvement in health. Response accuracy should be high when those surveyed have direct knowledge of the effects they are being asked to value. However, the hypothetical nature of the questions involved, and the fact that the respondents do not actually have to spend money, sometimes causes these results to be viewed with some skepticism. Nevertheless, surveys can provide information about relative economic values that cannot be obtained with other approaches, and are increasingly being used to assess the benefits of environmental policy.

Overall, morbidity values in the valuation literature range from as little as $4.50, to avoid a case of mild cough (Loehman et al., 1979), to $570,000 for cases of adult chronic bronchitis (Viscusi et al., 1991). In between, a case of hospitalization for respiratory conditions has been valued in the thousands, and other effects in the tens or hundreds of dollars. Basically, costs tend to vary with the extensiveness of medical treatment and the degree to which an effect impairs normal activities.

The Health Sciences Foundation

An extensive health science literature provides the basis for associating health damage with ozone and fine particles. Hundreds of studies, using several different investigative designs, have shown that air pollutants adversely affect health. These research designs include animal studies and controlled human exposure studies. Animal studies can demonstrate not only the existence of an adverse health effect, but also that different concentrations of pollution produce variations in the severity of these effects. In contrast, controlled human exposure studies, where pollutant exposure is well characterized and individual reactions are measured, may help us to understand whether thresholds (levels below which there are no ill effects) exist and approximately where they are, at least for the study sample, and what short-term effects can be expected to occur.

A third form of research design, epidemiological studies, must therefore be utilized to provide some of the most important data to support both standard setting and economic evaluation of the adverse health effects that will be avoided when air quality is improved. The science of epidemiology involves careful statistical investigation of the associations between population characteristics and factors that might reasonably be expected to contribute to these characteristics. In the study of air pollu- tion-related health effects, the relevant population characteristics include a wide range of health indicators, from eye irritation, to hospital admis- sions, to changes in death rates. Contributing factors include ambient concentrations of specific pollutants and potential confounding variables, such as weather, age, or smoking. A variety of statistical methods appropriate to the available data can then be used to test for the existence and significance of any association between health and pollution.

To study the role of fine particles in promoting illness or premature death, epidemiological researchers have used three basic study designs: *time-series*, *cross-sectional*, and *prospective* studies. Time-series studies consider one population over a period of time, and attempt to estimate the association between pollution levels and the frequency of acute daily health events, such as asthma attacks or hospital admissions. That is, over time, as pollution levels vary, these studies investigate whether short-term health effects also vary and by how much. Of course, other factors that vary with time, such as temperature, must also be controlled for, in order to isolate statistically significant associations between pollution and health effects. Cross-sectional studies, in contrast, examine populations at one time but in different places, where pollution levels vary across locations. The key investigative question here is whether a population exposed to higher concentrations of pollution experiences more frequent ill effects, and how frequency varies with pollution levels, after controlling for any other differences across regions (income, age, smoking, or climate, for example). Finally, prospective studies follow cohorts of the population from a starting point in time forward to determine how health status changes with pollution and other factors. These studies are often able to include chronic effects, such as prevalence of asthma and chronic bronchitis.

There now exists an extensive body of peer-reviewed health research, conducted by diverse research groups, over a long period of time, largely in the United States and Europe. Further, the use of this literature to set air quality standards is also a peer-reviewed process. Economic analysts studying the health benefits of reduced ozone and fine particle exposure utilize the same body of peer-reviewed studies as the basis for estimating the frequency of ill effects at different concentrations in different populations.

Which adverse health effects are quantified?

For the case of particulate matter, the epidemiological literature that associates particles, especially fine particles, with a large variety of health endpoints and mortality has grown rapidly in the last decade. (See, for example, Dockery et al., 1989; Dockery and Pope, 1994; Dockery et al., 1993; and Pope et al., 1995.) Most recent prospective studies (where a large group from the population is tracked over a period of time), and time-series studies, whose underlying analytical techniques are considered to be the most sophisticated and precise, yield very consistent findings about the existence and size of the association between fine particles and adverse health outcomes, including mortality.

For the case of ozone, both epidemiological studies and controlled human exposure studies have been conducted for many of the morbidity effects that have been observed. Where both types of studies can be compared, there is considerable agreement in the degree and pattern of association between ozone concentrations and adverse health effects (Kleinman et al., 1989; Kleinman, 1991). Perhaps more significantly, a group of recent epidemiological studies representing populations in multiple regions of Europe and the United States have indicated an association between ozone and premature mortality (Verhoeff et al., 1996; Anderson et al., 1996; Sartor et al., 1995; Kinney and Ozkaynak, 1991, 1992). Because the preponderance of the mortality literature is relatively new, most existing studies that have quantified the economic value of reduced health effects do not include any benefit from reducing ozone-related mortality. However, these effects are potentially large.

From this literature, a common body of research has emerged as the "consensus", or at least the most frequently referenced, group of studies that provide concentration-response relationships that are the most defensible scientifically and therefore, most suitable as a basis for quantifying dollar values.

3. EMPIRICAL AND CONCEPTUAL CHALLENGES

While the state of the art has advanced over more than two decades of experience and research, substantial challenges remain. In this section, we present some of the most pervasive empirical difficulties and discuss underlying conceptual challenges to benefit estimation.

Because society might rely on benefit assessments to determine or guide policies, it is incumbent on practitioners to be clear about potential weaknesses and uncertainties in the empirical work. For the case of evaluating air pollution-related health effects, we need robust air quality data, an understanding of how changes in emissions and air quality are related in the affected geographic region, useable dose or concentration-response functions, and generally accepted economic values for each relevant adverse health effect.

Air Quality

Without data that accurately represent current air quality exposure and reasonable estimates of how air quality in the future will change as a result of proposed emissions controls, it is not possible to estimate the health benefits that will result from those controls. Monitoring is expensive, however, and many regions lack systematic networks. Similarly, emissions inventories are often based on extrapolations from assumed levels of operation and emission rates. Forecasters must also make assumptions about future population and levels of economic activity, both closely correlated with emissions. The best models that support predictions of future air quality are data-intensive and expensive to maintain and to operate. Consequently, only richer communities are likely to be able to forecast air quality changes reliably. Further, the ways in which emissions of different pollutants interact in the atmosphere determine whether emissions reductions will result in proportionately cleaner air.

This challenge can be overcome to some degree if current air quality data are available. At least it is then possible to estimate the value of health gains that would result from some absolute level of improvement in the ambient air. It is not possible without additional data as discussed above to say with much confidence how specific emissions controls will improve air quality (Hall and Hall, 1997). The exception to this is lead, for which reduced emissions translate directly to reduced concentrations in the atmosphere.

Relating Air Quality to Health

Several key health science issues influence the economic valuation of health benefits. These include: the determination of pollution thresholds, the overlapping effects of ozone and particulate matter and their precursors, the double-counting of health effects, and the general question of who is at greatest risk. These issues need to be kept in mind as existing valuation studies are reviewed, and further explored as more studies are undertaken in the future.

The Existence and Location of Thresholds

The most important unresolved issue connected with health benefit valuation may be the existence of health effects thresholds, that is, pollution levels below which there are no further beneficial health benefits to be realized from increased controls. The fact that most empirical results have come from epidemiological studies, where researchers do not have "control" over the levels of pollution exposure, makes it particularly difficult to determine whether or not there are health effect threshold levels. A consistent association between particulate matter and health effects has been found by recent health studies, even at pollution levels well below most air quality standards (Schwartz & Dockery, 1992a,b, for example). The existence and level of thresholds remains an important source of uncertainty in health estimation, for if no threshold is assumed, but one exists, benefits will be overestimated. Conversely, if a threshold is imposed where one does not exist, the predicted health benefits resulting from an improvement in air quality could be seriously underestimated.

Overlapping Effects of Particulates and Ozone

Benefit assessments depend heavily on epidemiological studies, many of which show statistical associations between pollutants and a number of common health effects, including increased hospital admissions and mortality risk. What makes the use of these associations somewhat problematic is that significant overlap may exist in adding together the estimated benefits attributed separately to the reductions in particulate concentrations and in ozone concentrations. An additional source of overlap in benefit estimation involves the valuing of reductions in the common precursor emissions for particulates and ozone. Reductions in nitrogen oxides, for example, can reduce both particulates and ozone. Any calculation of health benefits per ton reduced, therefore, should account for reductions in effects related to both pollutants. In future valuation efforts, this overlap issue may carry further importance, as statistical associations are now being increasingly found between ozone and higher mortality risk – ozone-related mortality will increasingly be included in benefit assessments.

Double-Counting of Health Effects

In addition to the possibility of overlapping effects between particulate matter and ozone, overlapping health effects for each separate pollutant must also be considered. Wherever potentially overlapping health categories are valued, it becomes necessary to make adjustments in calculating total health effects. For example, epidemiological studies find statistical associations between particulate levels and a number of health endpoints, including hospital admissions, emergency room visits, and restricted activity days (RADs). But obviously, days spent in a hospital are also days of restricted activity, and should therefore be subtracted from RADs before aggregating monetary benefits.

In the case of ozone-related effects, it is likely that when air pollution levels are sufficient to trigger, say, headache or chest discomfort, there might also be occurrences of a number of more minor symptoms, such as sore throat, cough and eye irritation, since all of these symptoms result from the irritant action of ozone on exposed membranes. It follows that any results from exposure or dose-response functions that predict a variety of minor health effects must somehow be adjusted to account for this overlap. The most conservative approach, in the absence of more concrete pollution-specific data on the probability of symptom overlap, would be to assume that many of the effects occur together, and that their monetary values cannot simply be added together.

Determining How Society Values Reduced Health Risk

In the end, we conduct benefit assessments so that society can make collective decisions. What we want to know is: what it is worth to society to achieve an improvement in air quality? A number of empirical and ethical issues arise here, relating largely to issues of whether all individuals are valued equally and equity in the distribution of pollution and the benefits of reducing it.

Who is at Risk?

There are certain groups of people who are more likely to suffer adverse health effects than others following exposure to air pollution. For example, the health effects literature offers some quantitative evidence that a large portion (80%) of the individuals at risk of premature mortality are 65 or older, while 70% of all deaths in the U.S. occur in this age group. This has important implications for calculation of health effects, and for monetary valuation, since the value of changes in mortality risk might be different for the older population. Extrapolating findings from one age group to another introduces further uncertainty into an already challenging process. It is also useful to draw a distinction between persons who are merely "at risk" from exposure to air pollution and persons who are extremely sensitive to air pollution effects. Sensitive persons, who perhaps already have compromised heart of lung function, will react more dramatically to exposure than would individuals with no particular sensitivity.

An area of great concern to policy makers is obviously risk to children. Traditionally, most of the emphasis in developing data for setting air quality standards has been on adults. More recently, however, there has arisen an awareness that children cannot be considered "scaled-down" adults, and that more sophisticated approaches are necessary in order to accurately account for the effects of air pollution on them. While children inhale less mass of pollutant for a given exposure level than adults do, most physiological effects are dependent upon dose received. On this basis, the effective dose to a child's lung, in terms of pollutant received as a function of body weight, is usually greater than that for adults under similar exposure conditions. Moreover, lungs grow until the late teens or early twenties. If air pollution influences the growth process, resulting in smaller lungs, vitality is at risk. Some recent studies that have estimated health effects specifically for children include Dockery et al. (1989), who examined child bronchitis, and Ransom and Pope (1995) who considered hospital visits and lost school time in young people.

Children are more impacted by a given level of pollution because of their physiology and tendency to be active and out of doors. Children and members of ethnic minorities might also be more at risk because they live in sections of urban areas with worse than average air quality. A number of studies suggest that exposure to riskier levels of pollution is greater for lower income groups, ethnic groups, and children (Brajer and Hall, 1992; Korc, 1996.)

Are All Valued Equally?

Some recent valuation studies reflect the possibility that two-thirds or more of those affected may be over 65 years of age (USEPA, 1997). This has occurred in response to the argument that the value of a statistical life for the elderly should be significantly less than for younger people. There are two reasons for such adjustments. First, fewer years of life are lost if an older person dies than if a child dies. Second, the quality of life of the elderly may be poorer than the average person's quality of life. Therefore, less time is lost and the quality of that time is also assumed to be compromised, when the risk is greatest for the elderly. Recently, consideration of the years of life lost, and the quality of life, as well as the number of premature deaths, has become a consideration in benefit estimation.

Confounding this is recent research that shows that even very old people – 80 and older – with compromised quality of life place significantly greater value on even a limited amount of additional life that has been assumed. There are a number of reasons for this; a main one being that, given little remaining time, the marginal benefit of what remains is very high.

Benefit Transfer

The majority of health science and economic valuation work has been done in the United States and in Europe (Georgiou et al., 1997). In recent years, more epidemiological studies have been conducted in developing countries. This means that benefit assessment must of necessity rely heavily on an information base derived from populations that are relatively wealthy and industrialized, and largely western. For estimation of health effects, this raises issues regarding relative underlying states of health and health care, as well as differences in complex atmospheres across the world. Regarding the value placed on each effect, it is assumed that higher income produces higher willingness to pay, and that values based, for example, on U.S. preferences might overstate the value someone in Africa or Asia would place on avoiding an effect. While this seems straightforward and is consistent with economic theory, in fact we have almost no data on how cultural differences might also affect preferences and how this would relate to the effect of income on willingness to pay.

The Issue of Incompleteness

Unfortunately, the adverse health effects whose frequency in association with air pollution can be quantified and whose avoidance can also be valued in dollars is a limited subset of the adverse effects that have been observed or measured in epidemiological, human exposure or animal studies. Limitations of both health science and economics contribute to our inability to quantify these effects. For example, exposure to carbon monoxide is believed to be related with occurrences of heart problems, which can be valued quite easily in economic terms. Until recently, however, no specific dose response relationships had been developed by heath science researchers, thereby precluding the dollar valuation of this particular health endpoint. Reduced lung function, on the other hand, which has been linked to changing particulate levels in a number of health studies, cannot be easily valued in economic terms. Since at present we have no way to calculate the relative importance of what is measurable and what is not, it is impossible to determine how large the unquantified effects may be in economic terms. In addition, some of the unquantified effects may overlap some effects that are quantified. For example, changed pulmonary function accompanies chronic bronchitis. Nonetheless, it is important to recognize the number and nature of such unquantified effects to provide perspective when interpreting the meaning and comprehensiveness of estimates of the economic value of improved air quality.

Currently, the unquantified ozone-related effects include: lower respiratory symptoms, immunological changes, chronic respiratory damage and disease, inflammation of the lung, increased airway responsiveness, and changes in pulmonary function. Particle-related effects that cannot be quantified include: initiation of chronic asthma, chronic respiratory disease other than bronchitis, cancer, altered host defense mechanisms (which may be related to vulnerability to disease or injury), morphological changes, and changes in pulmonary function.

4. CONCLUSIONS

Real progress has been made over a period of more than two decades to provide a more robust foundation for estimating the benefits of environmental improvements. A number of limiting factors remains important. These limitations arise in all aspects of assessment - the air quality data and forecasts, the usefulness of the health literature for quantifying effects, and the existence and meaning of economic values for individual adverse health effects. Consequently, benefit assessments should probably not be relied on to make decisions about "close calls" or narrow programs, but rather should be viewed as offering guidance for broad policy issues. Decision makers must exercise their own judgment, based on consideration of the fundamental reasons why there are uncertainties, and on their assessment of society's objectives and preferences with regard to equity and related issues as well as efficiency. Still, benefit assessment can help to make uncertainties and their influence clear, to identify what is missing from the analysis, and to systematically present a complex set of information to make it more useful. Ultimately, benefit assessment can help to ensure that limited resources are used more effectively.

REFERENCES

Anderson, H.R., et al. (1996) "Air Pollution and Daily Mortality in London: 1987–92", *British Medical Journal*, 312: 665–669.

Atkinson, S.E. and Halvorsen, R. (1990) "The Valuation of Risks to Life: Evidence from the Market for Automobiles", *Review of Economics and Statistics*, 72(1): 133–136.

Bates, D. (1992) "Health Indices of the Adverse Effects of Air Pollution: The Question of Coherence", *Environmental Research*, 59: 336–349.

Brajer, V. and Hall, J. (1992) "Recent Evidence on the Distribution of Air Pollution Effects", *Contemporary Policy Issues*, Vol. 10, No. 2, pp. 63–71.

Chestnut, L.G., et al. (1988) *Heart Disease Patients' Averting Behavior, Costs of Illness, and Willingness to Pay to Avoid Angina Episodes*, Final Report to the Office of Policy Analysis, U.S. EPA, Washington, DC.

Crocker, T.D. and R.L. Horst, Jr. (1981) "Hours of Work, Labor Productivity, and Environmental Conditions: a Case Study", *The Review of Economics and Statistics*, 63: 361–368.

Dockery, D.W. Speizer, F.E., Stram, J.H., Spengler, J.D. and Ferris, B.G. Jr. (1989) "Effects of Inhalable Particles on Respiratory Health of Children", *American Review of Respiratory Diseases*, 139: 587–594.

Dockery, D.W., Pope III, C.A., Xu X., Spengler J., Ware J., Fay M., Ferris B. and Speizer F. (1993) "An Association Between Air Pollution and Mortality in Six U.S. Cities", *New England Journal of Medicine*: 329: 1753–1759.

Dockery, D.W. and Pope, C.A. III (1994) "Acute Respiratory Effects of Particulate Air Pollution" *Annual Review of Public Health*, Vol. 15, pp. 107–132.

Georgiou, S., Whittington, D., Pearce, D. and Moran, Dominic, *Economic Values and the Environment in the Developing World*, Edward Elgar, Cheltenham, U.K.

Hall, J.V., Winer A.M., Kleinman, M.T., Lurmann F.W., Brajer V. and Colome S.D. (1992) "Valuing the Health Benefits of Clean Air", *Science*, Vol. 255 No. 5046, pp. 812–817.

Hall, J. V. (1996a) "Estimating Environmental Health Benefits: Implications for Social Decision-Making", *International Journal of Social Economics*, 23(4/5/6): 282–295.

Hall, J.V. (1996b). "Assessing Health Effects of Air Pollution", *Atmospheric Environment*, 30(5): 743–746.

Hall, Darwin C. and Hall, Jane V. (1997) "Estimating the Benefits of Emissions Reductions in Complex Atmospheres", *International Journal of Global Energy Issues*, 9(4–6): 286–298.

Kinney, P.L. and Ozkaynak, H. (1991) "Associations of Daily Mortality and Air Pollution in Los Angeles County", *Environmental Research*, Vol. 54, pp. 99–120.

Kinney, P.L. and Ozkaynak, H. (1992) "Associations Between Ozone and Daily Mortality in Los Angeles and New York City", *American Review of Respiratory Disease*, 145.

Kleinman, M.T., Colome, S.D. and Foliart, D. (1989) *Effects on Human Health of Pollutants in the South Coast Air Basin*, Final Report to the South Coast Air Quality Management District, Diamond Bar, CA.

Kleinman, M.T. (1991) "Effects of Ozone on Pulmonary Function: The Relationship of Response to Dose", *Journal of Exposure Analysis and Environmental Epidemiology*, Vol. 1, pp. 309–324

Korc, M. (1996) "A Socioeconomic Assessment of Human Exposure to Ozone in the South Coast Air Basin", *Journal of the Air and Waste Management Association*, 46(6): 547–557.

Krupnick, A.J. and M.L. Cropper (1989) *Valuing Chronic Morbidity Damages: Medical Costs, Labor Market Effects, and Individual Valuations*, Final Report to U.S. EPA, Office of Policy Analysis, Washington, DC.

Loehman, E.T. et al. (1979) "Distribution Analysis of Regional Benefits and Cost of Air Quality Control", *Journal of Environmental Economics and Management*, 6: 222–243.

366

Pope, A.C.III. Thun, M.J., Namboodiri, M.M., Dockery, D.W., Evans, J.S., Speizer, F.E. and Heath C.W. (1995) "Particulate Air Pollution as a Predictor of Mortality in a Prospective Study of U.S. Adults", *American Journal of Respiratory Critical Care Medicine*, Vol. 151, pp. 669–674.

Ransom, M.B. and Pope, A. III. (1995) "External Health Costs of a Steel Mill", *Contemporary Economic Policy*, 13(2): 86–97.

Rowe, R.D. and T.N. Neithercut (1987) *Economic Assessment of the Impacts of Cataracts*, Prepared for U.S. Environmental Protection Agency, Office of Policy, Planning, and Evaluation, Washington, DC.

Sartor, F. et al. (1995) "Temperature, Ambient Ozone Levels, and Mortality during Summer, 1994, in Belgium", *Environmental Research*, 70: 105–113.

Schwartz, J. and Dockery D.W. (1992a) "Increased Mortality in Philadephia Associated with Daily Air Pollution Concentrations", *American Review of Respiratory Diseases*, 145: 600–604.

Schwartz, J. and Dockery D.W. (1992b) "Particulate Air Pollution and Daily Mortality in Steubenville. Ohio", *American Journal of Epidemiology*, 135: 12–19.

U.S. Environmental Protection Agency (1997) *The Benefits and Costs of the Clean Air Act, 1970 to 1990*, October.

Verhoeff, A.P. et al. (1996) "Air Pollution and Daily Mortality in Amsterdam", *Epidemiology*, 7(3): 225–230.

Viscusi, W.K. (1986) "The Valuation of Risks to Life and Health: Guidelines for Policy Analysis", in Bentkover, J.D., Covello, V. and Mumpower, J. (Eds.) *Benefits Assessment: State of the Art*, pp. 193–210, D. Reidel Publishing Co., Dordrecht.

Viscusi, W.K., Magat, W.A. and Forrest A. (1988) "Altruistic and Private Valuations of Risk Reduction", *Journal of Policy Analysis and Management*, Vol. 7 No. 2, pp. 227–245.

Viscusi, W.K., W.A. Magat and J. Huber (1991) "Pricing Environmental Health Risks: Survey Assessments of Risk-Risk and Risk-Dollar Trade-offs for Chronic Bronchitis", *Journal of Environmental Economics and Management*, 21(1): 32–51.

Viscusi, W.K. (1993) "The Value of Risks to Life and Health", *Journal of Economic Literature*, 31(4): 1912–1946.

CHAPTER - 21

THE IMPLICATIONS OF ECOLOGICAL ECONOMIC THEORIES OF VALUE TO COST-BENEFIT ANALYSIS: IMPORTANCE OF ALTERNATIVE VALUATION FOR DEVELOPING NATIONS WITH SPECIAL EMPHASIS ON CENTRAL AMERICA

Bernardo Aguilar and Thomas J. Semanchin

ABSTRACT

For the studious of environmental problems, economics has traditionally been a foreign science. Nevertheless, the need to harmonize the objectives of development has led to overcome this distance. The truth is that economics can be used as a science to promote conservation. This paper argues that the ecological economics theory of value and capital can be used to promote sustainable development in decision-making processes. We survey the existing trends in ecological economic literature regarding value estimating and their effect on Cost Benefit Analysis.

After presenting a cross-section of the literature, we try to show that the adoption of this young scientific position may be conducive to the sustainability of developing nations' patterns of development. We focus more specifically on the region of Central America. Through a series of examples and two brief case studies we hope to prove that the ecological economic position provides a good choice framework for public and private development decision making. Nevertheless, the complexity of the issue prevents us from drawing complete and definite conclusions. The goal is that this paper generates discussion around this issue among all involved in the scientific/practical processes of decision-making in/with the region.

I. INTRODUCTION: DEVELOPMENT MODELS AND
ECONOMIC DECISION MAKING

For the studious of environmental problems, economics has traditionally been a foreign science. Nevertheless, the need to harmonize the objectives of development has led to overcome this distance. The truth is that economics can be used as a science to promote conservation.

Those who identify economics with the value system of the capitalist society might want to dispute the validity of the last statement by blaming economic thought for the substantial environmental damage that we have caused to our planet. We cannot deny that the neoclassical biased application of this science has generated a substantial impact. Nevertheless, we can also bias economic analysis in favor of conservation. In essence we are dealing with a science that explains accountings within the context of human societies. The ethical base that supports value measurement choices resides essentially in the way that a specific social group views the world. From this perspective, economics can reflect the value system of sustainable development.

Sustainable development theoretically unifies the goals of economics and conservation. Necessary conditions for this balance to occur are intra and intergenerational human equity. Such conditions derive from the need to guarantee that all humans can have access to certain minimum conditions of life. The achievement of those conditions (nutrition, appropriate housing, education, political participation etc.) causes a reduction of the pressure exercised by the human capital base on the natural capital stock.

Ecological Economics has explicitly claimed these values as its foundation. Even if still young, this economic trend has taken the challenge of questioning the roots of the ruling neoclassic economic paradigm. Its goal is to promote a sustainable world, for which it confronts the notion of the economy as an isolated, ever growing system. As Robert Costanza (1989, 2) argues

> 'Current economic paradigms . . . are all based on the underlying assumption of continuing and unlimited growth. This assumption allows problems of intergenerational, and interspecies equity and sustainability to be ignored (or at least postponed), since they are seen to be most easily solved by additional growth.'

In contrast, this science has proposed alternative theories of capital and value. These theories seek to promote sustainability as a criterion for development.

This proposed paradigm shift would affect the essence of economic decision making and therefore cost-benefit analysis (CBA). CBA is used by policy makers nationally and internationally to decide which of alternative options provides the greatest contribution to the welfare of a nation. Welfare here is traditionally measured as the monetary relation between benefits and costs. Yet, as Demmel (1992, 35) says, the usefulness of this tool depends on **ALL** the costs and benefits being included. Therefore, 'though it makes the most precise statements about which policy choices are efficient, it also imposes the largest requirements for information in order to provide those statements' (Tietenberg 1996, 67).

The information requirements of CBA are directly related to the notion of value used to estimate benefits and costs. As Bingham et al. (1995, 79) state it 'at the most basic level, choice implies value. Whether the decision maker chooses to do something or not, the act of choice implicitly reveals a threshold for the value the decision maker has assigned to what is at stake'. So, the decision maker translates in his/her choices collective decisions, implicit values about the resources valued. In essence, what occurs is a predetermination of how costs and benefits will be weighted in making decisions. This paper seeks to survey the existing trends in ecological economic literature regarding value estimating and their effect on CBA. The survey does not seek to be complete. It will provide a foundation and show the applicability of these emerging techniques with specific examples. By concentrating on some important publications and recent editions of the Journal of Ecological Economics we hope to present a good cross-section of the literature.

The information requirements and structure of CBA are also affected by the context in which it is applied (Bingham et al., 1995, 85). The application of ecological economic analysis to developing nations is scarce. As Pearce et al. (1990, 186) acknowledge,

> 'The need to know something about environment, about the developing world and about economics makes it a fairly daunting subject to pursue. It may also be due to the generally 'fuzzy' nature of the subject. There are no real neat solutions, such as those that appear in the professional economics journals in respect of more abstract questions, and there are formidable problems of obtaining data and even greater ones of assessing the reliability of what there is'.

Nevertheless, ecological economics may be particularly applicable to developing nations (partly due to this ambiguity). In this paper we try to show that the adoption of this young scientific position may be conducive to the sustainability of developing nations' patterns of development. We focus more specifically on the region of Central America, to which we are tied physically and emotionally. Through a series of examples and two brief case studies we hope to prove that the ecological economic position provides a good choice framework for public and private development decision making. Nevertheless, the complexity of the issue prevents us from drawing complete and definite conclusions. This effort seeks to be a starting point that can generate discussion around this issue among all involved in the scientific/practical processes of decision-making in/with the region.

II. THE PROPOSAL OF ECOLOGICAL ECONOMICS: AN ALTERNATIVE VALUE THEORY

In the mid nineteenth century, economics saw the birth of what was called pure economy, or as later called, the neoclassical economic school. It embraced pure competition as the means to achieve social welfare. This made it seem similar to the classic school that preceded it. Yet, a distinction is found in the optimistic outlook it had for the future. This responded to the economic conditions that America and Europe were perceiving by the end of the century: abundance and prosperity because of the industrial revolution.

Neoclassical economics abandons the labor theory of value and adopts a position based on scarcity and the utility provided by a good. The relation between the two, which presupposes the capacity to appropriate goods, determines an equilibrium price.

Impossibility of full appropriation leaves many environmental functions out of the possibility of valuation. Environmental functions are understood as a part of the human economy that can be substituted by manufactured capital.

Further, the intra and intergenerational distribution implications of differences in consumer's willingness to pay and natural resource exhaustion are not accounted for. The institutional market base of the neoclassic proposal assumes a given distribution of endowments. Distributional problems are to be solved by the growth of the system, which, given its conception of capital, has no limits.

Based on this paradigm, economic decisions, using tools like CBA, are made with incomplete and insufficient information. This is a direct violation of the complete and perfect information assumption of the neoclassic free market model.

As a reaction, the ecological economic paradigm proposes an alternative value theory based on a broader and more comprehensive understanding of capital. This notion of capital is a direct consequence of a co-evolutionary paradigm between social and natural systems. In essence, the ecological economic conceptualization of capital presents it as a two level system. The first level is natural capital which is composed of all ecosystems (managed and non managed). Human systems are part of ecosystems and so is the second level of capital: human-made capital. The size of the natural capital and its capacity to adapt or renew in view of human activity determines the limits to growth of human-made capital. Materials and energy flow through human systems from the natural capital stock of environmental functions. This flow makes every productive process in human societies possible.

The interface between these two levels is cultural capital which helps the adaptation between one and the other (see Figure 1). Cultural capital includes all knowledge, conventions and formal/informal institutional agreements in human societies. An institutional framework is instrumental to the expression of knowledge and social conventions. It includes the legal and political systems, traditions, morality and all expressions of cultural continuity.

This conception of capital supports the paradigm shift toward sustainable development. By understanding the dimensions of natural and cultural capital depletion generated by economic decisions, the achievement of an efficient allocation of resources seems possible. The achievement of a fair distribution of resources, within and between human generations and other species, also seems possible. Implied also is the respect for the carrying capacity of ecosystems (See Daly, 1992, 186–187). Yet, as Victor (1991, 209) admits it, the applicability of sustainable development depends on its incorporation to decision making through measurability. For this, the development of an accompanying value theory has been a key issue for ecological economists.

We use the notion of value theory in a broad sense here. By theory we understand a dynamic explanatory scheme of ideas. By value we understand a recognition of the relevance that an energy or material entity has in relation to the system to which it belongs. In this sense, the relevance can be an expression of a role as part of the stock of natural

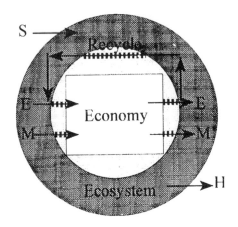

capital types:

S = solar energy   = human-made
H = heat
M= matter   = cultural
E = energy   = natural

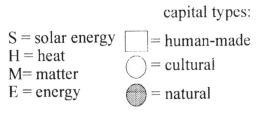

Figure 1.

capital. It can also be an expression of the relevance of the flows occurring within the system. In both cases, the value can be intrinsic or related to other entities. If the evaluation of relevance is done by a human being, it will imply moral and ethical assumptions, such as the desire to achieve a sustainable world.

The literature shows three trends regarding ecological economic valuation. The first trend we will discuss is known as the 'London School'. This effort seeks mostly to establish methods of value comparability. It does not abandon monetary units as the unit of measure. Yet, on a philosophical ground, it can be distinguished from neoclassic theory in its attempt to recognize non-anthropocentric sources of value and. It also incorporates of sustainability as the main criterion for decision making.

The second approach, the 'Thermodynamic School', appears more radical from a neoclassical perspective since it proposes a shift to commensurability of values between ecosystems and human systems. This is done through the recognition and quantification of energy and material stocks and flows as the basis of value.

A third group includes several options that try to capture the complexity of decision-making and do not recognize a unique source of 'value' as the appropriate basis. One of them proposes a combination of value measurements. The main idea is to incorporate multiple evaluation criteria that overcome the availability of information limitations that characterize the first two. This approach can have important implications through its applicability by policy makers who would require a longer time to digest the rationality of a total abandonment of the neoclassic approach to valuation.

Additionally, the literature shows another approach that proposes an integral theory based on the different ways in which human express end values. It seeks a method of decision making that can capture this multi-dimensional process.

The next sections briefly explain the main proposals behind these three groups and some criticism to them. This short presentation does not claim a great degree of depth. More detailed explanations can be found in the respective references.

A. MAKING SYSTEMS COMPARABLE: THE ALLOCATIVE APPROACH TO VALUATION.

The allocative approach to valuation has been developed, among others, by a group of leading economists at the London Centre for Environmental Economics. This group of economists has the common thread of 'trying to develop an appreciation of sustainable development in economic terms' (Victor, 1991, 201). As Pearce et al. (1990, 4) expressly recognize it, the main condition that defines sustainability is the maintenance of a constant stock of natural capital.

The need to maintain a sustainable stock of natural capital requires a means to measure it in economic analysis. According to Victor (1991, 203) the four options considered by this school are physical units; total value of stocks; unit value of natural resource services and the value of resource flows.

The first possibility is rejected due to the difficulty in understanding different units together. The other three are used as a 'rod to measure the gains or losses in welfare' (Pearce and Turner (1990, 121).

de Groot (1994) bases his adoption of this type of valuation in the benefits provided by environmental functions to human welfare. This idea is clarified by Costanza et al. (1998, 7)who point to the benefits of estimating 'how changes in the quantity or quality of various types of natural capital or ecosystem services may have an impact on humanwelfare'.

These ideas are formalized in the Total Value Equation (TVE) which expresses Total Economic Value (TEV). McNeely (1988) proposes that the values and benefits of biological diversity can be classified in two main groups: direct and indirect. In this section we rely strongly on his classification system. Direct values (DV) are related to the consumption of a good or service. Indirect values (IV) are usually related to environmental services. They measure human welfare that does not originate in consumption & they acknowledge the intrinsic value of nature (Aguilar, 1996a and 1996b).

According to McNeely (1988, 14) direct values can be divided into productive use values (PUV) and consumptive use values (CUV). The PUV is the value of goods and services that are commercially harvested. It is determined through a market (wholesale, retail). We believe that this is the market price even if some literature seems to imply it is not necessarily it. McNeely (1988, 17) for example says that 'where close substitutes are not available, there exists a "consumer surplus" beyond the market price. In this case, use of price data may severely underestimate productive use value'.

The CUV is the value of goods and services that are consumed without having been taken to the market for valuation (de Groot, 1994). This consumption implies an increase in welfare that arises from the utility derived and the savings from the potential value that would have been paid in the market. Consumption is understood in this scenario in its strict sense of ingesting, expending or using up.

Indirect Values are subdivided in non consumptive use values (NCUV), option values (OV) and existence values (EV). NCUVs derive from nature's services that provide increases in welfare without being consumed or traded in the marketplace (McNeely, 1988). They also derive from uses that do not imply consumption of the good or service involved such as recreation, tourism or education.

As de Groot (1994, 156) states it the 'option value is a type of life insurance for access to future services from natural ecosystems'. Pearce and Turner (1990) explain the need for this value in the uncertainty of future supply of determined environmental services and human risk aversion. The OV is an extra value that seeks to assure the future availability of resources. It includes the serendipity value for those goods and services that may be found to affect human welfare in the future (McNeely, 1988).

The EV is the intrinsic, intangible and ethical value of goods and services that is unrelated to any actual or potential use of the good. It stems from a feeling of stewardship for nonhuman entities and future generations of humans. This value implies a form of extensionism (Page, 1991, 59) in the 'recognition of value referents beside people'. It also implies a bequest value that is the 'vicarious benefit received now because someone who may not yet exist may benefit in some unidentified manner from the future existence' of some resource (McNeely, 1988, 24).

The Total Value Equation can then be expressed as:

$$TEV_t = DV_t + IV_t \qquad (1)$$

where

$$DV_t = PUV_t + CUV_t \qquad (2)$$

and,

$$IV_t = NCUV_t + OV_t + EV_t \qquad (3)$$

Summarizing the notion of value, this approach to valuation does not seem to challenge the main basis of the neoclassic theory of value in relation to human welfare being a source of value. Yet, it does broaden the possible sources of value by recognizing the effect on human welfare of those goods and services that are not owned or consumed. Probably its most radical proposals are the incorporation of use over time as a source of value (OV) and the recognition of value referents outside humans (EV).

Prugh et al. (1995, 96) point to the lack of universal agreement on the classification presented above. They tell us some systems overlap yet favor what they call the simplest scheme, proposed by Pearce and Turner (1990). This system is reduced to three components: Use Value (UV), OV and EV. The UV component is disaggregated in market captured and nonmarket captured values.

Others, as de Groot (1994, 155) disaggregate the values according to their ecological, social or economic nature. Within this framework,

NCUV is disaggregated as conservation value, health value and employment value. We favor the classifications which disaggregate the DV component between PUV and CUV in view of specific conditions of
developing nations. We will get back to this issue later. For now, we make
this claim to resolve the semantic difficulties associated with the terms
used in relation to the context we analyze. On the rest of the components,
the proposals appear uniform.

In Figures 2a. and 2b. we see a graphic summary of the total value of
ecosystem services, relying heavily on the presentation made by Costanza
et al. (1998, 8). The total value equation seeks to reveal preferences not
captured in market prices. It reveals willingness to pay for those services.
In Figure 2a. we see total economic value for a human-made good as the
sum of consumer and producer surplus, which is larger than the total
revenue accounted for by traditional methods (price times quantity).Figure 2b. presents the case where the consumers' surplus approaches infinity as the good or service becomes more scarce and supply
is fixed. This is the typical case of many natural resources, which can be
an obstacle to estimate the total allocative values for environmental
goods.

TVE estimation techniques depend on the available information. They
range from simple valuation (when prices are available) to shadow pricing
and survey based approaches (relying mostly on contingent valuation
methods) (see, e.g., Dixon et al. (1994), 42–103; Dixon and Sherman
(1990), 33–48).

The allocative approach to valuation has received several criticisms
that seem worth mentioning. The first of these criticisms relates to the
ethical implications of a 'commodification' of the environment. This is a
common criticism made by environmentalists that see this as an oversim-
plification of the environment. Yet, the response of the supporters of this
approach, (e.g., Prugh et al., 1995, 96; Pearce and Turner, 1990, 121) is
that even if it is an incomplete process, the assignment of monetary value
to components of natural capital is a useful yardstick. It allows comparisons to be made which by several decision making techniques yield a
quantified measure of peoples' preferences.

a

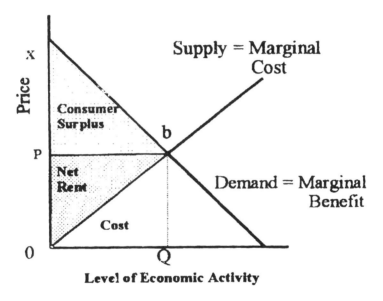

Figure 2.

b

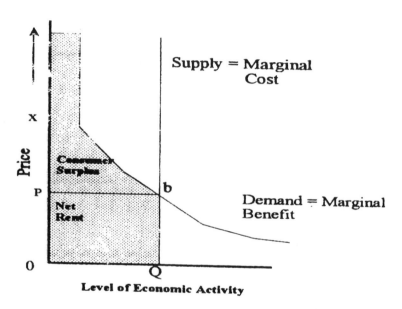

Figure 2.

Victor (1991, 202) summarizes other difficulties in measuring the value of the stock of natural capital. Some resources will not have a price or if a price exists it might be affected by many imperfections. Further, those prices do not measure the preferences of future generations for which they seem irrelevant to measure the value of stocks. Finally, net prices affect marginal conditions for which they are not accurate to measure stocks.

Despite this criticism, the value of this approach is still well accepted. Costanza et al. (1998, 4) reaffirm this in their recent paper when they write:

'The economies of the Earth would grind to a halt without the services of ecological life-support systems so in one sense their total value to the economy is infinite. However it can be instructive to estimate the 'incremental' or 'marginal' value of ecosystem services (the estimated rate of change of value compared with changes in ecosystem services from their current levels)'.

Testimony to the acceptance of this approach, the latter paper referenced estimated the total value of 17 global ecosystem services and natural capital for the first time ever. The estimate was of an average thirty-three trillion US Dollars per year, which amounts to almost twice the global GDP (Costanza et al., 1998, 12).

B. MAKING SYSTEMS COMMENSURABLE: THE BIOPHYSICAL APPROACH TO VALUATION

As said above, the second 'school' of ecological economics, has been concerned with finding methods to account for the environment and human societies using the same units. This effort for Commensurability has implied the incorporation of the laws of physics into economics, since the primary factors of production and common rods for measurement are energy, material and information flows (Christensen, 1989, 28).

The main principles for this approach are related to the laws of thermodynamics. Energy and mass conservation happens through open systems that only transform them, including human economies. Any form of valuation or accosting has to take into account this principle of energy/matter conservation.

Further, the transformation process done in the economy takes highly organized materials and energy flows from nature and converts it into high entropy materials/energy (second law of thermodynamics) (Victor,

1991, 206). This implies that degradation should be accounted for as the organization of these flows requires an effort that affects the stocks of natural capital.

Then, the source of value shifts from utility derived from the possibilities of consumption to the stocks and flows of energy/materials in different systems. As Odum (1996, 260) calls it, a measure of real wealth 'needs a donor determined value, a measure of what was required to make an item or generate a service'. The underlying ethical base of this approach is the long term welfare that can potentially be generated by sustainability for all species. In view of its 'thermodynamic nature', this is probably the most interdisciplinary approach. Distinguishing here between the fields of Economics and Systems Ecology is hard. One could say it is Ecological Economics in its purest sense.

As Daly (1990, 2) suggests it, sustainability will be assured by the maintenance of the life support systems of the planet (the capital base in its different levels). In specific terms, it implies that use of renewable and non-renewable resources needs to be maintained within the assimilative and regenerating capacity of the systems involved. Productivity needs to be measured as a function of value extracted per unit of resource instead of the increase in resource throughput.

Without being exhaustive, currently we can find three frequently used approaches to accounting in this school. One is mostly concerned with accounting for energy use both on its raw and embodied form. This has been called an 'embodied energy' approach (Patterson, 1996, 377–390). A second approach includes not only the quantities but also qualitative aspects of energy used in systems. It is known as the 'emergy approach' (Odum, 1996, 10–14). A third approach accounts for biophysical investment as the land/water productivity required to produce the resource flows employed by a region. This approach is known as the 'ecological footprint' (Rees and Wackernagel, 1994, 370).

The accounting of benefits and costs is done in the first approach mostly through the relation between outputs and inputs, in similar fashion to a benefit/cost ratio in energy terms. Hall & Hall (1993, 4), when analyzing economic efficiency concerning labor productivity, say,

'...an equally valid index of productivity is energy efficiency, or productivity per unit of energy used, since more than 99% of the energy used in the process of economic production is not human labor but industrial use (i.e., from fossil fuels, nuclear and hydro power)'.

This approach is also suggested in Daly (1994, 34) when he proposes an ecological economic efficiency measurement using the ratio between man made capital services gained and natural capital services sacrificed. This relationship of outputs and inputs can be formalized as

$$Energy\ Efficiency_t = \frac{QE_t}{EU_t}.$$ (4)

where,

QE_t = Output in energy units at time t, and,
EU_t = Energy used at time t.

All inputs and outputs are converted into energy units based on thermal efficiency, which allows to account for the quality differences between different energy sources. Cleveland (1991, 298 and 1995, 190) disaggregates the energy use component in

$$EU_t = DE_t + IE_t;$$ (5)

where,

DE_t = is the direct energy used (in fuels or electricity) in the economic activity at time t, and; IE_t = is the indirect energy used in the process at time t.

The indirect energy use is the energy used elsewhere in the economy to produce the inputs used in the economic activity. Here we see how this approach accounts for the embodied energy in the non direct energy inputs, which derives in a more comprehensive assessment of the energy involved in the processes analyzed.

The embodied energy approach has been widely used lately to measure the efficiency of managed and non managed systems and to make comparisons between them. The research ranges from overall analyses of the economies of developed nations (Cleveland et al., 1984; U.S. Congress, Office of Technology Assessment, 1990; Cleveland, 1991 and Hall, 1992 among others), to social-economic sectors specific analyses (e.g., Tiezzi et al., 1991 and Cleveland, 1995).

The 'emergy' approach is the second that we currently find in the literature. The main developer of this approach is Howard Odum from the University of Florida.

In his recent publication, which summarizes much of his previous work, Odum presents the main principles of his analytical proposal. He relies in the notion of emergy. He defines emergy as the 'available energy of one kind previously required directly and indirectly to make a product or service'. (Odum, 1996, 13).

This theory states that energy of one kind cannot be considered equivalent to energy of another kind. Some forms of energy can do more work due to factors like concentration. In this, Odum distinguishes his position from the embodied energy approach. As he says, 'there are several, quite different concepts under the name "embodied energy", so it was necessary to coin the terms "EMERGY" and "transformity" and rigorously define them to eliminate confusion'. (Odum, 1996, 266). He proposes standardization by using solar emergy. This standardization is done through solar transformity that he defines as the 'solar emergy required to make one joule of a service or product. Its unit is solar emjoules per joule'. (Odum, 1994, 203). An emjoule is a unit of emergy expressed in joules.

Two important contributions from this theory are its position regarding the measure of societal welfare and the analysis it makes of monetary evaluation impacts on sustainability. Odum recognizes that market values are not good measures of societal welfare. They are only important to the small scale transactions of individuals and businesses. He suggests the use of a form of macroeconomic values for this purpose. So, values of environmental resources (fluxes and storage of emergy) can be measured in what he calls the macroeconomic dollar value: 'solar emergy value divided by the emergy/money ratio for an economy in that year'. (Odum, 1994, 203). With this type of calculation, the value of the environmental resource is higher than with market values.

Further, Odum states another important contribution that has important implications for cost-benefit analysis (Odum, 1994, 205). In his view, 'market values are inverse to real wealth contributions from the environment'. This conclusion is derived from the fact that when resources from the environment are abundant, little effort is needed from the economy, prices are low, yet the contribution in natural wealth is the highest. The opposite happens when resources are scarce. This means that any type of valuation based on willingness to pay is going to be affected by this scarcity factor. So monetary valuation would be sending the wrong signals concerning natural wealth that would be valued lower per unit in stock. Since value does not reside anymore in scarcity according to this logic, the measurement using the money rod seems inappropriate.

Emergy analysis has been applied extensively. Its applications include many areas summarized in Odum (1996, 283–287).

The third approach that will be mentioned for the thermodynamic school is known as the "ecological footprint approach". This view has been mainly presented by William Rees and Mathis Wackernagel from the University of British Columbia.

The ecological footprint seeks to measure the biophysical feasibility of sustainable development by using human carrying capacity as a measuring tool. Human carrying capacity is the 'maximum rate of resource consumption and waste discharge that can be sustained indefinitely without progressively impairing the functional integrity and productivity of relevant ecosystems wherever the latter may be'. (Rees and Wackernagel, 1994, 370). The authors argue that this concept is an inverse of the traditional understanding of carrying capacity that seeks to find out the population of a given species that can be supported definitely in a habitat without damaging the underlying ecosystem. Given the differences caused by consumption patterns, this approach proposes to concentrate on the determination of human impact on the ecosphere:

$$THI_t = Pop t * Pc I, \qquad (6)$$

where,

THI_t = total human impact at time t; Pop_t = total population at time t; and, PcI_t = per capita impact at time t.

Per capita impact is defined by per capita rates of material consumption and waste output. What is sought is an estimate of natural capital requirements of productive landscape: 'How much productive land is required to support the region's population indefinitely at current consumption levels?' (Rees and Wackernagel, 1994, 370). This estimate of area is called that population's ecological footprint.

Through this proposal, the authors can estimate if an area goes below or beyond its physical capabilities given a technological state of things. For instance, they have estimated that the ecological footprint of the Vancouver-Lower Fraser Valley is of 8.7 million hectares whereas its area is only of 0.4 million hectares (ha). Therefore, the valley imports about 22 times its carrying capacity from other areas given its consumption patterns (Rees and Wackernagel, 1994, 371). If the whole world was to consume at this rate, the required ecological footprint would be of 28.5 billion ha. The total land area of the earth is only 13 billion ha of which only 8.8 billion is crop land, pasture or forest.

Summarizing, this approach, by using a land proxy for ecological functions, highlights the ecological-thermodynamic base of the productive process. It provides a biophysical interpretation of resource scarcity that also overcomes the limitations of monetary accountings pointed out before. In this sense, it shares the value base of the other thermodynamic approaches presented.

C. OTHER APPROACHES THAT AFFECT DECISION MAKING

Another branch that can be found in contemporary ecological economic decision making literature is the multicriteria evaluation approach. In essence, this approach does not embrace either a monetary or biophysical position of value. It concentrates in the development of processes by which both types of assessments can be harmonized for environmental management.

Munda, Nijkamp and Rietveld (1994, 97–112) summarize the work that they and other have developed on multicriteria evaluation for environmental management. Their starting point is the weakness of traditional decision making in view of the impossibility to count with all the necessary information to derive social welfare functions. This impossibility obstructs, according to the authors, the use of traditional cost-benefit analysis (Munda et al., 1994, 99).

In the field of environmental management, according to this position, decision making is immersed in an interaction between different kinds of value sources (political, technical, environmental, etc.). This justifies the use of flexible techniques that can assess the multidimensional effects of decisions (qualitative and quantitative). The authors propose that multicriteria techniques are optimal for this purpose (Munda et al., 1994, 99).

The use of this environmental-economic technique seeks to integrate differences in time and space scales. It also seeks to integrate differences in the measurement levels of the variables.

In this last sense, the incorporation of methods to assess qualitative information and the uncertainty it generates is essential. This approach recognizes two types of uncertainty: stochastic and fuzzy. The first arises from the impossibility to 'establish exactly the future state of a problem' (Munda et al., 1994, 102). Fuzziness refers to the ambiguity that is intrinsic to certain types of information (linguistic variables for instance).

The multicriteria model procedure depends on a careful definition and structuring of a problem. On this stage the handling and structuring of information add a subjective component. Defining and structuring the analysis as close to reality as possible is critical, since the effectiveness of Multiple Criteria Decision-Making (MCDM) is context dependent.

Secondly, the procedure implies the generation of alternatives and the choice of a set of evaluation criteria. The closest to the real world that the MCDM process is taken, the largest the set of criteria may be.

The subjectivity of the decision maker is accounted for by identifying his/her preference system. The process is ended following several aggregation techniques (listed in Munda et al., 1994, 107).

Through this procedure, large amounts of data of different nature are used to study a problem from different angles. Yet, the possibility of conflicting evaluations is very high, since being better against all others is rare for one criterion. So the tendency is to move from MCDM to MCDA (Multiple Criteria Decision Aid) whose aim is not to discover a solution, but to provide insight into the nature of the conflicts involved and in ways to arrive at compromises (Munda et al., 1994, 107).

We can finally mention the recent proposal of Michael Lockwood (1997, 83–93). His is an integrated value theory concentrating on end values. Its commonality with multiple criteria decision making is its use of qualitative information.

It identifies three modes of human value expression: weakly comparable, exchange and non compensatory. The first implies that a person can choose between alternatives without producing a general value ranking. If such a ranking exists, the expressions are called strongly comparable and are distinguished between exchange and non compensatory. A non compensatory preference implies the production of a value ranking but no willingness for tradeoffs between alternatives. Exchange value expressions are consistent with the neoclassical conception of value (see Lockwood, 1997, 85). This notion implies the continuity condition by which substitutability will compensate for the change in one good.

So, 'different individuals may ascribe different value types to the same policy proposal, and express these values in different ways'. (Lockwood, 1997, 85). Aggregating methods need to allow for this. This approach criticizes what it calls conventional methods of aggregation. Cost-benefit analysis assumes a structure of values that only accounts for exchange values. MCDM can encompass all expression modes, but does not provide a rule for discrimination.

This theory proposes to make a qualitative evaluation of the proportion of stakeholders that have non compensatory or weakly comparable value expressions against or in favor of the project. If this initial evaluation approves the project, then the methods to assess changes in economic welfare can be applied for a final decision (Lockwood, 1997, 92).

Summarizing, this theory still maintains human preferences at the center of justifications for value. Yet, it seeks to incorporate more information in the decision making process through a better understanding of the ways in which values are expressed.

Having presented the main trends in Ecological Economic theories of value, we can now examine the implications of their adoption for social-economic decision making in Central American developing nations.

III. MAIN IMPLICATIONS OF ECOLOGICAL ECONOMIC THEORIES OF VALUE FOR COST-BENEFIT ANALYSES IN CENTRAL AMERICAN DEVELOPING NATIONS

The ruling development paradigm has created conditions of intra generational inequity within and across nations. Cleveland presents three fundamental realities that involve developed and developing nations (Cleveland, 1993, 25):

- To keep their standard of living, developed nations consume large quantities of natural resources;
- World populations are explosively growing, and,
- A large disparity exists between rich and poor nations in these two realities.

These imbalances also have important consequences on intergenerational equity. The possibility for future generations of having the resources to achieve at least the same standard of living that we have is uncertain. Uncertainty is affected by the structural characteristics of each society. So, for instance, we can say that consumption per human in developed nations is the most influencing factor for future resource availability. Probably enough evidence exists in developing nations to consider population growth the main factor.

Globalization interconnects these realities. The complex consequences of mass consumption show us that sustainability is a global issue.

Within this context relying on decision making methods that yield sustainable results seems crucial. Barkin (1996, 199) questions the tools of economic decision making that are designed to examine marginal changes in productive systems (standard CBA) within the framework of development projects in third world countries. In projects that cause substantial structural changes, as the Hidrovia canal project in South America, the chance for external costs not to be accounted is large. He says that the first task is to define the context within which the analysis is conducted.

We agree with Barkin in the sense that the context defines the methodological needs. Although, to go a step further, we should adopt a value theory that helps unveil the real dimensions of the context. We believe that an ecological economic value theory is more comprehensive and appropriate for decision-making given the characteristics of many developing nations. The Central American context can be proof of this statement.

A. THE SOCIO-ECOLOGICAL REALITY: WHY IS THE ECOLOGICAL ECONOMIC THEORY OF VALUE MORE CONVENIENT FOR THE SUSTAINABILITY OF CENTRAL AMERICAN DEVELOPING NATIONS?

In this section we examine the applicability of an ecological economic position regarding value in view of the specific Central American context. We first examen the advantages of 'comparability' applications. We continue by presenting the advantages of 'commensurability' in relation to the reality of this part of the world. To illustrate these advantages we include two case studies of applications. Further examination takes us to aspects that are not easily measurable and the advantage of multicriteria analysis and the integrated theory of value.

1. ADVANTAGES OF COMPARABILITY

The allocative approach to ecological economic valuation provides the possibility of incorporating essential information in the framework of economic decision making. For the Central American reality highlighting the importance of the informal sectors of the economy seems important.

Also, this approach allows the calculation of non consumptive use and option benefits and costs, which are crucial in the structural reality of these countries.

a. The importance of Informal Sectors of the Economy
The Achilles heel of Latin America and the Caribbean is poverty. A growing population, an increase in urbanization, and an impoverishment of the agricultural sector contribute to this situation.

Central America is no exception to this trend. This reality is partially a result of structural adjustment policies that have caused changes in formal sector employment opportunities and supply cost of labor. As Reed (1996, 320) points it, when summarizing the results of case studies in Africa, Asia, Latin America and the Caribbean,

'Without employment prospects in the formal sector, unemployed workers pursue activities in the informal sector to ensure their survival. Urban vendors, artisans, and micro-entrepreneurs have proliferated. In peri urban areas of some countries, many underemployed families began cultivating food crops. In rural areas, families turned to using natural resources to survive through producing charcoal, capturing wildlife and brewing home beer'.

According to FLACSO (1993,18), Central American countries had a degree of urban informality of 24.5 % in the industrial sector, 43% in the trade sector and 18.3% in the service sector in 1989. The highest percentage of these informal workers was self employed (57.8%).

Another important component of the informal sector in Central America is the subsistence agriculture economy. It is concentrated in crops in which the region has production deficits, mostly staples such as beans, rice, subsistence fruits, tubers and corn. This agriculture is frequently complementary to export cash crops such as coffee, cacao and other export fruits. Such a situation is found frequently in the volcanic areas of the Pacific slopes, where large intensive monocrop farms are less common. Even in the lower areas of the Pacific, the separation between commercial and subsistence agriculture is not clear since the small subsistence units provide seasonal labor sources. This is the case of Guatemalan Indian small producers (Leonard, 1985, 88).

Overall, due to the region's topography, large scale export agricultural projects are difficult. Further, green revolution technologies require an investment capacity that is often beyond the economic possibilities of the region. Therefore, agricultural productivity, understood in traditional productive value terms, is low in Central America. The main grains produced for subsistence purposes in the early eighties had much lower productivity levels than the yields achieved in the United States in the same period.

So, agriculture normally only contributes about 25 percent of the nation's Gross Domestic Product in countries like Guatemala. Nevertheless, 50–60% of the workers depend on subsistence agriculture for survival. Such a pattern does not only suggest the lack of other economic opportunities where the working age population can find employment. As will be discussed later, culture can also play an important role in defining the desire of rural area inhabitants to remain under a subsistence pattern.

Additionally, socio-cultural factors have determined the existence of other activities done in an informal way, mostly for self consumption. This is the case of resource uses such as medicinal plants and wildlife related activities.

A high amount of the primary energy use in the region comes from consumptive uses. About 50% of the energy consumed comes from biomass resources (including firewood and agricultural residues) (Mc Neely 1988; 15, 16). This source of energy is highly used in certain key export activities such as coffee production.

As it becomes obvious, the CUV component of the total value equation is very relevant for these regions. The welfare of these countries seems dependent largely on this component that is not accounted for in the traditional notion of productivity and income. Yet, these contributions represent savings for Central American governments that, in absence of these uses, would have to make higher investments in social services. Also, labor supply costs would be higher.

b. Non-Consumptive Use Benefits

The most striking feature of the Central American region is its diversity at all levels. Geologically, the area has great diversity of surface forms because of its complex tectonic history and its position within a region of contemporary mountains.

Climatically, the area is also diverse within tropical climates. The climate ranges between seasonally dry (northwest Costa Rica and southwestern Nicaragua) to the highest precipitation levels in the New World (Atlantic lowlands of Costa Rica and Panama). Some areas are semideserts (east-central Guatemala) and others are cloud forests (Highlands of Guatemala and Costa Rica).

Result of these conditions is also an incredible diversity of flora and fauna. Costa Rica alone has an estimated 5 percent of the biodiversity in the world. Much of this diversity is endemic to the region (up to 80%). The highest floristic diversity occurs in humid regions. Yet, the highest amounts of endemism are present in dryer areas.

Cultural diversity of the area parallels this natural diversity. The topographical conditions have generated extreme cultural diversification. For instance, in Guatemala, even if most of the languages descend directly from the Proto-Mayan, dialect diversification is high. This is partially the result of the country's topography.

A mix of northern and southern hemispheres cultural influence is also present. Northern Mesoamerican cultures extended all the way to northwestern Costa Rica. From the south, a Macro-Chibcha influence exists. A combination of resource use patterns resulted. The Spanish conquest and colonization in the sixteenth century completed the mix. This blend resulted in unique patterns of domestication and utilization for plants used currently worldwide.

As it becomes clear, this diversity generates several non consumptive use benefits that contribute to the welfare of Central Americans. Consequently, they also need to be accounted for. We can find specific examples in different economic activities, environmental and cultural services.

(1) ECONOMIC ACTIVITIES

The emergence of economic activities that rely on the cultural-ecological NCUV services of the region is an important factor in the development of the area today. Two good examples of this are ecotourism and biodiversity information services.

Central America's attractive rain forests, coastline and biological wealth have created a new market for travelers seeking pristine ecosystems. Between 1987 and 1996, export revenue from tourism increased from 136.2 to 653.8 million dollars in Costa Rica, making it the first economic activity of the country. During the same period, visits to the National Parks System (SINAC) increased from 287,047 to 658,657. Out of this trend, foreigner visitations increased from 25 to 41% of total visitors. Travel cost estimations of recreational consumer surplus for two protected areas in Costa Rica show a much higher potential benefit for the country. Tobias and Mendehlson (1991, 91–93) estimated a consumer surplus per domestic visitor to the Monteverde Biological Reserve of $35 per visit.

Similarly, Besleme and Aguilar (1994, 11) estimated a consumer surplus of $31 per domestic visitor to Carara Biological Reserve. Given the assumptions in these studies, these two reserves account for a recreational consumer surplus value per hectare of protected land that ranges between $434–$1250 per year. Monteverde measures 10,569 ha, Carara 4,700 ha.

Biodiversity preservation and bioprospecting are also gaining importance. With increased scientific, pharmaceutical and biotechnological projects the technical service sector will expand as well. An example of a project attempting to develop this natural capital is the Instituto Nacional de Biodiversidad (INBio) in Costa Rica. They have been collecting and cataloging the vast insect gene pool of their country to monitor species diversity and secure genetic information (Blum, 1993, 17). The management of this information does not only provide a non consumptive benefit for the education and scientific community. As will be discussed later, it also has economic users that can constitute sources of funding for the biodiversity conservation initiatives (Gámez, 1992, 305).

(2) ENVIRONMENTAL SERVICES

Central America, and the tropics in general, provide globally essential environmental services, such as carbon sequestration and water conservation. Climate change has become a global priority and the risks associated with changing weather patterns and rising sea levels have become too serious to ignore. Carbon dioxide emissions are largely due to fossil fuel consumption and concentrated in developed countries. Yet, as Molly O'Meara (1997, 24) of the World Watch Institute states, 'deforestation accounts for as much as a third of the carbon dioxide added to the atmosphere from human activities. But if we halt deforestation and actually increase forest cover – through better conservation, management, and reforestation – then forests may be able to slow the buildup of atmoshperic carbon dioxide'. Tropical countries have the potential to be net consumers of carbon dioxide if given the incentive by accounting for benefits and future risks.

The value of these services can be estimated in several ways. Costanza et al. (1998, 10) summarize several studies that estimate climate regulation services for tropical forests. Those studies use mostly shadow pricing methodologies. The only specific reference to a Central American nation in this study is for Costa Rica with an estimated value of

$3046 per hectare of forest. The World Bank (1994, 5) estimates the value of Costa Rican forests' carbon sequestration service based on the economic losses associated with a marginal ton of carbon if the stock of carbon in the atmosphere is doubled. The estimated value is $1098 million for the 1.3 million hectares of forest in the country.

Tropical forests also contribute to watershed regulation, providing rural and urban populations with all their water. The above mentioned World Bank study (1994, 5)estimated a value of $47 per hectare of Costa Rican forest in urban and rural water conservation based on replacement and compensation costs.

(3) CULTURAL SERVICES

The wealth of local and regional knowledge/cultural practices increases general welfare, which is also not accounted for in conventional indicators. Native/traditional agricultural production systems and plant species domestication are examples of cultural capital benefits.

An example of a subsistence sustainable agricultural practice is the *frijol tapado* ("covered bean") system found throughout Central America. The common bean, *Phaseolus vulgaris*, is native to the region and this system predates the arrival of the Spanish. A farmer using the covered bean system takes a parcel of land covered in herbs, cuts them, mulches them and leaves them above the soil to be used as a substrate for the bean plants. This system maintains the stability of the agroecosystem and requires few to no agrochemicals (Arias and Amador, 1991, 12).

Nevertheless, assessments of the economic viability of this system are limited to traditional cost-benefit analysis (Bellows, 1992, 87). Bellows's study in Perez Zeledón, Costa Rica, compared benefit cost ratios for small farmers (less than 3 ha.). Those owning their farm that used using the more intensive method of *espeque*, a practice with bear soil and agrochemical inputs, had higher ratios (2.95), than those using the *tapado* system (2.4). Interestingly, the differences between the systems for tenants were not significant.

The use of an ecological economic approach to this problem might have yielded different results. We can extrapolate this conclusion from the estimates that the Tropical Science Center (Solórzano et al., 1991, 5) made of losses from soil erosion for Costa Rica (1970–1989). According to this study, annual crops contributed to approximately 60% of the total losses for the country (between 70 and 110 million metric tons per year). This loss had an average value based on nutrient replacement costs of $33.4 million in 1984 terms. This is equivalent to 1% of the total average GDP for the same period. It would be expectable that beans contributed significantly to this number since Costa Ricans consume 10% of their dietary protein (about 10–13 Kg annually) from this crop. Fifty per cent of the bean crop is Costa Rica produced through the *espeque* system. However, a specific study is pending.

The blend of Indigenous and Spanish cultural traditions also favors sustainable agriculture for export crops. Vandermeer and Perfecto (1995, 137) tell us that 'traditional coffee farms share many structural attributes normally associated with forests' due to the presence of shade trees interspersed with coffee. The benefits of this system include a rich biological community. Rice and Ward (1996, 8) document this cultural adaptation that occurred mainly in the 19th. century in all of northern Latin America. According to their account, this diversity is reflected in the variations of species composition and structure of these traditional systems. For instance, in Carazo, Nicaragua, traditional coffee holdings have at least 25 species of trees (fruit and timber), some of which are native to dry forest ecosystems that characterize the region. Farmers in the Pacific slopes of Guatemala intersperse citrus, bananas and native palms within their coffee. Producers in the region of Atenas, Costa Rica, use a mixture of citrus and nitrogen fixing trees such as Inga, Glyricidium and Erythrina. Modernized coffee plantations support far fewer bird, insect and tree species and require more inputs, such as pesticides and fertilizers.

These benefits have been quantified as part of a study by Boyce et al. (1993). They compared, through an ecological economic CBA, the profitability of organic and 'conventional' coffee. One main characteristic of the farms that they categorized as organic was the use of agroforestry techniques as the ones described above. Organic coffee showed a net private benefit for the 1992–93 crop of $123.37 per hectare (a benefit-cost ratio of 1.1). Conventional coffee reported an average net loss per hectare of $147.3 (a benefit-cost ratio of 0.91). When social costs were accounted for (pesticide impacts, soil erosion, etc.), the benefit-cost ratio of organic coffee remained virtually unchanged ($116.8 of net social benefit). For conventional coffee, the ratio decreased to 0.80 (a negative social benefit of $ 360.7 per hectare) (Boyce et al., 1993, 139–140).

c. The Valuable Preservation of Native Genetic Material

As already noted, biological diversity of the region has been given a great deal of attention. Another vital reason for preservation is that "many cultivated plants important for food and income in developing nations arose from tropical forests". (Smith et al., 1992, 1) As new pathogens threaten current agricultural varieties the wild strains can be crossbred to reintroduce natural resistence to the pests. As Smith et al. (1992, 2) explain, 'the ability of plants breeders to respond to such challenges rests in large part on the genetic resources they can fall back on to generate new resistant varieties'. If the habitats for the wild plants and trees disappear, the potential to create new varieties will diminish. All sectors of the Central American economies, from subsistence agriculture to export crops, depend on reliable harvests. Again, the future costs of biodiversity loss need to be accounted for when considering preservation proposals.

Capturing the option value – the benefits of future forest products for industrial, nutritional or medicinal uses – is another factor to be considered in economic decision making. Researchers, such as those at INBio, look to discover new species and screen them for economic viability. Many countries and companies, such as Merck Pharmaceuticals that has an agreement with INBio, are already aware of potential benefits and have invested in bioprospecting projects. Under this contract, INBio provides Merck's drug-screening program with chemical extracts from wild plants, insects, and microorganisms. In return, Merck gives INBio a research and sampling budget of $1.14 million, royalties on any commercial products that result, and technical assistance and training to help establish drug research in Costa Rica. INBio agreed to contribute 10 percent of the up-front payment from Merck and 50 percent of any royalties to Costa Rica's National Park Fund to help conserve national parks (Reid, 1994, 50).

The World Bank (1994, 5), based on this agreement, estimates the value for pharmaceutical use of Costa Rican forests in $2.3 per hectare. In reality, we believe that the value paid by the pharmaceutical companies is based on an expectation more than on tangible present benefits. In this sense, we prefer to understand the payment in this contract as option premium. This value can be added to the existing estimate of the World Bank. Based on donations for conservation areas, the bank estimates a value of $295 per hectare.

The payment of an option premium breaks the traditional trend of non compensation for the potential benefits obtained from tropical forest products by pharmaceutical companies. In this sense, these genetic resources give developing nations a political economic advantage if they maintain management of exploitation and allocation.

The intrinsic value of species is difficult to quantify, yet an awareness of this value will justify any projects that halt the mass extinctions occurring in tropical forests. We believe that the use of techniques as contingent valuation to estimate existence values, fails to recognize the real nature of this axiological component of the total value equation and contributes to semantic confusion. In the end, it uses a measure of human appreciation as a proxy for a non anthropocentric value. If we are to incorporate this component to the total value equation, truly non anthropocentric evaluations cannot yield monetary estimations. Probably a combination of valuation criterions, such as those suggested in multiple-criteria approaches, needs to be considered. Yet, this is a problem that overrides the scope of this article. So, we will consider enough to acknowledge the existence of this component.

d. Case Study: Subsistence farmers and Conservation in Guatemala

An interesting case study in which we participated took place in Guatemala (Brown et al., 1996). In this scenario, subsistence agriculture dependence was used as a justification for conservation.

(1) THE PROBLEM

This study was a collaboration between the RARE Center for Tropical Conservation, the Fundación Defensores de la Naturaleza (Guatemala) and the Fundación Ecologista "Hector Rodrigo Pastor Fasquelle" (Honduras). The objective was to quantify the hydrologic and economic benefits in the Sierra de las Minas Biosphere Reserve (SMBR), in Guatemala and Cusuco National Park, in Honduras.

The part of the study we are interested in took place in the SMBR. It is in the Central-South East region of Guatemala (see Figure 3). This area 'encompasses the watersheds of 63 permanent rivers, making it the largest producer of water in Guatemala. The socioeconomic value of water resources of the Sierra strongly influenced the decision to establish the reserve in 1990'. (Brown et al., 1996, 2). Surface water is extremely important in this region for economic relations, settlement patterns, land use, and agricultural productivity. This is specially true in the valleys of Motagua and San Jerónimo, where the Sierra has a shadow effect that results in annual precipitations as low as 500 mm.

394

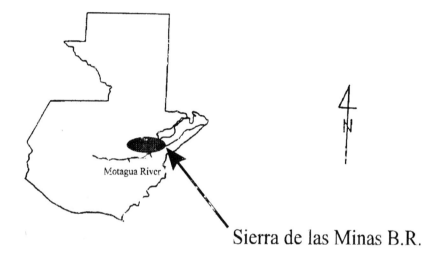

Motagua River

Sierra de las Minas B.R.

N

Figure 3.

Three ethnic groups are found in the 158 communities around the Sierra: two Mayan (Q'eqchi and Poqonchi) groups and one Ladino (white) group. Seventy-five percent of the Mayan population speaks only the language of their ethnic group. Ladino communities have higher literacy rates (58%, and the Mayas have 25%). The higher rates of population growth happen in Mayan communities where couples have an average of five children.

Occupation is higher in Ladino communities (45%) than their Maya counterparts (35%). The mode income in the region is between $ 396 and $600 per year. The mode household size is between five and seven members.

Fixed sources of employment are scarce in the region. Most families are involved in agricultural activities through subsistence crops. They combine this with cash crops as coffee, sugar cane, cardamom, fruits and other crops. They also work as laborers for large landowners or neighbors (Brown et al., 1996, 29). Other sources of revenue include commercial activities, crafts, the army and family members in the United States. This last source of revenue is very important especially in the Jones Watershed, in the southern range of the SMBR (Paiz, 1994, 29 and Brown et al., 1996, 29).

396

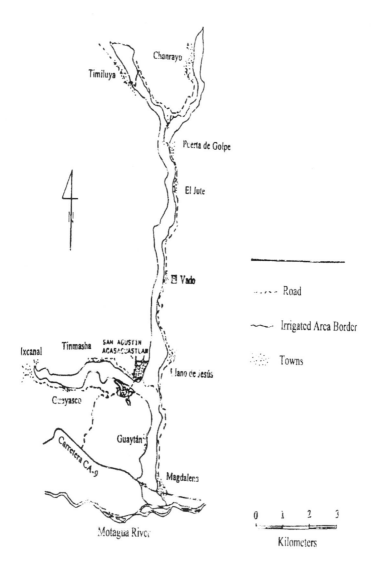

Figure 4.

For the populations in the semi-desertic region, the preservation of the reserve is extremely critical. They are dedicated to agricultural activities in areas that depend completely on irrigation. That is the case of the populations of San Agustín Acasaguastlán, which depend on the lower section of the Hato River watershed. The irrigated area in this region extends less than 1 kilometer parallel to the river bed (Paiz, 1994, 27) (Figure 4).

Summarizing, we have a scenario that combines families that are highly dependent on water environmental services from a protected area to generate their subsistence through agriculture. This happens within a very diverse cultural scenario.

Within this context, the study sought to value the environmental benefits generated by the SMBR as a justification to maintain and improve its conservation.

(2) METHODS

Since water resources appeared so critical to those involved in the main economic activity of the region, we thought of using a change in productivity approach to value the contribution of the water resources of the SMBR. We concentrated in the areas of the Hato and Jones watersheds. They gave us a good representation of the natural variability of the ecosystems surrounding the reserve, while also being areas where water resources are critical. Irrigation systems are very rustic in these areas, therefore, productive lands are concentrated close to the rivers. The value of irrigated real state in the Jones Watershed is 3.6 to nine times higher, whereas in the Hato Watershed it ranges from four to 6.8 times higher (Brown et al., 1996, 78, 88). They are both in the Motagua River Valley (see Figure 5), yet the Jones watershed is closer to the Caribbean and receives a higher amount of precipitation. The Hato watershed's lower section is within the semi-desertic region. The two areas also have diverse cultural characteristics. The Jones region is mainly of Ladino population, while the Hato watershed is mostly inhabited by Mayans.

A survey was conducted in both watersheds to estimate the significance of water used for irrigation, by comparing the productivity of irrigated and dry (rain-fed) land. 'This productivity analysis uses the market value of agricultural production to quantify the indirect value of an ecosystem service – in this case, watershed protection and maintenance of dry season flow'. (Brown et al., 1996, 43). To do this, communities were chosen at different points of the watersheds that represented the upper, middle and lower sections of the watersheds. Overall, 15

398

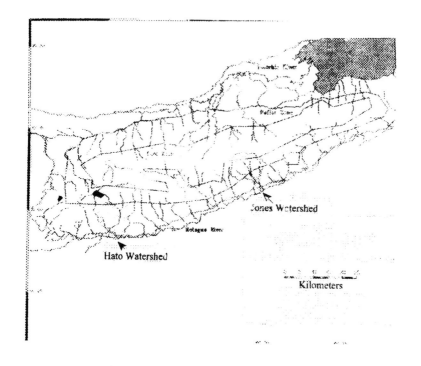

Figure 5.

percent of the farmers in each zone were interviewed (70 surveys in Jones and 89 in Hato).

The information gathered was used to quantify the benefits and costs of the farms. Since many farmers in the regions depend on their crops for subsistence (the average size of farms surveyed was 1.21 ha.) and do not have enough production to take it to the market, productivity was estimated using a combination of traditional accounting and a replacement cost approach. The savings from not having to buy products in the market were quantified as benefits of subsistence crops (CUV estimation). Since cattle are a long-term investment, the benefits of pasture lands were estimated by summing dairy earnings and the market value of annual weight gain (Brown et al., 1996, 45). We also estimated water productivity as a ratio of gross agricultural benefits and annual number of hours of irrigation.

We developed two simple semi-Cobb-Douglas functions to determine which factors affect gross productivity/area and water productivity as previously defined. The models used input costs, availability and percentage of irrigated land in the farms, crops planted and size of the farm, tenure, location, education and climate as dependent variables. From this estimation we derived the value of the irrigation service for the productivity of the farms.

(3) RESULTS AND IMPLICATIONS

The net productivity estimations showed us that in the Jones watershed 29.85% of the land, which is irrigated, produces 89.74% of the net agricultural profits (see Table 1). Irrigated land produces higher crop yields, supports more grazing and allows the production of crops that cannot be grown on dry land. For the Hato watershed, the 45.30% of irrigated land produces 84.48 % of the net agricultural productivity. The survey also showed that irrigated land is much higher in the Jones basin (1,406 ha. As opposed to 279 ha in Hato). This was also correlated to higher net benefits in Jones ($906,974 and $111,055 in Hato) (Brown et al., 1996, 79, 89).

The gross productivity models showed us that labor costs, percentage of area irrigated and the size of farms, were the most significant variables influencing both gross productivity per unit of area and water productivity (see Table 2). We used the models to simulate the potential change in productivity caused by introducing another hectare of irrigated land. This also implied that we had to forecast an increase in size from the average of 1.21 to 1.87 hectares per farm. The original average net productivity for both areas was $2254.12 per hectare per year. The resulting forecast yielded an increase in gross productivity per hectare of almost 50%, from a   fitted   value   of $399.07   to $587.79   per   hectare   per

Table 1

Comparative net productivity in irrigated and non-irrigated areas in the Jones and Hato watersheds. Source et al. (1996)

	Jones Watershed	Hato Watershed
Total Ha of Irrigated Land	1406	279
Total Ha of Non-irrigated Land	3305	337
Net Productivity Irrigated Land	$813922	$93819
Net Productivity Non-Irrigated Land	$93052	$17236

Table 2

Results of agricultural productivity and wate productivity models after stepwise elimination procedure. Source: Brown et al. (1996)

Variable	Agricultural productivity model coefficient (P value)	Water productivity model coefficient (P value)
Hours of irrigation	0.0576 (0.0438)	–
Inputs	0.0354 (0.1531)	−5.1357 (0.0004)
Percentage of irrigated land	0.0057 (0.0403)	0.1801 (0.007)
Size of farm	0.1322 (0.0400)	3.2638 (0.0119)
Mixed property tenure	−0.6488 (0.0043)	–
Zone of location	–	−4.44960 (0.0495)
Rain^2	0.0000018 (0.0537)	–
Intercept	2.8451	26.867

year. Through the average benefit-cost ratio of 6.74 estimated for the farmers of both areas we derive an increase in net productivity per hectare from a fitted value of $2689 per hectare to $3961.70 (a difference of $1272.70).

Our results seemed shocking to us. The net productivity per hectare that we estimated for both watersheds would derive in a net productivity per farm of $2727.48. This is not extremely far away from the average national GDP for 1995, which was $3080. Nevertheless, as we had mentioned before, the mode income for the region is between $396 and $600. After recently examining the data, we found four outliers in the Jones watershed that suggested that we could have overestimated the benefits generated by cattle. They had benefit-cost ratios of 49 and above, which took the average benefit-cost ratio to 12.39 for Jones. Yet, further examination of the data showed us that the benefit-cost ratio in Hato was of 3.38. This suggests that our estimation of productivity including the CUV also had an influence. Such observations call for a continuation ofresearch on this case study.

Nevertheless, we believe that from this case study we have enough evidence that shows the value of comparability in ecological economic accounting for these countries. For the Guatemalan subsistence producers of the region examined, this new approach can prove that SMBR provides a highly valuable environmental service that has an impact over their welfare. This, by allowing them a high CUV to supplement their scarce economic options. We feel those values would need to be taken into account in potential development project proposals that effect their livelihoods or the conservation of the Biosphere Reserve. We also feel they make a strong argument for the continuing preservation of the area.

2. ADVANTAGES OF COMMENSURABILITY

As previously suggested, the adoption of the ecological economic theory of capital has two important implications. First, the economy is an open system that is not isolated from the other systems that make our world. Second, the size of human capital cannot override the carrying capacity of the natural capital base. Since all ecosystems are interrelated, all economic transactions will affect the whole planet in some way. Stocks or flows of energy and materials will increase or diminish.

Under this framework, human beings must solve the problems generated by the standards of living of developed nations, the growing populations of developing nations and the inequity between the two. Daly (1991, 15–49) adds a limitation to the possibility of solving this problem when he claims that the limits of natural capital derive in an impossibility theorem. In essence, this theorem states that developed-nation style mass consumption cannot be afforded by the planet for all its inhabitants. Consequently, he proposes the desirability of a steady-state economy (SSE). A SSE is 'an economy with constant stocks of people and artifacts maintained at some desired, sufficient levels by low rates of maintenance throughput', that is, by the lowest feasible flows of materialsenergy from the first stage of production to the last stage of consumption.

Daly (1991, 148) recognizes that asking developing nations to achieve a SSE is morally backward before overdeveloped countries face the same issue. Nevertheless, in view of the links that a globalized world implies between the development patterns of these groups of nations, it is essential to model complete systems of trade. Only then can we understand the resource flows/stock depletion that international trade and multinational production imply.

As it was previously suggested, a traditional monetary economic valuation does not allow for a proper accounting of these processes. In the specific case of monetary CBA, its limitations come from the fact that it does not measure the real contribution to system wealth because monetary information does not measure scarcity of resources appropriately. Social and environmental costs and benefits are measured inappropriately due to price distortions or not measured at all. In the words of Hawken (1993, 76) 'gasoline is cheap in the United Sates because its price does not reflect the cost of smog, acid rain and their subsequent effects on health and the environment. Likewise, American food is the cheapest in the world, but the price does not reflect the fact that we have depleted the soil, reducing average topsoil from a depth of twenty-one to six inches over the past hundred years, contaminated our groundwater (farmers don't drink from wells in Iowa), and poisoned wildlife through the use of pesticides'. Even the ecological economic methods of monetary CBA lack the appropriate tools to measure the different effects on stocks that a choice between development options causes (Bingham et al., 1995, 81–82).

In many ways, this method of decision making has eased the consolidation of the inequitable relations between developed and developing nations. The lack of instruments to account for resource flows and effects on stocks has allowed developed nations to import carrying capacity and export environmental degradation to their underdeveloped counterparts. This is a key to maintain their high standard of living (Hawken, 1993, 135; Rees, 1993, 50–51). A concrete example of carrying capacity imports is clothes manufacturing in 'maquiladora plants'. Since labor costs have increased in developed nations, companies shift the assembly of clothing to developing countries where they can reduce their costs in two ways: labor is cheaper and worker condition regulations are less stringent. Korten (1996, 129) shows us that although the productivity of Mexican workers is comparable to that of U.S. workers, their average hourly wage is $1.64. At the same time, these companies are established in duty free zones where enforcement of labor regulations is 'unofficially' lax. So, the price of clothing is maintained for the consumer at the expense of a cheaper resource that can be degraded with fewer regulations. The lack of contact with the reality of these workers gives no incentive to clothes consumers to change their lifestyle. This pattern of 'development' became very common in Meso-american economies in the decade of the eighties and is still present in the nineties.

Within this framework of global resource scarcity and conflicting interests between developed and developing nations, the possibility of commensurability that the biophysical approaches to valuation provide is appropriate to understand the real costs and benefits of development alternatives. For Central American nations, two expressions of the usefulness of this method are in the fields of 'modern' technology transfer and fossil fuel energy where their degree of dependence is high.

a. Technological Dependence

As a whole, the agricultural sector is still the most important export revenue generator Central America. Several commodities as coffee, bananas, flowers, pineapples and sugar cane are the main cash crops of the region. Newer activities in the manufacturing (clothes, electronics) sectors are gradually becoming more important.

Many of those activities are controlled by multinational corporations (MNC). Technology transfer, occurs frequently through these companies. In the activities that are not controlled by MNCs, the matter remains that the highest Research and Development capabilities are concentrated in the developed world. The same situation happens with patents. Therefore, even when technology is acquired by less-developed countries, it usually comes from a developed nation.

Several authors as Sharan (1985, 80) questioned this model of technology transfer. The doubts around it arise from the potential non appropriateness that the technology may have for the conditions of the receiving nation. Also, the continued dependence on imported technology, and, the impacts that such imports have on the economy of the country are criticized. Environmentally, these limitations show up as potential damage to the natural resource stock and the need to rely on resource throughput to maintain such dependence.

In Central American agriculture, two expressions of the inappropriateness of such technologies are soil erosion, as we above mentioned, and agrochemical impacts. According to the Pesticide Action Network (1996,1), Latin America accounts for 9% of annual agrochemical uses. Of these sales, in 1994 Costa Rica had the fifth place in the region with agrochemical sales of $81 million dollars. In 1996, Nicaragua imported $30.5 million worth of agrochemicals and was announced by the U.S., government as one of the best prospects for agricultural sector U.S. exports and investment.

Simultaneously, intoxications from pesticides are common in the region. Cheminova Holding (1997, 5, 8) reported that between 1986 and 1995, a total of 7613 cases of acute pesticide intoxication were reported

404

in Guatemala. In Nicaragua, only in the Department of Chinandega, 559 cases of intoxication were reported in 1995–1996.

The technological packages of certain activities are specially intensive. Such is the case of banana production in Costa Rica (CORBANA, 1992, 18) with its high degree of chemical contamination of soil and water resources.

Nevertheless, the main indicator of the failure of the agricultural technological packages used is its biophysical efficiency. Using fertilizer use as an indicator of this process of technological change, we can see an increase from nine to 63 Kg/ha between 1961 and 1991 in the region (Figure 6). If we relate these figures to total production per hectare, we see that the efficiency of those applications has decreased from $24.11/kg to $7.10/kg of application. Obviously, more agrochemicals are applied to yield proportionally less agricultural productivity. Again, this suggests the inadequacy of the technological model to achieve its development objectives over time.

b. Energetic Dependence

A disadvantage of the technological dependence of the region is that the main base of such technologies is fossil fuel. Central American countries, with one exception, are completely fossil fuel dependent

As reported by the World Resources Institute (1997, 285–289) only Guatemala has proved recoverable reserves of crude oil. Simultaneously, the increase in commercial energy consumption per capita between 1973

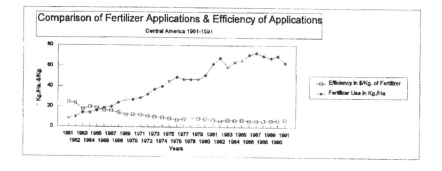

Figure 6.

and 1993 ranged between 4% and 90%. Further, even if the average per country consumption is 14.8 gigajoules per capita per year (4% of the consumption in the United States), between 67% and 100% is imported by Central American countries.

So, the possibilities to develop fossil fuel-based technologies are affected by the costs of importing them. Further, this circumstance generates a dependence effect over transportation, energy production and other factors that go beyond productive technologies and affect the general welfare of the population.

c. Case Study: Energy Efficiency of Coffee Production in Costa Rica

(1) THE PROBLEM

A recent case study, in which we also had a chance to participate, made a biophysical analysis of coffee production in Costa Rica. Our objective was to analyze the sustainability of coffee production by interrelating production to energy use.

This crop is one of the prime export revenue sources of Costa Rica. In the early part of the twentieth century it generated between 60% and 90% of all foreign exchange earnings. While coffee's economic importance has diminished, it still generated between 10–36% of this economic indicator between 1972 and 1996 (Aguilar and Klocker, in press.)

The sustainability of this economic activity in Central America has been discussed considerably in recent years. Several studies have examined the potential of organic production or agroforestry system methods to mitigate the impact of the 'modern' unshaded system (Boyce et al., 1993 among others). The social sustainability of the system has also been an object of attention. In Central American countries, to a lesser degree in Costa Rica, the wealth that the production and trade of this crop produce is concentrated in the hands of a few national or foreign processors/traders (Appropriate Technology International, 1993 among others).

The analysis examined the long-term sustainability of the production and processing of this crop. Through an analysis of the technological trends involved, we sought to depict the degree to which this activity degrades the natural environment and increases the energetic dependence of Costa Rica.

(B) METHODS

The study included an embodied energy biophysical benefit/cost accounting. This was done by quantifying the relation between outputs and inputs, similar to an economic benefit/cost ratio, but as discussed above, in energy terms.

Estimates of energy efficiency were done in two ways. First, we estimated it in metric tons produced per terajoules of inputs (TTT). In order to account separately for the combined effect of international price fluctuations and monetary policies in the country, we also estimated efficiency in dollars of revenue per terajoules of inputs (TDT).

To understand the different influences that different inputs have on each stage of the cycle fully, two versions of energy efficiency for the production and processing stages were calculated. Therefore, estimates for efficiency in dollars per terajoule in production (EDTP) and processing (EDTR) were reported. The same division was done for efficiency in tons per terajoule in production (ETTP) and efficiency in tons per terajoule in processing (ETTR).

We analyzed production for the 1980/81 through 1995/96 harvest year. Accounts included energy consumed directly in the transportation of the beans to the beneficio and materials to the farms. Estimates of the indirect energy included in fertilizers and other agrochemicals (fungicides, nematicides, insecticides, herbicides and moisturizers) were done.

Data for coffee processing efficiency (1984/85–1995/96) were taken and modified from Cague et al. (1997). They gathered data for all of the processing plants in Costa Rica from the Costa Rican Coffee Bureau (ICAFE). This study converted their data to dollars and tons per terajoule of input for consistency. Such figures accounted only for direct energy inputs (Aguilar and Klocker, in press).

(C) RESULTS AND DISCUSSION

The coffee cycle can be divided in two main subsystems, or stages: production and processing (Figure 7). Energy and materials flow into the subsystems and yield green coffee beans as a final product plus waste and heat emissions as byproducts (Aguilar and Klocker, in press).

Results from this research showed that the efficiency of coffee production in dollars per terajoule of energy used (EDTP)decreased by 57% between 1980/81 and 1995/96 (Figure 8 and Table 3). We found a

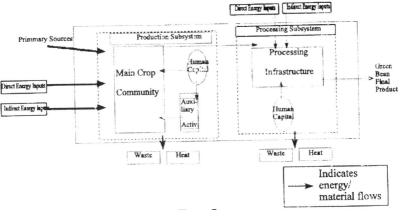

Figure 7.

Energy Efficiency for Coffee Production

in relation to Prices 1980/81 - 1995/96

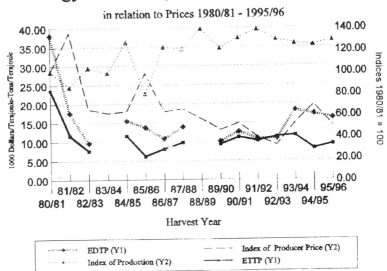

Figure 8.

Table 3

Comparative figures for energy efficiency in dollars per energy used in coffee production and processing and cost rican agriculture. Source: Aguilar and Klocker (in press)

Harvest Year	Production Coffee $/TJ (EDTP)	Production Coffee $/TJ Direct	Process Coffee $/TJ (EDTR)	Process Coffee $/TJ Direct	Total Coffee $/TJ (TDT)	Total Coffee $/TJ Direct	Agriculture $/TJ Direct
1980/81	38104.14	838128.98	N/A	N/A	N/A	N/A	101700.00
1981/82	17526.98	740421.37	N/A	N/A	N/A	N/A	100840.00
1982/83	8603.83	535828.19	N/A	N/A	N/A	N/A	126460.00
1983/84	N/A	N/A	N/A	N/A	N/A	N/A	138950.00
1984/85	15490.43	477236.86	156506.77	156506.77	14095.53	117920.42	140590.00
1985/86	13669.17	497773.28	178922.28	178922.88	12669.00	131692.50	144850.00
1986/87	10792.02	436918.62	108277.84	108277.84	9813.87	86901.69	137360.00
1987/88	13893.03	533111.20	116238.52	116238.52	12366.69	95512.98	135030.00
1988/89	N/A	N/A	113681.58	113681.58	N/A	N/A	141420.00
1989/90	10060.53	215451.36	87210.57	87210.57	9020.00	62100.54	145730.00
1990/91	12468.54	248620.54	91667.43	91667.43	10975.64	66996.32	139770.00
1991/92	10789.56	232853.11	86281.28	86281.28	9590.29	62970.10	151270.00
1992/93	10834.91	171806.36	78901.69	78901.69	9526.69	54089.12	153210.00
1993/94	18263.26	242446.07	126190.93	126190.93	15954.25	83024.56	N/A
1994/95	17296.28	201665.77	174064.40	174064.40	15732.94	93447.47	N/A
1995/96	16266.31	207045.91	N/A	N/A	N/A	N/A	N/A

similar trend for tons produced per terajoule of energy used (ETTP), where the decline was of 60% (Table 4). This decrease in efficiency was accompanied by a 29 percent increase in production (Q) and 50 percent decline in real producer prices (RP).

To understand this trend better we disaggregated ETTP according to the different inputs used. Fertilizer inputs were the largest component of ETTP, on average, 72 percent of the total energy used throughout the period (Figure 9). Their use increases over time from 34 to 73 gigajoules per ton produced (a 114% increase).

Other agrochemical inputs account for an average 23 percent of the total energy use. They increased by 300% from 6.4 to 25.6 gigajoules used per ton of production. Fossil fuel intensity also grew through the period, going from 1.9 to 10.5 gigajoules per metric ton produced (a 443 percent increase). It accounted for 4.6 percent of the energy costs on the average for the period.

Table 4

Energy efficiency in tons per megajoule of energy used in the coffee cycle*. source: Aguilar and Klocker (in press)

Harvest Year	Ton/TJ Firewood Process	Ton/TJ Endocarps Process	Ton/TJ Electricity Process	Ton/TJ Fossil Fuels Process	Total Ton/TJ Processing (ETTR)	Total Ton/TJ (TTT)
1980/81	N/A	N/A	N/A	N/A	N/A	N/A
1981/82	N/A	N/A	N/A	N/A	N/A	N/A
1982/83	N/A	N/A	N/A	N/A	N/A	N/A
1983/84	N/A	N/A	N/A	N/A	N/A	N/A
1984/85	167.99	233.93	1184.31	938.35	82.67	10.13
1985/86	167.99	233.93	1026.23	801.40	80.27	5.71
1986/87	167.99	233.93	1103.64	829.24	80.90	7.33
1987/88	167.99	233.93	1072.33	946.96	81.79	8.70
1988/89	167.99	233.93	1131.15	887.66	81.65	N/A
1989/90	167.99	233.93	1067.28	729.99	80.42	8.32
1990/91	167.99	233.93	1106.32	912.66	81.76	8.32
1991/92	167.99	233.93	1090.37	855.83	81.19	9.79
1992/93	167.99	233.93	1023.91	969.21	81.70	9.02
1993/94	167.99	233.93	1037.97	814.35	80.49	9.86
1994/95	167.99	233.93	1225.92	921.94	82.43	7.45
1995/96	N/A	N/A	N/A	N/A	N/A	N/A

Coffee production is very reactive to price fluctuations. It is clear though that after the recuperation in prices in the middle nineties, EDTP increased up to $16266.31/TJ. Each ton of the product was worth more. Yet, the level production was maintained through a more than proportional increase in energy use, that actually lowered the levels of ETTP to 9.32 tons/TJ of energy used.

Results of the processing stage do not show much variance in energy efficiency in tons processed per terajoules used (ETTR) (Table 4). The highest components of the energy expense accounted for in the processing stage are firewood and endocarps (an average 84% of the energy cost per metric ton (Figure 10). Efficiency, in US dollars per terajoule of energy used in processing (EDTR), decreases consistently between 1985/86 and 1992/93 (from 178922.88 to 78901.69 $/TJ). This 126% decrease is correlated to price fluctuations that showed a significant influence on EDTR during the period analyzed (Figure 11).

Estimates for the efficiency of the complete coffee cycle in Costa Rica from combining the above data for the 1984/85–94/95 period

410

Energy Inputs, Production and Prices

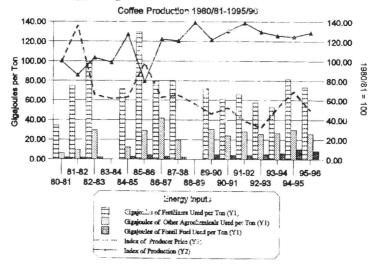

Figure 9.

Energy Inputs and Producer Prices

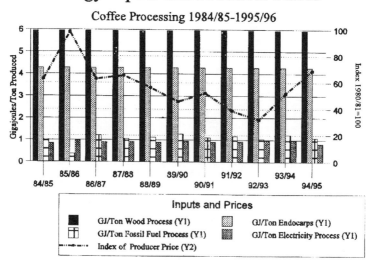

Figure 10.

411

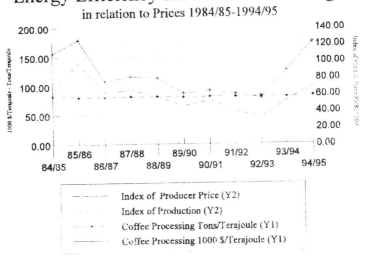

Figure 11.

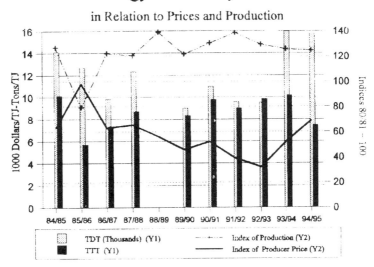

Figure 12.

412

(Figure 12). Total efficiency in tons (TTT) per terajoule had a significant dependence on the levels of production, showing a parallel trend to production variations. It followed then that TTT varied inversely to price changes. Total efficiency in dollars per terajoule of energy use (TDT) did not show a clear pattern or significant correlation to production or producer prices. This was probably an effect of inflation distortions.

The main energy costs for coffee are imported inputs. The inclusion of machinery costs would increase this. Biomass sources and electricity, which might be seen as more sustainable sources of energy in Costa Rica, came out among the lowest components of TMT.

Fertilizers represented 46.8 percent on average of the total energy cost of each metric ton produced and processed. Other agrochemicals used are second (15.3 percent). Direct fossil fuel use is 12.8 percent, firewood 12.5 percent, endocarps 8.95 percent, and electricity 1.9 percent follow. Agrochemicals are 74 percent of EMDP (Aguilar and Klocker, in press).

These results made us conclude that farmers were becoming less efficient in view of declining prices, and were trying to increase their revenue by increasing production with lower energy efficiency methods. This was not the case for processing, where accounting for machinery expenses seemed necessary to get a clearer picture. Nevertheless, the study did highlight the fact that the biomass sources of energy used in processing could be considered sustainable if their rate of use does not surpass the capacity of the systems to generate them. This is, since the endocarps and firewood come from the coffee systems themselves. Drying technologies can be intensive depending on the efficiency of ovens.

The study compared the direct energy efficiency between Costa Rican agriculture as a whole and coffee production. Total energy use per dollar of income in coffee proved much higher than overall agriculture (Figure 13). On average, coffee resulted 1.85 times higher in energy intensity than the agricultural sector as a whole. Such difference in ntensity can be in large part because fertilizer applications (kilograms per hectare) for coffee production are higher compared with general Costa Rican agriculture (Figure 14) (Aguilar and Klocker, in press).

As we can see, accounting for energy costs questions the comparative advantages of producing this crop in Costa Rica. From the conclusions of this case study we can see to what degree the crop is dependent on a fossil fuel based technological package that guarantees a continued situation of dependence.

Comparison of Direct Energy Efficiency

Coffee Cycle - Agriculture 84/85-92/93

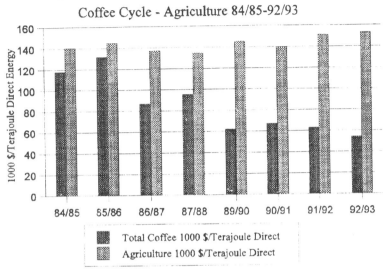

Figure 13.

Comparison of Fertilizer Applications

Coffee Cycle - Costa Rican Agriculture

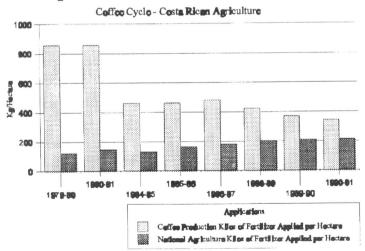

Figure 14.

Other considerations stem from the fact that coffee has played an important role in the conformation of Costa Rican democracy and it is an icon in the culture of the country. It also contributes to a higher distribution of social welfare because it is controlled mostly by nationals and has a more benign land and capital distribution pattern (Aguilar and Klocker, in press). These are characteristics that a sole application of an allocative or a biophysical method of ecological economic valuation would not reveal. This is why, we also need to explore briefly some advantages of applying multicriteria decision making procedures.

3. UNDERSTANDING DIFFERENT VALUE SCALES

A brief mention must be done about an issue that needs much more research on it. The admission of qualitative assessments of value appears important to capture the notion of value in regions like Central America fully. When traditional scientists or economists try to ascribe a means of exchange (be it money or energy) to value, in regions where cultural development is so complex, they miss the importance that cultural roots can have over decisions in social groups. In this way, we ignore the value of cultural diversity.

We had already mentioned the value of traditional knowledge concerning the service it can provide for wise management of natural resources. Yet, often when we use traditional knowledge in development, we do not completely apply its meaning and we end up eroding cultural diversity.

An example of this would be to encourage in Mayan populations to go back to more traditional systems of production for their sustainability, without recognizing the values implicit in their cosmology. For the Maya all things were alive and had a meaning. Sometimes farmers would offer a gourd bowl of water and white corn gruel to the spirits of his field for better crops (Schele and Friedel, 1990, 94). If we value these productive systems only for their physical sustainability without recognizing this wealth of spiritual cultural continuity, our development decisions will be as flawed as when we do not account for environmental impact.

This is where the value of multicriteria analysis and an integral theory of value come in place. If we are to value according to the welfare needs of all potential stakeholders (Opschoor, 1998, 43) we need to consider ranking according to qualitative considerations.

IV. BRIEF CONCLUSION

415

The adoption of the ecological economic position, within the specific context of these countries, opens a whole set of structural questions. Those questions are probably valid for research around this issue in all developing nations.

Also, some concerns that relate to what Bingham et al. (1995, 85–89) call challenges, remain unanswered. As they put it, these issues relate to the complexity of environmental decisions rather than to specific valuation techniques. Decision-making needs to deal with uncertainty and account for irreversibility.

All these issues affect cost-benefit analysis in a structural way. They will affect the methodological choices and decision rules chosen to decide finally.

The uncertainty about ecosystem effects is extremely large. Further, changes in the conditions of the natural capital base are sometimes irreversible (Bingham et al., 1995, 87). Then, if we accept the applicability of these value theories within this context, we want to minimize risk and prevent negative irreversible effects, what decision rules are the most adequate? Is the maximum net present value a desirable rule? These questions call for a continuation of this issue.

Nevertheless, we believe that the clearest conclusion that arises from the examples we have presented here is that development decision making in these nations will benefit substantially from having more and better information. We do not advocate for the adoption of any of the three approaches, since all will provide benefits. In the words of Patterson (1998, 124) 'A monolithic approach based on a single theory of value is not being proposed. Neoclassical economics has fallen into this trap and ecological economics should avoid it'.

Yet, just an increase in information would have important political economic consequences for the countries analyzed. More information would help to solve the inequity in international relations since a main reason for such inequity has been the undervaluation of natural and cultural capital assets and informal economies.

Within this context, free trade and globalization have acted as stimulants of an increase in throughput and opened the possibility, as we previously suggested, of 'importing carrying capacity in the form of raw materials and waste absorption capacities in exchange for production' (Daly, 1993, 155). The resulting situation is a dependency cycle with con-

416

stant unfavorable terms of trade for developing nations that can hardly afford sustainable development models.

As Brown et al. (1996, 15) state it, 'the resource depletion and loss of biodiversity that result form the conversion of tropical forest to agricultural land or pasture has often been justified by developing country governments as unavoidable consequences of the need for development. These governments are faced with rapid growth of a largely uneducated population, foreign debt and little industrial capacity'.

Given those conditions, the proper accounting of costs is essential for countries that depend highly on the export of primary commodities and their cultural-natural resource base. Sustainable comparative advantages can be better assessed with this information.

Therefore, we propose that the application of ecological economic theories of value would be the best means to recognize the decision framework needed for decision-making in these countries. We hope this proposal develops into a comprehensive discussion that encompasses all the options analyzed and more.

REFERENCES

Aguilar, B. and Klocker, J. (In press) 'The Costa Rica Coffee Industry', in Hall, C. (Ed.), *The Environment of Tropical Economies: A Biophysical Analysis of Sustainability,* Academic Press, San Diego, California.

Aguilar, B. (1996a) 'Economía Ecológica', *El Heraldo,* San José, Costa Rica, November 5, 1996. pp. 10.

Aguilar, B. (1996b) 'La Valoración Económica Ecológica: Más Allá de un Concepto Estático y Disciplinario de Biodiversidad' in Consejo Nacional de Rectores, Comisión de Vicerrectores de Investigación, *El Papel de las Universidades Estatales en el Estudio y Conservación de la Diversidad Biológica-Memoria*,OPES, San José, Costa Rica, pp. 9–14.

Appropriate Technology International (1993) *Central American Coffee Initiative Regional Program to Increase Value Added by Small Producers and Reduce Environmental Impact of Processing*, ATI, Washington, D.C.

Arias, F. and Amadar, M. (1991) 'Frijol Tapado, Un Sistema Ventajoso para el Pequeño Productor', *Memoria del I Encuentro Nacional Campesino de Frijol Tapado*, Julio 1991, Colegio Agropecuario San Ignacio de Acosta.

Barkin, D. (1996) 'Macro Changes and Micro Analysis: Methodological Issues in Ecological Economics', *Ecological Economics*, December, 1996, pp. 197–200.

Bellows, B. (1992) *Sustainability of Steep Land Bean (Phaseolus vulgaris L.) Farmin in Costa Rica: An Agronomic and Socio-Economic Assesment*, Unpublished thesis, University of Florida, USA.

Besleme, K. and Aguilar, B. (1994) *An Economic Valuation of Carara Biological Reserve: Potential Tourism Values as an Incentive for Conservation*, in Inter-American Institute for Cooperation on Agriculture/ International Society for Ecological Economics, *III Biennial Meeting of the International Society for Ecological Economics "Down to Earth, Practical Applications of Ecological Economics*, October 24–28, 1994, San José, Costa Rica, IICA, 1994.

Bingham, G., et al. (1995) 'Issues in Ecosystem Valuation: Improving Information for Decision Making.'*Ecological Economics* , August, 1995, pp. 73–90.

Blum, E. (1993) 'Conservation Profitable: a case study of the Merk/INBio agreement', *Environment*, May 1993

Boyce, J.K., et al. (1993) *Sustentabilidad de la Producción Cafetalera Costarricense y Conveniencia del Café Orgánico como Alternativa*, Universidad Nacional-Asociación Alternativas de Desarrollo, Heredia, Costa Rica.

Brown, M., et al. (1996) *A Valuation Analysis of the Role of Cloud Forests in Watershed Protection. Sierra de las Minas Biosphere Reserve, Guatemala and Cusuco National Park, Honduras*, RARE Center for Tropical Conservation, Fundación Defensores de la Naturaleza and Fundación Ecológista "Hector Rodrigo Pastor Fasquelle" (Honduras), Research Report, Guatemala.

Cheminova Holding A/S (1997) *Statement to the Coopenhagen Stock Exchange-Report Based on Visits to Central America (10–18 May 1997), http://www.cheminova.com/holding/meddelse013.html.*

Christensen, P. (1989) 'Historical Roots for Ecological Economics-Biophysical Versus Allocative Approaches', *Ecological Economics* (1) 1989, pp. 17–36.

Cleveland, C. (1993) 'Basic Principles and Evolution of Ecological Economics', in Institute for Research on Environment and the Economy (org.) *Ecological Economics. Emergence of a New Paradigm*, IREE, Ottawa, pp. 25–41.

Cleveland, C. (1991) 'Natural Resource Scarcity and Economic Growth Revisited: Economic and Biophysical Perspectives', in R. Costanza (ed.) *Ecological Economics. The Science and Management of Sustainability*, Columbia University Press, New York, pp. 289–318.

Cleveland, C. (1995)'Resource Degradation, Technical Change, and the Productivity of Energy in U.S. Agriculture', *Ecological Economics*, June 1995, pp. 185–201.

CORBANA (1992) 'Conferencia: La Actividad Bananera y el Medio Ambiente', *II Congreso Bananero Nacional-Memorias*, CORBANA, San José, Costa Rica, pp. 16–34.

Costanza, R., et al.. (1998) 'The Value of the World's Ecosystem Services and Natural Capital', *Ecological Economics*, April 1998, pp. 3–15.

Costanza, R. (1989) 'What is Ecological Economics?', *Ecological Economics*,1990, pp. 1–7.

Daly, H. (1994) 'Operationalizing Sustainable Development by Investing in Natural Capital', in A. Jansson, M. Hammer, C. Folke and R. Costanza (ed.) *Investing in Natural Capital. The Ecological Economics Approach to Sustainability*, Island Press, Washington, D.C., pp. 22–37.

Daly, H. (1991) *Steady-State Economics*, Island Press, Covelo, California.

Daly, H. (1992) 'Allocation, Distribution and Scale: Towards an Ecomomics that is Efficient, Just and Sustainable', *Ecological Economics*, 1992, pp. 185–193.

Daly, H. (1993) 'Problems with Free Trade: Neoclassical anmd Steady-state Perspectives', in D. Zaelke, P. Orbuch and R. Housman (ed) *Trade and the Environment. Law Economics, and Policy*, Island Press, Washington, DC.

418

Daly, H. (1990) 'Toward some Operational Principles of Sustainable Development', *Ecological Economics*, 1990, pp. 1–6.

de Groot, R. (1994) 'Environmental Functions and the Economic Value of Natural Ecosystems', in A. Jansson, M. Hammer, C. Folke and R. Costanza (ed.) *Investing in Natural Capital. The Ecological Economics Approach to Sustainability*, Island Press, Washington, DC., pp. 151–168.

Demmel, U. (1992) 'Evaluación de la Carretera San José-Siquirres: Una Crítica al Análisis Costo-Beneficio en Proyectos Financiados por el Banco Mundial', *Ciencias Económicas*, July 1992, pp. 35–60.

Dixon, J., et al. (1994) *Economic Analysis of Environmental Impacts*, Earthscan, London.

Dixon, J. and Sherman, P. (1990) *Economics of Protected Areas. A New Look at Benefits and Costs*, Island Press, Washington, DC.

Gámez, R. (1992) 'El Instituto Nacional de Biodiversidad', in Segura, O. (ed.) *Desarrollo Sostenible y Políticas Económicas en América Latina*, DEI, San José, Costa Rica, pp. 303–308.

Hall, C. and Hall, M. (1993) 'The Efficiency of Land and Energy Use in Tropical Economies and Agriculture', *Agriculture, Ecosystems and the Environment*, 46 (1993) 1–30.

Hall, C. (1992) 'Economic Development or Developing Economics: What are our Priorities?', in Wali, M. (ed.) *Ecosystem Rehabilitation*, SPB Academic Publishing bv, The Hague, pp. 101–126.

Hawken, P. (1993) *The Ecology of Commerce*, Harper Collins, New York.

Korten, D. (1995) *When Corporations Rule the World*, Kumarian Press-Barrett-Koehler Publishers, Inc., West Hartford, Connecticut-San Francisco, California.

Leonard, H.J. (1985) *Recursos Naturales y Desarrollo Económico en América Central*, IIED, Washington, DC.

Lockwood, M. (1997) 'Integrated Value Theory for Natural Areas', *Ecological Economics*, January, 1997, pp. 83–93.

McNeely, J. (1988) *Economics and Biological Diversity. Developing and Using Economic IOncentives to Conserve Biological Resources*, IUCN, Gland, Switzerland.

Munda, G., et al. (1994) 'Qualitative Multicriteria Evaluation for Environmental Management', *Ecological Economics*, July, 1994, pp. 97–112.

O'Meara, M. (1997) 'The Risks of Disrupting Climate', *World Watch*, Nov/Dec 1997, pp. 20–28.

Odum, H. (1994) 'The Emergy of Natural Capital', in A. Jansson, M. Hammer, C. Folke and R. Costanza (ed.) *Investing in Natural Capital. The Ecological Economics Approach to Sustainability*, Island Press, Washington, DC., pp. 200–214.

Odum, H. (1996) *Environmental Accounting. Emergy and Environmental Decision Making*, John Wiley & Sons, New York.

Opschoor, J.B. (1998) 'The Value of Ecosystem Services: Whose Values?', *Ecological Economics*, April 1998.

Page, T. (1991) 'Sustainability and the Problem of Valuation', in R. Costanza (ed.) *Ecological Economics. The Science and Management of Sustainability*, Columbia University Press, New York, pp. 58.74.

Paiz, C. (1994) *Caracterización de las Areas Irrigadas en la Cuenca del Río Hato, San Agustín Acasaguastlan, El Progreso*, Unpublished thesis, Universidad de San Carlos, Guatemala.

Patterson, M. (1998) 'Commensuration and Theories of Value in Ecological Economics', *Ecological Economics*, April, 1998, pp. 105–126.

419

Patterson, M. (1996) 'What is Energy Efficiency? Concepts, Indicators and Methodological Issues', *Energy Policy*, October, 1996, pp. 377–390.

Pearce, D., et al. (1990) *Sustainable Development. Economics and Environment in the Third World*.Edward Elgar, Hants, England.

Pearce, D. and Turner, R. (1990) *Economics of Natural Resources and the Environment*, John Hopkins, Baltimore.

Pesticide Action Network (1996) *Pesticides in Latin America, http://csf.colrado.edu/lists/elan/96/apr96/0075.html*.

Prugh, T., et al. (1995) *Natural Capital and Human Economic Survival*, ISEE Press, Solomons, Maryland.

Reed, D. (1996) 'Conclusions: Short-Term Environmental Impacts of Structural Adjustment Programs', in D. Reed (ed.) *Structural Adjustment, the Environment and Sustainable Development, E*arthscan, London, pp. 335–354.

Rees, W. and Wackernagel, M. (1994) 'Ecological Footprints and Appropriated Carrying Capacity: Measuring the Natural Capital Requirements of the Human Economy', in A. Jansson, M. Hammer, C. Folke and R. Costanza (ed.) *Investing in Natural Capital. The Ecological Economics Approach to Sustainability*, Island Press, Washington D.C., pp. 362–390.

Rees, W. (1993) 'Natural Capital in Relation to Regional/Global Concepts of Carrying Capacity', in Institute for Research on Environment and the Economy (org.) *Ecological Economics. Emergence of a New Paradigm*, IREE, Ottawa, pp. 42–60.

Reid, J. (1994) 'The Economic Realities of Biodiversity', *Issues in Science and Technology*, Winter issue 1993–94, pp. 48–55.

Rice, R. and Ward, J. (1996) *Coffee, Conservation and Comerce in the Western Hemisphere. How Individuals and Institutions can Promote Ecologically Sound Farming and Forest Management in Northern Latin America*, Natural Resources Defense Council-Smithsonian Migratory Bird Center, New York.

Schele, L. and Freidel, D. (1990) *A Forest of Kings: The Untold Story of the Ancient Maya*, William Morrow and Company, New York.

Sharan, V. (1985) *International Economic Order and Less Developed Countries*, Stehrling Publishers Private Limited, New Dehli.

Smith, N., et al. (1992) *Tropical Forests and Their Crops*, 1992 Cornell University Press.

Solórzano, R., et al. (1991) *Accounts Overdue:Natural Resource Depreciation in Costa Rica*, World Resources Institute, Washington, D.C.

Tietenberg, T. (1996) *Environmental and Natural Resou*rce *Economics*, Harper Collins, New York.

Tiezzi, E., Marchettini, N. and Ugliatti, S. (1991) 'Integrated Agro–Industrial Ecosystems: An Assesment of the Sustainability of a Cogenerative Approach to Food, Energy and Chemical Production by Photosynthesis', in R. Costanza (ed.) *Ecological Economics. The Science and Management of Sustainability*, Columbia University Press, New York, pp. 459–473.

Tobias, D. and Mendehlson, R. (1991) 'Valuing Ecotourism in a Tropical Rain-Forest Reserve', *Ambio*, April, 1991, pp 91–93

U.S. Congress, Office of Technology Asseement (1990) *Energy Use and the U.S. Economy*, OTA-BP-E-57, Government Printing Office, Washington, DC.

Vandermeer, J. and Perfecto, I. (1995) *Breakfast of Biodiversity: The Truth about Rainforest Destruction*, A Food First Book, The Institute for Food and Dvelopment Policy, Oakland, California.

Victor, P. (1991) 'Indicators of Sustainable Development: Some Lessons from Capital Theory', *Ecological Economics*, 4(1991), pp. 191–213.

World Resources Institute (1997) *World Resources 1996–97*, World Resources Institute. Washington, D.C.

World Bank (1994) *Costa Rica. Forest Sector Review*, World Bank Report N. 11516-CR.

INDEX

422

426

428